A Sole Survivor

Ambrose Bierce

A Sole Survivor

Bits of Autobiography

**Edited by S. T. Joshi
and David E. Schultz**

The University of Tennessee Press
Knoxville

Copyright © 1998 by The University of Tennessee Press / Knoxville.
All Rights Reserved. Manufactured in the United States of America.
First Edition.

Frontispiece: Ambrose Bierce in the early 1870s, reproduced courtesy of the
Bancroft Library, University of California, Berkeley.

The paper in this book meets the minimum requirements of the American
National Standard for Permanence of Paper for Printed Library Materials.
∞ The binding materials have been chosen for strength and durability.
✹ Printed on recycled paper.

Library of Congress Cataloging-in-Publication Data
Bierce, Ambrose, 1842–1914?
A sole survivor : bits of autobiography / Ambrose Bierce;
edited by S. T. Joshi and David E. Schultz. —1st ed.
      p.   cm.
ISBN 1-57233-018-X (cloth: alk. paper)
1. Bierce, Ambrose, 1842–1914?—Biography. 2. Authors,
American—19th century—Biography. 3. Journalists—United
States—Biography.
I. Joshi, S. T., 1958–   II. Schultz, David E., 1952–   III. Title.
PS1097.Z5 A3   1998
813'.4—ddc21
[B]   98-8981

Contents

Introduction

Ambrose Bierce was a private man. For all the millions of words he wrote in more than forty years as a journalist, and the hundreds of thousands of words he penned as a prolific correspondent, he made few direct statements about many of his most deeply held beliefs, and he was not given to chatting about his daily activities. To this degree, and to this alone, Ambrose Bierce matches the popular caricature of him—the misanthropic recluse spewing venom at the world.

And yet, it was Bierce himself who wrote his "memoirs" (as he termed them in a letter of 1908), by which he presumably meant the eleven essays he published in the first volume of his *Collected Works* under the general title "Bits of Autobiography." Most of these pieces had appeared in the newspapers and magazines for which Bierce wrote, the earliest (and best) of them, "What I Saw of Shiloh," as early as 1881. But if Bierce meant "Bits of Autobiography" to constitute his memoirs, are we to believe that nothing significant occurred in his life after 1875? For although the last item, "A Sole Survivor," is clearly the rumination of an old man who has seen his friends die one by one, the chronological sequence of "Bits of Autobiography" ends with his English visit of 1872–75.

Fortunately, there is in the remarkable richness of Bierce's literary work a wealth of autobiographical material—interpreting that phrase in a wider sense than merely a chronicle of the bare events of his life, to cover his piquant and challenging views of society and politics and his dicta on the principles of literature—that allows us to augment those "Bits of Autobiography" and present a few further glimpses into the long life and career of the saturnine journalist and master of the short story.

It is not surprising that Bierce offers little information about his upbringing. The youngest of ten children (each with a first name beginning with the letter A), he was born in 1842 to a poor and religiously (perhaps even fanatically) devout family of farmers in Meigs County, Ohio. In all likelihood, he spent the years of his youth attempting to earn a hard living from the earth. Although he proclaimed himself a lifelong atheist, Bierce must have absorbed some elements of his parents' extreme Christian views, for he exhibited a lifelong puritanical intolerance for unchastity (especially in women) and judged friend and foe alike by an unwavering and rigid moral standard that took no account of differing customs or changing times.

It was mere circumstance that allowed Bierce to expand his physical and mental horizons beyond the narrow confines of his youthful environment. He first stayed briefly with his uncle Lucius Verus Bierce, a well-known politician and lawyer who took Bierce in at his residence in Akron, Ohio, in 1859, more than a decade after Bierce's own family had moved to Indiana. Later that year Bierce enrolled for a year at the Kentucky Military Institute, but of his tenure there nothing is known. Then, while Bierce was idling at home in Indiana in the spring of 1861, the Civil War broke out.

Bierce's immediate enlistment in the 9th Indiana Volunteers appears to bespeak more a wish to be where "something was going on" (as he put it late in his life, when he was preparing to go to Mexico) than any devotion to one side or the other of the conflict. It is true that Bierce had served in 1857 as a printer's devil on an abolitionist newspaper, the *Northern Indianan,* but, again, little is known of that experience. Throughout his life Bierce would express a rueful wistfulness over the horrific struggle and his role in it. When, in 1903, he returned to West Virginia, the scene of his earliest fighting in the war, he told a correspondent that the grave of a Confederate soldier had recently been found and remarked: "I'm going over to beg his pardon."[1]

If nothing else, Bierce's participation in some of the bloodiest battles of the Civil War—Shiloh, Chickamauga, Franklin—allowed him in later years to set down some of the most memorable accounts we have of those conflicts; and although several were written more than forty years after the events, they harmonize in every significant particular with the known facts. Bierce's memories of the war are found not only in his formal essays; many shorter and more informal recollections scattered throughout his journalistic work, reprinted here for the first time, substantially augment our knowledge of Bierce's involvement in the war.

Eight of the eleven "Bits of Autobiography" concern Bierce's experiences during and immediately following the war; did he, perhaps, believe that the most exciting period of his life had been lived by 1865? In a sense it was: physically he would never be the same (the gunshot wound in the head, received in 1864, was nearly fatal, and for the rest of his life he was susceptible to searing headaches as a result of his injury), while his psychological state as a veteran who had somehow survived when so many of his companions had perished can only be conjectured. Although Bierce left the army for good in 1866, for the whole of his life he considered himself more soldier than civilian, and it is no surprise that his first collection of tales focuses on that distinction in its very title.

But for the immediate future there was work to be considered. A stint as an aide to the Treasury Department in Alabama during Reconstruction proving markedly unsatisfactory, Bierce joined his old friend and erstwhile commander, Gen. William B. Hazen, in a trip to the uncharted wilderness of the West on an exploratory mission. He abandoned the party at San Francisco in early 1867; although he did not know it then, he would, for the next thirty years, be intimately identified with the Bay Area. What led Bierce to become a writer is unclear; certainly, his earliest pieces—a few poems and an essay on female suffrage for the *Californian*—are stiff and undistinguished. But he got a needed break when, after writing a number of unsigned items for the *San Francisco News Letter and California Advertiser,* he was hired as its regular columnist late in 1868. Bierce's career as an editorialist had begun.

The paragraphs of random commentary Bierce wrote for the *News Letter* are a testament more to his energy than to his emotional maturity, for the twenty-five-hundred-word columns that appeared weekly almost without a break for more than three years are, in actual substance, very much the callow reflections of a young man eager to prove to the world—or, at least, to the local community—his wit, his outrageousness, and his defiance of convention. In the rough-and-tumble world of post–forty-niner San Francisco, where several other newspapers competed with the *News Letter,* including the *Chronicle,* the *Bulletin,* the *Call,* and the *Alta California,* Bierce's provocative opinions on religion, women, and politics found a receptive audience; and, as early as the summer of 1869, they also found recognition in the pages of so august a journal as the *Nation,* which felt that the Western firebrand was worth introducing to its refined readership.

It was in the *News Letter* that Bierce articulated a defense of the unrelenting satire that would consume much of the rest of his career. From the beginning he was faced with the naive criticism that satire of his sort—the tart, at times biting satire of Juvenal, Swift, and Voltaire, which did not refrain from naming names, which disdained the tickle of a feather and stung with the rapier's slash—was somehow inherently improper, beyond the bounds of civilized discourse, and the product of personal spite. It may be true that some of Bierce's earlier and cruder work is mere vilification, although even this has its amusing qualities; but the overwhelming bulk of his work features satire that is both pungent and thought-provoking, marked by a carefully considered intellectual stance even at its most vicious. Few perceived that the objects of Bierce's scorn were condemned in such a way as clearly to suggest his approval of their opposites.

Given Bierce's notoriety, it is perhaps not surprising that he courted and won the well-bred society lady Mary Ellen ("Mollie") Day for his wife, marrying her on Christmas Day of 1871. Bierce's silence about his wife, and about the course of their long and often troubled marriage, is telling; even in private correspondence she is rarely mentioned, although we have several affecting letters by Bierce to his three children as well as to the wife of his nephew Carlton, whom he seemed to regard with as much tenderness as his own offspring. As with his relations with his parents, Bierce's attitude toward Mollie can only be inferred with caution from his creative work—from his celebrated definition of "Marriage" in *The Devil's Dictionary* ("The state or condition of a community consisting of a master, a mistress and two slaves, making in all, two") to the numerous paragraphs in the *News Letter* and elsewhere on the miseries of married couples, the loathsomeness of babies, and the alarmingly frequent suicides, homicides, and infanticides within the family circle.

By the spring of 1872, Bierce apparently found himself discontented with the narrow literary horizon of San Francisco and boldly resettled in England. Although the dozen letters he wrote to the *Alta California* in the fall and winter of 1872 read in part like the notes of a wide-eyed tourist, it is likely that he felt the move to be permanent—dependent, of course, upon his success as a writer. His stay lasted only a little more than three years, but it proved remarkably fertile. He wrote hundreds of columns for the semiweekly magazine *Figaro,* dozens of stories and sketches for Tom Hood's comic paper *Fun* (and also *Tom Hood's Comic Annual*), as well as work (not yet traced) for at least two other periodicals. He and Mollie also found time to begin their family: a son, Day, was born in December 1872, while another, Leigh, arrived in April 1874. It was at this time that Bierce's first books appeared, albeit pseudonymously: *The Fiend's Delight* (1873), *Nuggets and Dust* (1873), and *Cobwebs from an Empty Skull* (1874), consisting of various scraps derived from his earlier California work and from his *Fun* contributions. In later years Bierce wished upon these little books an oblivion he felt they deserved; but, if nothing else, they exhibited his sardonic wit in a form more permanent than newspapers or magazines. It is not to be denied that in some ways these books shared the celebrity enjoyed in England at that time by California writers, among them Bierce's longtime friend Joaquin Miller (whose *Songs of the Sierras* was the sensation of 1871) and Mark Twain, who was sojourning in England concurrently with Bierce and whom Bierce met on a few occasions.

Perhaps the most peculiar of Bierce's experiences in England was his work in 1874 on two issues of a paper entitled the *Lantern*. Bierce wrote every word of the paper, unaware that it was secretly funded by the exiled empress of France as a vehicle for attacking her bitter enemy, Henri Rochefort. Bierce later found out about the charade, writing up the event in "Working for an Empress." After the paper folded he resumed his work for *Figaro* and *Fun*.

Bierce clearly enjoyed dallying with the English literati of Grub Street and hopping from London to Bath to Leamington, with an occasional jaunt into France; but when, in the spring of 1875, Mollie became pregnant with their third child (Helen, born in October) and returned to San Francisco, Bierce regretfully followed to tend to his family. For the next two years there is silence, although we know that Bierce worked for the U.S. mint in San Francisco, where he had been briefly employed in 1867.

The next stage of his career was shaped by Frank Pixley, who in the spring of 1877 founded a weekly paper named the *Argonaut* and invited Bierce to write for it. Bierce resumed the writing of a column of miscellaneous comment. In the *News Letter* Bierce had taken over a column called "The Town Crier," a title he retained in *Figaro*. Now he revived the name he had used previously for only a single column in the short-lived *Lantern*—"Prattle." For the next twenty years— in three different papers—the Prattler would be the terror of San Francisco: no politician, cleric, writer, actor, or private individual could know whether he or she would be skewered with Bierce's pen. The *Argonaut* columns reveal both considerable expansion of Bierce's horizons—his London stay had shown him that the world, not just California, was a bountiful haven of fools and scoundrels— and a marked advance in style. Bierce quickly became a master of the most condensed literary forms—fables, epigrams, definitions, poetic couplets and quatrains—but he occasionally ventured into more expansive ruminations on the world around him and on his own three and a half decades of life. His earliest memories of the Civil War and of his English stay appear in the *Argonaut*.

In the summer of 1879 Bierce's contributions to the *Argonaut* ended abruptly. For the next year and a half we find him mired in the frustrating proposition known as the Black Hills Placer Mining Company. Gold had been discovered in the Dakota Territory, and Bierce's old colleague Gen. Sherburne B. Eaton (who had supervised his work as a Treasury aide in 1865 and who was the company's New York attorney) urged Bierce to come out and share in the wealth expected from the venture. In the summer of 1880 Bierce was sent there by Eaton and John McGinnis Jr., the company's vice president, to be the general agent overseeing the progress of the mining. Romantic as this may sound, one should not picture Bierce sitting by a trickling stream panning for gold; this was big business. It was, unfortunately, a very badly run business, as Eaton and McGinnis provided almost no support to Bierce against the machinations of the company's president, Gen. Alexander Shaler; the duplicitous treasurer, Marcus Walker; and various other individuals who appeared to resent Bierce's authority—indeed, his very presence—perhaps because of his inexperience in the business and what may have been his cantankerous attitude. Although we have little evidence of the nature of the enterprise besides that contained in Bierce's letters to Eaton and McGinnis, it appears the company was very poorly operated—with sometimes too many people in charge, at other times none at all. Bierce lasted as long as he could in the face of poor (or nonexistent) pay, hostility from workers whose salaries were far in arrears, lawsuits from all sides, and the ever-present physical danger of robbery or death at the hands of brigands. Bierce left the job in late 1880, and some years later the company collapsed; but for years thereafter Bierce was vexed by a lawsuit that emerged from the boondoggle.

Upon his return to San Francisco, Bierce found that Frank Pixley would not rehire him. But shortly thereafter, in March 1881, another weekly paper, the *Wasp*, offered Bierce his usual page of "Prattle." For the next five and a half years Bierce worked tirelessly on the *Wasp*, contributing his usual commentary on the follies of the world, along with poems, humorous sketches, and—in small numbers— actual short stories. Bierce's first real story, "The Haunted Valley," had appeared in the *Overland Monthly* in 1871. The many brief comic pieces he wrote for *Fun* in England, few longer than a thousand words, qualify as stories only for lack of anything else to call them. During his *Argonaut* stint he wrote only two stories, "The Night-Doings at 'Deadman's'" and "The Famous Gilson Bequest," but for the *Wasp* he produced such tales of horror and the Civil War as "A Holy Terror," "George Thurston," and "An Imperfect Conflagration." How Bierce became attracted to the horror tale is not entirely clear; certainly he must have read Poe, and he retained Poe's devotion to the short story and the short poem for the whole of his life. Perhaps the morbid humor he displayed in both his journalism and his comic sketches required little alteration for transition into tales of supernatural or psychological horror. Whatever the case, Bierce began to achieve recognition in another arena: his journalism may have attracted the notice of contemporary San Franciscans, but his tales garnered readers who knew nothing of the local personalities lambasted every week by the Prattler.

Politics—both local and national—came increasingly under Bierce's scrutiny during his *Wasp* years. His political convictions clearly developed over the course of his life, and it is impossible to pin him down to any specific party line. In the end he came to believe that hypocrisy and "rascality" owed allegiance to no party, and that his stance—"a pox on both your houses"—was the one that best accorded with political reality. To say that Bierce's political satire—or his satire as a whole—was merely the product of an inflexible "misanthropy" is shortsighted and superficial. There is no reason to disbelieve his declaration: "I like many things in this world and a few persons."[2] But there is good reason to believe that his witnessing of the increasing corruption of American politics had much to do with his increasing censoriousness. The assassination of President Garfield in 1881 seemed to confirm all Bierce's fears.

By the fall of 1886 Bierce again found himself out of a job; perhaps the *Wasp*'s purchase in 1885 by Col. J. P. Jackson, not a man after Bierce's heart, rendered continued work untenable. For years he had struggled with increasingly severe asthma, and he moved continually from one rural or mountain locale (Auburn, Angwin, Los Gatos) to another; not coincidentally, he found in these moves a convenient opportunity to escape from his wife and the burdens of child rearing. It was while living in Oakland in the spring of 1887 that Bierce's life took its most dramatic turn; for it was then that the twenty-three-year-old William Randolph Hearst knocked at his door and asked him to become the chief editorial writer for the *San Francisco Examiner*.

Hearst readily dropped out of Harvard when his father gave him a chance to run the paper, and he immediately hired the best-known local journalists of the day. It is a testament to Bierce's local fame that his "Prattle" column was for several years the only signed contribution on the editorial page of the *Examiner*, which at that time was rather more subdued than its flamboyant incarnation of the late 1890s. Bierce plunged into his work with renewed vigor, producing not only weekly columns of unprecedented length (sometimes longer than three thousand words) and wondrously scintillating wit, but also many short stories. In his first four years at the *Examiner*, he published such tales as "One of the Missing," "A Son of the Gods," "A Tough Tussle," "Chickamauga," "A Horseman in the Sky," "The Coup de Grâce," "The Suitable Surroundings," "A Watcher by the Dead," "An Occurrence at Owl Creek Bridge," "The Realm of the Unreal," as well as the little-known "The Fall of the Republic," a long political satire later rewritten as "Ashes of the Beacon." Bierce's continuing outspokenness embroiled him in many controversies, but he gave as well as he got—usually better. It is noteworthy, however, that two personal dilemmas—his separation from Mollie in 1888 over his discovery of what he took to be love letters to her from a Danish admirer, and the death the next year of his sixteen-year-old son, Day, in a sordid duel over a girl—find virtually no mention in either his published work or his surviving correspondence.

The 1890s were, at least on paper, a decade of triumph for Bierce. His *Tales of Soldiers and Civilians* was published locally (the edition is dated 1891, but it probably appeared in early 1892) after being rejected by major houses in New York; it was reprinted in 1892 in England as *In the Midst of Life*, and although Bierce then used that title in subsequent editions, several remarks in letters lead one to believe that he preferred his original title. In 1892 his translation (with G. A. Danziger) of Richard Voss's *The Monk and the Hangman's Daughter* appeared in book form, as did his first collection of verse (culled from his newspaper columns), *Black Beetles in Amber*. The volume emerged under the imprint of the

Western Authors Publishing Association, a firm he and Danziger had established; for the next decade he would wrangle with Danziger over the profits of the book and the rights to the *Monk*. In 1893 his collection of horror tales, *Can Such Things Be?*, was published; in 1898 an augmented edition of *In the Midst of Life* appeared from Putnam's, and the next year that publisher issued his *Fantastic Fables*.

Following these literary successes (tempered by the fact that three of the publishing houses folded a year or two after the books they published appeared), Bierce found himself at the nation's political center. In early 1896 Hearst sent Bierce to Washington to lobby against the efforts of Collis P. Huntington, one of the most notorious of the "railroad barons," to pass a funding bill that would give Huntington nearly a century to repay a debt to the government for the building and maintenance of the Southern and Central Pacific Railroad. Bierce, for once agreeing with Hearst on a point of policy, believed Huntington to be a mere thief who had already pocketed too much of the government's money, and he entered the fray with gusto. His sixty or so articles on the matter, from February to May, were written for both the *San Francisco Examiner* and the *New York Journal*, which Hearst had recently acquired; most of the pieces were apparently sent to the newspaper offices by telegraph. There is little doubt that Bierce's articles were instrumental in swaying both the public and members of Congress (many of whom had initially been inclined to vote for the Huntington bill) to defeat the measure. These pieces alone are sufficient to establish Bierce as a forerunner of the muckraker movement of the following generation.

Bierce claimed to suffer health problems upon the completion of his work in Washington, but his contributions to the *Examiner* continued unabated. By November he had returned to San Francisco. The next year, 1897, Bierce tendered his resignation from the Hearst staff, on this occasion because he objected to the severe editing and rewriting of his contributions in the New York paper. (It was probably not the first occasion for such an act, and it definitely was not the last.) Hearst, having many other concerns and probably not wishing to exercise rigid supervision of his staff, managed to lure Bierce back to work, but the editorial tampering continued.

In 1898 Bierce commenced a long series of articles on the Spanish-American War and its ramifications in the Philippines and on American relations with China. Here he was manifestly not in Hearst's corner, seeing the war as merely a naked grab for power.[3] These articles, if perhaps less superficially dramatic than his broadsides against Huntington, reveal a seasoned understanding of political reality that was exceptionally rare for their period, and leagues beyond the impish abuse of local politicians that characterized Bierce's earliest work. They may stand as his most distinguished newspaper writing.

In December 1899 Bierce's work for the *Examiner* again lapsed briefly; but this time it was not because he went on strike. Bierce had finally decided for health reasons to uproot himself from his adopted hometown, the town that had stood in mingled terror and admiration of him for thirty years. He settled in Washington, D.C., where his contributions were wired to both the *New York Journal*, which in early 1902 became the *New York American*, and the *Examiner*. His literary output declined both in quantity and in substance: the columns became skimpier ("Prattle" gave way to "The Passing Show," which in turn gave way to "The Views of One" and other brief pieces), and relatively few works of fiction appeared, with the notable exception of the revised "Ashes of the Beacon," which took up an entire page of the *American* and *Examiner* in February 1905. Another personal tragedy—the death of his son Leigh of pneumonia in March 1901—is mentioned tersely in a few letters.

In 1905 Hearst finally put forward to Bierce a proposal that seemed promising: Bierce would eventually cease his newspaper work and write exclusively for the newly purchased magazine, *Cosmopolitan*. At first Bierce jumped to the task, writing an array of stories as well as several additional satires of the "Ashes of the Beacon" type. But Bierce's regular column, "The Passing Show," proved to be unsatisfying, as he found himself unable to discuss contemporary affairs pertinently in a column that would be published a month or two after the items were written. A shift to a less topical column, "Small Contributions," proved no more satisfactory, and the title unwittingly reflected both the size and nature of his work for the magazine. The only book publication of note during this period was *The Devil's Dictionary*, which Doubleday issued in 1906; Bierce did not care for the lackluster title *The Cynic's Word Book*, used to avoid offending readers' religious sensibilities.[4] It was also at this time that Bierce attempted valiantly to secure the publication of his young pupil George Sterling's remarkable poem of fantasy and imagination, "A Wine of Wizardry"; after being rejected by many standard magazines, it appeared in *Cosmopolitan*, accompanied by an essay on it by Bierce. Perhaps Bierce felt indebted to Sterling for his financing of Bierce's second collection of verse, *Shapes of Clay* (1903). Whatever the case, the Hearst papers used the occasion to create a kind of literary tempest in a teapot, with many of Bierce's enemies upbraiding him for advocating a poem so out of tune with the placid decorum of the verse of the day.

By the spring of 1909 Bierce had had all he could stomach of *Cosmopolitan*, and his resignation signaled the definitive end of his work for Hearst. For more than twenty years Bierce had given the best years of his literary life to the Hearst publications, and in his rumination on those years, "A Thumb-Nail Sketch," which curiously does not appear among the "Bits of Autobiography," Bierce concluded that the relation had been of mutual benefit. Certainly, his contributions of 1887–99 represent the pinnacle of his journalistic work, and a case could be made that they constitute the most remarkable American journalism of the century.

It was tragically shortsighted of Bierce not to reprint much of this material in the twelve volumes of his *Collected Works*, which his friend, the publisher

Walter Neale, issued between 1909 and 1912. Bierce's low view of journalism in general clearly skewed his assessment of his own work; and of course his journalism has now gained added historical value as the commentary of a keen mind on the political and social events of the period. But no reader of this body of work—which makes up the bulk of the latter two-thirds of this book—can come away unimpressed with the verbal witchery, the glittering wit, the merciless satire, the towering rhetorical fire, and, most important, the depth of thought and keenness of perception of Bierce's editorial columns. One must compare them with the average run of work written in the newspapers at this time to gain a true sense of their superiority. Even if Bierce on occasion embodies his own definition of "positive" ("mistaken at the top of one's voice"), there can be little doubt that most of his views are well considered, sincerely held, and expressed with dazzling wit and acerbity.

For the last eight or nine years of Bierce's life we are largely reliant on his correspondence, which either was more voluminous during this time or merely happens to survive more copiously than for earlier periods. Bierce continued to play his hand close to the vest, treating in a sentence or a phrase matters we would like to see dealt with in paragraphs or pages; but it is all we have. The assembling, editing, and proofreading of the *Collected Works* was occupying much of his time, but Bierce found occasion to return triumphantly, and a little ruefully, to San Francisco in 1910 and 1912; he had overcome his resolve not to visit the city after its destruction by the earthquake and fire of 1906, of which he heard much from friends like Sterling.

By 1913 Bierce was tiring of his idle life in Washington. He was writing little, save letters, and, although now past seventy, felt the need to involve himself in something. The Mexican Civil War offered an opportunity. Many of his letters of the latter half of 1913 speak of his inclination to see what was going on there and then to continue to South America. Was this merely an elaborate deception? Did Bierce in fact not go to Mexico (beyond a brief foray in November 1913)? The puzzle of Bierce's disappearance—attested by the provocative "1842–1914?" that follows his name in library catalogues—has certainly augmented his reputation as a mystery man of American letters, and in all likelihood the truth will never be known. His most recent biographer, Roy Morris Jr., has argued that Bierce did not in fact go to Mexico; but the existence of a letter written from Chihuahua on December 26, 1913, of which Morris was evidently unaware, makes such a view unlikely. What exactly happened to Bierce may never be known for certain, but the evidence suggests that he perished in very early 1914, possibly mistaken for a spy.

Bierce's frequent strictures on the uselessness, even the perniciousness, of literary biography extended to autobiography, but they did not prevent him from writing of his own life from time to time. Perhaps he did not have the energy or inclination to chronicle the entirety of his life; perhaps he felt that much of his life was not worth writing about. Perhaps, too, he did not have the patience to wade through the oceans of his journalism over forty years to abstract items that might flesh out the high points of his literary and personal existence beyond those harrowing days as a raw soldier and the intoxicating few years as a man of letters in London. But at least that journalism has been left for future hands to sift, and we hope that the following volume presents some bits of autobiography of which Bierce might have approved.

It is true that some of this material is not "autobiographical" in the narrowest sense; but surely a writer's opinions on the world around him—and, especially, the evolution of those opinions from youth to maturity—are as much a part of his life as the bare physical events he experienced. It is indisputable that the "life" of many a writer is largely made up of writing; but for such persons the life of the mind can certainly rival that of the body in compelling interest. We make no apologies, therefore, for presenting what amounts to an anthology of Bierce's journalistic work in addition to his consciously autobiographical writing; for this work provides as transparent an index to Bierce's literary and philosophical development as anyone could wish. Perhaps, too, it will help expand the general understanding of Bierce beyond that of a skilled writer of short stories; for those stories, brilliant as they are, are dwarfed at least in quantity by the editorial commentary Bierce expounded over nearly half a century of newspaper work. Such diligent and untiring work, which brought him his share of fame, notoriety, and obloquy, should not be forgotten.

A Note on the Text

The items in this volume are derived from Bierce's *Collected Works* (1909–12), columns in newspapers and magazines, and personal letters.

Full bibliographical information for all items is given in the Sources section. That listing is arranged in the order the items occur in this volume. In instances where a given section consists of more than one item, each item is numbered in the text (the number appearing in square brackets at the end of the extract), and bibliographical information for it can be found under the corresponding number in the Sources.

The eleven items from "Bits of Autobiography" ("On a Mountain," "What I Saw of Shiloh," "A Little of Chickamauga," "The Crime at Pickett's Mill," "Four Days in Dixie," "What Occurred at Franklin," "Across the Plains," "The Mirage," "'Way Down in Alabam'," "Working for an Empress," and "A Sole Survivor") are taken from *Collected Works*, volume 1. The texts have been compared with Bierce's manuscript copy sent to the typesetter, now at the Huntington Library. The items are arranged chronologically in the order of the events they describe; Bierce's other discussions of his Civil War experiences, derived from his newspaper columns, are incorporated within this chronological framework.

For extracts from letters, we have derived our texts from manuscript sources where possible. We are grateful to the following libraries for permission to publish these extracts: the Bancroft Library, University of California, Berkeley; the Huntington Library, San Marino, California; Henry W. and Albert A. Berg Collection, New York Public Library, Astor, Lenox and Tilden Foundations; Bailey Millard Papers, Ax 431, Department of Special Collections and University Archives, Knight Library, University of Oregon; the James S. Copley Library Collection, La Jolla, California; Ella Strong Library, Scripps College, Claremont, California; Rare Book Collection, University of Louisville; the Yale Collection of American Literature, Beinecke Rare Book and Manuscript Library, Yale University; and Special Collections, University of Pennsylvania Library. Some letters have been derived from *The Letters of Ambrose Bierce,* edited by Bertha Clark Pope (San Francisco: Book Club of California, 1922). The letter to Bernice Wright (June 8, 1864) has been taken from Carey McWilliams, "Ambrose Bierce's First Love," in *Bookman* (New York, June–July 1932).

We have done most of our research at the New York Public Library, New York University Library, Beinecke Rare Book and Manuscript Library, Yale University, Los Angeles Public Library, and Princeton University. We are grateful to librarians at St. Cloud State University (St. Cloud, Minnesota), Arizona State University (Tempe), and the Milwaukee Public Library for assistance with this volume. John D. Beatty contributed much to the notes on Bierce's Civil War writings. Lawrence I. Berkove, Scott D. Briggs, Perry M. Grayson, Marc Michaud, Alan Gullette, and Mindi Rayner also lent valuable assistance.

Chronology

1842	June 24: Ambrose Gwinnett Bierce born in Meigs County, Ohio, the youngest of ten children of Marcus Aurelius and Laura (Sherwood) Bierce.
1846	Family moves to Koskiusco County, Indiana; Bierce attends school; meets Bernice ("Fatima") and Clara Wright.
1857	Leaves family, moving to Warsaw, Indiana, and working as printer's devil for *Northern Indianan* (abolitionist newspaper).
1859	Comes to live with uncle Lucius Verus Bierce in Akron, Ohio. Fall: Begins attending Kentucky Military Institute at Franklin Springs.
1860	Drops out of Kentucky Military Institute; settles in Elkhart, Indiana, working at odd jobs.
1861	April: Outbreak of Civil War. May: Bierce enlists for three-month stint with 9th Indiana Volunteers. May 29: Leaves for western Virginia. June 3: Fights in battle of Philippi. July 11: Fights in battle of Rich Mountain and Laurel Hill. Late July: Mustered out; reenlists for three years; promoted to sergeant major. Returns to Virginia. Participates in reconnaissance

mission at Cheat Mountain (October 3) and battle of Buffalo Mountain (December).

1862   Joins Gen. William Nelson's division at Nashville, where he meets William B. Hazen, then colonel under Nelson. April 6–8: Battle of Shiloh. December 1: Promoted to second lieutenant. December 31: Battle of Stones River.

1863   April 25: Promoted to first lieutenant. May: Joins General Hazen's staff as topographical engineer. September 19–20: Battle of Chickamauga. November 23–25: Battle of Missionary Ridge. December: Returns home to Warsaw, Indiana, on furlough; becomes engaged to Bernice Wright.

1864   February: Returns to front. May: Moves to Georgia with Army of the Cumberland. May 14–15: Battle of Resaca. May 27: Battle of Pickett's Mill. June 27: Shot in head at battle of Kennesaw Mountain. July–September: Furlough in Warsaw; engagement with Bernice Wright broken off. Late September: Returns to Hazen's brigade. Mid-October: Captured by Confederates near Gaylesville, Alabama, but escapes. November 30: Battle of Franklin. December 15–16: Battle of Nashville.

1865   January 25: Declared unfit for military service because of head wound; accepts job with Treasury Department. September: Visits Panama.

1866   July: Joins William B. Hazen's expedition to explore western forts.

1867   Resigns from army, angered at receiving only a second lieutenant's commission; settles in San Francisco, where he secures job at U.S. mint. Fall: First published work—prose and poetry in *Californian*.

1868   Writes for *Golden Era* and *San Francisco News Letter*. December: Becomes regular columnist ("The Town Crier") for *News Letter*.

1871   Occasional contributions to *Overland Monthly,* including first story, "The Haunted Valley." December 25: Marries Mary Ellen ("Mollie") Day.

1872	March: Resigns from *News Letter*. Summer: Leaves for England; begins writing stories for Tom Hood's *Fun* and columns ("The Town Crier," "The Passing Show") for *Figaro*. Fall–Winter: Letters on England to *Alta California*. December: Birth of son, Day.
1873	First book, *The Fiend's Delight* (John Camden Hotten). *Nuggets and Dust* (Chatto and Windus) published later that year.
1874	*Cobwebs from an Empty Skull* (Routledge). April 29: Birth of son, Leigh. Writes both issues of *Lantern*.
1875	April: Mollie, Day, and Leigh return to San Francisco. September: Bierce leaves England; resumes work at U.S. mint. October 30: Birth of daughter, Helen.
1876	February: Death of Marcus Aurelius Bierce.
1877	Associate editor and columnist ("Prattle") of *Argonaut*, founded by Frank Pixley. Writes *The Dance of Death* with Thomas A. Harcourt.
1878	May: Death of Laura Bierce.
1879	Resigns from *Argonaut*.
1880	July: Becomes general agent for Black Hills Placer Mining Company in Rockerville, Dakota Territory. October: Resigns; spends several months in New York. Writes occasional articles for *San Francisco Call*.
1881	January: Returns to San Francisco. March: Joins staff of *Wasp* as columnist ("Prattle") and associate editor. Begins publishing *The Devil's Dictionary* serially; also fables and stories.
1886	May: Resigns from *Wasp*.
1887	March: Joins staff of William Randolph Hearst's *San Francisco Examiner* as chief editorial writer. Writes occasional stories: "The Fall of the Republic" (March 25, 1888, later "Ashes of the Beacon"), "A Son of the Gods" (July 29, 1888), "A Tough Tussle" (September 30, 1888), etc.

1888–89   Winter: Separates from Mollie over his discovery of what he
                 believes to be love letters to her from another man.

1889   July 27: Day killed in duel over girl. Bierce publishes
                 "Chickamauga" (January 20), "A Horseman in the Sky"
                 (April 14), "The Coup de Grâce" (June 30), "The Suitable
                 Surroundings" (July 14), "The Affair at Coulter's Notch"
                 (October 20), and "A Watcher by the Dead" (December
                 29), all in the *Examiner*.

1890   Publishes "The Man and the Snake" (June 29), "An Oc-
                 currence at Owl Creek Bridge" (July 13), "The Realm of
                 the Unreal" (July 20), "The Middle Toe of the Right Foot"
                 (August 17).

1891   Contributes stories to the *Wave*: "Haïta the Shepherd" (Janu-
                 ary 24), "The Death of Halpin Frayser" (December 19). Trans-
                 lation (with G. A. Danziger) of Richard Voss's *The Monk and
                 the Hangman's Daughter* serialized in *Examiner* (September 13–
                 27). *Tales of Soldiers and Civilians* (E. L. G. Steele) (dated 1891,
                 but probably published January 1892).

1892   *The Monk and the Hangman's Daughter* (F. J. Schulte); *Black
                 Beetles in Amber* (Western Authors Publishing Association).
                 Chatto and Windus reprints *Tales of Soldiers and Civilians* un-
                 der title *In the Midst of Life*.

1893   *Can Such Things Be?* (Cassell). "The Damned Thing" pub-
                 lished in *Town Topics* (December 7).

1896   January: Sent to Washington to lobby against funding bill for
                 Collis P. Huntington. February–May: Writes many articles at-
                 tacking Huntington (mostly for *Examiner*, but some for *New
                 York Journal*, now owned by Hearst). June: Funding bill de-
                 feated. November: Returns to San Francisco.

1897   "The Eyes of the Panther" (October 17) and "An Affair of Out-
                 posts" (December 19) published in *Examiner*.

1898   Articles on Spanish-American War in *Examiner*. Augmented
                 edition of *In the Midst of Life* (Putnam).

1899   *Fantastic Fables* (Putnam). December: Leaves for Washington to write simultaneously for *New York Journal* (later *American*) and *San Francisco Examiner.*

1901   March 31: Leigh Bierce dies of pneumonia.

1903   *Shapes of Clay* (W. E. Wood), funded by George Sterling. *Can Such Things Be?* reprinted by Neale Publishing Co.

1904   December: Mollie Bierce files for divorce.

1905   "Ashes of the Beacon" published in *New York American* (February 19) and *San Francisco Examiner* (February 26). April 27: Mollie dies before divorce proceedings can be finalized. May: Bierce begins writing for Hearst's *Cosmopolitan* (newspaper work continues, but ends in summer of 1906). Many stories written for the magazine: "One Summer Night" (March 1906), "Staley Fleming's Hallucination" (March 1906), "The Moonlit Road" (January 1907), "Beyond the Wall" (December 1907), "A Resumed Identity" (September 1908), "The Stranger" (February 1909).

1906   *The Devil's Dictionary* published in book form as *The Cynic's Word Book* (Doubleday, Page).

1907   *The Monk and the Hangman's Daughter* reprinted by Neale Publishing Co. Succeeds in several-year effort to publish George Sterling's "A Wine of Wizardry"; furor over its appearance and over Bierce's praise of it. Winter: Visits S. O. Howes in Galveston, Texas.

1908   April: Walter Neale broaches plan to publish Bierce's *Collected Works* in ten volumes (later extended to twelve). Bierce begins compilation.

1909   May: Bierce resigns from *Cosmopolitan,* definitively ending association with Hearst. *Collected Works* begins to appear. *The Shadow on the Dial* (A. M. Robertson), essay collection assembled by S. O. Howes. *Write It Right* (Neale).

1910   May–October: Returns to California for extended visit.

1911   Summer: Spends a month in Sag Harbor, Long Island, with
                relatives of George Sterling.

1912   Final two volumes of *Collected Works* appear. June–October:
                Second and last visit to California.

1913   October: Leaves Washington; visits Civil War battlefields;
                settles in Texas. November: Brief foray into Mexico (Juarez,
                Chihuahua); returns to Texas. December 26: Last surviving let-
                ter by Bierce, expressing intent to go to Ojinaga. Is never heard
                from again.

■

(1 8 6 1 – 1 8 6 5)

The Civil War

■

A Bivouac of the Dead

[In the summer of 1903 Bierce undertook the
first of several reminiscent journeys over old
Civil War battlefields. In this instance he came
upon a cemetery in Grafton, West Virginia,
where comrades from his earliest days of
fighting were buried. Two works emerged
from this trip: a long letter written for a re-
union of the 9th Indiana Volunteers in 1904,
and a condensed and revised version of it, "A
Bivouac of the Dead," published in the *New
York American* for November 22, 1903, and
revised for volume 11 (1912) of his *Collected
Works*. We present the latter piece first.]

Away up in the heart of the Allegheny mountains, in
Pocahontas county, West Virginia, is a beautiful little valley
through which flows the east fork of the Greenbrier river. At
a point where the valley road intersects the old Staunton and
Parkersburg turnpike, a famous thoroughfare in its day, is a
postoffice in a farm house. The name of the place is Travelers' Repose, for it was once a tavern. Crowning some low
hills within a stone's throw of the house are long lines of old

Confederate fortifications, skilfully designed and so well "preserved" that an hour's work by a brigade would put them into serviceable shape for the next civil war. This place had its battle—what was called a battle in the "green and salad days" of the great rebellion. A brigade of Federal troops, the writer's regiment among them, came over Cheat mountain, fifteen miles to the westward, and, stringing its lines across the little valley, felt the enemy all day; and the enemy did a little feeling, too. There was a great cannonading, which killed about a dozen on each side; then, finding the place too strong for assault, the Federals called the affair a reconnaissance in force, and burying their dead withdrew to the more comfortable place whence they had come. Those dead now lie in a beautiful national cemetery at Grafton, duly registered, so far as identified, and companioned by other Federal dead gathered from the several camps and battlefields of West Virginia. The fallen soldier (the word "hero" appears to be a later invention) has such humble honors as it is possible to give.

> His part in all the pomp that fills
> The circuit of the Summer hills
> Is that his grave is green.

True, more than a half of the green graves in the Grafton cemetery are marked "Unknown," and sometimes it occurs that one thinks of the contradiction involved in "honoring the memory" of him of whom no memory remains to honor; but the attempt seems to do no great harm to the living, even to the logical.

A few hundred yards to the rear of the old Confederate earthworks is a wooded hill. Years ago it was not wooded. Here, among the trees and in the undergrowth, are rows of shallow depressions, discoverable by removing the accumulated forest leaves. From some of them may be taken (and reverently replaced), small thin slabs of the split stone of the country, with rude and reticent inscriptions by comrades. I found only one with a date, only one with full names of man and regiment. The entire number found was eight.

In these forgotten graves rest the Confederate dead—between eighty and one hundred, as nearly as can be made out. Some fell in the "battle;" the majority died of disease. Two, only two, have apparently been disinterred for reburial at their homes. So neglected and obscure in this *campo santo*[1] that only he upon whose farm it is—the aged postmaster of Travelers' Repose—appears to know about it. Men living within a mile have never heard of it. Yet other men must be still living who assisted to lay these Southern soldiers where they are, and could identify some of the graves. Is there a man, North or South, who would begrudge the expense of giving to these fallen brothers the tribute of green graves? One would rather not think so. True, there are several hundreds of such places still discoverable in the track of the great war. All the stronger is the dumb demand—the silent plea of these fallen brothers to what is "likest God within the soul."

They were honest and courageous foemen, having little in common with the political madmen who persuaded them to their doom and the literary bearers of false witness in the aftertime. They did not live through the period of honorable strife into the period of vilification—did not pass from the iron age to the brazen—from the era of the sword to that of the tongue and pen. Among them is no member of the Southern Historical Society. Their valor was not the fury of the non-combatant; they have no voice in the thunder of the civilians and the shouting. Not by them are impaired the dignity and infinite pathos of the Lost Cause. Give them, these blameless gentlemen, their rightful part in all the pomp that fills the circuit of the summer hills.

Battlefields and Ghosts

I passed the greater part of the summer before the last at the little village of Aurora, West Virginia, just west of the Maryland line, and overlooking the Cheat River valley in the Alleghany Mountains. Through Aurora a part of the Confederate force retreated after the engagement at Carrick's Ford,[2] a few miles to the southwest, and the older inhabitants still tell many tales of that to them memorable event. From some of the peaks near Aurora I could see down into several of the blue and purple valleys, where, with some of the comrades who, I hope, will be with you when this paper is read, I campaigned in the distant days of '61 and '62.

That region had ever since been to me, as I suppose it has to them, a kind of dreamland. I was reluctant to descend into it for fear of dispelling the illusion, but finally I did so, and passed a few of the most interesting weeks of my life, following the track of the Ninth, visiting its camps, the forts that it helped to build, those that it assisted to take, or try to take, the graves of its fallen and those of the misguided gentlemen whom it sent to their long rest, and who, doubtless, sleep not less soundly than the others.

At Grafton is a beautiful National Cemetery, where lie some twelve hundred of the Federal dead, removed to that place from their scattered graves in that part of the state. About one-half of them are marked "unknown." Many of the Ninth, however, were identified, and I forward herewith some notes concerning them which I copied from the records of the cemetery.

Some of the entries doubtless are incorrect, or at least inaccurate. The very first on the books stood thus:

"Abbott, E. J. (Ind.). Removed July 17, 1867, from Geo. Burns' farm, Travelers' Repose, Pocahontas Co. Head southeast, 150 yards from road."

This entry I took to refer to James A. Abbott of my company (C), who fell at the battle of Greenbrier River—Travelers' Repose being a wayside inn and postoffice on the field of engagement. Afterward I was shown the grave from which the body had been removed. On returning to Washington I went to the War Department and had the record corrected in accordance with my belief, although I was not present at the engagement.

Of the other dead members of Company C the Grafton Cemetery has no record, though doubtless some of them are there among the "unknown."

Philippi, where we had our first affair with the enemy,[3] is now a considerable town. It was easy to identify the road by which we entered, in the belief that we had the enemy's camp surrounded. The high hill from which a battery of ours pitched shells into the startled Confederate camp (and I believe flung a few at us by mistake) is still there, as is the way of hills, and looked quite familiar. We afterward camped on it, among the trees in a field. It is still a field, but the trees are mostly gone. By the way, that battery of ours did nothing worse than take off a young Confederate's leg. He was living near there a year ago, a prosperous and respectable gentleman, but still minus the leg; no new one had grown on.

The "three months' men" will remember Belington well enough. I think it was little but a blacksmith's shop at a cross-roads. It is now a pleasant little village. Two or three miles out is where we fought the battle of Laurel Hill.[4] It was not much of a battle—none of them were—but it gave us something to think about during the few days that it kept us pegging away at Garnett's[5] men, with or without orders. None of the enemy's earthworks remain except an emplacement for guns on the summit of a hill; the rifle pits cannot now be traced. They were lower down the hill in the woods. With the exception of a strip of trees at the very bottom, held by our skirmishers, the forest is gone. In this strip of trees occurred, just before nightfall one day, the only really sharp little fight that we had. It has been represented as a victory for us, but it was not. A few dozens of us, who had been swapping shots with the enemy's skirmishers, grew tired of the resultless quarrel, and by a common impulse, and I think without orders or officers, ran forward into the woods and attacked the Confederate works. We did well enough, considering the hopeless folly of the movement, but we came out of the woods faster than we went in, a good deal. This was the affair in which Corporal Dyson Boothroyd of Company A fell with a mortal wound. I found the very rock against which he lay.[6]

Our camp is now a race track.

On the reorganization of the regiment for the three years' service it returned to this region and lay for weeks at Huttonsville, near the foot of Cheat Mountain, where many of the men died of disease. Their bodies are at Grafton. Then, after the Greenbrier affair, we went to the summit of the mountain. It will be remembered that we built a row of big log houses, one for each company, all connected for mutual protection and loopholed for rifle firing. These military defenses commanded the road—almost straddled it. I fancy we feared that if the enemy got a chance he would sneak by us at arm's length and conquer all the country in our rear. Certainly there was many a prediction of disaster when we went into an earthwork a considerable distance from the road.

The stone foundations of the houses are still there, as are all the stone and earth elements of the fort. Everything wooden has disappeared. The parapet of the fort is in so good condition that an hour's work by a regiment would make it serviceable. The old cemetery on the hillside opposite (I think none of our regiment was buried there) shows twenty-five or thirty graves from which all the bodies have been removed. One headstone remains, propped against a rock and rudely carved: "W. Walkerson. Died Aug. 9, 1861."

For many square miles the forests on the slopes of the mountains have been thinned by the lumbermen, with their sawmills. But the old wooden covered bridge across the Cheat River looks hardly a day older, and is still elaborately decorated with the soldiers' names carven with jack-knives. I think the summit used to be a farm, with a farm house. There is now neither field nor dwelling— just a desolate area of rock and scanty grass, where nothing dwells but memories and ghosts.

At Greenbrier River Confederate earthworks are almost good as new. If they were all there at the time of the engagement the wisdom of not assaulting them cannot be doubted. The best thing to do was to call it a "reconnaissance in force," and let it go at that. I found a number of opened graves besides that of Abbott, and a few undisturbed ones which had apparently been overlooked. Back of the fortifications is the burial ground of the Confederates. It is nearly obliterated. The graves are in rows that can hardly be traced in the dense undergrowth. Persons living within a mile did not know of its existence. I made out between eighty and a hundred graves—depressions that had been mounds. Fallen into them were eight or ten rude headstones with inscriptions that I copied. It did not seem quite fair that these poor fellows should lie there under the forest leaves, their graves forgotten even by their own people, while our dead were so well housed under the big flag at Grafton, with monuments and flowers, music and Memorial days.

The last place that I visited was the old Confederate fort at the summit of Buffalo Mountain. Officially, in the postoffice department, the name is "Top of Alleghany," and it *is* the top of the main ridge. Here the regiment had its hardest fight in Western Virginia, and was most gloriously thrashed. When I saw the place (with better opportunities for observation than we had then) I knew why. The works are skilfully constructed and nearly a half mile in length, with emplacements for several batteries. They are built on a narrow ridge and are hardly more than one hundred and fifty yards wide at any point. At the rear, where our attack was made (after the garrison, having defeated our co-operating force in front, had got "good and ready" for us to "surprise" them) there was but one approach, and that was by a narrow road, through acres of slashed timber, impenetrable to a cat. The trunks of the trees are still there, all pointing away from the fort, all decaying and none of them having even their largest branches. A big head-log across the embrasure commanding the road is so rotten that one can pick it to pieces with the fingers. I fancy the Yankee bullets have all been picked out of it; I found none.

The slashed timber, which prevented us from attacking in line, saved our lives—most of them—when we attacked in column. We took cover in it and pot-shotted the fellows behind the parapet all day, as I recollect it, and then withdrew and began our long retreat in a frame of mind that would have done credit to an imp of Satan.

The road that penetrated the slashed timber is easily traced; I recognized the spot where Captain Madden fell, at the extreme head of the column. Lord! how close to the works it was—I had thought it farther away.

This fortification is distant from our camp at the summit of Cheat Mountain some twenty miles, with nothing intervening but valleys and low hills. In those winter days of '61 we used to watch the blue smoke of the Confederate camp with intense interest, but that was all we could see of our enemies. But from their position they could see all that we did, if they had glasses of moderate power. They could see our houses, our fort, our parade ground, all our movements; for our position was a little over on their side of the summit. Both camps guarded the old Staunton and Parkersburg turnpike, a fine and famous road in its day, but now fallen into disuse and no longer a "main traveled road." But the whole region is wild and grand, and if any one of the men who in his golden youth soldiered through its sleepy valleys and over its gracious mountains will revisit it in the hazy season when it is all aflame with the autumn foliage I promise him sentiments that he will willingly entertain and emotions that he will care to feel. Among them, I fear, will be a haunting envy of those of his comrades whose fall and burial in that enchanted land he once bewailed.

On a Mountain

[Bierce's account of his experiences at Cheat Mountain (in what is now West Virginia) was first published in the "Bits of Autobiography" section of his *Collected Works,* volume 1 (1909). On October 3, 1861, Bierce took part in a reconnaissance mission at Cheat Mountain (the battle had taken place on September 10–15), shortly after Bierce's regiment, the 9th Indiana Volunteer Infantry, had enlisted for three years (its first three-month enlistment had extended from May to July).]

They say that the lumberman has looked upon the Cheat Mountain country and seen that it is good, and I hear that some wealthy gentlemen have been there and made a game preserve. There must be lumber and, I suppose, sport, but some

things one could wish were ordered otherwise. Looking back upon it through the
haze of near half a century, I see that region as a veritable realm of enchantment;
the Alleghanies as the Delectable Mountains. I note again their dim, blue billows,
ridge after ridge interminable, beyond purple valleys full of sleep, "in which it
seemèd always afternoon."⁷ Miles and miles away, where the lift of earth meets
the stoop of sky, I discern an imperfection in the tint, a faint graying of the blue
above the main range—the smoke of an enemy's camp.

It was in the autumn of that "most immemorial year,"⁸ the 1861st of our
Lord, and of our Heroic Age the first, that a small brigade of raw troops—
troops were all raw in those days—had been pushed in across the Ohio border
and after various vicissitudes of fortune and mismanagement found itself,
greatly to its own surprise, at Cheat Mountain Pass, holding a road that ran
from Nowhere to the southeast. Some of us had served through the summer in
the "three-months' regiments," which responded to the President's first call for
troops. We were regarded by the others with profound respect as "old soldiers."
(Our ages, if equalized, would, I fancy, have given about twenty years to each
man.) We gave ourselves, this aristocracy of service, no end of military airs;
some of us even going to the extreme of keeping our jackets buttoned and our
hair combed. We had been in action, too; had shot off a Confederate leg at
Philippi, "the first battle of the war,"⁹ and had lost as many as a dozen men at
Laurel Hill and Carrick's Ford, whither the enemy had fled in trying, Heaven
knows why, to get away from us. We now "brought to the task" of subduing the
Rebellion a patriotism which never for a moment doubted that a rebel was a
fiend accursed of God and the angels—one for whose extirpation by force and
arms each youth of us considered himself specially "raised up."

It was a strange country. Nine in ten of us had never seen a mountain, nor a
hill as high as a church spire, until we had crossed the Ohio River. In power upon
the emotions nothing, I think, is comparable to a first sight of mountains. To a
member of a plains-tribe, born and reared on the flats of Ohio or Indiana, a
mountain region was a perpetual miracle. Space seemed to have taken on a new
dimension; areas to have not only length and breadth, but thickness.

Modern literature is full of evidence that our great grandfathers looked upon
mountains with aversion and horror. The poets of even the seventeenth century
never tire of damning them in good, set terms. If they had had the unhappiness
to read the opening lines of "The Pleasures of Hope," they would assuredly have
thought Master Campbell had gone funny and should be shut up lest he do
himself an injury.¹⁰

The flatlanders who invaded the Cheat Mountain country had been suckled
in another creed, and to them western Virginia—there was, as yet, no West Virginia—was an enchanted land. How we reveled in its savage beauties! With what
pure delight we inhaled its fragrances of spruce and pine! How we stared with
something like awe at its clumps of laurel!—real laurel, as we understood the

matter, whose foliage had been once accounted excellent for the heads of illustrious Romans and such—mayhap to reduce the swelling. We carved its roots into
finger-rings and pipes. We gathered spruce-gum and sent it to our sweethearts
in letters. We ascended every hill within our picket-lines and called it a "peak."

And, by the way, during those halcyon days (the halcyon was there, too, chatter-
ing above every creek, as he is all over the world) we fought another battle. It has
not got into history, but it had a real objective existence, although by a felicitous af-
terthought called by us who were defeated a "reconnaissance in force." Its short and
simple annals are that we marched a long way and lay down before a fortified camp
of the enemy at the farther edge of a valley. Our commander had the forethought to
see that we lay well out of range of the small-arms of the period. A disadvantage of
this arrangement was that the enemy was out of reach of us as well, for our rifles
were no better than his. Unfortunately—one might almost say unfairly—he had a
few pieces of artillery very well protected, and with those he mauled us to the eminent satisfaction of his mind and heart. So we parted from him in anger and returned to our own place, leaving our dead—not many.

Among them was a chap belonging to my company, named Abbott; it is not
odd that I recollect it, for there was something unusual in the manner of Abbott's
taking off. He was lying flat upon his stomach and was killed by being struck in
the side by a nearly spent cannon-shot that came rolling in among us. The shot
remained in him until removed. It was a solid round-shot, evidently cast in some
private foundry, whose proprietor, setting the laws of thrift above those of ballis-
tics, had put his "imprint" upon it: it bore, in slightly sunken letters, the name
"Abbott." That is what I was told—I was not present.

It was after this, when the nights had acquired a trick of biting and the
morning sun appeared to shiver with cold, that we moved up to the summit of
Cheat Mountain to guard the pass through which nobody wanted to go. Here
we slew the forest and built us giant habitations (astride the road from Nowhere to the southeast) commodious to lodge an army and fitly loopholed for
discomfiture of the adversary. The long logs that it was our pride to cut and
carry! The accuracy with which we laid them one upon another, hewn to the
line and bullet-proof! The Cyclopean doors that we hung, with sliding bolts fit
to be "the mast of some great ammiral"![11] And when we had "made the pile
complete"[12] some marplot[13] of the Regular Army came that way and chatted a
few moments with our commander, and we made an earthwork away off on
one side of the road (leaving the other side to take care of itself) and camped
outside it in tents! But the Regular Army fellow had not the heart to suggest the
demolition of our Towers of Babel, and the foundations remain to this day to
attest the genius of the American volunteer soldiery.

We were the original game-preservers of the Cheat Mountain region, for although we hunted in season and out of season over as wide an area as we dared
to cover we took less game, probably, than would have been taken by a certain

single hunter of disloyal views whom we scared away. There were bear galore and deer in quantity, and many a winter day, in snow up to his knees, did the writer of this pass in tracking bruin to his den, where, I am bound to say, I commonly left him. I agreed with my lamented friend, the late Robert Weeks, poet:

> Pursuit may be, it seems to me,
> Perfect without possession.[14]

There can be no doubt that the wealthy sportsmen who have made a preserve of the Cheat Mountain region will find plenty of game if it has not died since 1861. We left it there.

Yet hunting and idling were not the whole of life's programme up there on that wild ridge with its shaggy pelt of spruce and firs, and in the riparian lowlands that it parted. We had a bit of war now and again. There was an occasional "affair of outposts";[15] sometimes a hazardous scout into the enemy's country, ordered, I fear, more to keep up the appearance of doing something than with a hope of accomplishing a military result. But one day it was bruited about that a movement in force was to be made on the enemy's position miles away, at the summit of the main ridge of the Alleghanies—the camp whose faint blue smoke we had watched for weary days. The movement was made, as was the fashion in those 'prentice days of warfare, in two columns, which were to pounce upon the foeman from opposite sides at the same moment. Led over unknown roads by untrusty guides, encountering obstacles not foreseen—miles apart and without communication, the two columns invariably failed to execute the movement with requisite secrecy and precision. The enemy, in enjoyment of that inestimable military advantage known in civilian speech as being "surrounded," always beat the attacking columns one at a time or, turning red-handed from the wreck of the first, frightened the other away.

All one bright wintry day we marched down from our eyrie; all one bright wintry night we climbed the great wooded ridge opposite. How romantic it all was; the sunset valleys full of visible sleep; the glades suffused and interpenetrated with moonlight; the long valley of the Greenbrier stretching away to we knew not what silent cities; the river itself unseen under its "astral body" of mist! Then there was the "spice of danger."

Once we heard shots in front; then there was a long wait. As we trudged on we passed something—some things—lying by the wayside. During another wait we examined them, curiously lifting the blankets from their yellow-clay faces. How repulsive they looked with their blood-smears, their blank, staring eyes, their teeth uncovered by contraction of the lips! The frost had begun already to whiten their deranged clothing. We were as patriotic as ever, but we did not wish to be that way. For an hour afterward the injunction of silence in the ranks was needless.

· · · · ·

Repassing the spot the next day, a beaten, dispirited and exhausted force, feeble from fatigue and savage from defeat, some of us had life enough left, such as it was, to observe that these bodies had altered their position. They appeared also to have thrown off some of their clothing, which lay near by, in disorder. Their expression, too, had an added blankness—they had no faces.

As soon as the head of our straggling column had reached the spot a desultory firing had begun. One might have thought the living paid honors to the dead. No; the firing was a military execution; the condemned, a herd of galloping swine. They had eaten our fallen, but—touching magnanimity!—we did not eat theirs.[16]

The shooting of several kinds was very good in the Cheat Mountain country, even in 1861.

What I Saw of Shiloh

[This imperishable account of the battle of Shiloh—which Roy Morris Jr. calls the finest single work Bierce ever wrote—was first published in two parts in the *Wasp* (Dec. 23 and 30, 1881). It later appeared in a revised version in the *San Francisco Examiner* for June 19 and 26, 1898, and was revised again for "Bits of Autobiography." The first version, therefore, antedates Gen. U. S. Grant's "The Battle of Shiloh" (*Century Magazine,* Feb. 1885) by several years.

The battle was named for a rustic log meetinghouse near the Tennessee River's Pittsburg Landing in southwestern Tennessee. The Confederate Army of Mississippi[17] under A. S. Johnston surprised Grant's largely untested and exhausted Union Army of the Tennessee[18] at dawn on April 6, 1862. Bierce's 9th Indiana Infantry regiment division (part of the 2d Brigade, 4th Division, Army of the Ohio) moved from its camp on the eastern side of the Tennessee River, some ten miles from Pittsburg Landing, on the afternoon of the sixth, and across the river that night, moving into line during the night. After two days of ferocious fighting, the Union forces gained a tenuous victory. The battle was one of the worst of the war, with more than ten thousand Union and thirteen thousand Confederate killed, wounded, and missing.]

I.

This is a simple story of a battle; such a tale as may be told by a soldier who is no writer to a reader who is no soldier.

The morning of Sunday, the sixth day of April, 1862, was bright and warm. Reveille had been sounded rather late, for the troops, wearied with long marching, were to have a day of rest. The men were idling about the embers of their bivouac fires; some preparing breakfast, others looking carelessly to the condition of their arms and accoutrements, against the inevitable inspection; still others were chatting with indolent dogmatism on that never-failing theme, the end and object of the campaign. Sentinels paced up and down the confused front with a lounging freedom of mien and stride that would not have been tolerated at another time. A few of them limped unsoldierly in deference to blistered feet. At a little distance in rear of the stacked arms were a few tents out of which frowsy-headed officers occasionally peered, languidly calling to their servants to fetch a basin of water, dust a coat or polish a scabbard. Trim young mounted orderlies, bearing dispatches obviously unimportant, urged their lazy nags by devious ways amongst the men, enduring with unconcern their good-humored raillery, the penalty of superior station. Little negroes of not very clearly defined status and function lolled on their stomachs, kicking their long, bare heels in the sunshine, or slumbered peacefully, unaware of the practical waggery prepared by white hands for their undoing.

Presently the flag hanging limp and lifeless at headquarters was seen to lift itself spiritedly from the staff. At the same instant was heard a dull, distant sound like the heavy breathing of some great animal below the horizon. The flag had lifted its head to listen. There was a momentary lull in the hum of the human swarm; then, as the flag drooped the hush passed away. But there were some hundreds more men on their feet than before; some thousands of hearts beating with a quicker pulse.

Again the flag made a warning sign, and again the breeze bore to our ears the long, deep sighing of iron lungs. The division, as if it had received the sharp word of command, sprang to its feet, and stood in groups at "attention." Even the little blacks got up. I have since seen similar effects produced by earthquakes; I am not sure but the ground was trembling then. The mess-cooks, wise in their generation, lifted the steaming camp-kettles off the fire and stood by to cast out. The mounted orderlies had somehow disappeared. Officers came ducking from beneath their tents and gathered in groups. Headquarters had become a swarming hive.

The sound of the great guns now came in regular throbbings—the strong, full pulse of the fever of battle. The flag flapped excitedly, shaking out its blazonry of stars and stripes with a sort of fierce delight. Toward the knot of officers in its shadow dashed from somewhere—he seemed to have burst out of the ground in a cloud of dust—a mounted aide-de-camp, and on the instant rose the sharp, clear notes of a bugle, caught up and repeated, and passed on by other bugles, until the level reaches of brown fields, the line of woods trending away to far hills, and the unseen valleys beyond were "telling of the sound,"[19] the farther, fainter strains half drowned in ringing cheers as the men ran to range themselves behind the stacks of arms. For this call was not the wearisome "general" before which the tents go down; it was the exhilarating "assembly," which goes to the heart as wine and stirs the blood like the kisses of a beautiful woman. Who that has heard it calling to him above the grumble of great guns can forget the wild intoxication of its music?

II.

The Confederate forces in Kentucky and Tennessee had suffered a series of reverses, culminating in the loss of Nashville. The blow was severe: immense quantities of war material had fallen to the victor, together with all the important strategic points. General Johnston[20] withdrew Beauregard's[21] army to Corinth, in northern Mississippi, where he hoped so to recruit and equip it as to enable it to assume the offensive and retake the lost territory.[22]

The town of Corinth was a wretched place—the capital of a swamp. It is a two days' march west of the Tennessee River, which here and for a hundred and fifty miles farther, to where it falls into the Ohio at Paducah, runs nearly north. It is navigable to this point—that is to say, to Pittsburg Landing,[23] where Corinth got to it by a road worn through a thickly wooded country seamed with ravines and bayous, rising nobody knows where and running into the river under sylvan arches heavily draped with Spanish moss. In some places they were obstructed by fallen trees. The Corinth road was at certain seasons a branch of the Tennessee River. Its mouth was Pittsburg Landing. Here in 1862 were some fields and a house or two; now there are a national cemetery and other improvements.

It was at Pittsburg Landing that Grant[24] established his army, with a river in his rear and two toy steamboats as a means of communication with the east side, whither General Buell[25] with thirty thousand men was moving from Nashville to join him. The question has been asked, Why did General Grant occupy the enemy's side of the river in the face of a superior force before the arrival of Buell? Buell had a long way to come; perhaps Grant was weary of waiting. Certainly Johnston was, for in the gray of the morning of April 6th, when Buell's leading division was *en bivouac* near the little town of Savannah, eight or ten miles below, the Confederate forces, having moved out of Corinth two days before, fell upon Grant's advance brigades and destroyed them. Grant was at Savannah, but hastened to the Landing in time to find his camps in the hands of the enemy and the remnants of his beaten army cooped up with an impassable river at their

backs for moral support. I have related how the news of this affair came to us at
Savannah. It came on the wind—a messenger that does not bear copious details.

III.

On the side of the Tennessee River, over against Pittsburg Landing, are some
low bare hills, partly inclosed by a forest. In the dusk of the evening of April 6
this open space, as seen from the other side of the stream—whence, indeed, it
was anxiously watched by thousands of eyes, to many of which it grew dark long
before the sun went down—would have appeared to have been ruled in long,
dark lines, with new lines being constantly drawn across. These lines were the
regiments of Buell's leading division, which having moved up from Savannah
through a country presenting nothing but interminable swamps and pathless
"bottom lands," with rank overgrowths of jungle, was arriving at the scene of
action breathless, footsore and faint with hunger. It had been a terrible race;
some regiments had lost a third of their number from fatigue, the men dropping from the ranks as if shot, and left to recover or die at their leisure. Nor was
the scene to which they had been invited likely to inspire the moral confidence
that medicines physical fatigue. True, the air was full of thunder and the earth
was trembling beneath their feet; and if there is truth in the theory of the conversion of force, these men were storing up energy from every shock that burst
its waves upon their bodies. Perhaps this theory may better than another explain the tremendous endurance of men in battle. But the eyes reported only
matter for despair.

Before us ran the turbulent river, vexed with plunging shells and obscured in
spots by blue sheets of low-lying smoke. The two little steamers were doing their
duty well. They came over to us empty and went back crowded, sitting very low
in the water, apparently on the point of capsizing. The farther edge of the water
could not be seen; the boats came out of the obscurity, took on their passengers
and vanished in the darkness. But on the heights above, the battle was burning
brightly enough; a thousand lights kindled and expired in every second of time.
There were broad flushings in the sky, against which the branches of the trees
showed black. Sudden flames burst out here and there, singly and in dozens.
Fleeting streaks of fire crossed over to us by way of welcome. These expired in
blinding flashes and fierce little rolls of smoke, attended with the peculiar metallic ring of bursting shells, and followed by the musical humming of the fragments
as they struck into the ground on every side, making us wince, but doing little
harm. The air was full of noises. To the right and the left the musketry rattled
smartly and petulantly; directly in front it sighed and growled. To the experienced ear this meant that the death-line was an arc of which the river was the
chord. There were deep, shaking explosions and smart shocks; the whisper of

stray bullets and the hurtle of conical shells; the rush of round shot. There were faint, desultory cheers, such as announce a momentary or partial triumph. Occasionally, against the glare behind the trees, could be seen moving black figures, singularly distinct but apparently no longer than a thumb. They seemed to me ludicrously like the figures of demons in old allegorical prints of hell. To destroy these and all their belongings the enemy needed but another hour of daylight; the steamers in that case would have been doing him fine service by bringing more fish to his net. Those of us who had the good fortune to arrive late could then have eaten our teeth in impotent rage. Nay, to make his victory sure it did not need that the sun should pause in the heavens; one of the many random shots falling into the river would have done the business had chance directed it into the engine-room of a steamer. You can perhaps fancy the anxiety with which we watched them leaping down.

But we had two other allies besides the night. Just where the enemy had pushed his right flank to the river was the mouth of a wide bayou, and here two gunboats had taken station. They too were of the toy sort, plated perhaps with railway metals, perhaps with boiler-iron. They staggered under a heavy gun or two each. The bayou made an opening in the high bank of the river. The bank was a parapet, behind which the gunboats crouched, firing up the bayou as through an embrasure. The enemy was at this disadvantage: he could not get at the gunboats, and he could advance only by exposing his flank to their ponderous missiles, one of which would have broken a half-mile of his bones and made nothing of it. Very annoying this must have been—these twenty gunners beating back an army because a sluggish creek had been pleased to fall into a river at one point rather than another. Such is the part that accident may play in the game of war.

As a spectacle this was rather fine. We could just discern the black bodies of these boats, looking very much like turtles. But when they let off their big guns there was a conflagration. The river shuddered in its banks, and hurried on, bloody, wounded, terrified! Objects a mile away sprang toward our eyes as a snake strikes at the face of its victim. The report stung us to the brain, but we blessed it audibly. Then we could hear the great shell tearing away through the air until the sound died out in the distance; then, a surprisingly long time afterward, a dull, distant explosion and a sudden silence of small-arms told their own tale.

IV.

There was, I remember, no elephant on the boat that passed us across that evening, nor, I think, any hippopotamus. These would have been out of place. We had, however, a woman. Whether the baby was somewhere on board I did not learn. She was a fine creature, this woman; somebody's wife. Her mission, as she understood it, was to inspire the failing heart with courage; and when she selected mine I felt less flattered by her preference than astonished by her penetration. How did she learn? She stood on the upper deck with the red blaze of battle bathing her beautiful face, the twinkle of a thousand rifles mirrored in her eyes; and displaying a small ivory-handled pistol, she told me in a sentence punctuated by the thunder of great guns that if it came to the worst she would do her duty like a man! I am proud to remember that I took off my hat to this little fool.[26]

V.

Along the sheltered strip of beach between the river bank and the water was a confused mass of humanity—several thousands of men. They were mostly unarmed; many were wounded; some dead. All the camp-following tribes were there; all the cowards; a few officers. Not one of them knew where his regiment was, nor if he had a regiment. Many had not. These men were defeated, beaten, cowed. They were deaf to duty and dead to shame. A more demented crew never drifted to the rear of broken battalions. They would have stood in their tracks and been shot down to a man by a provost-marshal's guard, but they could not have been urged up that bank. An army's bravest men are its cowards. The death which they would not meet at the hands of the enemy they will meet at the hands of their officers, with never a flinching.

Whenever a steamboat would land, this abominable mob had to be kept off her with bayonets; when she pulled away, they sprang on her and were pushed by scores into the water, where they were suffered to drown one another in their own way. The men disembarking insulted them, shoved them, struck them. In return they expressed their unholy delight in the certainty of our destruction by the enemy.

By the time my regiment had reached the plateau night had put an end to the struggle. A sputter of rifles would break out now and then, followed perhaps by a spiritless hurrah. Occasionally a shell from a far-away battery would come pitching down somewhere near, with a whir crescendo, or flit above our heads with a whisper like that made by the wings of a night bird, to smother itself in the river. But there was no more fighting. The gunboats, however, blazed away at set intervals all night long, just to make the enemy uncomfortable and break him of his rest.

For us there was no rest. Foot by foot we moved through the dusky fields, we knew not whither. There were men all about us, but no camp-fires; to have made a blaze would have been madness. The men were of strange regiments; they mentioned the names of unknown generals. They gathered in groups by the wayside, asking eagerly our numbers. They recounted the depressing incidents of the day. A thoughtful officer shut their mouths with a sharp word as he passed; a wise one coming after encouraged them to repeat their doleful tale all along the line.

Hidden in hollows and behind clumps of rank brambles were large tents, dimly lighted with candles, but looking comfortable. The kind of comfort they supplied was indicated by pairs of men entering and reappearing, bearing litters; by low moans from within and by long rows of dead with covered faces outside. These tents were constantly receiving the wounded, yet were never full; they were continually ejecting the dead, yet were never empty. It was as if the helpless had been carried in and murdered, that they might not hamper those whose business it was to fall to-morrow.

The night was now black-dark; as is usual after a battle, it had begun to rain. Still we moved; we were being put into position by somebody. Inch by inch we crept along, treading on one another's heels by way of keeping together. Commands were passed along the line in whispers; more commonly none were given. When the men had pressed so closely together that they could advance no farther they stood stock-still, sheltering the locks of their rifles with their ponchos. In this position many fell asleep. When those in front suddenly stepped away those in the rear, roused by the tramping, hastened after with such zeal that the line was soon choked again. Evidently the head of the division was being piloted at a snail's pace by some one who did not feel sure of his ground. Very often we struck our feet against the dead; more frequently against those who still had spirit enough to resent it with a moan. These were lifted carefully to one side and abandoned. Some had sense enough to ask in their weak way for water. Absurd! Their clothes were soaken, their hair dank; their white faces, dimly discernible, were clammy and cold. Besides, none of us had any water. There was plenty coming, though, for before midnight a thunderstorm broke upon us with great violence. The rain, which had for hours been a dull drizzle, fell with a copiousness that stifled us; we moved in running water up to our ankles. Happily, we were in a forest of great trees heavily "decorated" with Spanish moss, or with an enemy standing to his guns the disclosures of the lightning might have been inconvenient. As it was, the incessant blaze enabled us to consult our watches and encouraged us by displaying our numbers; our black, sinuous line, creeping like a giant serpent beneath the trees, was apparently interminable. I am almost ashamed to say how sweet I found the companionship of those coarse men.

So the long night wore away, and as the glimmer of morning crept in through the forest we found ourselves in a more open country. But where? Not a sign of battle was here. The trees were neither splintered nor scarred, the underbrush was unmown, the ground had no footprints but our own. It was as if we had broken into glades sacred to eternal silence. I should not have been surprised to see sleek leopards come fawning about our feet, and milk-white deer confront us with human eyes.

A few inaudible commands from an invisible leader had placed us in order of battle. But where was the enemy? Where, too, were the riddled regiments that we had come to save? Had our other divisions arrived during the night and passed the river to assist us? or were we to oppose our paltry five thousand breasts to an army flushed with victory? What protected our right? Who lay upon our left? Was there really anything in our front?

There came, borne to us on the raw morning air, the long, weird note of a bugle. It was directly before us. It rose with a low, clear, deliberate warble, and seemed to float in the gray sky like the note of a lark. The bugle calls of the Federal and the Confederate armies were the same: it was the "assembly"! As it died away I observed that the atmosphere had suffered a change; despite the equilibrium established by the storm, it was electric. Wings were growing on blistered feet. Bruised muscles and jolted bones, shoulders pounded by the cruel knapsack, eyelids leaden from lack of sleep—all were pervaded by the subtle fluid, all were unconscious of their clay. The men thrust forward their heads, expanded their eyes and clenched their teeth. They breathed hard, as if throttled by tugging at the leash. If you had laid your hand in the beard or hair of one of these men it would have crackled and shot sparks.

VI.

I suppose the country lying between Corinth and Pittsburg Landing could boast a few inhabitants other than alligators. What manner of people they were it is impossible to say, inasmuch as the fighting dispersed, or possibly exterminated them; perhaps in merely classing them as non-saurian I shall describe them with sufficient particularity and at the same time avert from myself the natural suspicion attaching to a writer who points out to persons who do not know him the peculiarities of persons whom he does not know. One thing, however, I hope I may without offense affirm of these swamp-dwellers—they were pious. To what deity their veneration was given—whether, like the Egyptians, they worshiped the crocodile, or, like other Americans, adored themselves, I do not presume to guess. But whoever, or whatever, may have been the divinity whose ends they shaped, unto Him, or It, they had builded a temple. This humble edifice, centrally situated in the heart of a solitude, and conveniently accessible to the supersylvan crow, had been christened Shiloh Chapel, whence the name of the battle. The fact of a Christian church—assuming it to have been a Christian church—giving name to a wholesale cutting of Christian throats by Christian hands need not be dwelt on here; the frequency of its recurrence in the history of our species has somewhat abated the moral interest that would otherwise attach to it.

VII.

Owing to the darkness, the storm and the absence of a road, it had been impossible to move the artillery from the open ground about the Landing. The privation was much greater in a moral than in a material sense. The infantry soldier feels a confidence in this cumbrous arm quite unwarranted by its actual achievements in thinning out the opposition. There is something that inspires confidence in the way a gun dashes up to the front, shoving fifty or a hundred men to one side as if it said, "Permit *me!*" Then it squares its shoulders, calmly dislocates a joint in its back, sends away its twenty-four legs and settles down with a quiet rattle which says as plainly as possible, "I've come to stay." There is a superb scorn in its grimly defiant attitude, with its nose in the air; it appears not so much to threaten the enemy as deride him.

Our batteries were probably toiling after us somewhere; we could only hope the enemy might delay his attack until they should arrive. "He may delay his defense if he like," said a sententious young officer to whom I had imparted this natural wish. He had read the signs aright; the words were hardly spoken when a group of staff officers about the brigade commander shot away in divergent lines as if scattered by a whirlwind, and galloping each to the commander of a regiment gave the word. There was a momentary confusion of tongues, a thin line of skirmishers detached itself from the compact front and pushed forward, followed by its diminutive reserves of half a company each—one of which platoons it was my fortune to command. When the straggling line of skirmishers had swept four or five hundred yards ahead, "See," said one of my comrades, "she moves!" She did indeed, and in fine style, her front as straight as a string, her reserve regiments in columns doubled on the center, following in true subordination; no braying of brass to apprise the enemy, no fifing and drumming to amuse him; no ostentation of gaudy flags; no nonsense. This was a matter of business.

In a few moments we had passed out of the singular oasis that had so marvelously escaped the desolation of battle, and now the evidences of the previous day's struggle were present in profusion. The ground was tolerably level here, the forest less dense, mostly clear of undergrowth, and occasionally opening out into small natural meadows. Here and there were small pools—mere discs of rainwater with a tinge of blood. Riven and torn with cannonshot, the trunks of the trees protruded bunches of splinters like hands, the fingers above the wound interlacing with those below. Large branches had been lopped, and hung their green heads to the ground, or swung critically in their netting of vines, as in a hammock. Many had been cut clean off and their masses of foliage seriously impeded the progress of the troops. The bark of these trees, from the root upward to a height of ten or twenty feet, was so thickly pierced with bullets and grape that one could not have laid a hand on it without covering several punctures. None had escaped. How the human body survives a storm like this must be explained by the fact that it is exposed to it but a few moments at a time, whereas these grand old trees had had no one to take their places, from the rising to the going down of the sun. Angular bits of iron, concavo-convex, sticking in the sides of muddy depressions, showed where shells had exploded in their furrows. Knapsacks, canteens, haversacks distended with soaken and swollen biscuits, gaping to disgorge, blankets beaten into the soil by the rain, rifles with bent barrels or splintered stocks, waist-belts, hats and the omnipresent sardine-box—all the wretched débris of the battle still littered the spongy earth as far as one could see, in every direction. Dead horses were everywhere; a few disabled caissons, or limbers, reclining on one elbow, as it were; ammunition wagons standing disconsolate behind four or six sprawling mules. Men? There were men enough; all dead, apparently, except one, who lay near where I had halted my platoon to await the slower movement of the line—a Federal sergeant, variously hurt, who had been a fine giant in his time. He lay face upward, taking in his breath in convulsive, rattling snorts, and blowing it out in sputters of froth which crawled creamily down his cheeks, piling itself alongside his neck and ears. A bullet had clipped a groove in his skull, above the temple; from this the brain protruded in bosses, dropping off in flakes and strings. I had not previously known one could get on, even in this unsatisfactory fashion, with so little brain. One of my men, whom I knew for a womanish fellow, asked if he should put his bayonet through him. Inexpressibly shocked by the cold-blooded proposal, I told him I thought not; it was unusual, and too many were looking.[27]

VIII.

It was plain that the enemy had retreated to Corinth. The arrival of our fresh troops and their successful passage of the river had disheartened him. Three or four of his gray cavalry videttes[28] moving amongst the trees on the crest of a hill in our front, and galloping out of sight at the crack of our skirmishers' rifles, confirmed us in the belief; an army face to face with its enemy does not employ cavalry to watch its front. True, they might be a general and his staff. Crowning this rise we found a level field, a quarter of a mile in width; beyond it a gentle acclivity, covered with an undergrowth of young oaks, impervious to sight. We pushed on into the open, but the division halted at the edge. Having orders to conform to its movements, we halted too; but that did not suit; we received an intimation to proceed. I had performed this sort of service before, and in the exercise of my discretion deployed my platoon, pushing it forward at a run, with trailed arms, to strengthen the skirmish line, which I overtook some thirty or forty yards from the wood. Then—I can't describe it—the forest seemed all at once to flame up and disappear with a crash like that of a great wave upon the beach—a crash that expired in hot hissings, and the sickening "spat" of lead against flesh. A dozen of my brave fellows tumbled over like ten-pins. Some struggled to their feet, only to go down again, and yet again. Those who stood fired into the smoking brush and doggedly retired. We had expected to find, at most, a line of skirmishers similar to our own; it was with a view to overcoming them by a sudden *coup* at the moment of collision that I had thrown forward my little reserve. What we had found was a line of battle, coolly holding its fire till it could count our teeth. There was no more to be done but get back across the open ground, every superficial yard of which was throwing up its little jet of mud provoked by an impinging bullet. We got back, most of us, and I shall never forget the ludicrous incident of a young officer who had taken part in the affair walking up to his colonel, who had been a calm and apparently impartial spectator, and gravely reporting: "The enemy is in force just beyond this field, sir."

IX.

In subordination to the design of this narrative, as defined by its title, the incidents related necessarily group themselves about my own personality as a center; and, as this center, during the few terrible hours of the engagement, maintained a variably constant relation to the open field already mentioned, it is important that the reader should bear in mind the topographical and tactical features of the local situation. The hither side of the field was occupied by the front of my brigade—a length of two regiments in line, with proper intervals for field batteries. During the entire fight the enemy held the slight wooded acclivity beyond. The debatable ground to the right and left of the open was broken and thickly wooded for miles, in some places quite inaccessible to artillery and at very few points offering opportunities for its successful employment. As a consequence of this the two sides of the field were soon studded thickly with confronting guns, which flamed away at one another with amazing zeal and rather startling effect. Of course, an infantry attack delivered from either side was not to be thought of when the covered flanks offered inducements so unquestionably superior; and I believe the riddled bodies of my poor skirmishers were the only ones left on this "neutral ground" that day. But there was a very pretty line of dead continually growing in our rear, and doubtless the enemy had at his back a similar encouragement.

The configuration of the ground offered us no protection. By lying flat on our faces between the guns we were screened from view by a straggling row of brambles, which marked the course of an obsolete fence; but the enemy's grape was sharper than his eyes, and it was poor consolation to know that his gunners could not see what they were doing, so long as they did it. The shock of our own pieces nearly deafened us, but in the brief intervals we could hear the battle roaring and stammering in the dark reaches of the forest to the right and left, where our other divisions were dashing themselves again and again into the smoking jungle. What would we not have given to join them in their brave, hopeless task! But to lie inglorious beneath showers of shrapnel darting divergent from the unassailable sky—meekly to be blown out of life by level gusts of grape—to clench our teeth and shrink helpless before big shot pushing noisily through the consenting air—this was horrible! "Lie down, there!" a captain would shout, and then get up himself to see that his order was obeyed. "Captain, take cover, sir!" the lieutenant-colonel would shriek, pacing up and down in the most exposed position that he could find.

O those cursed guns!—not the enemy's, but our own. Had it not been for them, we might have died like men. They must be supported, forsooth, the feeble, boasting bullies! It was impossible to conceive that these pieces were doing the enemy as excellent a mischief as his were doing us; they seemed to raise their "cloud by day"[29] solely to direct aright the streaming procession of Confederate missiles. They no longer inspired confidence, but begot apprehension; and it was with grim satisfaction that I saw the carriage of one and another smashed into matchwood by a whooping shot and bundled out of the line.

X.

The dense forests wholly or partly in which were fought so many battles of the Civil War, lay upon the earth in each autumn a thick deposit of dead leaves and stems, the decay of which forms a soil of surprising depth and richness. In dry weather the upper stratum is as inflammable as tinder. A fire once kindled in it will spread with a slow, persistent advance as far as local conditions permit, leaving a bed of light ashes beneath which the less combustible accretions of previous years will smolder until extinguished by rains. In many of the engagements of the war the fallen leaves took fire and roasted the fallen men. At Shiloh, during the first day's fighting, wide tracts of woodland were burned over in this way and scores of wounded who might have recovered perished in slow torture. I remember a deep ravine a little to the left and rear of the field I have described, in which, by some mad freak of heroic incompetence, a part of an Illinois regiment had been surrounded, and refusing to surrender was destroyed, as it very well deserved. My regiment having at last been relieved at the guns and moved over to the heights above this ravine for no obvious purpose, I obtained leave to go down into the valley of death and gratify a reprehensible curiosity.

Forbidding enough it was in every way. The fire had swept every superficial foot of it, and at every step I sank into ashes to the ankle. It had contained a thick undergrowth of young saplings, every one of which had been severed by a bullet, the foliage of the prostrate tops being afterward burnt and the stumps charred. Death had put his sickle into this thicket and fire had gleaned the field. Along a line which was not that of extreme depression, but was at every point significantly equidistant from the heights on either hand, lay the bodies, half buried in ashes; some in the unlovely looseness of attitude denoting sudden death by the bullet, but by far the greater number in postures of agony that told of the tormenting flame. Their clothing was half burnt away—their hair and beard entirely; the rain had come too late to save their nails. Some were swollen to double girth; others shriveled to manikins. According to degree of exposure, their faces were bloated and black or yellow and shrunken. The contraction of muscles which had given them claws for hands had cursed each countenance with a hideous grin. Faugh! I cannot catalogue the charms of these gallant gentlemen who had got what they enlisted for.

XI.

It was now three o'clock in the afternoon, and raining. For fifteen hours we had been wet to the skin. Chilled, sleepy, hungry and disappointed—profoundly disgusted with the inglorious part to which they had been condemned—the men of my regiment did everything doggedly. The spirit had gone quite out of them. Blue sheets of powder smoke, drifting amongst the trees, settling against the hillsides and beaten into nothingness by the falling rain, filled the air with their peculiar pungent odor, but it no longer stimulated. For miles on either hand could be heard the hoarse murmur of the battle, breaking out near by with frightful distinctness, or sinking to a murmur in the distance; and the one sound aroused no more attention than the other.

We had been placed again in rear of those guns, but even they and their iron antagonists seemed to have tired of their feud, pounding away at one another with amiable infrequency. The right of the regiment extended a little beyond the field. On the prolongation of the line in that direction were some regiments of another division, with one in reserve. A third of a mile back lay the remnant of somebody's brigade looking to its wounds. The line of forest bounding this end of the field stretched as straight as a wall from the right of my regiment to Heaven knows what regiment of the enemy. There suddenly appeared, marching down along this wall, not more than two hundred yards in our front, a dozen files of gray-clad men with rifles on the right shoulder. At an interval of fifty yards they were followed by perhaps half as many more; and in fair supporting distance of these stalked with confident mien a single man! There seemed to me something indescribably ludicrous in the advance of this handful of men upon an army, albeit with their left flank protected by a forest. It does not so impress me now. They were the exposed flanks of three lines of infantry, each half a mile in length. In a moment our gunners had grappled with the nearest pieces, swung them half round, and were pouring streams of canister into the invaded wood. The infantry rose in masses, springing into line. Our threatened regiments stood like a wall, their loaded rifles at "ready," their bayonets hanging quietly in the scabbards. The right wing of my own regiment was thrown slightly backward to threaten the flank of the assault. The battered brigade away to the rear pulled itself together.

Then the storm burst. A great gray cloud seemed to spring out of the forest into the faces of the waiting battalions. It was received with a crash that made the very trees turn up their leaves. For one instant the assailants paused above their dead, then struggled forward, their bayonets glittering in the eyes that shone behind the smoke. One moment, and those unmoved men in blue would be impaled. What were they about? Why did they not fix bayonets? Were they stunned by their own volley? Their inaction was maddening! Another tremendous crash!—the rear rank had fired! Humanity, thank Heaven! is not made for this, and the shattered gray mass drew back a score of paces, opening a feeble fire. Lead had scored its old-time victory over steel; the heroic had broken its great heart against the commonplace. There are those who say that it is sometimes otherwise.

All this had taken but a minute of time, and now the second Confederate line swept down and poured in its fire. The line of blue staggered and gave way; in those two terrific volleys it seemed to have quite poured out its spirit. To this deadly work our reserve regiment now came up with a run. It was surprising to see it spitting fire with never a sound, for such was the infernal din that the ear could take in no more. This fearful scene was enacted within fifty paces of our toes, but we were rooted to the ground as if we had grown there. But now our commanding officer rode from behind us to the front, waved his hand with the courteous gesture that says *après vous,* and with a barely audible cheer we sprang into the fight. Again the smoking front of gray receded, and again, as the enemy's third line emerged from its leafy covert, it pushed forward across the piles of dead and wounded to threaten with protruded steel. Never was seen so striking a proof of the paramount importance of numbers. Within an area of three hundred yards by fifty there struggled for front places no fewer than six regiments; and the accession of each, after the first collision, had it not been immediately counterpoised, would have turned the scale.

As matters stood, we were now very evenly matched, and how long we might have held out God only knows. But all at once something appeared to have gone wrong with the enemy's left; our men had somewhere pierced his line. A moment later his whole front gave way, and springing forward with fixed bayonets we pushed him in utter confusion back to his original line. Here, among the tents from which Grant's people had been expelled the day before, our broken and disordered regiments inextricably intermingled, and drunken with the wine of triumph, dashed confidently against a pair of trim battalions, provoking a tempest of hissing lead that made us stagger under its very weight. The sharp onset of another against our flank sent us whirling back with fire at our heels and fresh foes in merciless pursuit—who in their turn were broken upon the front of the invalided brigade previously mentioned, which had moved up from the rear to assist in this lively work.

As we rallied to reform behind our beloved guns and noted the ridiculous brevity of our line—as we sank from sheer fatigue, and tried to moderate the terrific thumping of our hearts—as we caught our breath to ask who had seen such-and-such a comrade, and laughed hysterically at the reply—there swept past us and over us into the open field a long regiment with fixed bayonets and rifles on the right shoulder. Another followed, and another; two—three—four! Heavens! where do all these men come from, and why did they not come before? How grandly and confidently they go sweeping on like long blue waves of ocean chasing one another to the cruel rocks! Involuntarily we draw in our weary feet beneath us as we sit, ready to spring up and interpose our breasts when these gallant lines shall come back to us across the terrible field, and sift brokenly through among the trees with spouting fires at their backs. We still our breathing to catch the full grandeur of the volleys that are to tear them to shreds. Minute after minute passes and the sound does not come. Then for the first time we note that the silence of the whole region is not comparative, but absolute. Have we become stone deaf? See; here comes a stretcher-bearer, and there a surgeon! Good heavens! a chaplain!

The battle was indeed at an end.

XII.

And this was, O so long ago! How they come back to me—dimly and brokenly, but with what a magic spell—those years of youth when I was soldiering! Again I hear the far warble of blown bugles. Again I see the tall, blue smoke of camp-fires ascending from the dim valleys of Wonderland. There steals upon my sense the ghost of an odor from pines that canopy the ambuscade. I feel upon my cheek the morning mist that shrouds the hostile camp unaware of its doom, and my blood stirs at the ringing rifle-shot of the solitary sentinel. Unfamiliar landscapes, glittering with sunshine or sullen with rain, come to me demanding recognition, pass, vanish and give place to others. Here in the night stretches a wide and blasted field studded with half-extinct fires burning redly with I know not what presage of evil. Again I shudder as I note its desolation and its awful silence. Where was it? To what monstrous inharmony of death was it the visible prelude?

O days when all the world was beautiful and strange; when unfamiliar constellations burned in the Southern midnights, and the mocking-bird poured out his heart in the moon-gilded magnolia; when there was something new under a new sun; will your fine, far memories ever cease to lay contrasting pictures athwart the harsher features of this later world, accentuating the ugliness of the longer and tamer life? Is it not strange that the phantoms of a blood-stained pe-

riod have so airy a grace and look with so tender eyes?—that I recall with difficulty the danger and death and horrors of the time, and without effort all that
was gracious and picturesque? Ah, Youth, there is no such wizard as thou! Give
me but one touch of thine artist hand upon the dull canvas of the Present; gild
for but one moment the drear and somber scenes of to-day, and I will willingly
surrender another life than the one that I should have thrown away at Shiloh. [1]

Appendix

[Even after writing his lengthy account of the battle of Shiloh,
Bierce continued to defend General Buell against those who would
deprive him of due credit in that vicious conflict.]

The death of Gen. Don Carlos Buell provoked hardly a ripple of interest. To many
of the present generation he was hardly known as an historical figure. Yet he was a
notable person in his day, and by many of the old Army men he was regarded as the
ablest soldier of the Civil War. The whiskered pandours and the fierce hussars of
the non-combatant contingent in Washington and elsewhere, the iron-handed
Stanton[30] and his fiery following, thought that Buell's treatment of the Southern
people had too much rose-water in it; many of his men and officers resented being
put on guard over the property of their enemies, and the seraphim and cherubim
of Abolition continually did cry. So his magnificent "Army of the Ohio" was taken
away from him, he was denied another opportunity and resigned before the close
of the war; but if ever that turbulent time have a competent historian who had nothing to do with it the name of Don Carlos Buell will not need to be shouted in letters
of brass to obtain an honorable mention.

Buell's most notable service was the rescue of Grant's army from the consequences of its commander's astonishing fatuity at Shiloh, or more accurately
Pittsburg Landing. And in the ensuing controversy he showed literary qualities
of the highest order. One has only to read this controversy between Buell on one
side and Grant and Sherman[31] on the other to get an abiding consciousness of the
man's immeasurable superiority to them in clarity of mind and conscience.[32]
Grant was no more a match for him in logic and veracity than upon that memorable field he was for Sidney Johnston in arms.

The facts are simple. At the close of the first day's battle Grant's camps were
held by the enemy and his army had been driven (withdrawn he says) to the river.
Night had put an end to the fighting. Buell arrived that evening and crossing
thirty thousand men attacked next morning. It required an all day's fight of incomparable severity for the united Federal armies to retake the lost ground and
win a victory which was merely not a defeat. These facts are conceded by all—
there is no dispute about them and they decide the question. Grant says he would
have won without Buell, although with him he did no more than save himself. If

that is true Buell's thirty thousand fresh troops counted for nothing, their labors and losses were needless, their assistance did not assist! That is the absurd position to which Grant's apologists are driven without their opponents having to make a single disputed statement. Let it be said in justice to them that they have never signified the faintest consciousness of the bog into which they have been herded. [2]

Stones River and Missionary Ridge

[This extract relates to the battle of Stones River (also Murfreesboro) in central Tennessee on December 31, 1862, and January 2, 1863.[33] Union General Rosecrans,[34] moving south from his base at Nashville with the Army of the Cumberland (formerly Buell's Army of the Ohio), met with Bragg's[35] Army of Tennessee as it was moving north. The ensuing battle was first thought by Bragg to have been a Confederate victory, but later was deemed a defeat because Bragg had to abandon Murfreesboro at its end.

Bierce fictionalized some elements of the battle in "A Resumed Identity" (*Cosmopolitan Magazine,* Sept. 1908; also in *Can Such Things Be?* [1909]).]

A correspondent has directed my attention to some recent utterances of Mr. Jerome B. Cox, concerning his services as commander of a field battery[36] at the great battle of Stone's River, or Murfreesboro. Mr. Cox has had the vanity to join "the innumerable caravan"[37] of "day-savers." The peculiarity of the day-saver is that, while he is but one of a mighty multitude each of whom believes himself to have "turned the tide of battle" by his personal efforts, he steadfastly ignores or passionately denies the existence (as day-savers) of all the rest. Captain Cox, it appears, saved the day at Stone's River by "mowing down" the enemy, who, with astonishing improvidence, came up to the mowing "nine battalions deep." "You can say," says Captain Cox, in conclusion of his story, "that our stubborn resistance changed the tide of victory and gave Rosecrans time to rally his men and Bragg got licked." Now I happen to be an eye-witness in this case: I saw the enemy's charge, the resistance, Captain Cox and all of it. Captain Cox was a brave and efficient officer: he fought his little battery with skill and discretion. But he was aided by several brigades of infantry which, veracity compels me to add, did most of the "mowing." In fact the incident was of such magnitude that Captain Cox and his guns cut a very small figure in it. And, after all, Bragg was not "licked" and the day was saved by the night.

It has seldom been my good fortune to meet a man who took part in a military engagement whose command did not signally distinguish itself in the action.

The insupportable vanity which so easily persuades itself of its own importance in the scheme of the universe finds in the obscurity and tumult of battle its freest field and opportunity. This disagreeable phenomenon of self-magnification makes nearly all personal narrative of military service practically valueless. No battle of the civil war was so prolific of day-savers and tide-turners as the engagement at Stone's River. The history of that action is exceedingly simple. The two armies, nearly equal in strength, confronted one another on level ground at daybreak. As the Federal left was preparing to attack the Confederate right the Confederate left took the initiative and attacked the Federal right. By nightfall, which put an end to the engagement, the whole Federal line had been turned upon its left, as upon a hinge, till it lay at a right angle to its first direction. Yet I have heard at least a dozen commands of regiments, brigades and divisions of the beaten right make strenuous claims to the distinction of having resisted enough longer than the rest to save the army. Their conviction was undoubtedly shared by nearly every man and officer in their commands. The late Senator Miller,[38] whose brigade was driven from the field along with the others, always declared that its heroism stayed Bragg's whole army and wrested the victory from his hands. Two days later Bragg made a feeble attempt with six thousand men upon our left and rear. After it had been repulsed by our artillery alone, Miller's brigade and four or five others crossed a creek and assailed its retreat—to them an easy and almost bloodless operation. Miller was, I am convinced, fully persuaded that he again saved the army; and so persistently did his partisans repeat the tale that it became his chief public claim to political preferment. It was not until after his death that Mr. Cox ventured to stand forth in defense of the everlasting truth! [1]

> [The incident described below probably took place in early 1863, shortly after the battle of Stones River, since Readyville, the small town mentioned by Bierce as the site of the event, is a few miles east of Murfreesboro.]

In an article on military punishments a writer in "Chambers' Journal" describes various brutalities practiced in the English army during the last century. Among them was that known as riding the wooden horse. For back the steed had a plank edge upward and the horseman was not permitted the luxury of stirrups, but in order that he might have a certain stability and augment the firmness of his session in the no saddle various material objects of a considerable weight were annexed to the ankles of him. We are assured with an almost audible sigh for the depravity of our forefathers that the remains of a wooden horse were standing on the parade at Portsmouth as lately as 1760. The wooden horse it will be observed differs from the ordinary domestic horse (*Equus penalis Hobarti*) even in death: its remains will stand alone, whereas the strongest man cannot stand those of the other beast.

Well, as lately as 1863 in this land of light and law the spectacle of a wooden horse carrying double or even triple was for weeks a familiar one to this present writer. Indeed, I have seen the animal serving as charger to as many as a half-dozen American warriors, the two legs of each thoughtfully provided with ballast of rock. This was at the little Tennessee village of Readyville, where I dare say tradition still babbles imperfect witness of the military phenomenon. I do not know if the wooden horse is still extant in American military life.[39] If so it would seem singularly suited to the moral needs of the headless horseman of the retired list who are now so anxious to avert the horrors of peace by charging the British battleships. I am not sure but the fiery Dimond himself would, as a spectacular extravaganza, have an added picturesqueness if given an oaken mount; and in default of something better and heavier to keep him from falling off, I should not mind serving my country in the humble character of ballast by clinging to his legs. [2]

> [Bierce's opinion of General Grant was not high, but as a vigorous
> imbiber himself he was at pains to defend Grant against the charge
> of immoderate drinking. In so doing he brings up memories of the
> battle of Missionary Ridge on November 23–25, 1863.]

A deal of indignation is in course of discharge upon the memory of the late General Halleck[40] because he is said to have telegraphed to McClellan,[41] soon after the capture of Fort Donelson,[42] that Grant was "somewhere in the rear of his army, drunk." Defenders of Halleck are not lacking. They say he never sent such a telegram. They say that if he did he may honestly have erred. They say he was, anyhow, a competent commander—which is not so. They say this and they say that. So far, nobody seems to have thought to inquire if the telegram was true. For my part, I know of nothing in great military or civic abilities incompatible with a love of strong drink, nor any reason to suppose that a true patriot may not have the misfortune to be dissipated. Alexander the Great was a drunkard, and died of it. Webster was as often drunk as sober. The instances are numberless. When the nation's admiration of Grant, who was really an admirable soldier, shall have accomplished its fermentation and purged itself of toadyism, men of taste will not be ashamed to set it before their guests at a feast of reason. I present it as an intellectual tipple that one offers with an apology.

Old army men and old Californians need not be told that in Grant's early days of service he swallowed a good deal more than he chewed. With them the question whether he reformed before the battle at Donelson or afterward is not of sufficient importance to enlist their enthusiasm on the one side or the other. My own observation—take it for what it is worth—is that it was some time afterward. As late as the battle of Mission Ridge (November 25, 1863) it was my privilege to be close to him for six or seven hours, on Orchard Knob—him and his staff and a variable group of other general and staff officers, including Thomas, Granger, Sheridan, Wood and Hazen. They looked upon the wine when it was red, these tall fellows— they bit glass. The poisoned chalice went about and about. Some of them did not kiss the dragon; my recollection is that Grant commonly did. I don't think he took enough to comfort the enemy—not more than I did myself from another battle— but I was all the time afraid he would, which was ungenerous, for he did not appear at all afraid I would. This confidence touched me deeply.

Many times since then I have read with pleasure and approval the warmest praises of Grant's total abstinence from some of the gentlemen then and there present.

> "Such virtues as we have
> Our piety doth grace the gods withal."

These gentlemen were themselves total abstainers from the truth. [3]

A Little of Chickamauga

["A Little of Chickamauga" first appeared (as "Chickamauga") in the *San Francisco Examiner* for April 24, 1898, and in slightly revised form in "Bits of Autobiography."[43]

On the heels of a swift and fairly bloodless (by Civil War standards) Federal campaign from Nashville to Chattanooga, the battle of Chickamauga took place on September 19-20, 1863, in northwestern Georgia and southern Tennessee. Bragg's Army of Tennessee, reinforced by a corps from Lee's Army of Northern Virginia, struck Rosecrans's Army of the Cumberland incautiously advancing south from Chattanooga and cut the Federal force nearly in half. The battle was distinguished not only by its bloodiness but also by the peculiar topography of the area, vine-choked woods interspersed with open farmland.

Bierce later dramatized the battle in one of his finest stories, "Chickamauga" (*San Francisco Examiner*, Jan. 20, 1889; in *Tales of Soldiers and Civilians* [1891]).]

The history of that awful struggle is well known—I have not the intention to record it here, but only to relate some part of what I saw of it; my purpose not instruction, but entertainment.

I was an officer of the staff of a Federal brigade. Chickamauga was not my first battle by many, for although hardly more than a boy in years, I had served at the front from the beginning of the trouble, and had seen enough of war to give me a fair understanding of it. We knew well enough that there was to be a fight: the fact that we did not want one would have told us that, for Bragg always retired when we wanted to fight and fought when we most desired peace. We had manœuvred him out of Chattanooga, but had not manœuvred our entire army into it, and he fell back so sullenly that those of us who followed, keeping him actually in sight, were a good deal more concerned about effecting a junction with the rest of our army than to push the pursuit. By the time that Rosecrans[44] had got his three scattered corps together we were a long way from Chattanooga, with our line of communication with it so exposed that Bragg turned to seize it. Chickamauga was a fight for possession of a road.

Back along this road raced Crittenden's corps, with those of Thomas[45] and McCook,[46] which had not before traversed it.[47] The whole army was moving by its left.[48]

There was sharp fighting all along and all day, for the forest was so dense that the hostile lines came almost into contact before fighting was possible. One instance was particularly horrible. After some hours of close engagement my brigade, with foul pieces and exhausted cartridge boxes, was relieved and withdrawn to the road to protect several batteries of artillery—probably two dozen pieces—which commanded an open field in the rear of our line. Before our weary and virtually disarmed men had actually reached the guns the line in front gave way, fell back behind the guns and went on, the Lord knows whither. A moment later the field was gray with Confederates in pursuit. Then the guns opened fire with grape and canister and for perhaps five minutes—it seemed an hour—nothing could be heard but the infernal din of their discharge and nothing seen through the smoke but a great ascension of dust from the smitten soil. When all was over, and the dust cloud had lifted, the spectacle was too dreadful to describe. The Confederates were still there—all of them, it seemed—some almost under the muzzles of the guns. But not a man of all these brave fellows was on his feet, and so thickly were all covered with dust that they looked as if they had been reclothed in yellow.

"We bury our dead," said a gunner, grimly, though doubtless all were afterward dug out, for some were partly alive.

To a "day of danger" succeeded a "night of waking."[49] The enemy, everywhere held back from the road, continued to stretch his line northward in the hope to overlap us and put himself between us and Chattanooga. We neither saw nor heard his movement, but any man with half a head would have known that he was making it, and we met it by a parallel movement to our left. By morning we had edged along a good way and thrown up rude intrenchments at a little distance from the road, on the threatened side. The day was not very far advanced when we were attacked furiously all along the line, beginning at the left. When repulsed, the enemy came again and again—his persistence was dispiriting. He seemed to be using against us the law of probabilities: of so many efforts one would eventually succeed.

One did, and it was my luck to see it win. I had been sent by my chief, General Hazen,[50] to order up some artillery ammunition and rode away to the right and rear in search of it. Finding an ordnance train I obtained from the officer in charge a few wagons loaded with what I wanted, but he seemed in doubt as to our occupancy of the region across which I proposed to guide them. Although assured that I had just traversed it, and that it lay immediately behind Wood's division,[51] he insisted on riding to the top of the ridge behind which his train lay and overlooking the ground. We did so, when to my astonishment I saw the entire country in front swarming with Confederates; the very earth seemed to be moving toward us! They came on in thousands, and so rapidly that we had barely time to turn tail and gallop down the hill and away, leaving them in possession of the train, many of the wagons being upset by frantic efforts to put them about. By what miracle that officer had sensed the situation I did not learn, for we parted company then and there and I never again saw him.

By a misunderstanding Wood's division had been withdrawn from our line of battle just as the enemy was making an assault. Through the gap of half a mile the Confederates charged without opposition, cutting our army clean in two. The right divisions were broken up and with General Rosecrans in their midst fled how they could across the country, eventually bringing up in Chattanooga, whence Rosecrans telegraphed to Washington the destruction of the rest of his army.[52] The rest of his army was standing its ground.

A good deal of nonsense used to be talked about the heroism of General Garfield,[53] who, caught in the rout of the right, nevertheless went back and joined the undefeated left under General Thomas. There was no great heroism in it; that is what every man should have done, including the commander of the army. We could hear Thomas's guns going—those of us who had ears for them—and all that was needful was to make a sufficiently wide detour and then move toward the sound. I did so myself, and have never felt that it ought to make me President. Moreover, on my way I met General Negley,[54] and my duties as topographical engineer having given me some knowledge of the lay of the land offered to pilot him back to glory or the grave. I am sorry to say my good offices were rejected a little uncivilly, which I charitably attributed to the general's obvious absence of mind. His mind, I think, was in Nashville, behind a breastwork.

Unable to find my brigade, I reported to General Thomas, who directed me to remain with him. He had assumed command of all the forces still intact and was pretty closely beset. The battle was fierce and continuous, the enemy extending his lines farther and farther around our right, toward our line of retreat. We could not meet the extension otherwise than by "refusing" our right flank and letting him inclose us; which but for gallant Gordon Granger[55] he would inevitably have done.

This was the way of it. Looking across the fields in our rear (rather longingly) I had the happy distinction of a discoverer. What I saw was the shimmer of sunlight on metal: lines of troops were coming in behind us! The distance was too great, the atmosphere too hazy to distinguish the color of their uniform, even with a glass. Reporting my momentous "find" I was directed by the general to go and see who they were. Galloping toward them until near enough to see that they were of our kidney I hastened back with the glad tidings and was sent again, to guide them to the general's position.

It was General Granger with two strong brigades of the reserve, moving soldier-like toward the sound of heavy firing. Meeting him and his staff I directed him to Thomas, and unable to think of anything better to do decided to go visiting. I knew I had a brother in that gang—an officer of an Ohio battery.[56] I soon found him near the head of a column, and as we moved forward we had a comfortable chat amongst such of the enemy's bullets as had inconsiderately been fired too high. The incident was a trifle marred by one of them unhorsing another officer of the battery, whom we propped against a tree and left. A few moments later Granger's force was put in on the right and the fighting was terrific!

By accident I now found Hazen's brigade—or what remained of it—which had made a half-mile march to add itself to the unrouted at the memorable Snodgrass Hill.[57] Hazen's first remark to me was an inquiry about that artillery ammunition that he had sent me for.

It was needed badly enough, as were other kinds: for the last hour or two of that interminable day Granger's were the only men that had enough ammunition to make a five minutes' fight. Had the Confederates made one more general attack we should have had to meet them with the bayonet alone. I don't know why they did not; probably they were short of ammunition. I know, though, that while the sun was taking its own time to set we lived through the agony of at least one death each, waiting for them to come on.

At last it grew too dark to fight. Then away to our left and rear some of Bragg's people set up "the rebel yell." It was taken up successively and passed round to our front, along our right and in behind us again, until it seemed almost to have got to the point whence it started. It was the ugliest sound that any mortal ever heard—even a mortal exhausted and unnerved by two days of hard fighting, without sleep, without rest, without food and without hope. There was, however, a space somewhere at the back of us across which that horrible yell did not prolong itself; and through that we finally retired in profound silence and dejection, unmolested.

To those of us who have survived the attacks of both Bragg and Time, and who keep in memory the dear dead comrades whom we left upon that fateful field, the place means much. May it mean something less to the younger men whose tents are now pitched where, with bended heads and clasped hands, God's great angels stood invisible among the heroes in blue and the heroes in gray, sleeping their last sleep in the woods of Chickamauga. [1]

Appendix

> [On several occasions Bierce had reason to return to his discussion of the battle of Chickamauga. The first occurred when a reader commented on one facet of Bierce's essay when it was published in the *Examiner*.]

I have the following letter from a well-known physician of San Francisco:

"Dear sir—I read your article in 'The Examiner' on 'some personal recollections of Chickamauga' with a great deal of interest . . . from the fact that I had heard a description of that battle from a personal friend who was on the staff of General Jeff. C. Davis.[58] Your account differs from his in this particular: he characterizes Rosecrans' retreat with his staff from the battlefield as cowardly and ignominious in the extreme, of which you say nothing, possibly because Rosecrans so recently passed away. I should be more than pleased, if this was not the case, to have you relate the battle more fully, telling us why and through whom it was so nearly lost, also through whom the army was saved, although I have always understood that it was through the consummate skill of General Thomas and his brave supporters."

Rosecrans' retirement from the field was not cowardly: he was caught in the rout of the right and naturally supposed that the entire army had given way. His error lay in accepting that view of the disaster without inquiry and endeavoring to repair his broken fortunes by holding the reorganized fugitives at Chattanooga instead of leading them back to the support of his unbeaten left. If that was impracticable he should at least have gone himself, though Thomas undoubtedly did better work without him. There is no reason to doubt that he acted on his best judgment, which, however, was never very good. Rosecrans was many kinds of a brilliant crank, but his personal courage was beyond question. The action was lost, as I explained, by withdrawal of Wood's division from its center just as the enemy was attacking. That was Rosecrans' fault, for his order, in obedience to which Wood withdrew, was made under an unpardonable misconception. Wood was directed to close on the right of another division, which was supposed to be next to him on the left. It was not, and in order to reach it he left the front line to move behind the troops intervening. Rosecrans had forgotten his own dispositions. Under these circumstances, Wood would have been justified in deferring obedience and apprising his commander of the situation. As to who saved the army there can be no two intelligent opinions: it was saved by the superb obstinacy of Thomas and the soldierly instinct of Gordon Granger in marching toward the sound of cannon. [2]

> [More than a decade later, Bierce received an inquiry from Col. Archibald Gracie, who was writing a book on the battle, published as *The Truth about Chickamauga* (1911).[59] Bierce's response, in a letter to Gracie, follows.]

From the trouble that you took to consult me regarding certain phases of the battle of Chickamauga I infer that you are really desirous of the truth, and that your book is not to belong to that unhappily too large class of books written by "bad losers" for disparagement of antagonists. Sympathies and antipathies are disabilities in an historian that are hard to overcome. That you believe yourself devoid of this disability I do not doubt; yet your strange views of Thomas, Granger and Brannan,[60] and some of the events in which they figured, are (to me) so obviously erroneous that I find myself unable to account for them on the hypothesis of an entirely open mind. All defeated peoples are "bad losers"—history supplies no examples to the contrary, though there are always individual exceptions. (General D. H. Hill[61] is an example of the "good loser," and, with reference to the battle of Chickamauga, the good winner. I assume your familiarity with his account of that action, and his fine tribute of admiration to some of the men whom he fought—Thomas and others.) The historians who have found, and will indubitably continue to find, general acceptance are those who have most generously affirmed the good faith and valor of their enemies. All this, however, you have of course considered. But consider it again.

My very humble personal relation to the events at and about the Snodgrass house I partly explained to you, and you can get the rest from the little unmilitary sketch in the book that I lent you for the purpose. It seems to me that it gave me entirely adequate opportunities for observation. I passed almost the entire afternoon at and near the Snodgrass house, with nothing to do but look on, and, as a topographical officer, with some natural interest in, and knowledge of, "the lay of the land." Of my credibility as a witness you have of course no knowledge—no more than you can have of that of many others whom you quote, and must quote. But since you have asked for my views, I will set them down here a little more definitely than was possible in conversation, and you may take them for what they may seem to be worth.

I believe (and gave you some reasons for believing) that Granger did not arrive on the field until well along in the afternoon—I should say (with Hill—see *Battles and Leaders*)[62] not earlier than three o'clock.

I believe that Hazen was already in the Snodgrass field when Granger arrived, and had detached the Ninth Indiana, which was then on the ridge west of the

Snodgrass house; that it was among the men of that regiment that an ineffectual attempt was made to place a section of Aleshire's battery.[63] The facts that the section was commanded by my brother and that the Ninth Indiana was my regiment have given the incident unusual interest to me and tended to fix it in my mind.

There was at no time during the afternoon any organized body of troops occupying ground in the rear (north) of the Snodgrass house. Granger's were the only ones that even moved across it. We had no reserves—all our men were on the firing-line.

There is no hill, bald or otherwise, immediately to the north of the Snodgrass house. All is, and was then, open, level country for miles.

Hazen's fire was at no time directed toward what I think you call Horse-shoe Ridge. He faced due south and all his fire was in that direction.

The ridge immediately south of the Snodgrass house (I do not know if that is the one that you call Horse-shoe Ridge) was at no time, until after nightfall, occupied by the Confederates, nor was any other part of the ridges that our forces had held. Nobody was "driven" from this position; all retired in perfect order in the evening, there having been no fighting here for a long time—I should say an hour or two.

I do not share the belief of some of the officers of my regiment that the regiment was intentionally "sacrificed" by General Brannan. There was no occasion, no need, to "sacrifice" anybody, for, as said above, we were not at all pressed. I mingled freely, naturally, with the officers and men of my regiment for many months afterward, at Chattanooga and elsewhere, yet never heard a hint of such a thing. Nor did I see anything in what you read me from your manuscript to fortify such a charge.

The commonly accepted account of the second day's battle on our right is true if my eyes were normal. We were defeated all right, cleanly and gallantly, but not as some of your "authorities" say. [3]

[This extract was written a decade before "A Little of Chickamauga."]

Altogether apart from politics—which I abhor—I am sincerely sorry that Illinois "went" Republican, for that defeats General John M. Palmer,[64] the Democratic candidate for Governor. I knew General Palmer in the civil war and served in his division. He was a magnificent fellow in those days (the old man is about seventy-two now), courageous to the marrow in his bones, competent in command and with a perfectly ghastly frankness which kept every one about him in a white doubt as to what truth he would tell next. I believe he was the only commander on either side who ever made a mistake: he made a good one at the battle of Chickamauga. Yet the man's modesty was such that he did not at all glorify himself on account of it, but in his official report just mentioned as he would have mentioned anything else that came under his observation, and precisely as if it were a common, every-day occurrence—something that constituted no distinction and no more than anybody could do. His words are these, the officers mentioned being commanders of brigades:

> Hazen had been relieved by General Turchin,[65] who had formed on Cruft's[66] left, and he (Hazen) had retired to fill his boxes and protect some artillery which was threatened from the rear. I then committed the error of directing Gross to move to the right to engage in a severe fight going on in that direction.

There were greater soldiers than General Palmer, but as the author of the only error of the war which was not committed by the other fellow, he had, in my judgment, a just and reasonable claim to the distinction of governing Illinois, which is not much of a State anyhow.

While on the subject of great soldiers I may as well enlighten my editor about Colonel J. P. Jackson, the fiery soul who is accused of trying to incite a mob to hang a political opponent last Tuesday evening; the EXAMINER inquires who he is. In his civil capacity he is apparently a seller of experience to capitalists. As a warrior he says he "raised, equipped and commanded" the Twenty-third Kentucky Infantry during the war. When the panorama of the Battle of Missionary Ridge was first opened I had the pleasure of reading "Colonel" Jackson's glowing account of how he led that regiment up the ridge. The regiment was led up the ridge by Colonel James C. Foy, to whom I myself conveyed the order to go. It was in Hazen's brigade of Wood's division at that time and long before and after. I was an officer of Hazen's staff and naturally had to know the field-officers of the regiments. I knew those of the Twenty-third Kentucky, but I did not know Jackson, nor did I ever hear of him. It is my opinion that he was never a soldier at all or he would have known better than to make statements so easily refuted. He is not the only military impostor in California whose bubble of glory I can prick when so disposed. I have hitherto abstained because the bubbles are so gorgeous that I admire them myself.[67]

Colonel Foy, who, by the way, was killed during the Atlanta campaign, was a good fellow and a brave man but not a very clear thinker, of which fact he seemed guiltily conscious. A few weeks before he was knocked over we were cautiously moving against the enemy's line, through a thick wood. Foy's little battalion got lost and I was sent to look it up. It was found about a half-mile away, utterly isolated and marching straight to kingdom come. Foy had not the faintest notion of where he came from, where he was nor where he was going to. "What are you doing here, Colonel?" I asked, biting my lips to keep from laughing. He looked at me for a moment in a helpless and bewildered way, then pulled on a grave face and replied: "O, I'm sort o' flankin' 'em." [4]

The Crime at Pickett's Mill

["The Crime at Pickett's Mill: A Plain Account of a Bad Half Hour With Jo. Johnston" was published in the *San Francisco Examiner* for May 27, 1888, and reprinted in "Bits of Autobiography." It recounts the battle of Pickett's Mill on May 27, 1864, at a mill on Little Pumpkin Vine Creek, thirty miles northwest of Atlanta.

The battle is considered a part of the much larger Dallas Line/ New Hope Church battle, and because of its relatively small size does not often gain more than passing mention. It was an embarrassing failure for the Union forces. General Sherman had ordered Maj. Gen. Oliver O. Howard to attack what he believed to be the enemy's exposed flank; only one brigade at a time charged the enemy, and General Hazen's brigade—in which Bierce was an officer—was chosen first. The Confederates, however, were ready for the charge, and Hazen's troops were massacred. Both Sherman and Howard later minimized the action, leading Bierce to write his account.][68]

There is a class of events which by their very nature, and despite any intrinsic interest that they may possess, are foredoomed to oblivion. They are merged in the general story of those greater events of which they were a part, as the thunder of a billow breaking on a distant beach is unnoted in the continuous roar. To how many having knowledge of the battles of our Civil War does the name Pickett's Mill suggest acts of heroism and devotion performed in scenes of awful carnage to accomplish the impossible? Buried in the official reports of the victors there are indeed imperfect accounts of the engagement: the vanquished have not thought it expedient to relate it. It is ignored by General Sherman in his memoirs, yet Sherman ordered it. General Howard[69] wrote an account of the campaign of which it was an incident, and dismissed it in a single sentence; yet General Howard planned it, and it was fought as an isolated and independent action under his eye. Whether it was so trifling an affair as to justify this inattention let the reader judge.

The fight occurred on the 27th of May, 1864, while the armies of Generals Sherman and Johnston confronted each other near Dallas, Georgia, during the memorable "Atlanta campaign." For three weeks we had been pushing the Confederates southward, partly by manœuvring, partly by fighting, out of Dalton, out of Resaca, through Adairsville, Kingston and Cassville.[70] Each army offered battle everywhere, but would accept it only on its own terms. At Dallas Johnston made another stand and Sherman, facing the hostile line, began his customary manœuvring for an advantage. General Wood's division of Howard's corps occupied a position opposite the Confederate right. Johnston finding himself on the 26th overlapped by Schofield,[71] still farther to Wood's left, retired his right (Polk[72]) across a creek, whither we followed him into the woods with a deal of desultory bickering, and at nightfall had established the new lines at nearly a right angle with the old—Schofield reaching well around and threatening the Confederate rear.

The civilian reader must not suppose when he reads accounts of military operations in which relative positions of the forces are defined, as in the foregoing passages, that these were matters of general knowledge to those engaged. Such statements are commonly made, even by those high in command, in the light of later disclosures, such as the enemy's official reports. It is seldom, indeed, that a subordinate officer knows anything about the disposition of the enemy's forces—except that it is unaimable—or precisely whom he is fighting. As to the rank and file, they can know nothing more of the matter than the arms they carry. They hardly know what troops are upon their own right or left the length of a regiment away. If it is a cloudy day they are ignorant even of the points of the compass. It may be said, generally, that a soldier's knowledge of what is going on about him is coterminous with his official relation to it and his personal connection with it; what is going on in front of him he does not know at all until he learns it afterward.

At nine o'clock on the morning of the 27th Wood's division was withdrawn and replaced by Stanley's.[73] Supported by Johnson's division, it moved at ten o'clock to the left, in the rear of Schofield, a distance of four miles through a forest, and at two o'clock in the afternoon had reached a position where General Howard believed himself free to move in behind the enemy's forces and attack them in the rear, or at least, striking them in the flank, crush his way along their line in the direction of its length, throw them into confusion and prepare an easy victory for a supporting attack in front. In selecting General Howard for this bold adventure General Sherman was doubtless not unmindful of Chancellorsville, where Stonewall Jackson had executed a similar manœuvre for Howard's instruction.[74] Experience is a normal school: it teaches how to teach.

There are some differences to be noted. At Chancellorsville it was Jackson who attacked; at Pickett's Mill, Howard. At Chancellorsville it was Howard who was assailed; at Pickett's Mill, Hood.[75] The significance of the first distinction is doubled by that of the second.

The attack, it was understood, was to be made in column of brigades, Hazen's brigade of Wood's division leading. That such was at least Hazen's understanding I learned from his own lips during the movement, as I was an officer of his staff. But after a march of less than a mile an hour and a further delay of three hours at the end of it to acquaint the enemy of our intention to surprise him, our single shrunken brigade of fifteen hundred men was sent forward without support to double up the army of General Johnston. "We will put in Hazen and see what success he has." In these words of General Wood to General Howard we were first apprised of the true nature of the distinction about to be conferred upon us.

General W. B. Hazen, a born fighter, an educated soldier, after the war Chief Signal Officer of the Army and now long dead, was the best hated man that I ever knew, and his very memory is a terror to every unworthy soul in the service. His was a stormy life: he was in trouble all round. Grant, Sherman, Sheridan[76] and a countless multitude of the less eminent luckless had the misfortune, at one time and another, to incur his disfavor, and he tried to punish them all. He was always—after the war—the central figure of a court-martial or a Congressional inquiry, was accused of everything, from stealing to cowardice, was banished to obscure posts, "jumped on" by the press, traduced in public and in private, and always emerged triumphant. While Signal Officer, he went up against the Secretary of War and put him to the controversial sword. He convicted Sheridan of falsehood, Sherman of barbarism, Grant of inefficiency. He was aggressive, arrogant, tyrannical, honorable, truthful, courageous—a skillful soldier, a faithful friend and one of the most exasperating of men. Duty was his religion, and like the Moslem he proselyted with the sword. His missionary efforts were directed chiefly against the spiritual darkness of his superiors in rank, though he would turn aside from pursuit of his erring commander to set a chicken-thieving orderly astride a wooden horse, with a heavy stone attached to each foot. "Hazen," said a brother brigadier, "is a synonym of insubordination." For my commander and my friend, my master in the art of war, now unable to answer for himself, let this fact answer: when he heard Wood say they would put him in and see what success he would have in defeating an army—when he saw Howard assent—he uttered never a word, rode to the head of his feeble brigade and patiently awaited the command to go. Only by a look which I knew how to read did he betray his sense of the criminal blunder.

The enemy had now had seven hours in which to learn of the movement and prepare to meet it. General Johnston says:

"The Federal troops extended their intrenched line [we did not intrench] so rapidly to their left that it was found necessary to transfer Cleburne's[77] division to Hardee's[78] corps to our right, where it was formed on the prolongation of Polk's line."[79]

General Hood, commanding the enemy's right corps, says:

"On the morning of the 27th the enemy were known to be rapidly extending their left, attempting to turn my right as they extended. Cleburne was deployed to meet them, and at half-past five P.M. a very stubborn attack was made on this division, extending to the right, where Major-General Wheeler [80] with his cavalry division was engaging them. The assault was continued with great determination upon both Cleburne and Wheeler."[81]

That, then, was the situation: a weak brigade of fifteen hundred men, with masses of idle troops behind in the character of audience, waiting for the word to march a quarter-mile up hill through almost impassable tangles of underwood, along and across precipitous ravines, and attack breastworks constructed at leisure and manned with two divisions of troops as good as themselves. True, we did not know all this, but if any man on that ground besides Wood and Howard expected a "walkover" his must have been a singularly hopeful disposition. As topographical engineer it had been my duty to make a hasty examination of the ground in front. In doing so I had pushed far enough forward through the forest to hear distinctly the murmur of the enemy awaiting us, and this had been duly reported; but from our lines nothing could be heard but the wind among the trees and the songs of birds. Some one said it was a pity to frighten them, but there would necessarily be more or less noise. We laughed at that: men awaiting death on the battlefield laugh easily, though not infectiously.

The brigade was formed in four battalions, two in front and two in rear. This gave us a front of about two hundred yards. The right front battalion was commanded by Colonel R. L. Kimberly of the 41st Ohio, the left by Colonel O. H. Payne of the 124th Ohio, the rear battalions by Colonel J. C. Foy, 23d Kentucky,[82] and Colonel W. W. Berry, 5th Kentucky—all brave and skillful officers, tested by experience on many fields. The whole command (known as the Second Brigade, Third Division, Fourth Corps) consisted of no fewer than nine regiments, reduced by long service to an average of less than two hundred men each. With full ranks and only the necessary details for special duty we should have had some eight thousand rifles in line.

We moved forward. In less than one minute the trim battalions had become simply a swarm of men struggling through the undergrowth of the forest, pushing and crowding. The front was irregularly serrated, the strongest and bravest in advance, the others following in fan-like formations, variable and inconstant, ever defining themselves anew. For the first two hundred yards our course lay along the left bank of a small creek in a deep ravine, our left battalions sweeping along its steep slope. Then we came to the fork of the ravine. A part of us crossed below, the rest above, passing over both branches, the regiments inextricably intermingled, rendering all military formation impossible. The color-bearers kept well to the front with their flags, closely furled, aslant backward over their shoulders. Displayed, they would have been torn to rags by the boughs of the trees. Horses were all sent to the rear; the general and staff and all the field officers toiled along on foot as best they could. "We shall halt and form when we get out of this," said an aide-de-camp.

Suddenly there were a ringing rattle of musketry, the familiar hissing of bullets, and before us the interspaces of the forest were all blue with smoke. Hoarse, fierce yells broke out of a thousand throats. The forward fringe of brave and hardy assailants was arrested in its mutable extensions; the edge of our swarm grew dense and clearly defined as the foremost halted, and the rest pressed forward to align themselves beside them, all firing. The uproar was deafening; the air was sibilant with streams and sheets of missiles. In the steady, unvarying roar of small-arms the frequent shock of the cannon was rather felt than heard, but the gusts of grape which they blew into that populous wood were audible enough, screaming among the trees and cracking against their stems and branches. We had, of course, no artillery to reply.

Our brave color-bearers were now all in the forefront of battle in the open, for the enemy had cleared a space in front of his breastworks. They held the colors erect, shook out their glories, waved them forward and back to keep them spread, for there was no wind. From where I stood, at the right of the line—we had "halted and formed," indeed—I could see six of our flags at one time. Occasionally one would go down, only to be instantly lifted by other hands.

I must here quote again from General Johnston's account of this engagement, for nothing could more truly indicate the resolute nature of the attack than the Confederate belief that it was made by the whole Fourth Corps, instead of one weak brigade:

"The Fourth Corps came on in deep order and assailed the Texans with great vigor, receiving their close and accurate fire with the fortitude always exhibited by General Sherman's troops in the actions of this campaign. . . . The Federal troops approached within a few yards of the Confederates, but at last were forced to give way by their storm of well-directed bullets, and fell back to the shelter of a hollow near and behind them. They left hundreds of corpses within twenty paces of the Confederate line. When the United States troops paused in their advance within fifteen paces of the Texan front rank one of their color-bearers planted his colors eight or ten feet in front of his regiment, and was instantly shot dead. A soldier sprang forward to his place and fell also as he grasped the color-staff. A second and third followed successively, and each received death as speedily as his predecessors. A fourth, however, seized and bore back the object of soldierly devotion."[83]

Such incidents have occurred in battle from time to time since men began to venerate the symbols of their cause, but they are not commonly related by the enemy. If General Johnston had known that his veteran divisions were throwing their successive lines against fewer than fifteen hundred men his glowing tribute to his enemy's valor could hardly have been more generously expressed. I can attest the truth of his soldierly praise: I saw the occurrence that he relates and regret that I am unable to recall even the name of the regiment whose colors were so gallantly saved.

Early in my military experience I used to ask myself how it was that brave troops could retreat while still their courage was high. As long as a man is not disabled he can go forward; can it be anything but fear that makes him stop and finally retire? Are there signs by which he can infallibly know the struggle to be hopeless? In this engagement, as in others, my doubts were answered as to the fact; the explanation is still obscure. In many instances which have come under my observation, when hostile lines of infantry engage at close range and the assailants afterward retire, there was a "dead-line" beyond which no man advanced but to fall. Not a soul of them ever reached the enemy's front to be bayoneted or captured. It was a matter of the difference of three or four paces—too small a distance to affect the accuracy of aim. In these affairs no aim is taken at individual antagonists; the soldier delivers his fire at the thickest mass in his front. The fire is, of course, as deadly at twenty paces as at fifteen; at fifteen as at ten. Nevertheless, there is the "dead-line," with its well-defined edge of corpses—those of the bravest. Where both lines are fighting without cover—as in a charge met by a counter-charge—each has its "dead-line," and between the two is a clear space—neutral ground, devoid of dead, for the living cannot reach it to fall there.

I observed this phenomenon at Pickett's Mill. Standing at the right of the line I had an unobstructed view of the narrow, open space across which the two lines fought. It was dim with smoke, but not greatly obscured: the smoke rose and spread in sheets among the branches of the trees. Most of our men fought kneeling as they fired, many of them behind trees, stones and whatever cover they could get, but there were considerable groups that stood. Occasionally one of these groups, which had endured the storm of missiles for moments without perceptible reduction, would push forward, moved by a common despair, and wholly detach itself from the line. In a second every man of the group would be down. There had been no visible movement of the enemy, no audible change in the awful, even roar of the firing—yet all were down. Frequently the dim figure of an individual soldier would be seen to spring away from his comrades, advancing alone toward that fateful interspace, with leveled bayonet. He got no farther than the farthest of his predecessors. Of the "hundreds of corpses within twenty paces of the Confederate line," I venture to say that a third were within fifteen paces, and not one within ten.

It is the perception—perhaps unconscious—of this inexplicable phenomenon that causes the still unharmed, still vigorous and still courageous soldier to retire without having come into actual contact with his foe. He sees, or feels, that he *cannot*. His bayonet is a useless weapon for slaughter; its purpose is a moral one.

Its mandate exhausted, he sheaths it and trusts to the bullet. That failing, he re-treats. He has done all that he could do with such appliances as he has.

No command to fall back was given, none could have been heard. Man by man, the survivors withdrew at will, sifting through the trees into the cover of the ravines, among the wounded who could drag themselves back; among the skulkers whom nothing could have dragged forward. The left of our short line had fought at the corner of a cornfield, the fence along the right side of which was parallel to the direction of our retreat. As the disorganized groups fell back along this fence on the wooded side, they were attacked by a flanking force of the enemy moving through the field in a direction nearly parallel with what had been our front. This force, I infer from General Johnston's account, consisted of the brigade of General Lowrey,[84] or two Arkansas regiments under Colonel Baucum.[85] I had been sent by General Hazen to that point and arrived in time to witness this formidable movement. But already our retreating men, in obe-dience to their officers, their courage and their instinct of self-preservation, had formed along the fence and opened fire. The apparently slight advantage of the imperfect cover and the open range worked its customary miracle: the assault, a singularly spiritless one, considering the advantages it promised and that it was made by an organized and victorious force against a broken and retreating one, was checked. The assailants actually retired, and if they afterward renewed the movement they encountered none but our dead and wounded.

The battle, as a battle, was at an end, but there was still some slaughtering that it was possible to incur before nightfall; and as the wreck of our brigade drifted back through the forest we met the brigade (Gibson's) which, had the attack been made in column, as it should have been, would have been but five minutes behind our heels, with another five minutes behind its own. As it was, just forty-five minutes had elapsed, during which the enemy had destroyed us and was now ready to perform the same kindly office for our successors. Nei-ther Gibson nor the brigade which was sent to his "relief" as tardily as he to ours accomplished, or could have hoped to accomplish, anything whatever. I did not note their movements, having other duties, but Hazen in his "Narrative of Mili-tary Service" says:

"I witnessed the attack of the two brigades following my own, and none of these (troops) advanced nearer than one hundred yards of the enemy's works. They went in at a run, and as organizations were broken in less than a minute."[86]

Nevertheless their losses were considerable, including several hundred pris-oners taken from a sheltered place whence they did not care to rise and run. The entire loss was about fourteen hundred men, of whom nearly one-half fell killed and wounded in Hazen's brigade in less than thirty minutes of actual fighting.

General Johnston says:

"The Federal dead lying near our line were counted by many persons, officers and soldiers. According to these counts there were seven hundred of them."[87]

This is obviously erroneous, though I have not the means at hand to ascertain the true number. I remember that we were all astonished at the uncommonly large proportion of dead to wounded—a consequence of the uncommonly close range at which most of the fighting was done.

The action took its name from a water-power mill near by. This was on a branch of a stream having, I am sorry to say, the prosaic name of Pumpkin Vine Creek. I have my own reasons for suggesting that the name of that water-course be altered to Sunday-School Run. [1]

Appendix

[Six years after writing his account of Pickett's Mill, Bierce was still seething over the needless loss of life, and he took occasion to hurl one more salvo at General Howard.]

The Magazine of American History is to be revived, with General O. O. Howard as editor. General Howard's hardihood in accentuating his connection with American history transcends the limits of human effrontery and passes into the circumcluding domain of infinite gall. This military Quaker, spirited sheeply and skilled in the tactics of confusion and the strategy of retreat, will hardly try to keep up with his pen the place in American history that he won with his heels. I do not mean to affirm a lack of courage in General Howard; his crayfish charges were due to a lukewarm support on the part of the enemy—whose woful state of sin caused him the liveliest and most prayerful concern. The piety of the man is touching. When struck by a spent bullet he would knuckle down upon his Marybones and thank the God of Battles for letting him off with all his limbs; when his arm went he made a handsome acknowledgment of the divine goodness in thinking him worthy to keep his life. If he had incurred a bellyful of grapeshot he would have expended his last breath in gratitude for the safety of his hat. Of his patriotism there can be no question: this is a country of religious cant, and he loves it—a land of holy snuffle and he will fight for it as long as it has an enemy out of sight and hearing. He is about to retire, however, being sixty-four years old. If he had been born sixty-four years old it would have been greatly to the advantage of his military reputation outside church circles, and would have saved us two years of war.

I once had the honor to serve as a staff officer under this consummate master of the art of needless defeat, and he made the critical Confederate eye familiar with my back—which is not handsome. I said then that I would get even if spared, and Heaven having spared me for the good work, these remarks are in part performance of that pious vow. This explanation seems proper in order that they may be taken with whatever allowances the reader may think right and just in a matter not devoid of personal feeling. I should be sorry indeed to discredit any of my private animosities by disguising them as history.

Down in Georgia is a little forest where the blood of six hundred of my fifteen hundred battlemates utters a mute demand for recognition and place in this revenge. It took them only twenty minutes to fall, but it has taken General Howard thirty years to ignore their hopeless heroism, and he has not finished. He was probably the only officer present who expected a different result; but as humble testimony to the sustaining power of religion, I am bound to confess that he has borne his disappointment with a more unfailing cheerfulness than the rest of us have felt in the memory of our fulfilled expectations. *Vale,* General Howard!—may you live forever! And may every unctuous smile of your life cover a warm and comfortable consciousness of your soldierly generosity in enriching American history with *one line* about the affair at Pickett's Mill. [2]

A Letter from the Front Lines

[While he was attending school in Warsaw, Indiana, several years before the outbreak of the Civil War, Bierce struck up a friendship with Bernice Wright (whom Bierce called Fatima) and her sister Clara. Very little is known about this relationship, but by the time of Bierce's furlough in December 1863, when he returned to Warsaw for several months, he had become engaged to Fatima. In early June 1864 he wrote a long letter to Clara, vividly describing the rigors of military life and expressing his continuing esteem for both Fatima and Clara. The engagement, however, was broken off later that year.]

Hd. Qrs. 2nd Brig. 3d Div. 4th A.C.
Ackworth, Ga., June 8th, 1864.

My Dear Clara:

Will you be very much displeased to hear from me by letter?

If I thought so I would never touch pen again. 'Tis true you never asked me to write to you, but the knowledge that I still live cannot be unwelcome to one who professed to regard me as a *friend.* I don't know Clare what the word *friend* means to you who have so many, but to *me* friendship has a meaning deeper than the definition of Webster or Worcester.[88] And my friendship for you is a feeling which no language can define. Do you call this flattery? If so you do not know me and I forgive you.

I have not written to you before, but my neglect was not caused by indifference. I knew Tima would sometimes mention my name to you. But I want to hear from you very much; not because you will tell me of Tima, but of yourself. You always seemed to think, Clare, that I never cared for you except as Tima's sister—a sort of necessary evil. (*Vide*—our carriage ride by Eagle lake.) Is it necessary for me to say you were unjust to me? No, Clare, except our sweet Tima, I love you better than any one on this earth.

Perhaps this is not right;—perhaps my mother and sister should be first in my affections,—but so it is.

I am getting very tired of my present life and weary of the profession of arms. Not because of its horrors or dangers; not because its hardships affect me, but because I wish to be with you and my darling. The pleasant weeks with you, so like a dream, have nearly spoiled the soldier to make the—pensive individual.

Ask Tima why I get no more letters from her. Have I offended her? I may have written something as heartless and cruel as I used to say to her. If I have I hope she will forgive me. Her last letter was dated May 11th.

Do you think that there is a probability of my letters getting into other hands than hers? Please tell me for the thought troubles me very much. Oh, if I could be with you both again my measure of happiness would be full. I do not see how I could have been so unhappy as I sometimes was when with you.

But I ought rather to be thankful for being allowed so much happiness with you—so much more than I deserved—than to repine at the fate which withholds more. I hardly expect ever to see you again, and perhaps it is better so. Every day some one is struck down who is so much better than I. Since leaving Cleveland Tenn. my brigade has lost nearly one third its numbers killed and wounded.

Among these were so many good men who could ill be spared from the army and the world. And yet *I* am left. But my turn will come in time. Oh, how pleasant would death be were it for you and Tima, instead of for my country—for a cause which may be right and may be wrong. Do you think I lack patriotism for talking this way? Perhaps so. Soldiers are not troubled with that sort of stuff.

May I talk to you about D—? Do you love him yet? or think you do?

Is that a blunt question? You know you told me you did once. Please answer it.

Oh, I wish I could help you. You who have been so good to me. But my hands are tied. I can only warn you. There is a metal among the rocks here which viewed at a distance has all the appearances of gold. A close inspection shows it to be the basest dross. You are an admirer of pebbles I believe.

Do tell me all about yourself and Tima. What books you read, what society you have, and if you have lots of fun. Capt. Webster desired to be remembered to you and Tima if I ever wrote you. By the way is Jo Williams at W.? The less you have to do with him the better you will please me. If you require reasons I will give them. Do you know my mother yet, and does Tima call on her as she promised me? How is Lyde C.?

Now Clare if you don't write to me at once I shall take it as proof that you don't wish to hear from me again.

Give my kindest regards to 'Slissa and the girls.

Take my darling in your arms, and kiss her a thousand times for me.

With more love than I can tell, I am

Your friend
A. G. Bierce

P.S. Do you hear from Ol? I can get no word from him.

B—

It is raining very hard and I am very lonely. In looking over my valise just now I found tucked away snugly a little embroidered handkerchief. Do you remember it? Then there were also some little pebbles; common looking things enough, but each one is transparent, and looking into it I see two tiny figures with skirts just *slightly* elevated, showing such delicate little—feet, stepping along the soft sand, and picking up these little nothings for me. What delicate little tracks they leave behind them. But these tracks will all be erased by the next rain. Not so the impressions left on the hard and stony soil of my heart. Every examination shows me how some mischievous persons have crept into the garden of my soul, and tracked it up worse than a melon patch by school-boys.

But not one of the little tracks shall be blotted out by the rude gardener Time. The amount of it all is, Clare, that I love you and Tima so I can't find language to tell it.

I just wish I could pass my whole life with you both, and have nothing to do but give myself up to the delicious intoxication of your society. For that, I would renounce the whole world and all the ties of kindred; throw away every ambition or aim in life, and make a fool of myself in the most approved style generally.

Brady.

Four Days in Dixie

[In this essay—first published in the *San Francisco Examiner* (Nov. 4, 1888) and reprinted in "Bits of Autobiography"—Bierce briefly mentions the serious head wound he received at the battle of

Kennesaw Mountain on June 27, 1864, and recounts in detail his
brief capture by and escape from the rebel army during a rather
reckless reconnaissance mission near Gaylesville, Alabama, in October of that year.][89]

During a part of the month of October, 1864, the Federal and Confederate
armies of Sherman and Hood respectively, having performed a surprising and
resultless series of marches and countermarches since the fall of Atlanta,[90] confronted each other along the separating line of the Coosa River in the vicinity
of Gaylesville, Alabama. Here for several days they remained at rest—at least
most of the infantry and artillery did; what the cavalry was doing nobody but
itself ever knew or greatly cared. It was an interregnum of expectancy between
two régimes of activity.

I was on the staff of Colonel McConnell,[91] who commanded an infantry brigade in the absence of its regular commander. McConnell was a good man, but
he did not keep a very tight rein upon the half dozen restless and reckless young
fellows who (for his sins) constituted his "military family." In most matters we
followed the trend of our desires, which commonly ran in the direction of adventure—it did not greatly matter what kind. In pursuance of this policy of es-
capades, one bright Sunday morning Lieutenant Cobb, an aide-de-camp, and I
mounted and set out to "seek our fortunes," as the story books have it. Striking
into a road of which we knew nothing except that it led toward the river, we
followed it for a mile or such a matter, when we found our advance interrupted
by a considerable creek, which we must ford or go back. We consulted a moment and then rode at it as hard as we could, possibly in the belief that a high
momentum would act as it does in the instance of a skater passing over thin ice.
Cobb was fortunate enough to get across comparatively dry, but his hapless
companion was utterly submerged. The disaster was all the greater from my
having on a resplendent new uniform, of which I had been pardonably vain. Ah,
what a gorgeous new uniform it never was again!

A half-hour devoted to wringing my clothing and dry-charging my revolver,
and we were away. A brisk canter of a half-hour under the arches of the trees
brought us to the river, where it was our ill luck to find a boat and three soldiers of our brigade. These men had been for several hours concealed in the
brush patiently watching the opposite bank in the amiable hope of getting a
shot at some unwary Confederate, but had seen, none. For a great distance up
and down the stream on the other side, and for at least a mile back from it, extended cornfields. Beyond the cornfields, on slightly higher ground, was a thin
forest, with breaks here and there in its continuity, denoting plantations, probably. No houses were in sight, and no camps. We knew that it was the enemy's
ground, but whether his forces were disposed along the slightly higher country
bordering the bottom lands, or at strategic points miles back, as ours were, we

knew no more than the least curious private in our army. In any case the river line would naturally be picketed or patrolled. But the charm of the unknown was upon us: the mysterious exerted its old-time fascination, beckoning to us from that silent shore so peaceful and dreamy in the beauty of the quiet Sunday morning. The temptation was strong and we fell. The soldiers were as eager for the hazard as we, and readily volunteered for the madmen's enterprise. Concealing our horses in a cane-brake, we unmoored the boat and rowed across unmolested.

Arrived at a kind of "landing" on the other side, our first care was so to secure the boat under the bank as to favor a hasty re-embarking in case we should be so unfortunate as to incur the natural consequence of our act; then, following an old road through the ranks of standing corn, we moved in force upon the Confederate position, five strong, with an armament of three Springfield rifles and two Colt's revolvers. We had not the further advantage of music and banners. One thing favored the expedition, giving it an apparent assurance of success: it was well officered—an officer to each man and a half.

After marching about a mile we came into a neck of woods and crossed an intersecting road which showed no wheel-tracks, but was rich in hoof-prints. We observed them and kept right on about our business, whatever that may have been. A few hundred yards farther brought us to a plantation bordering our road upon the right. The fields, as was the Southern fashion at that period of the war, were uncultivated and overgrown with brambles. A large white house stood at some little distance from the road; we saw women and children and a few negroes there. On our left ran the thin forest, pervious to cavalry. Directly ahead an ascent in the road formed a crest beyond which we could see nothing.

On this crest suddenly appeared two horsemen in gray, sharply outlined against the sky—men and animals looking gigantic. At the same instant a jingling and tramping were audible behind us, and turning in that direction I saw a score of mounted men moving forward at a trot. In the meantime the giants on the crest had multiplied surprisingly. Our invasion of the Gulf States had apparently failed.

There was lively work in the next few seconds. The shots were thick and fast— and uncommonly loud; none, I think, from our side. Cobb was on the extreme left of our advance, I on the right—about two paces apart. He instantly dived into the wood. The three men and I climbed across the fence somehow and struck out across the field—actuated, doubtless, by an intelligent forethought: men on horseback could not immediately follow. Passing near the house, now swarming like a hive of bees, we made for a swamp two or three hundred yards away, where I concealed myself in a jungle, the others continuing—as a defeated commander would put it—to fall back. In my cover, where I lay panting like a hare, I could hear a deal of shouting and hard riding and an occasional shot. I heard some one calling dogs, and the thought of bloodhounds added its fine suggestiveness to the other fancies appropriate to the occasion.

Finding myself unpursued after the lapse of what seemed an hour, but was probably a few minutes, I cautiously sought a place where, still concealed, I could obtain a view of the field of glory. The only enemy in sight was a group of horsemen on a hill a quarter of a mile away. Toward this group a woman was running, followed by the eyes of everybody about the house. I thought she had discovered my hiding-place and was going to "give me away." Taking to my hands and knees I crept as rapidly as possible among the clumps of brambles directly back toward the point in the road where we had met the enemy and failed to make him ours. There I dragged myself into a patch of briars within ten feet of the road, where I lay undiscovered during the remainder of the day, listening to a variety of disparaging remarks upon Yankee valor and to dispirit-ing declarations of intention conditional on my capture, as members of the Opposition passed and repassed and paused in the road to discuss the morning's events. In this way I learned that the three privates had been headed off and caught within ten minutes. Their destination would naturally be Andersonville;[92] what further became of them God knows. Their captors passed the day making a careful canvass of the swamp for me.

When night had fallen I cautiously left my place of concealment, dodged across the road into the woods and made for the river through the mile of corn. Such corn! It towered above me like a forest, shutting out all the starlight except what came from directly overhead. Many of the ears were a yard out of reach. One who has never seen an Alabama river-bottom cornfield has not exhausted nature's surprises; nor will he know what solitude is until he explores one in a moonless night.

I came at last to the river bank with its fringe of trees and willows and canes. My intention was to swim across, but the current was swift, the water forbid-dingly dark and cold. A mist obscured the other bank. I could not, indeed, see the water more than a few yards out. It was a hazardous and horrible undertak-ing, and I gave it up, following cautiously along the bank in search of the spot where we had moored the boat. True, it was hardly likely that the landing was now unguarded, or, if so, that the boat was still there. Cobb had undoubtedly made for it, having an even more urgent need than I; but hope springs eternal in the human breast, and there was a chance that he had been killed before reaching it. I came at last into the road that we had taken and consumed half the night in cautiously approaching the landing, pistol in hand and heart in mouth. The boat was gone! I continued my journey along the stream—in search of another.

My clothing was still damp from my morning bath, my teeth rattled with cold, but I kept on along the stream until I reached the limit of the cornfields and en-tered a dense wood. Through this I groped my way, inch by inch, when, suddenly emerging from a thicket into a space slightly more open, I came upon a smolder-ing camp-fire surrounded by prostrate figures of men, upon one of whom I had almost trodden. A sentinel, who ought to have been shot, sat by the embers, his carbine across his lap, his chin upon his breast. Just beyond was a group of unsaddled horses. The men were asleep; the sentinel was asleep; the horses were asleep. There was something indescribably uncanny about it all. For a moment I believed them all lifeless, and O'Hara's familiar line, "The bivouac of the dead,"[93] quoted itself in my consciousness. The emotion that I felt was that inspired by a sense of the supernatural; of the actual and imminent peril of my position I had no thought. When at last it occurred to me I felt it as a welcome relief, and stepping silently back into the shadow retraced my course without having awakened a soul. The vividness with which I can now recall that scene is to me one of the marvels of memory.

Getting my bearings again with some difficulty, I now made a wide detour to the left, in the hope of passing around this outpost and striking the river beyond. In this mad attempt I ran upon a more vigilant sentinel, posted in the heart of a thicket, who fired at me without challenge. To a soldier an unexpected shot ringing out at dead of night is fraught with an awful significance. In my circumstances—cut off from my comrades, groping about an unknown country, surrounded by invisible perils which such a signal would call into eager activity—the flash and shock of that firearm were unspeakably dreadful! In any case I should and ought to have fled, and did so; but how much or little of conscious prudence there was in the prompting I do not care to discover by analysis of memory. I went back into the corn, found the river, followed it back a long way and mounted into the fork of a low tree. There I perched until the dawn, a most uncomfortable bird.

In the gray light of the morning I discovered that I was opposite an island of considerable length, separated from the mainland by a narrow and shallow channel, which I promptly waded. The island was low and flat, covered with an almost impenetrable cane-brake interlaced with vines. Working my way through these to the other side, I obtained another look at God's country—Shermany, so to speak. There were no visible inhabitants. The forest and the water met. This did not deter me. For the chill of the water I had no further care, and laying off my boots and outer clothing I prepared to swim. A strange thing now occurred—more accurately, a familiar thing occurred at a strange moment. A black cloud seemed to pass before my eyes—the water, the trees, the sky, all vanished in a profound darkness. I heard the roaring of a great cataract, felt the earth sinking from beneath my feet. Then I heard and felt no more.

At the battle of Kennesaw Mountain in the previous June I had been badly wounded in the head, and for three months was incapacitated for service. In truth, I had done no actual duty since, being then, as for many years afterward, subject to fits of fainting, sometimes without assignable immediate cause, but mostly when suffering from exposure, excitement or excessive fatigue. This combination of them all had broken me down—most opportunely, it would seem.

When I regained my consciousness the sun was high. I was still giddy and half blind. To have taken to the water would have been madness; I must have a raft. Exploring my island, I found a pen of slender logs: an old structure without roof or rafters, built for what purpose I do not know. Several of these logs I managed with patient toil to detach and convey to the water, where I floated them, lashing them together with vines. Just before sunset my raft was complete and freighted with my outer clothing, boots and pistol. Having shipped the last article, I returned into the brake, seeking something from which to improvise a paddle. While peering about I heard a sharp metallic click—the cocking of a rifle! I was a prisoner.

The history of this great disaster to the Union arms is brief and simple. A Confederate "home guard," hearing something going on upon the island, rode across, concealed his horse and still-hunted me. And, reader, when you are "held up" in the same way may it be by as fine a fellow. He not only spared my life, but even overlooked a feeble and ungrateful after-attempt upon his own (the particulars of which I shall not relate), merely exacting my word of honor that I would not again try to escape while in his custody. Escape! I could not have escaped a new-born babe.

At my captor's house that evening there was a reception, attended by the élite of the whole vicinity. A Yankee officer in full fig—minus only the boots, which could not be got on to his swollen feet—was something worth seeing, and those who came to scoff remained to stare. What most interested them, I think, was my eating—an entertainment that was prolonged to a late hour. They were a trifle disappointed by the absence of horns, hoof and tail, but bore their chagrin with good-natured fortitude. Among my visitors was a charming young woman from the plantation where we had met the foe the day before—the same lady whom I had suspected of an intention to reveal my hiding-place. She had had no such design; she had run over to the group of horsemen to learn if her father had been hurt—by whom, I should like to know. No restraint was put upon me; my captor even left me with the women and children and went off for instructions as to what disposition he should make of me. Altogether the reception was "a pronounced success," though it is to be regretted that the guest of the evening had the incivility to fall dead asleep in the midst of the festivities, and was put to bed by sympathetic and, he has reason to believe, fair hands.

The next morning I was started off to the rear in custody of two mounted men, heavily armed. They had another prisoner, picked up in some raid beyond the river. He was a most offensive brute—a foreigner of some mongrel sort, with just sufficient command of our tongue to show that he could not control his own. We traveled all day, meeting occasional small bodies of cavalrymen, by whom, with one exception—a Texan officer—I was civilly treated. My guards said, however, that if we should chance to meet Jeff Gatewood he would probably take me from them and hang me to the nearest tree; and once or twice, hearing horsemen approach, they directed me to stand aside, concealed in the brush, one of them remaining near by to keep an eye on me, the other going forward with my fellow-prisoner, for whose neck they seemed to have less tenderness, and whom I heartily wished well hanged.

Jeff Gatewood was a "guerrilla" chief of local notoriety, who was a greater terror to his friends than to his other foes. My guards related almost incredible tales of his cruelties and infamies. By their account it was into his camp that I had blundered on Sunday night.

We put up for the night at a farmhouse, having gone not more than fifteen miles, owing to the condition of my feet. Here we got a bite of supper and were permitted to lie before the fire. My fellow-prisoner took off his boots and was soon sound asleep. I took off nothing and, despite exhaustion, remained equally sound awake. One of the guards also removed his footgear and outer clothing, placed his weapons under his neck and slept the sleep of innocence; the other sat in the chimney corner on watch. The house was a double log cabin, with an open space between the two parts, roofed over—a common type of habitation in that region. The room we were in had its entrance in this open space, the fireplace opposite, at the end. Beside the door was a bed, occupied by the old man of the house and his wife. It was partly curtained off from the room.

In an hour or two the chap on watch began to yawn, then to nod. Pretty soon he stretched himself on the floor, facing us, pistol in hand. For a while he supported himself on his elbow, then laid his head on his arm, blinking like an owl. I performed an occasional snore, watching him narrowly between my eyelashes from the shadow of my arm. The inevitable occurred—he slept audibly.

A half-hour later I rose quietly to my feet, particularly careful not to disturb the blackguard at my side, and moved as silently as possible to the door. Despite my care the latch clicked. The old lady sat bolt upright in bed and stared at me. She was too late. I sprang through the door and struck out for the nearest point of woods, in a direction previously selected, vaulting fences like an accomplished gymnast and followed by a multitude of dogs. It is said that the State of Alabama has more dogs than school-children, and that they cost more for their keep. The estimate of cost is probably too high.

Looking backward as I ran, I saw and heard the place in a turmoil and uproar; and to my joy the old man, evidently oblivious to the facts of the situation, was lifting up his voice and calling his dogs. They were good dogs: they went back; otherwise the malicious old rascal would have had my skeleton. Again the traditional bloodhound did not materialize. Other pursuit there was no reason to fear; my foreign gentleman would occupy the attention of one of the soldiers, and in the darkness of the forest I could easily elude the other, or, if need be, get him at a disadvantage. In point of fact there was no pursuit.

I now took my course by the north star (which I can never sufficiently bless), avoiding all roads and open places about houses, laboriously boring my way through forests, driving myself like a wedge into brush and bramble, swimming every stream I came to (some of them more than once, probably), and pulling myself out of the water by boughs and briars—whatever could be grasped. Let any one try to go a little way across even the most familiar country on a moonless night, and he will have an experience to remember. By dawn I had probably not made three miles. My clothing and skin were alike in rags.[94]

During the day I was compelled to make wide detours to avoid even the fields, unless they were of corn; but in other respects the going was distinctly better. A light breakfast of raw sweet potatoes and persimmons cheered the inner man; a good part of the outer was decorating the several thorns, boughs and sharp rocks along my sylvan wake.

Late in the afternoon I found the river, at what point it was impossible to say. After a half-hour's rest, concluding with a fervent prayer that I might go to the bottom, I swam across. Creeping up the bank and holding my course still northward through a dense undergrowth, I suddenly reeled into a dusty highway and saw a more heavenly vision than ever the eyes of a dying saint were blessed withal—two patriots in blue carrying a stolen pig slung upon a pole!

Late that evening Colonel McConnell and his staff were chatting by a campfire in front of his headquarters. They were in a pleasant humor: some one had just finished a funny story about a man cut in two by a cannon-shot. Suddenly something staggered in among them from the outer darkness and fell into the fire. Somebody dragged it out by what seemed to be a leg. They turned the animal on its back and examined it—they were no cowards.

"What is it, Cobb?" said the chief, who had not taken the trouble to rise.

"I don't know, Colonel, but thank God it is dead!"

It was not.

What Occurred at Franklin

[Bierce's account of the battle of Franklin first appeared in *Cosmopolitan Magazine* for December 1906 under the title "What May Happen Along a Road," and later in "Bits of Autobiography."

When Sherman took Atlanta in September 1864 and cut free of his supply lines in his famous "March to the Sea," Hood, commanding the venerable Rebel Army of Tennessee, moved back into Tennessee in an ill-planned diversion. The Army of the Cumberland under Thomas and the Army of the Ohio (actually no more than XXIII Corps) under Schofield hurried in unseasonably bad weather to try to stay ahead of him.

On November 29, 1864, a small part of Schofield's army met Wheeler's cavalry near the small south-central Tennessee town of

Spring Hill and thought that they had lost the race. Hood failed to
give orders for deployment, and as Wheeler and the rest of the
army watched, Schofield's army was allowed to pass—sometimes
within earshot—the Army of Tennessee during the night and into
the city of Franklin.

The next day the Confederates made a frontal attack over open
country against Schofield's well-fortified position. The result was a
foregone conclusion—the Confederates suffered more than eight
thousand casualties in a few hours.]

For several days, in snow and rain, General Schofield's little army had crouched
in its hastily constructed defenses at Columbia, Tennessee. It had retreated in hot
haste from Pulaski, thirty miles to the south, arriving just in time to foil Hood,
who, marching from Florence, Alabama, by another road, with a force of more
than double our strength, had hoped to intercept us. Had he succeeded, he would
indubitably have bagged the whole bunch of us. As it was, he simply took position in front of us and gave us plenty of employment, but did not attack; he knew
a trick worth two of that.

Duck River was directly in our rear; I suppose both our flanks rested on it.
The town was between them. One night—that of November 27, 1864—we pulled
up stakes and crossed to the north bank to continue our retreat to Nashville,
where Thomas and safety lay—such safety as is known in war. It was high time
too, for before noon of the next day Forrest's[95] cavalry forded the river a few miles
above us and began pushing back our own horse toward Spring Hill, ten miles in
our rear, on our only road. Why our infantry was not immediately put in motion toward the threatened point, so vital to our safety, General Schofield could
have told better than I. Howbeit, we lay there inactive all day.

The next morning—a bright and beautiful one—the brigade of Colonel P.
Sidney Post[96] was thrown out, up the river four or five miles, to see what it could
see. What it saw was Hood's head-of-column coming over on a pontoon bridge,
and a right pretty spectacle it would have been to one whom it did not concern.
It concerned us rather keenly.

As a member of Colonel Post's staff, I was naturally favored with a good view
of the performance. We formed in line of battle at a distance of perhaps a half-
mile from the bridge-head, but that unending column of gray and steel gave us
no more attention than if we had been a crowd of farmer-folk. Why should it?
It had only to face to the left to be itself a line of battle. Meantime it had more
urgent business on hand than brushing away a small brigade whose only offense
was curiosity; it was making for Spring Hill with all its legs and wheels. Hour
after hour we watched that unceasing flow of infantry and artillery toward the
rear of our army. It was an unnerving spectacle, yet we never for a moment
doubted that, acting on the intelligence supplied by our succession of couriers,

our entire force was moving rapidly to the point of contact. The battle of Spring Hill was obviously decreed. Obviously, too, our brigade of observation would be among the last to have a hand in it. The thought annoyed us, made us restless and resentful. Our mounted men rode forward and back behind the line, nervous and distressed; the men in the ranks sought relief in frequent changes of posture, in shifting their weight from one leg to the other, in needless inspection of their weapons and in that unfailing resource of the discontented soldier, audible damning of those in the saddles of authority. But never for more than a moment at a time did any one remove his eyes from that fascinating and portentous pageant.

Toward evening we were recalled, to learn that of our five divisions of infantry, with their batteries, numbering twenty-three thousand men, only one—Stanley's, four thousand weak—had been sent to Spring Hill to meet that formidable movement of Hood's three veteran corps! Why Stanley was not immediately effaced is still a matter of controversy. Hood, who was early on the ground, declared that he gave the needful orders and tried vainly to enforce them; Cheatham,[97] in command of his leading corps, that he did not. Doubtless the dispute is still being carried on between these chieftains from their beds of asphodel and moly in Elysium. So much is certain: Stanley drove away Forrest and successfully held the junction of the roads against Cleburne's division, the only infantry that attacked him.

That night the entire Confederate army lay within a half mile of our road, while we all sneaked by, infantry, artillery, and trains. The enemy's camp-fires shone redly—miles of them—seemingly only a stone's throw from our hurrying column. His men were plainly visible about them, cooking their suppers—a sight so incredible that many of our own, thinking them friends, strayed over to them and did not return. At intervals of a few hundred yards we passed dim figures on horseback by the roadside, enjoining silence. Needless precaution; we could not have spoken if we had tried, for our hearts were in our throats. But fools are God's peculiar care, and one of his protective methods is the stupidity of other fools. By daybreak our last man and last wagon had passed the fateful spot unchallenged, and our first were entering Franklin, ten miles away. Despite spirited cavalry attacks on trains and rear-guard, all were in Franklin by noon and such of the men as could be kept awake were throwing up a slight line of defense, inclosing the town.

Franklin lies—or at that time did lie; I know not what exploration might now disclose—on the south bank of a small river, the Harpeth by name. For two miles southward was a nearly flat, open plain, extending to a range of low hills through which passed the turnpike by which we had come. From some bluffs on the precipitous north bank of the river was a commanding overlook of all this open ground, which, although more than a mile away, seemed almost at one's feet. On this elevated ground the wagon-train had been parked and General Schofield had stationed himself—the former for security, the latter for outlook. Both were guarded by General Wood's infantry division, of which my brigade was a part. "We are in beautiful luck," said a member of the division staff. With some prevision of what was to come and a lively recollection of the nervous strain of helpless observation, I did not think it luck. In the activity of battle one does not feel one's hair going gray with vicissitudes of emotion.

For some reason to the writer unknown General Schofield had brought along with him General D. S. Stanley, who commanded two of his divisions—ours and another, which was not "in luck." In the ensuing battle, when this excellent officer could stand the strain no longer, he bolted across the bridge like a shot and found relief in the hell below, where he was promptly tumbled out of the saddle by a bullet.

Our line, with its reserve brigades, was about a mile and a half long, both flanks on the river, above and below the town—a mere bridge-head. It did not look a very formidable obstacle to the march of an army of more than forty thousand men. In a more tranquil temper than his failure at Spring Hill had put him into Hood would probably have passed around our left and turned us out with ease—which would justly have entitled him to the Humane Society's great gold medal. Apparently that was not his day for saving life.

About the middle of the afternoon our field-glasses picked up the Confederate head-of-column emerging from the range of hills previously mentioned, where it is cut by the Columbia road. But—ominous circumstance!—it did not come on. It turned to its left, at a right angle, moving along the base of the hills, parallel to our line. Other heads-of-column came through other gaps and over the crests farther along, impudently deploying on the level ground with a spectacular display of flags and glitter of arms. I do not remember that they were molested, even by the guns of General Wagner,[98] who had been foolishly posted with two small brigades across the turnpike, a half-mile in our front, where he was needless for apprisal and powerless for resistance. My recollection is that our fellows down there in their shallow trenches noted these portentous dispositions without the least manifestation of incivility. As a matter of fact, many of them were permitted by their compassionate officers to sleep. And truly it was good weather for that: sleep was in the very atmosphere. The sun burned crimson in a gray-blue sky through a delicate Indian-summer haze, as beautiful as a daydream in paradise. If one had been given to moralizing one might have found material a-plenty for homilies in the contrast between that peaceful autumn afternoon and the bloody business that it had in hand. If any good chaplain failed to "improve the occasion" let us hope that he lived to lament in sackcloth-of-gold and ashes-of-roses his intellectual unthrift.

The putting of that army into battle shape—its change from columns into lines—could not have occupied more than an hour or two, yet it seemed an eternity. Its leisurely evolutions were irritating, but at last it moved forward

with atoning rapidity and the fight was on. First, the storm struck Wagner's isolated brigades, which, vanishing in fire and smoke, instantly reappeared as a
confused mass of fugitives inextricably intermingled with their pursuers. They
had not stayed the advance a moment, and as might have been foreseen were
now a peril to the main line, which could protect itself only by the slaughter of
its friends. To the right and left, however, our guns got into play, and simultaneously a furious infantry fire broke out along the entire front, the paralyzed
center excepted. But nothing could stay those gallant rebels from a hand-to-
hand encounter with bayonet and butt, and it was accorded to them with hearty
good-will.

Meantime Wagner's conquerors were pouring across the breastwork like water over a dam. The guns that had spared the fugitives had now no time to fire;
their infantry supports gave way and for a space of more than two hundred yards
in the very center of our line the assailants, mad with exultation, had everything
their own way. From the right and the left their gray masses converged into the
gap, pushed through, and then, spreading, turned our men out of the works so
hardly held against the attack in their front. From our viewpoint on the bluff we
could mark the constant widening of the gap, the steady encroachment of that
blazing and smoking mass against its disordered opposition.

"It is all up with us," said Captain Dawson, of Wood's staff; "I am going to
have a quiet smoke."

I do not doubt that he supposed himself to have borne the heat and burden
of the strife. In the midst of his preparations for a smoke he paused and looked
again—a new tumult of musketry had broken loose. Colonel Emerson Opdycke[99]
had rushed his reserve brigade into the *mêlée* and was bitterly disputing the
Confederate advantage. Other fresh regiments joined in the countercharge,
commanderless groups of retreating men returned to their work, and there ensued a hand-to-hand contest of incredible fury. Two long, irregular, mutable,
and tumultuous blurs of color were consuming each other's edge along the line
of contact. Such devil's work does not last long, and we had the great joy to see
it ending, not as it began, but "more nearly to the heart's desire."[100] Slowly the
mobile blur moved away from the town, and presently the gray half of it dissolved into its elemental units, all in slow recession. The retaken guns in the
embrasures pushed up towering clouds of white smoke; to east and to west
along the reoccupied parapet ran a line of misty red till the spitfire crest was
without a break from flank to flank. Probably there was some Yankee cheering,
as doubtless there had been the "rebel yell," but my memory recalls neither.
There are many battles in a war, and many incidents in a battle: one does not
recollect everything. Possibly I have not a retentive ear.

While this lively work had been doing in the center, there had been no lack of
diligence elsewhere, and now all were as busy as bees. I have read of many "successive attacks"—"charge after charge"—but I think the only assaults after the

first were those of the second Confederate lines and possibly some of the reserves; certainly there were no visible abatement and renewal of effort anywhere except where the men who had been pushed out of the works backward tried to reënter. And all the time there was fighting.

After resetting their line the victors could not clear their front, for the baffled assailants would not desist. All over the open country in their rear, clear back to the base of the hills, drifted the wreck of battle, the wounded that were able to walk; and through the receding throng pushed forward, here and there, horsemen with orders and footmen whom we knew to be bearing ammunition. There were no wagons, no caissons: the enemy was not using, and could not use, his artillery. Along the line of fire we could see, dimly in the smoke, mounted officers, singly and in small groups, attempting to force their horses across the slight parapet, but all went down. Of this devoted band was the gallant General Adams, whose body was found upon the slope, and whose animal's forefeet were actually inside the crest. General Cleburne lay a few paces farther out, and five or six other general officers sprawled elsewhere. It was a great day for Confederates in the line of promotion.[101]

For many minutes at a time broad spaces of battle were veiled in smoke. Of what might be occurring there conjecture gave a terrifying report. In a visible peril observation is a kind of defense; against the unseen we lift a trembling hand. Always from these regions of obscurity we expected the worst, but always the lifted cloud revealed an unaltered situation.

The assailants began to give way. There was no general retreat; at many points the fight continued, with lessening ferocity and lengthening range, well into the night. It became an affair of twinkling musketry and broad flares of artillery; then it sank to silence in the dark.

Under orders to continue his retreat, Schofield could now do so unmolested: Hood had suffered so terrible a loss in life and *morale* that he was in no condition for effective pursuit. As at Spring Hill, daybreak found us on the road with all our impedimenta except some of our wounded, and that night we encamped under the protecting guns of Thomas, at Nashville. Our gallant enemy audaciously followed, and fortified himself within rifle-reach, where he remained for two weeks without firing a gun and was then destroyed. [1]

Appendix

[The following two extracts relate to the events before and after the battle of Franklin. The second extract was written nearly two decades before Bierce's exhaustive treatment of the battle.]

An editorial writer in this paper said in last Wednesday's issue: "There were not many famous Generals who went with Sherman to the sea, but of the few

Schofield was one." This is an error which my collaborator will not mind having corrected. While Sherman was moving on Savannah from Atlanta, Schofield was moving on Nashville from Pulaski. Schofield was moving faster than Sherman, for Hood was hard after him. I happen to have some knowledge of this movement, for I was a part of it, and it is one of the proudest recollections of my life that although the movement was one of the most rapid and persistent that occurred during the war, I was strong, hardy and resolute enough to keep up with the procession. At Franklin, where we stopped long enough to have a bit of a debate with Hood, I was perched on a bluff on the safe side of a river, overlooking the "forum," and acted as one of the judges. My notion was that Hood failed to maintain the affirmative of the proposition that we were "his'n." That was Schofield's decision too; and he had good opportunities to judge, for he was right with me through the thickest of it. We were guarding the wagons, he and I, and the only property we lost was a mule, which straggled off across the bridge toward the field of glory and we couldn't call it back. The loss of that mule is the only stain upon General Schofield's military escutcheon: he, as Commander-in-Chief, ought to have followed it a little way, and if he couldn't persuade it to return he would have been justified in using violence. [2]

One of the cleverest writers that we have in the Golden Out Here is Mr. E. H. Clough, who has recently set up in Oakland a weekly paper named the *Paragraph,* which is as clever as he. But Mr. Clough is a man of peace, and if ever his paper becomes a great military authority, such as the *Century* was before it got a pension and retired to civil life, it is more likely to be through fits in the office than facts in the paper. It has occurred to Mr. Clough that a certain Mr. J. G. Edwards would be a good man for the Pension Agency—or, possibly, that the Pension Agency would be a good office for Mr. Edwards; and the *Paragraph* gives him "a good send-off" by publishing his military "record." According to the paper's account, it was an honorable one, and I do not doubt that it was; but I do doubt that the brigade to which he was attached was detailed at Jonesboro, Georgia, "to accompany Hood to Franklin, where the hardest battle of the war was fought, and where over 10,000 brave men were killed in four hours." My recollection of this matter is that none of our fellows "accompanied" General Hood on that expedition: we went a few miles ahead of him, to show him the way. The distance between him and us was always as great as we could make it and as little as he could make it. Hood was a sociable sort of chap on that march, but we did not encourage his advances; in fact, we felled trees in his way to impede them. If Mr. Edwards ever "accompanied" him it must have been after the war, on the piano.

Franklin was a stubborn little fight, but by no means "the hardest battle of the war." There were no 10,000 men killed in it, nor a quarter of that number. Ten thousand men have not been killed in any modern battle.[102] There were that many killed in some of the ancient ones, but the mortality of battles decreases with the precision and destructiveness of weapons. There have been no improvements in the sword, however, since the siege of Troy, and General Dimond would kill as many men to-day as he did twenty-five years ago. General Barnes was no more fatal at Gettysburg than he would be at Temescal Creek.[103] But see how it is with other weapons. General Turnbull, whose cheap three-inch field piece mowed down the enemy at Chickamauga faster than they could get up, would probably do so little execution with the Lick telescope that invalids would storm the slopes of Mt. Hamilton in search of longevity.

But modern warfare is not altogether sanitary. Mr. Clough's Mr. Edwards, for example, was in an engagement in which his detachment of 124 Federals was ambushed by 3,500 Confederates, "and in fifteen minutes 117 corpses were stretched upon the field"—all Federals, apparently—at least that is the implication and the way it would naturally be in case of ambush. As the proportion of wounded to dead is commonly about five to one, it is clear that the Federal detachment must have lost all its men and owed the enemy a balance of about 572.

Mr. Clough is truthful and sincere, but, as I said, a man of peace, and he was not there. Evidently enough, he got all this stuff from the Edwards, and had the misfortune to believe it; I was born lucky and do not. It is noticed here as a fair sample of the things that men are willing to say when relating their military experiences. As a rule, they are not to be believed. One would think war horrible enough without the monstrous exaggerations that seem inseparable from the story of it. Nothing is more common than to hear and read about "mowing down" the enemy or being mown down by them, projectiles cutting "wide gaps" through charging columns, "heaps of slain" that clog the cannon wheels, "rivers of blood" and the rest of it. All this is absurd: nothing of the kind occurs—nothing, rather, of the degree. These are phenomena of the camp-fire, the hearthstone, the "rostrum" and the writing-desk. They are subjective—deeds of memory in a frame of mind. They have a fine literary effect when skillfully employed, and in purely literary work are allowable in landscape painting to aggrandize the mountains. Outside of literature their use is to humbug the civilian, frighten the children and grapple the women's hearts with hooks of steel—all tending to the magnification of the narrator. The women, by the way, are worth a word of caution: let them remember how Othello got Desdemona—and what Desdemona got.

Nothing more frightful (and fascinating) than a great battle can be conceived, but it is not frightful in just the way that its historians love to describe it. Men do not fight as heroically as they are said to fight: they are not as brave as they are said to be. If they were, two hostile lines would fight until all of one were down. As long as a man is not disabled he can go forward or stand his ground. When two lines of battle are fighting face to face on even terms and one is "forced back" (which always occurs unless it is ordered back) it is fear that forces it: the men could have stood if they had wanted to. In our civil war I saw scores of such instances. Sometimes the Federals fled, sometimes the Confederates. As a rule the Confederates fought better than our men. On even terms they commonly defeated us; nearly all our victories were won by superior numbers, better arms and advantages of position. [3]

The Battle of Nashville

[The following two extracts relate to the battle of Nashville on December 15–16, 1864. The Confederates' defeat here resulted in the effective destruction of the Army of Tennessee.]

A line in last Tuesday's dispatches, to the effect that a French colony in Senegal has been attacked by typhus fever, recalls an incident of the civil war. After the battle of Nashville I happened to be serving on the staff of the illustrious General Sam Beatty, of Ohio.[104] His command was at one time greatly scattered in pursuit of the enemy, who retired sullenly, and one brigade of it held a peculiarly exposed position some ten miles from General Sam's headquarters. There was a telegraph, however, and one day the commander of this brigade sent the general a dispatch which read thus: "Please relieve me; I am suffering from an attack of General Debility." "The ablest cavalry officer in the Confederate army," said my honored chief, showing me the telegram. "I served under him in Mexico." And he promptly prescribed three regiments of infantry and a battery of Rodman guns.

I was directed to pilot that expedition to the scene of the disaster to our arms. I never felt so brave in all my life. I rode a hundred yards in advance, prepared to expostulate single-handed with the victorious enemy at whatever point I might encounter him. I dashed forward through every open space into every suspicious looking wood and spurred to the crest of every hill, exposing myself recklessly to draw the Confederates' fire and disclose their position. I told the commander of the relief column that he need not throw out any advance guard as a precaution against an ambuscade—I would myself act in that perilous capacity, and by driving in the rebel skirmishers gain time for him to form his line of battle in case I should not be numerically strong enough to scoop up the entire opposition at one wild dash. I begged him, however, to recover my body if I fell.

There was no fighting: the forces of General Debility had conquered nobody but the brigade commander—his troops were holding their ground nobly, reading dime novels and playing draw poker pending the arrival of our succoring command. The official reports of this affair explained, a little obscurely, that there had been a misunderstanding; but my unusual gallantry elicited the highest commendation in general orders, and will never, I trust, be forgotten by a grateful country. [1]

A skeptical correspondent asks me for an opinion of the fighting qualities of our colored regiments. Really I had thought the question settled long ago. The Negro will fight and fight well. From the time when we began to use him in civil war, through all his service against Indians on the frontier, to this day he has not failed to acquit himself acceptably to his White officers. I the more cheerfully testify to this because I was at one time a doubter. Under a general order from the headquarters of the Army, or possibly from the War Department, I once in a burst of ambition applied for rank as a field officer of colored troops, being then a line officer of white troops. Before my application was acted on I had repented and persuaded myself that the darkies would not fight; so when ordered to report to the proper board of officers, with a view to gratification of my wish, I "backed out" and secured "influence" which enabled me to remain in my humbler station. But at the battle of Nashville it was borne in upon me that I had made a fool of myself. During the two days of that memorable engagement the only reverse sustained by our arms was in an assault upon Overton Hill, a fortified salient of the Confederate line on the second day. The troops repulsed were a brigade of Beatty's division and a colored brigade of raw troops which had been brought up from a camp of instruction at Chattanooga. I was serving on Gen. Beatty's staff, but was not doing duty that day, being disabled by a wound—just sitting in the saddle and looking on. Seeing the darkies going in on our left I was naturally interested and observed them closely. Better fighting was never done. The front of the enemy's earthworks was protected by an intricate abatis of felled trees denuded of their foliage and twigs. Through this obstacle a cat would have made slow progress; its passage by troops under fire was hopeless from the first—even the inexperienced black chaps must have known that. They did not hesitate a moment: their long lines swept into that fatal obstruction in perfect order and remained there as long as those of the white veterans on their right. And as many of them in proportion remained until borne away and buried after the action. It was as pretty an example of courage and discipline as one could wish to see. In order that my discomfiture and humiliation might lack nothing of completeness I was told afterward that one of their field officers succeeded in forcing his horse through a break in the abatis and was shot to rags on the slope on the parapet. But for my abjuration of faith in the Negroes' fighting qualities I might perhaps have been so fortunate as to be that man! [2]

Further Memories of the Civil War

[Scattered throughout Bierce's journalism are other ruminations about his involvement in the Civil War that relate to incidents of uncertain date. As with nearly the whole of Bierce's work, these memories are tinged with his customary sardonic wit.]

I am reminded of an execution I once witnessed, at which a brace of miscreants assisted on the scaffold, and some thousands of not very sympathetic soldiers below it and about. It was in Murfreesboro, Tennessee, in war-time, and the fellows were hanged by the military for a murder of revolting atrocity, committed without orders. At the crucial moment one of them began a self-righteous assertion that he was "going home to Jesus." As the words left his mouth a railway engine standing near by uttered a loud and unmistakably derisive *Hoot—hoot!* It may have been accident, it may have been design; at any rate it expressed the "sense of the meeting" better than a leg's length of resolutions; and when the drop fell from beneath the feet of that pious assassin and his mate the ropes about their necks were actually kept slack for some seconds by the gusts of laughter ascending from below. They are the only persons I know in the other world who enjoyed the ghastly distinction of leaving this to the sound of inextinguishable merriment.

I once saw a cavalry soldier shot for desertion. He was seated *astride* his coffin, a black bandage about his eyes, his arms bound behind his back. The officer of the firing squad gave the commands "Ready—aim!" and a dozen loaded carbines were leveled at his breast. We heard him call out, up went the guns and the officer was seen to step forward and bend his ear to the man's lips. Then the officer stepped back, repeated the commands, and a second later the poor fellow was a thing of shreds and patches. "What did he say to you?" I afterward asked the officer. "Wanted to know if he couldn't have a saddle." [1]

The *Kreuz Zeitung,* according to a telegram, expresses a doubt if the Czar has a sufficiently powerful army to preserve the peace. The trouble is that his troops are not well armed. It is obvious that you can not prevent as much warfare with an old-fashioned muzzle-loading rifle that will not carry a hundred yards down hill as you can with an improved repeater with which you can pick off a dozen men a minute a quarter of a mile away. The Czar's artillery, too, is good for nothing in the way of peace-making; he ought to replace his old pot-metal cannon with some kind that will just mow down and stack up the fellows who believe in bloodshed.

I am here reminded of a command I once heard given in the civil war. There was a good deal of desultory skirmishing going on one day about a half mile from where General T. J. Wood sat awaiting the issue of certain movements that were making to the right of his division. All at once a lively clatter of musketry broke out, and Wood, with marked impatience, turned to one of his brigade commanders, saying: "General, send a couple of regiments and your battery out there and put an end to that fighting." [2]

Faith in the authenticity of distinguished men's "last words" is an amiable infirmity; but if those of Jefferson Davis were "Pray excuse me," they were exceedingly appropriate, not especially upon his lips, but upon those of any one engaged in dying. To leave life with a courteous apology to those remaining, as one leaves

a drawing-room to go to bed, evinces thoughtfulness and good breeding. The finest "last words" (and they are pretty well authenticated) were those of Stonewall
Jackson: "Let us pass over the river and rest in the shade of the trees." It is not
creditable to American poets that these beautiful words have not been embalmed
in immortal verse. Given the poet, the pen and such a theme, and one would
think the great poem would write itself.

Jefferson Davis died impenitent, a political outlaw, but there are some who
feel that loyalty does not require his execration. When beaten it is best to submit, and this he did; but it is not always well that all should fraternize with the
victors. In this world are as good things as goodwill, and constantly may be,
under certain circumstances, one of them. It is not always, and in the large way,
a practicable virtue. An individual may rightly enough practice political devotion as an example—to keep alive the sentiment of devotion in general; but a
community can hardly afford the luxury of a needless and unprofitable heroism, sacrificing its material interest to its moral. Davis's attitude toward the
Government was less ignoble than we of the North are disposed to admit; and
many a Southern leader, brave, able and wise, must have felt in his presence that
life had something higher if not better than expediency—a loftier spiritual plane
than is attained by the smooth and easy gradients of common sense. Davis
stood upon his height alone, as it was fitting that he should stand. He asked
none of his vanquished people to share his chill and comfortless eminence; and
with an intuitive sense of his Great Obligation, they abstained from affection's
importunities, nor besought him to be as they. His isolation was no doubt distasteful to loyalty's hot-gospellers, who see in their fad the supreme good and
goal; but no generous antagonist to the lost, and justly lost, cause could have
wished to mitigate, even by gentle means, the stony immobility of that sole human monument, which death alone could overthrow. [3]

If a man is good he thinks all men are more or less worthy; if bad he makes all
mankind co-defendants. That comes of looking into his own heart and fancy-
ing that he surveys the world. Naturally the Rev. W. S. Hubbell, Chaplain in the
Loyal Legion, is a praying man, as befits him. When in trouble he asks God to
help him out. So he assumes that all others do the same. At a recent meeting of
a Congregational Club to do honor to General Howard on that gentleman's sev-
entieth birthday (may he have a seventy-first) Dr. Hubbell said: "I bear personal
testimony that if ever a man prays in his life it is in the midst of battle."

My personal testimony is the other way. I have been in a good many
battles, and in my youth I used some times to pray—when in trouble. But I
never prayed in battle. I was always too much preoccupied to think about
it. Probably Dr. Hubbell was misled by hearing in the battle the sacred
Name spoken on all sides with great frequency and fervency. And probably
he was too busy with his own devotions to observe, or, observing, did not

understand the mystic word that commonly followed—which, as nearly as
I can recollect, was "Dammit." [4]

The Hesitating Veteran

[This poem first appeared in the *San Francisco Examiner* for August 16, 1901, and was reprinted in *Shapes of Clay* (1903). Its rueful
reflections on serving in the war and the freeing of the slaves form
a fitting capstone to Bierce's Civil War memories.]

> When I was young and full of faith
>   And other fads that youngsters cherish
> A cry rose as of one that saith
>   With emphasis: "Help or I perish!"
> 'Twas heard in all the land, and men
>   The sound were each to each repeating.
> It made my heart beat faster then
>   Than any heart can now be beating.
>
> For the world is old and the world is gray—
>   Grown prudent and, I think, more witty.
> She's cut her wisdom teeth, they say,
>   And doesn't now go in for Pity.
> Besides, the melancholy cry
>   Was that of one, 'tis now conceded,
> Whose plight no one beneath the sky
>   Felt half so poignantly as he did.
>
> Moreover, he was black. And yet
>   That sentimental generation
> With an austere compassion set
>   Its face and faith to the occasion.
> Then there were hate and strife to spare,
>   And various hard knocks a-plenty;
> And I ('twas more than my true share,
>   I must confess) took five-and-twenty.
>
> That all is over now—the reign
>   Of love and trade stills all dissensions,
> And the clear heavens arch again
>   Above a land of peace and pensions.

The black chap—at the last we gave
    Him everything that he had cried for,
Though many white chaps in the grave
    'Twould puzzle to say what they died for.

I hope he's better off—I trust
    That his society and his master's
Are worth the price we paid, and must
    Continue paying, in disasters;
But sometimes doubts press thronging round
    ('Tis mostly when my hurts are aching)
If war for Union was a sound
    And profitable undertaking.

'Tis said they mean to take away
    The Negro's vote for he's unlettered.
'Tis true he sits in darkness day
    And night, as formerly, when fettered;
But pray observe—howe'er he vote
    To whatsoever party turning,
He'll be with gentlemen of note
    And wealth and consequence and learning.

With saints and sages on each side,
    How could a fool through lack of knowledge,
Vote wrong? If learning is no guide
    Why ought one to have been in college?
O Son of Day, O Son of Night!
    What are your preferences made of?
I know not which of you is right,
    Nor which to be the more afraid of.

The world is old and the world is bad,
    And creaks and grinds upon its axis;
And man's an ape and the gods are mad!—
    There's nothing sure, not even our taxes.
No mortal man can Truth restore,
    Or say where she is to be sought for.
I know what uniform I wore—
    O, that I knew which side I fought for!

The Aftermath of the War

'Way Down in Alabam'

> [The following essay, first published in "Bits of Autobiography," vividly relates the difficulties Bierce encountered as a Treasury aide in Alabama in the months immediately following the end of the Civil War.]

At the break-up of the great Rebellion I found myself at Selma, Alabama, still in the service of the United States, and although my duties were now purely civil my treatment was not uniformly so, and I am not surprised that it was not. I was a minor official in the Treasury Department, engaged in performance of duties exceedingly disagreeable not only to the people of the vicinity, but to myself as well. They consisted in the collection and custody of "captured and abandoned property." The Treasury had covered pretty nearly the entire area of "the States lately in rebellion" with a hierarchy of officials, consisting, as nearly as memory serves, of one supervising agent and a multitude of special agents. Each special agent held dominion over a collection district and was allowed an "agency aide" to assist him in his purposeful activity, besides such clerks, laborers and so forth as he could persuade himself to need. My humble position was that of agency aide. When the special agent was present for duty I was his chief executive officer; in his absence I represented him (with greater or less fidelity to the original and to my conscience) and was invested with his powers. In the Selma agency the property that we were expected to seize and defend as best we might was mostly plantations (whose owners had disappeared; some were dead, others in hiding) and cotton. The country was full of cotton which had been sold to the Confederate Government, but not removed from the plantations to take its chance of export through the blockade. It had been decided that it now belonged to the United States. It was worth about five hundred dollars a bale—say one dollar a pound. The world agreed that that was a pretty good price for cotton.

Naturally the original owners, having received nothing for their product but Confederate money which the result of the war had made worthless, manifested an unamiable reluctance to give it up, for if they could market it for themselves it would more than recoup them for all their losses in the war. They had therefore exercised a considerable ingenuity in effacing all record of its transfer to the Confederate Government, obliterating the marks on the bales, and hiding these away in swamps and other inconspicuous places, fortifying their claims to private ownership with appalling affidavits and "covering their tracks" in an infinite variety of ways generally.

In effecting their purpose they encountered many difficulties. Cotton in bales is not very portable property; it requires for movement and concealment a good deal of coöperation by persons having no interest in keeping the secret and easily accessible to the blandishments of those interested in tracing it. The negroes, by whom the work was necessarily done, were zealous to pay for emancipation by fidelity to the new *régime*, and many poor devils among them forfeited their lives by services performed with more loyalty than discretion. Railways—even those having a more than nominal equipment of rails and rolling stock—were unavailable for secret conveyance of the cotton. Navigating the Alabama and Tombigbee rivers were a few small steamboats, the half-dozen pilots familiar with these streams exacting one hundred dollars a day for their services; but our agents, backed by military authority, were at all the principal shipping points and no boat could leave without their consent. The port of Mobile was in our hands and the lower waters were patrolled by gunboats. Cotton might, indeed, be dumped down a "slide" by night at some private landing and fall upon the deck of a steamer idling innocently below. It might even arrive at Mobile, but secretly to transfer it to a deep-water vessel and get it out of the country—that was a dream.

On the movement of private cotton we put no restrictions; and such were the freight rates that it was possible to purchase a steamboat at Mobile, go up the river in ballast, bring down a cargo of cotton and make a handsome profit, after deducting the cost of the boat and all expenses of the venture, including the wage of the pilot. With no great knowledge of "business" I venture to think that in Alabama in the latter part of the year of grace 1865 commercial conditions were hardly normal.

Nor were social conditions what I trust they have now become. There was no law in the country except of the unsatisfactory sort known as "martial," and that was effective only within areas covered by the guns of isolated forts and the physical activities of their small garrisons. True, there were the immemorial laws of self-preservation and retaliation, both of which were liberally interpreted. The latter was faithfully administered, mostly against straggling Federal soldiers and too zealous government officials. When my chief had been ordered to Selma he had arrived just in time to act as sole mourner at the funeral of his predecessor—who had had the bad luck to interpret his instructions in a sense that was disagreeable to a gentleman whose interests were affected by the interpretation. Early one pleasant morning shortly afterward two United States marshals were observed by the roadside in a suburb of the town. They looked comfortable enough there in the sunshine, but each

> had that across his throat
> Which you had hardly cared to see.

When dispatched on business of a delicate nature men in the service of the agency had a significant trick of disappearing—they were of "the unreturning brave." Really the mortality among the unacclimated in the Selma district at that time was excessive. When my chief and I parted at dinner time (our palates were not in harmony) we commonly shook hands and tried to say something memorable that was worthy to serve as "last words." We had been in the army together and had many a time gone into battle without having taken that precaution in the interest of history.

Of course the better class of the people were not accountable for this state of affairs, and I do not remember that I greatly blamed the others. The country was full of the "elements of combustion." The people were impoverished and smarting with a sense of defeat. Organized resistance was no longer possible, but many men trained to the use of arms did not consider themselves included in the surrender and conscientiously believed it both right and expedient to prolong the struggle by private enterprise. Many, no doubt, made the easy and natural transition from soldiering to assassination by insensible degrees, unconscious of the moral difference, such as it is. Selma was little better than a ruin; in the concluding period of the war General Wilson's cavalry had raided it and nearly destroyed it, and the work begun by the battery had been completed by the torch. The conflagration was generally attributed to the negroes, who certainly augmented it, for a number of those suspected of the crime were flung into the flames by the maddened populace. None the less were the Yankee invaders held responsible.

Every Northern man represented some form or phase of an authority which these luckless people horribly hated, and to which they submitted only because, and in so far as, they had to. Fancy such a community, utterly without the restraints of law and with no means of ascertaining public opinion—for newspapers were not—denied even the moral advantage of the pulpit! Considering what human nature has the misfortune to be, it is wonderful that there was so little of violence and crime.

As the carcass invites the vulture, this prostrate land drew adventurers from all points of the compass. Many, I am sorry to say, were in the service of the United States Government. Truth to tell, the special agents of the Treasury were themselves, as a body, not altogether spotless. I could name some of them, and some of their assistants, who made large fortunes by their opportunities. The special agents were allowed one-fourth of the value of the confiscated cotton for expenses of collection—none too much, considering the arduous and perilous character of the service; but the plan opened up such possibilities of fraud as have seldom been accorded by any system of conducting the public business, and never without disastrous results to official morality. Against bribery no provision could have provided an adequate safeguard; the magnitude of the interests involved was too great, the administration of the trust too loose and irresponsible. The system as it was, hastily devised in the storm and stress of a closing war, broke down in the end, and it is doubtful if the Government might not more profitably have let the "captured and abandoned property" alone.

As an instance of the temptations to which we were exposed, and of our tactical dispositions in resistance, I venture to relate a single experience of my own. During an absence of my chief I got upon the trail of a lot of cotton—seven hundred bales, as nearly as I now recollect—which had been hidden with so exceptional ingenuity that I was unable to trace it. One day there came to my office two well-dressed and mannerly fellows who suffered me to infer that they knew all about this cotton and controlled it. When our conference on the subject ended it was past dinner time and they civilly invited me to dine with them, which, in hope of eliciting information over the wine, I did. I knew well enough that they indulged a similar selfish hope, so I had no scruples about using their hospitality to their disadvantage if I could. The subject, however, was not mentioned at table, and we were all singularly abstemious in the matter of champagne—so much so that as we rose from a rather long session at the board we disclosed our sense of the ludicrousness of the situation by laughing outright. Nevertheless, neither party would accept defeat, and for the next few weeks the war of hospitality was fast and furious. We dined together nearly every day, sometimes at my expense, sometimes at theirs. We drove, rode, walked, played at billiards and made many a night of it; but youth and temperance (in drink) pulled me through without serious inroads on my health. We had early come to an understanding and a deadlock. Failing to get the slenderest clew to the location of the cotton I offered them one-fourth if they would surrender it or disclose its hiding-place; they offered me one-fourth if I would sign a permit for its shipment as private property.

All things have an end, and this amusing contest finally closed. Over the remains of a farewell dinner, unusually luxurious, as befitted the occasion, we parted with expressions of mutual esteem—not, I hope, altogether insincere, and the ultimate fate of the cotton is to me unknown. Up to the date of my departure from the agency not a bale of it had either come into possession of the Government or found an outlet. I am sometimes disloyal enough to indulge myself in the hope that they baffled my successors as skilfully as they did me. One cannot help feeling a certain tenderness for men who know and value a good dinner.

Another corrupt proposal that I had the good fortune to be afraid to entertain came, as it were, from within. There was a dare-devil fellow whom, as I know him to be dead, I feel justified in naming Jack Harris. He was engaged in all manner of speculative ventures on his own account, but the special agent had so frequently employed him in "enterprises of great pith and moment"[1] that he was in a certain sense and to a certain extent one of us. He seemed to me at the time unique, but shortly afterward I had learned to classify him as a type of the Californian adventurer with whose peculiarities of manner, speech and disposition most of us are to-day familiar enough. He never spoke of his past, having doubtless good reasons for reticence, but any one learned in Western slang—a knowledge then denied me—would have catalogued him with infallible accuracy. He was a rather large, strong fellow, swarthy, blackbearded, black-eyed, blackhearted and entertaining, no end; ignorant with an ignorance whose frankness redeemed it from offensiveness, vulgar with a vulgarity that expressed itself in such metaphors and similes as would have made its peace with the most implacable refinement. He drank hard, gambled high, swore like a parrot, scoffed at everything, was openly and proudly a rascal, did not know the meaning of fear, borrowed money abundantly, and squandered it with royal disregard. Desiring one day to go to Mobile, but reluctant to leave Montgomery and its pleasures— unwilling to quit certainty for hope—he persuaded the captain of a loaded steamboat to wait four days for him at an expense of $400 a day; and lest time should hang too heavy on the obliging skipper's hands, Jack permitted him to share the orgies gratis. But that is not my story.

One day Jack came to me with a rather more sinful proposal than he had heretofore done me the honor to submit. He knew of about a thousand bales of cotton, some of it private property, some of it confiscable, stored at various points on the banks of the Alabama. He had a steamboat in readiness, "with a gallant, gallant crew," and he proposed to drop quietly down to the various landings by night, seize the cotton, load it on his boat and make off down the river. What he wanted from me, and was willing to pay for, was only my official signature to some blank shipping permits; or if I would accompany the expedition and share its fortunes no papers would be necessary. In declining this truly generous offer I felt that I owed it to Jack to give him a reason that he was capable of understanding, so I explained to him the arrangements at Mobile, which would prevent him from transferring his cargo to a ship and getting the necessary papers permitting her to sail. He was astonished and, I think, pained by my simplicity. Did I think him a fool? He did not purpose—not he—to tranship at all: the perfected plan was to dispense with all hampering formality by slipping through Mobile Bay in the black of the night and navigating his laden river craft across the Gulf to Havana! The rascal was in dead earnest, and that natural timidity of disposition which compelled me to withhold my coöperation greatly lowered me in his esteem, I fear.

It was in Cuba, by the way, that Jack came to grief some years later. He was one of the crew of the filibustering vessel *Virginius,* and was captured and shot along with the others. Something in his demeanor as he knelt in the line to receive the fatal fusillade prompted a priest to inquire his religion. "I am an atheist, by God!" said Jack, and with this quiet profession of faith that gentle spirit winged its way to other tropics.

Having expounded with some particularity the precarious tenure by which I held my office and my life in those "thrilling regions" where my duties lay, I ought to explain by what unhappy chance I am still able to afflict the reader. There lived in Selma a certain once wealthy and still influential citizen, whose two sons, of about my own age, had served as officers in the Confederate Army. I will designate them simply as Charles and Frank. They were types of a class now, I fear, almost extinct. Born and bred in luxury and knowing nothing of the seamy side of life—except, indeed, what they had learned in the war—well educated, brave, generous, sensitive to points of honor, and of engaging manners, these brothers were by all respected, by many loved and by some feared. For they had quick fingers upon the pistol-trigger withal, and would rather fight a duel than eat—nay, drink. Nor were they over-particular about the combat taking the form of a duel—almost any form was good enough. I made their acquaintance by chance and cultivated it for the pleasure it gave me. It was long afterward that I gave a thought to its advantages; but from the time that I became generally known as their friend my safety was assured through all that region; an army with banners could not have given me the same immunity from danger, obstruction or even insult in the performance of my disagreeable duties. What glorious fellows they were, to be sure—these my late antagonists of the dark days when, God forgive us, we were trying to cut one another's throat. To this day I feel a sense of regret when I think of my instrumentality, however small, in depriving the world of many such men in the criminal insanity that we call battle.

Life in Selma became worth living even as the chance of living it augmented. With my new friends and a friend of theirs, whose name—the more shame to me—I cannot now recall, but should not write here if I could, I passed most of my leisure hours. At the houses of themselves and their friends I did most of my dining; and, heaven be praised! there was no necessity for moderation in wine. In their society I committed my sins, and together beneath that noble orb unknown to colder skies, the Southern moon, we atoned for them by acts of devotion performed with song and lute beneath the shrine window of many a local divinity.

One night we had an adventure. We were out late—so late that it was night only astronomically. The streets were "deserted and drear," and, of course, unlighted—the late Confederacy had no gas and no oil. Nevertheless, we saw that we were followed. A man keeping at a fixed distance behind turned as we turned, paused as we paused, and pursued as we moved on. We stopped, went back and remonstrated; asked his intentions in, I dare say, no gentle words. He gave us no reply, but as we left him he followed. Again we stopped, and I felt my pistol plucked out of my pocket. Frank had unceremoniously possessed himself of it and was advancing on the enemy. I do not remember if I had any wish to interpose a protest—anyhow there was no time. Frank fired and the man fell. In a moment all the chamber-windows in the street were thrown open with a head visible (and audible) in each. We told Frank to go home, which to our surprise he did; the rest of us, assisted by somebody's private policeman—who afterward apprised us that we were in arrest—carried the man to a hotel. It was found that his leg was broken above the knee, and the next day it was amputated. We paid his surgeon and his hotel bill, and when he had sufficiently recovered sent him to an address which he gave us in Mobile; but not a word could anybody get out of him as to who he had the misfortune to be, or why he had persisted, against the light, in following a quartet of stray revelers.

On the morning of the shooting, when everything possible had been done for the comfort of the victim, we three accomplices were released on our own recognizance by an old gentleman of severe aspect, who had resumed his function of justice of the peace where he had laid it down during the war. I did not then know that he had no more legal authority than I had myself, and I was somewhat disturbed in mind as I reflected on the possibilities of the situation. The opportunity to get rid of an offensive Federal official must of course be very tempting, and after all the shooting was a trifle hasty and not altogether justifiable.

On the day appointed for our preliminary examination, all of us except Frank were released and put on the witness-stand. We gave a true and congruent history of the affair. The holdover justice listened to it all very patiently and then, with commendable brevity and directness of action, fined Frank five dollars and costs for disorderly conduct. There was no appeal.

There were queer characters in Alabama in those days, as you shall see. Once upon a time the special agent and I started down the Tombigbee River with a steamboat load of government cotton—some six hundred bales. At one of the military stations we took on a guard of a dozen or fifteen soldiers under command of a non-commissioned officer. One evening, just before dusk, as we were rounding a bend where the current set strongly against the left bank of the stream and the channel lay close to that shore, we were suddenly saluted with a volley of bullets and buckshot from that direction. The din of the firing, the rattle and crash of the missiles splintering the woodwork and the jingle of broken glass made a very rude arousing from the tranquil indolence of a warm afternoon on the sluggish Tombigbee. The left bank, which at this point was a trifle higher than the hurricane deck of a steamer, was now swarming with men who, almost near enough to jump aboard, looked unreasonably large and active as they sprang about from cover to cover, pouring in their fire. At the first volley the pilot had deserted his wheel, as well he might, and the boat, drifting in to the bank under the boughs of a tree, was helpless. Her jackstaff and yawl were carried away, her guards broken in, and her deck-load of cotton was tumbling into the stream a dozen bales at once. The captain was nowhere to be seen, the engineer had evidently abandoned his post and the special agent had gone to hunt up the soldiers. I happened to be on the hurricane deck, armed with a revolver, which I fired as rapidly as I could, listening all the time for the fire of the soldiers—and listening in vain. It transpired later that they had not a cartridge among them; and of all helpless mortals a soldier without a cartridge is the most imbecile. But all this time the continuous rattle of the enemy's guns and the petulant pop of my own pocket firearm were punctuated, as it were, by pretty regularly recurring loud explosions, as of a small cannon. They came from somewhere forward—I supposed from the opposition, as I knew we had no artillery on board.

The failure of our military guard made the situation somewhat grave. For two of us, at least, capture meant hanging out of hand. I had never been hanged in all my life and was not enamored of the prospect. Fortunately for us the bandits had selected their point of attack without military foresight. Immediately below them a bayou, impassable to them, let into the river. The moment we had drifted below it we were safe from boarding and capture. The captain was found in hiding and an empty pistol at his ear persuaded him to resume command of his vessel; the engineer and pilot were encouraged to go back to their posts and after some remarkably long minutes, during which we were under an increasingly long-range fire, we got under way. A few cotton bales piled about the pilot-house made us tolerably safe from that sort of thing in the future and then we took account of our damages. Nobody had been killed and only a few were wounded. This gratifying result was attributable to the fact that, being unarmed, nearly everybody had dived below at the first fire and taken cover among the cotton bales. While issuing a multitude of needless commands from the front of the hurricane-deck I looked below, and there, stretched out at full length on his stomach, lay a long, ungainly person, clad in faded butternut, bareheaded, his long, lank hair falling down each side of his neck, his coat-tails similarly parted, and his enormous feet spreading their soles to the blue sky. He had an old-fashioned horse-pistol, some two feet long, which he was in the act of sighting across his left palm for a parting shot at the now distant assailants. A more ludicrous figure I never saw; I laughed outright; but when his weapon went off it was matter for gratitude to be above it instead of before it. It was the "cannon" whose note I had marked all through the unequal fray.

The fellow was a returned Confederate whom we had taken on at one of the upper landings as our only passenger; we were deadheading him to Mobile. He was undoubtedly in hearty sympathy with the enemy, and I at first suspected him of collusion, but circumstances not necessary to detail here rendered this impossible. Moreover, I had distinctly seen one of the "guerrillas" fall and remain down after my own weapon was empty, and no man else on board except the passenger had fired a shot or had a shot to fire. When everything had been made snug again, and we were gliding along under the stars, without apprehension; when I had counted fifty-odd bullet holes through the pilot-house (which had not received the attention that by its prominence and importance it was justly entitled to) and everybody was variously boasting his prowess, I approached my butternut comrade-in-arms and thanked him for his kindly aid. "But," said I, "how the devil does it happen that *you* fight *that* crowd?"

"Wal, Cap," he drawled, as he rubbed the powder grime from his antique artillery,—"I allowed it was mouty clever in you-all to take me on, seein' I hadn't ary cent, so thought I'd jist kinder work my passage."

Across the Plains

[In the summer of 1866 Bierce accepted an offer by his old commander, General Hazen, to join him on an exploratory mission through the Indian country. Bierce was to be the mapmaker for the expedition, utilizing the skills he had developed during the war. The two essays relating his experiences on the Hazen expedition, "Across the Plains" and "The Mirage," were published in "Bits of Autobiography." The former essay first appeared in the *Oakland Daily Evening Tribune* for November 8, 1890, the latter in the *Examiner* for August 14, 1887.]

That noted pioneer, General John Bidwell, of California, once made a longish step up the western slope of our American Parnassus by an account of his journey "across the plains" seven years before the lamented Mr. Marshall had found the least and worst of all possible reasons for making the "trek."[2] General Bidwell had not the distinction to be a great writer, but in order to command admiration and respect in that province of the Republic of Letters which lies in the Sacramento Valley above the mouth of the Yuba the gift of writing greatly is a needless endowment. Nevertheless I read his narrative with an interest which on analysis turns out to be a by-product of personal experience: among my youthful indiscretions was a journey over much of the same ground, which I took in much the same way—as did many thousands before and after.

It was a far cry from 1841 to 1866, yet the country between the Missouri River and the Sierra Nevada had not greatly improved: civilization had halted at the river, awaiting transportation. A railroad had set out from Omaha westward, and another at Sacramento was solemnly considering the impossible suggestion of going eastward to meet it. There were lunatics in those days, as there are in these. I left the one road a few miles out of the Nebraskan village and met the other at Dutch Flat, in California.

Waste no compassion on the loneliness of my journey: a thriving colony of Mormons had planted itself in the valley of Salt Lake and there were "forts" at a few points along the way, where ambitious young army officers passed the best years of their lives guarding live stock and teaching the mysteries of Hardee's tactics[3] to that alien patriot, the American regular. There was a dusty wagon road, bordered with bones—not always those of animals—with an occasional mound, sometimes dignified with a warped and rotting headboard bearing an illegible inscription. (One inscription not entirely illegible is said to have concluded with this touching tribute to the worth of the departed: "He was a good egg." Another was: "He done his damnedest.") In other particulars the "Great American Desert" of our fathers was very like what it was when General Bidwell's party traversed it with that hereditary instinct, that delicacy of spiritual nose which served the Western man of that day in place of a map and guide-book. Westward the course of empire had taken its way, but excepting these poor vestiges it had for some fifteen hundred miles left no trace of its march. The Indian of the plains had as yet seen little to unsettle his assurance of everlasting dominion. Of the slender lines of metal creeping slowly toward him from East and West he knew little; and had he known more, how could he have foreseen their momentous effect upon his "ancient solitary reign"?[4]

I remember very well, as so many must, some of the marked features of the route that General Bidwell mentions. One of the most imposing of these is Court House Rock, near the North Platte. Surely no object of such dignity ever had a more belittling name—given it in good faith no doubt by some untraveled wight whose county court-house was the most "reverend pile"[5] of which he had any conception. It should have been called the Titan's Castle. What a gracious memory I have of the pomp and splendor of its aspect, with the crimson glories of the setting sun fringing its outlines, illuminating its western walls like the glow of Mammon's fires for the witches' revel in the Hartz, and flung like banners from its crest!

I suppose Court House Rock is familiar enough and commonplace enough to the dwellers in that land (riparian tribes once infesting the low lands of Ohio and Indiana and the flats of Iowa), but to me, tipsy with youth, full-fed on Mayne

Reid's romances,[6] and now first entering the enchanted region that he so charmingly lied about, it was a revelation and a dream. I wish that anything in the heavens, on the earth, or in the waters under the earth would give me now such an emotion as I experienced in the shadow of that "great rock in a weary land."[7]

I was not a pilgrim, but an engineer *attaché* to an expedition through Dakota and Montana, to inspect some new military posts. The expedition consisted, where the Indians preserved the peace, of the late General W. B. Hazen, myself, a cook and a teamster; elsewhere we had an escort of cavalry. My duty, as I was given to understand it, was to amuse the general and other large game, make myself as comfortable as possible without too much discomfort to others, and when in an unknown country survey and map our route for the benefit of those who might come after. The posts which the general was to inspect had recently been established along a military road, one end of which was at the North Platte and the other—there was no other end; up about Fort C. F. Smith at the foot of the Big-Horn Mountains the road became a buffalo trail and was lost in the weeds. But it was a useful road, for by leaving it before going too far one could reach a place near the headwaters of the Yellowstone, where the National Park is now.

By a master stroke of military humor we were ordered to return (to Washington) via Salt Lake City, San Francisco and Panama. I obeyed until I got as far as San Francisco, where, finding myself appointed to a second lieutenancy in the Regular Army, ingratitude, more strong than traitors' arms, quite vanquished me: I resigned, parted from Hazen more in sorrow than in anger and remained in California.

I have thought since that this may have been a youthful error: the Government probably meant no harm, and if I had served long enough I might have become a captain. In time, if I lived, I should naturally have become the senior captain of the Army; and then if there were another war and any of the field officers did me the favor to paunch a bullet I should become the junior major, certain of another step upward as soon as a number of my superiors equal to the whole number of majors should be killed, resign or die of old age—enchanting prospect! But I am getting a long way off the trail.

It was near Fort C. F. Smith that we found our first buffaloes, and abundant they were. We had to guard our camp at night with fire and sword to keep them from biting us as they grazed. Actually one of them half-scalped a teamster as he lay dreaming of home with his long fair hair commingled with the toothsome grass. His utterances as the well-meaning beast lifted him from the ground and tried to shake the earth from his roots were neither wise nor sweet, but they made a profound impression on the herd, which, arching its multitude of tails, absented itself to pastures new like an army with banners.

At Fort C. F. Smith we parted with our *impedimenta,* and with an escort of about two dozen cavalrymen and a few pack animals struck out on horseback through an unexplored country northwest for old Fort Benton, on the upper Missouri. The journey was not without its perils. Our only guide was my compass; we knew nothing of the natural obstacles that we must encounter; the Indians were on the warpath, and our course led us through the very heart of their country. Luckily for us they were gathering their clans into one great army for a descent upon the posts that we had left behind; a little later some three thousand of them moved upon Fort Phil Kearney, lured a force of ninety men and officers outside and slaughtered them to the last man. This was one of the posts that we had inspected, and the officers killed had hospitably entertained us.

In that lively and interesting book, "Indian Fights and Fighters," Dr. Cyrus Townsend Brady says of this "outpost of civilization":

"The most careful watchfulness was necessary at all hours of the day and night. The wood trains to fetch logs to the sawmills were heavily guarded. There was fighting all the time. Casualties among the men were by no means rare. At first it was difficult to keep men within the limits of the camp; but stragglers who failed to return, and some who had been cut off, scalped and left for dead, but who had crawled back to die, convinced every one of the wisdom of the commanding officer's repeated orders and cautions. To chronicle the constant succession of petty skirmishes would be wearisome; yet they often resulted in torture and loss of life on the part of the soldiers, although the Indians in most instances suffered the more severely."[8]

In a footnote the author relates this characteristic instance of the Government's inability to understand: "Just when the alarms were most frequent a messenger came to the headquarters, announcing that a train *en route* from Fort Laramie, with special messengers from that post, was corraled by Indians, and demanded immediate help. An entire company of infantry in wagons, with a mountain howitzer and several rounds of grapeshot, was hastened to their relief. It proved to be a train with mail from the Laramie Commission, announcing the confirmation of a 'satisfactory treaty of peace with all the Indians of the Northwest,' and assuring the district commander of the fact. The messenger was brought in in safety, and *peace* lasted until his message was delivered. So much was gained—that the messenger did not lose his scalp."[9]

Through this interesting environment our expeditionary force of four men had moved to the relief of the beleaguered post, but finding it impossible to "raise the siege" had—with a score of troopers—pushed on to Fort C. F. Smith, and thence into the Unknown.

The first part of this new journey was well enough; there were game and water. Where we swam the Yellowstone we had an abundance of both, for the entire river valley, two or three miles wide, was dotted with elk. There were hundreds. As we advanced they became scarce; buffalo became scarce; bear, deer, rabbits, sage-hens, even prairie dogs gave out, and we were near starving. Water gave out too, and starvation was a welcome state: our hunger was so much less disagreeable than our thirst that it was a real treat.

However, we got to Benton, Heaven knows how and why, but we were a sorry-looking lot, though our scalps were intact. If in all that region there is a mountain that I have not climbed, a river that I have not swum, an alkali pool that I have not thrust my muzzle into, or an Indian that I have not shuddered to think about, I am ready to go back in a Pullman sleeper and do my duty.

From Fort Benton we came down through Helena and Virginia City, Montana—then new mining camps—to Salt Lake, thence westward to California. Our last bivouac was on the old camp of the Donner party,[10] where, in the flickering lights and dancing shadows made by our camp-fire, I first heard the story of that awful winter, and in the fragrance of the meat upon the coals fancied I could detect something significantly uncanny. The meat which the Donner party had cooked at that spot was not quite like ours. Pardon: I mean it was not like that which we cooked.

The Mirage

Since the overland railways have long been carrying many thousands of persons across the elevated plateaus of the continent the mirage in many of its customary aspects has become pretty well known to great numbers of persons all over the Union, and the tales of early observers who came "der blains agross" are received with a less frigid inhospitality than they formerly were by incredulous pioneers who had come "der Horn aroundt," as the illustrious Hans Breitmann phrases it;[11] but in its rarer and more marvelous manifestations, the mirage is still a rock upon which many a reputation for veracity is wrecked remediless. With an ambition intrepidly to brave this disaster, and possibly share it with the hundreds of devoted souls whose disregard of the injunction never to tell an incredible truth has branded them as hardy and impenitent liars, I purpose to note here a few of the more remarkable illusions by which my own sense of sight has been befooled by the freaks of the enchanter.

It is apart from my purpose to explain the mirage scientifically, and not altogether in my power. Every schoolboy can do so, I suppose, to the satisfaction of his teacher if the teacher has not himself seen the phenomenon, or has seen it only in the broken, feeble and evanescent phases familiar to the overland passenger; but for my part I am unable to understand how the simple causes affirmed in the text-books sufficiently account for the infinite variety and complexity of some of the effects said to be produced by them. But of this the reader shall judge for himself.

One summer morning in the upper North Platte country I rose from my blankets, performed the pious acts of sun-worship by yawning toward the east, kicked together the parted embers of my camp-fire, and bethought me of water for my ablutions. We had gone into bivouac late in the night on the open plain, and without any clear notion of where we were. There were a half-dozen of us, our chief on a tour of inspection of the new military posts in Wyoming. I accompanied the expedition as surveyor. Having an aspiration for water I naturally looked about to see what might be the prospect of obtaining it, and to my surprise and delight saw a long line of willows, apparently some three hundred yards away. Willows implied water, and snatching up a camp-kettle I started forward without taking the trouble to put on my coat and hat. For the first mile or two I preserved a certain cheerful hopefulness; but when the sun had risen farther toward the meridian and began to affect my bare head most uncomfortably, and the picketed horses at the camp were hull down on the horizon in the rear, and the willows in front increased their pace out of all proportion to mine, I began to grow discouraged and sat down on a stone to wish myself back. Perceiving that the willows also had halted for breath I determined to make a dash at them, leaving the camp-kettle behind to make its way back to camp as best it could. I was now traveling "flying light," and had no doubt of my ability to overtake the enemy, which had, however, disappeared over the crest of a low sandhill. Ascending this I was treated to a surprise. Right ahead of me lay a barren waste of sand extending to the right and left as far as I could see. Its width in the direction that I was going I judged to be about twenty miles. On its farther border the cactus plain began again, sloping gradually upward to the horizon, along which was a fringe of cedar trees—the willows of my vision! In that country a cedar will not grow within thirty miles of water if it knows it.

On my return journey I coldly ignored the appeals of the camp-kettle, and when I met the rescuing party which had been for some hours trailing me made no allusion to the real purpose of my excursion. When the chief asked if I purposed to enter a plea of temporary insanity I replied that I would reserve my defense for the present; and in fact I never did disclose it until now.

I had afterward the satisfaction of seeing the chief, an experienced plainsman, consume a full hour, rifle in hand, working round to the leeward of a dead coyote in the sure and certain hope of bagging a sleeping buffalo. Mirage or no mirage, you must not too implicitly trust your eyes in the fantastic atmosphere of the high plains.

I remember that one forenoon I looked forward to the base of the Big Horn Mountains and selected a most engaging nook for the night's camp. My good opinion of it was confirmed when we reached it three days later. The deception in this instance was due to nothing but the marvelous lucidity of the atmosphere and the absence of objects of known dimensions, and these sources of

error are sometimes sufficient of themselves to produce the most incredible illusions. When they are in alliance with the mirage the combination's pranks are
bewildering.

One of the most grotesque and least comfortable of my experiences with the
magicians of the air occurred near the forks of the Platte. There had been a tremendous thunder-storm, lasting all night. In the morning my party set forward
over the soaken prairie under a cloudless sky intensely blue. I was riding in advance, absorbed in thought, when I was suddenly roused to a sense of material
things by exclamations of astonishment and apprehension from the men behind.
Looking forward, I beheld a truly terrifying spectacle. Immediately in front, at a
distance, apparently, of not more than a quarter-mile, was a long line of the most
formidable looking monsters that the imagination ever conceived. They were
taller than trees. In them the elements of nature seemed so fantastically and dis-
cordantly confused and blended, compounded, too, with architectural and mechanical details, that they partook of the triple character of animals, houses and
machines. Legs they had, that an army of elephants could have marched among;
bodies that ships might have sailed beneath; heads about which eagles might have
delighted to soar, and ears—they were singularly well gifted with ears. But wheels
also they were endowed with, and vast sides of blank wall; the wheels as large as
the ring of a circus, the walls white and high as cliffs of chalk along an English
coast. Among them, on them, beneath, in and a part of them, were figures and
fragments of figures of gigantic men. All were inextricably interblended and su-
perposed—a man's head and shoulders blazoned on the side of an animal; a
wheel with legs for spokes rolling along the creature's back; a vast section of wall,
having no contact with the earth, but (with a tail hanging from its rear, like a note
of admiration) moving along the line, obscuring here an anatomical horror and
disclosing there a mechanical nightmare. In short, this appalling procession,
which was crossing our road with astonishing rapidity, seemed made up of unas-
signed and unassorted units, out of which some imaginative god might be about
to create a world of giants, ready supplied with some of the appliances of a high
civilization. Yet the whole apparition had so shadowy and spectral a look that the
terror it inspired was itself vague and indefinite, like the terror of a dream. It affected our horses as well as ourselves; they extended their necks and threw forward their ears. For some moments we sat in our saddles surveying the hideous
and extravagant spectacle without a word, and our tongues were loosened only
when it began rapidly to diminish and recede, and at last was resolved into a train
of mules and wagons, barely visible on the horizon. They were miles away and
outlined against the blue sky.

I then remembered what my astonishment had not permitted me closely to
note—that this pageant had appeared to move along parallel to the foot of a slope
extending upward and backward to an immense height, intersected with rivers
and presenting all the features of a prairie landscape. The mirage had in effect

contracted the entire space between us and the train to a pistol-shot in breadth, and had made a background for its horrible picture by lifting into view Heaven knows how great an extent of country below our horizon. Does refraction account for all this? To this day I cannot without vexation remember the childish astonishment that prevented me from observing the really interesting features of the spectacle and kept my eyes fixed with a foolish distension on a lot of distorted mules, teamsters and wagons.

One of the commonest and best known tricks of the mirage is that of overlaying a dry landscape with ponds and lakes, and by a truly interesting and appropriate coincidence one or more travelers perishing of thirst seem always to be present, properly to appreciate the humor of the deception; but when a gentleman whose narrative suggested this article averred that he had seen these illusory lakes navigated by phantom boats filled with visionary persons he was, I daresay, thought to be drawing the long bow, even by many miragists in good standing. For aught I know he may have been. I can only attest the entirely credible character of the statement.

Away up at the headwaters of the Missouri, near the British possessions, I found myself one afternoon rather unexpectedly on the shore of an ocean. At less than a gunshot from where I stood was as plainly defined a seabeach as one could wish to see. The eye could follow it in either direction, with all its bays, inlets and promontories, to the horizon. The sea was studded with islands, and these with tall trees of many kinds, both islands and trees being reflected in the water with absolute fidelity. On many of the islands were houses, showing white beneath the trees, and on one which lay farthest out seaward was a considerable city, with towers, domes and clusters of steeples. There were ships in the offing whose sails glistened in the sunlight and, closer in, several boats of novel but graceful design, crowded with human figures, moved smoothly among the lesser islands, impelled by some power invisible from my point of view, each boat attended by its inverted reflection "crowding up beneath the keel." It must be admitted that the voyagers were habited after a somewhat uncommon fashion—almost unearthly, I may say—and were so grouped that at my distance I could not clearly distinguish their individual limbs and attitudes. Their features were, of course, entirely invisible. None the less, they were plainly human beings—what other creatures would be boating? Of the other features of the scene—the coast, islands, trees, houses, city and ships hull-down in the offing—I distinctly affirm an absolute identity of visible aspect with those to which we are accustomed in the realm of reality; imagination had simply nothing to do with the matter. True, I had not recently had the advantage of seeing any such objects, except trees, and these had been mighty poor specimens, but, like Macduff, I "could not but remember such things were,"[12] nor had I forgotten how they looked.

Of course I was not for an instant deceived by all this: I knew that under it all lay a particularly forbidding and inhospitable expanse of sagebrush and cactus, peopled with nothing more nearly akin to me than prairie dogs, ground owls and jackass rabbits—that with these exceptions the desert was as desolate as the environment of Ozymandias' "vast and trunkless legs of stone."[13] But as a show it was surely the most enchanting that human eyes had ever looked on, and after more years than I care to count it remains one of memory's most precious possessions. The one thing which always somewhat impairs the illusion in such instances— the absence of the horizon water-line—did not greatly abate the *vraisemblance* in this, for the large island in the distance nearly closed the view seaward, and the ships occupied most of the remaining space. I had but to fancy a slight haze on the farther water, and all was right and regular. For more than a half-hour this charming picture remained intact; then ugly patches of plain began to show through, the islands with their palms and temples slowly dissolved, the boats foundered with every soul on board, the sea drifted over the headlands in a most unwaterlike way, and inside the hour since,

> like stout Cortez, when with eagle eyes
>   He stared at the Pacific, and all his men
> Looked at each other with a wild surmise,
>   Silent upon a peak in Darien,[14]

I had discovered this unknown sea all this insubstantial pageant had faded like the baseless fabric of the vision that it was and left not a rack behind.

In some of its minor manifestations the mirage is sometimes seen on the western coast of our continent, in the bay of San Francisco, for example, causing no small surprise to the untraveled and unread observer, and no small pain to the spirits of purer fire who are fated to be caught within earshot and hear him pronounce it a "mirridge." I have seen Goat Island without visible means of support and Red Rock suspended in mid-air like the coffin of the Prophet. Looking up toward Mare Island one most ungracious morning when a barbarous norther had purged the air of every stain and the human soul of every virtue, I saw San Pablo Bay margined with cliffs whose altitude must have exceeded considerably that from whose dizzy verge old eyeless Gloster, falling in a heap at his own feet, supposed himself to have sailed like a stone.

One more instance and "I've done, i' faith."[15] Gliding along down the Hudson River one hot summer afternoon in a steamboat, I went out on the afterguard for a breath of fresh air, but there was none to be had. The surface of the river was like oil and the steamer's hull slipped through it with surprisingly little disturbance. Her tremor was for once hardly perceptible; the beating of her paddles was subdued to an almost inaudible rhythm. The air seemed what we call "hollow" and had apparently hardly enough tenuity to convey sounds. Everywhere on the surface of the glassy stream were visible undulations of heat, and the light steam of evaporation lay along the sluggish water and hung like a veil between the eye and the bank. Seated in an armchair and overcome by the heat and the droning of some prosy passengers near by, I fell asleep. When I awoke the guards were crowded with passengers in a high state of excitement, pointing and craning shoreward. Looking in the same direction I saw, through the haze, the sharp outlines of a city in gray silhouette. Roofs, spires, pinnacles, chimneys, angles of wall—all were there, cleanly cut out against the air.

"What is it?" I cried, springing to my feet.

"That, sir," replied a passenger stolidly, "is Poughkeepsie."

It was.

An Unexpected Encounter

[A very piquant episode during Bierce's expedition through the Indian country was told only twenty years after the event.]

The Northern Indian is quick at names; he has a notable knack at hitting off the outward and visible characteristics of a thing the moment he sees it. Show to a number of them, severally, something the like of which they could never before have seen or dreamed of, and nine in ten of them will give it the same name without a moment's hesitation. On reflection, you will be struck with the apt and felicitous significance of that name for that thing. This is true, too, with regard to persons, as an anecdote will attest. Ages and ages ago, near Fort Laramie, my curiosity was lured by the grave of Chief Spotted Tail's daughter, which I proceeded to sketch. This grave, by the way, consisted of an oblong wooden box draped with the tatters of a rotting blanket and supported on four poles. To two of these at one end of the box were affixed the heads of two ponies, "beated and chopped with tanned antiquity,"[16] and by the shrinking of the skins each cursed with a grin indescribably ghastly. At a corresponding height on the other poles dangled the ponies' tails. Upon the backs of these two chargers the deceased young woman was visible to the eye of faith, riding to the happy hunting grounds, though she did not show up in my picture.

Having made the sketch I took it to camp, and seated on a stool in the open, was finishing it, when by some mysterious intuition I became conscious of the presence directly behind me of a stalwart Indian chief, and to this day I shudder to think what his name may have been. He did not speak—I don't think he made a gesture; these people have some way, unknown and incomprehensible to us, of communicating with one another at a distance. I have observed the same thing in certain birds, whole flocks of which, widely separated, with hills and forests intervening, and in profound silence or all clamoring alike, will instantaneously spring to flight. Whales have the trick of it, too; from the masthead an entire "school," some of its individuals leagues apart, with the convexity of the sea between, have been seen to dive at the same instant. However these things be, a few seconds after I became aware that Chief Blank Dash was looking over my shoulder, I found myself the focal point of a few hundred converging Indians of both ·sexes, many ages and all conditions except the more desirable ones.

They came from beyond acres of tall willows, impervious to sight, and poured over the crests of long hills. Some advanced from the river's edge and behind others, as about the statue of Ozymandias, "the lone and level sands stretched far away."[17] I distinctly saw several in the act of rising out of the ground, or never believe me more! They came, they saw, they concurred; they were of one mind regarding the merits of my sketch, and by a thousand grunts attested their approval. A thousand thumb-marks perpetuated the record of the scrutiny. When it was all over we shook hands, and with spontaneous and unanimous assent, out of the fullness of their hearts, they gave me a name by which I was ever afterward known throughout their country, even to Indians whom I accidentally met hundreds of miles away and who had never before seen me. The name was descriptive; it took account of my skill with my pencil and of my youth. I confess a certain foolish pride in it. It is impossible to give it in the original—we have not the right kind of letters. Accurately translated it is The Magical Calf.

Early Days in San Francisco

A Wry Self-Portrait

[About a year after he began his "Town Crier" column, Bierce evidently became the object of curiosity from many sides. Here he presents a self-portrait that, although clearly written with tongue in cheek, perhaps presents far more truth than falsity.]

Whereas the *Town Crier's* lady admirers are always bothering him with notes asking for his photograph, and whereas the proprietor of this paper with unexampled meanness declines to have any struck off at his own expense, the *T. C.* hopes to satisfy all parties by the following meager description of his charms. In person he is rather thin early in the morning, and a trifle corpulent after dinner; in complexion pale, with a suspicion of ruby about the gills. He wears his hair brown, and parted crosswise of his remarkably fine head. His eyes are of various colors, but mostly bottle-green, with a glare in them reminding one of incipient hydrophobia—from which he really suffers. A permanent depression in the bridge of his nose was inherited from a dying father what time the *Town Crier* mildly petitioned for a division of the estate to which he and his seventeen brothers were about to become the heirs. The mouth is gentlemanly capacious, indicative of high breeding and feeding; the under jaw projects slightly, forming a beautiful natural reservoir for the reception of beer and other liquids. The forehead retreats rapidly whenever a creditor is met or an offended reader espied coming toward the office. His legs are of unequal length, owing to his constant habit of using one of them to kick members of the Young Men's Christian or other Associations who may happen to present a fairer mark than the nearest dog. His hand is remarkably slender and white, and is usually inserted in another man's pocket. In dress he is wonderfully fastidious; preferring to wear nothing but what is given him. His gait is something between those of a mud turtle and a jackass rabbit, verging closely on to the latter at periods of supposed personal danger, as before intimated. In conversation, he is animated and brilliant, some of his lies being quite equal to those of Coleridge or Bolingbroke;[1] but in repose he resembles nothing so much as a heap of old clothes. In conclusion, his respect for letter-writing ladies is so great that he would not touch one of them with a ten-foot pole. [1]

Justifications for Satire

[It is not surprising that Bierce was frequently asked to provide
justifications for satire, particularly the brand of satire—biting,
unrelenting, and specific—that he practiced. The following passages supply some phases of his answer.]

A correspondent writes us a deprecating letter, and wishes to know what fiend possesses us to lash everybody so unsparingly. Dear "Veritas" we do nothing of the kind. We lash the Evil-disposed only and commend the Good alone. The Good are the friends of the *News Letter,* and, like kings, can do no wrong; the Evil-disposed are its enemies, and can do little else. Some of them may occasionally stumble upon a good act, but it's a scratch if they do, and we never see it. If any of "our shafts" strike our friends, as "Veritas" says they sometimes do, they never penetrate the triple steel with which the clear conscience of all patrons of the *News Letter* are protected. That which when applied to an enemy is biting and malicious satire, becomes merely harmless fun and good-natured criticism when directed against a friend. The form of target makes all the difference in the world in the nature of the projectile. This is a truth which has never yet been explained, and we believe has never before been stated. But it *is* a truth: our saying so makes it such. "Veritas" says we cause pain to many "amiable" men. Very likely. Though none of our enemies are of the Good—goodness depending entirely upon a certain relation to the *News Letter*—we are willing to believe there are many who are of the Amiable. Whenever their general Amiability shall fructify into specific Virtue, the lion—N. L.—and the lamb—Am.—shall lie down together, and our dog Jack shall lead them. [2]

We have become intolerably tired of scolding the rogues and dunces of this village to no purpose. The more shrilly we clamor against them the more irreclaimable they become. It has just dawned upon us in the light of a revelation, that mere verbal satire is a delusion and a cheat—that the battles of intellect are waged with stuffed clubs—that the pen is not only less mighty than the sword, but is even inferior to a well-wielded hand-saw. In accordance with this new and wholly original view, we have decided upon a course of action designed, we prayerfully hope, to exterminate knavery and folly, in the brief period required for a complete oscillation in the tail of a lively lamb. Our abusive personalities will be continued for our own private delectation, but for the actual punishment of crime and stupidity we shall send round a man with a shotgun. It is hoped this will suffice for secular sinners; clerical offenders will be dealt with in a more summary manner. We shall lay an assessment of one dollar per week upon them, and vigorously enforce the demand with an ax-handle. With shameless ballet girls we shall plead eloquently with a boot-jack, and shall labor for the reform of the Board of Supervisors with a cart-rung. To prevent the incursions of our shotgun satirist into the various newspaper offices, and the consequent disturbance of the editorial tranquility, it will be necessary for each of our contemporaries to dispatch a delegate to this establishment every week to be killed. Monday morning will be most convenient for us. The *Workingman's Journal* is excused. It is earnestly hoped this new manifestation of humor may meet with general approval and support, and that it may be the means under Divine Providence of effecting a complete revolution in local morals. It is believed to be based upon sounder principles of criticism than any system of censorship that has yet been adopted. In the terse diction of a practical people, it means business. [3]

> "Satire should not be a saw, but a sword; it should cut, not
> mangle."
>
> —*Exchange.*

O, certainly; it should be "delicate." Every man of correct literary taste will tell you it should be "delicate"; and so will every scoundrel who fears it. If there is one main quality in satire to which everything should be subordinate—which should be kept constantly in view as solely worthy of achieving, it is "delicacy"— that is, obscurity—that is, ineffectiveness. Your satire, my young reader, should not mangle; our contemporary has *told* you it should not mangle. He has not explained why a thing that is a legitimate object of satire—that is, a thing that is bad and worthy of extermination—ought not to be mangled; but it is doubtless true that it ought not. It ought only to be made to slightly wince—"delicately." A man who is exposed to satire must not be made unhappy—O dear, no! He must find it very good reading—a little pungent and peculiar, but upon the whole invigorating and breezy. Don't mangle him. If he is a thief, don't call him so by name, but insinuate darkly—and "delicately"—that "possibly some gentleman to whose outward seeming his own aspect conforms, might justly be suspected of confusion in his conception of *meum* and *tuum*." Don't mangle the man, like that coarse Juvenal, and that horrid Swift, but touch him up neatly, like Horace or a modern magazinist. Then, in faith, you shall be in fashion, and every critic shall glow—"delicately"—with admiration of your niceness and polish; and your victim shall give your censures into the hands of his young daughter to read to him, that he may be free to writhe. It was not long ago that the *Atlantic* gravely praised somebody's satire, because it was "so subtle as to leave a half doubt of its intent!" What a jackass-taste is this. Gad! if Miss Nancy is going to "sentence letters" much longer, there will be little tatting made. Let us mangle! [4]

The Town Crier's Increasing Fame

[It was not long after Bierce commenced his column that his reputation as a wit began to spread far beyond the city limits: his paragraphs were copied in other periodicals; note was taken of his outrageous wit (one of the earliest articles being in the *Nation* for June 17, 1869); poems were written about him; and, of course, the objects of his attacks howled their protests far and wide.]

The New York *Nation* insinuates that the *Town Crier* possesses "the power at mental detachment," and intimates that he is even guilty of "spiritual sympathy." The editor of that paper may think it very fine fun to slander an inoffensive stranger, but how would *he* like to be accused of "spiritual sympathy"? As to "mental detachment," the *Town Crier* pleads guilty; his mind has long been detached from the harrowing task of perusing the *Nation*. [5]

The *Town Crier* will be happy to confer with his professional brethren of the daily papers regarding the merits of any of his little jokes as to the wit of which they may be undecided. This arrangement will save these gentlemen from two to four weeks time. Under the present system they do not dare to copy these paragraphs as they appear in this paper, and are compelled to await their indorsement by the Atlantic side and European press before transferring them to their own columns without credit. As the *Town Crier* writes principally for posterity, he flatters himself his wit is always fresh and sweet, but he is unable to see any marked improvement in it after a trip overland to New York and re-

turn; though the charming mystery then veiling its parentage may add an evanescent interest to its intrinsic excellence. Upon the whole, we think that in
waiting to correct their judgment by that of their Eastern contemporaries, our
San Francisco editors exhibit a just appreciation of their own intelligence, but
that in so doing they throw away a splendid opportunity of presenting their
readers with the freshest current thought. As it appears they *must* have our little
paragraphs, it would seem more sensible to take them from the fountain head.
As above intimated the *Town Crier* is a fair judge of his own work, and will be
happy to inform his careful brethren what portions of it are suited to the stomachs of their mentally dyspeptic readers. No charge for consultation. [6]

The following from an eastern paper is peculiarly soothing: "The *Town Crier* of
the San Francisco *News Letter* is said to be a gentleman named Spider, who was
formerly an officer in the Confederate Army. Being asked by his Colonel to resign, on account of laziness, he flatly declined unless he were furnished with a
blank resignation. So he remained, and in the next battle had a part of his brain
shot away, including the organ of common sense. Thus qualified for the vocation of a wit, his career has been a very enviable one; there are only about a thousand men in California who have sworn to take his life, and the number is constantly decreasing, from his habit of taking their's. He is a very polished and
scholarly blackguard, and every lover of polite deviltry will honestly deplore the
necessity of shooting him." This is very unkind, coming from the editor of the
Titusville *Herald*,[2] for whom we have never entertained any other feeling than the
kindest contempt. Will somebody tell us where the city of Titusville is, and who
the editor of the *Herald* is—and why? [7]

In the course of some bitter-sweet remarks upon the *Town Crier,* the Springfield
Republican intimates that a residence in the same city with him must be regarded
by the editor of the *Bulletin* as a penalty for some terrible crime committed in a
former state of existence. Not at all; the crime for which the gentleman suffers is
of somewhat later date, and consists simply in continuing to exist without adequate excuse. His sufferings, however, are somewhat overestimated by our Massachusetts admirer: the *Bulletin* is profoundly unaware of any such person as the
Town Crier. We hope, in the course of a decade or two, to impress him with a
comforting sense of our presence. [8]

The Follies of Religion

[Bierce quickly became notorious for his unrelenting attacks on
religion in all its forms: the intellectual failures of preachers; instances of religious fanaticism; and, in particular, the hypocrisy

revealed by a failure on the part of both clerics and ordinary
Christians to practice the tenets they purport to believe.]

Sunday schools for the Chinese have been established in various parts of the city.
Inside, the Chinamen master the theory of Christianity by means of the New Testament; outside, they are made acquainted with its practice through the agency
of loose building material. For Christianizing the heathen, the Bible and the
Brick-bat go hand in hand. The persuasive eloquence of the former is beautifully
supplemented by the convincing logic of the latter. *Vive* Bible, *vive* Brick-bat![3] [9]

The Rev. Eli Corwin, in his lecture a few evenings since, said it was "unaccount-
able to us how Jupiter, a swifter and vastly larger planet than the earth, should
spin erect like a top, while the earth was whirling with what the children designate a wabbling motion." The wabbling motion of the earth is certainly not due
to the weight of the Rev. Eli Corwin's brain upon the California side. [10]

We have received from a prominent clergyman a long letter of earnest remon-
strance against what he is pleased to term our "unprovoked attacks upon God's
elect." We emphatically deny that we have ever made any unprovoked attacks
upon them. "God's elect" are always irritating us. They are eternally lying in wait
with some monstrous absurdity, to spring it upon us at the very moment when
we are least prepared. They take a fiendish delight in torturing us with tantrums,
galling us with gammon, and pelting us with platitudes. Whenever we disguise
ourselves in the seemly toggery of the godly, and enter meekly into the tabernacle,
hoping to pass unobserved, the parson is sure to detect us and explode a bomb-
ful of bosh upon our devoted head. No sooner do we pick up a religious weekly
than we stumble and sprawl through a bewildering succession of inanities, manufactured expressly to ensnare our simple feet. If we pick up a tract we are laid out
cold by an apostolic knock straight from the clerical shoulder. We cannot walk
out on a pleasant Sunday without being keeled over by a stroke of pious lightning flashed from the tempestuous eye of an irate churchman at our secular attire. Should we cast our thoughtless glance upon the demure Methodist Rachel
we are paralyzed by a scowl of disapprobation, which prostrates like the shock of
a gymnotus; and any of our mild pleasantry at the expense of young Squaretoes
is cut short by a Bible rebuke, shot out of his mouth like a rock from a catapult.
Is it any wonder that we wax gently facetious in conversing of "the elect?"—that
in our weak way we seek to get even on them? Now, good clergyman, go thou to
the devil, and leave us to our own devices; or the *Town Crier* shall skewer thee
upon his spit, and roast thee in a blaze of righteous indignation. [11]

The editor of the *Barnacle* has a hobby which he has ridden for a number of years,
to the perfect satisfaction of his readers and the unspeakable delight of ourselves.

That hobby—now somewhat sore in the back—is the Darwinian theory. How much the rider knows about his horse will be seen from the following, upon the freedom of thought: "One man is not to be deterred from advocating the Darwinian theory because his neighbor is shocked at the idea that man is a development of the monkey." Very true, but he ought to be debarred from advocating it if he shocks his neighbor at his utter ignorance of what it really is. The Darwinian theory, James, does *not* imply that man is "a development of the monkey," but that both are descended from a common parent. See the difference? Your error is the same as if you should claim to be the offspring of a mule, instead of admitting that the ass is the father of both the mule and yourself. In the one case you would assert a physical impossibility, in the other you would simply support an extremely probable hypothesis. [12]

The clergy, poor devils, cannot divest themselves of the hallucination that we bear malice to the church. Not a Sunday passes but some of them project from the pulpit a blinding beam of Gospel calcium light in the direction of our humble lair, lest at any time some benighted lamb should stray hitherward and fall a prey to our jaws dropping with the blood of masticated innocents. And we blink placidly in the cheerful ray, gape good-naturedly and stretch our claws in this artificial sunshine, with a dreamy sense of ineffable repose. 'Tis sweet to be remembered in their prayers, albeit we do suspect there is a mental reservation of profound significance behind their touching appeals for mercy in our behalf. But it is a pity that all this kindly solicitude should be unworthily bestowed—that the elect should waste upon our careless feet the precious ointment that might be sold and the money given to the poor. Remember, good practitioners with pious pills for physicking our soul, we are not wholly without hope of ultimate recovery. The Lord helps those who help themselves, and lo! we help ourselves to the blessed bread and consecrated wine of thy holy communion with a liberal and unsparing hand. We walk unfaltering into thy sacred places and cram our honest pockets with thy golden images, thy costly censers and thy priestly ephods, which straightway we do stock our cabinet of curiosities withal. May the Lord forgive us, for we know not what we do! Nor, in good sooth, do we much care. [13]

A correspondent who admits that he has a biographical design against us, asks us, among other things, what is our religion—the only one of his inquiries to which he will get a civil answer. Owing to active business engagements, we have not as yet completed our system of religious belief, but so far as we have got, it is briefly as follows: These are the things that we believe: A Trinity—three Gods united by a rope at the waist; that being about the only method of *Tria Juncta in Uno* that our humble intelligence can accurately comprehend. This triple Deity is flesh and blood, for spirit, if it is anything, is breath; and in this case the question, Whose breath? would be utterly answerable. The remission of sins—that is, after they have been painfully expiated in the person of the sinner. Otherwise we should have to relinquish a belief in justice. There is a Heaven; the same as described by St. John. This is wholly uninhabited, except by the angels who were born there; for only a limited number of human beings have ever been good enough to go there, and these do not wish to spend an eternity of useless indolence. There is a hell; but its climate has undergone such a change in the last one hundred years that it may be called salubrious. In fact, it has been so modified in every respect that it is difficult to say what it is. There are four cardinal points in our theology. *Au reste,* we believe the doctrine of election without understanding it, and revere the doctrine of redemption without believing it. We believe the world was created out of nothing, but don't know how the nothing was held together, and don't think it could be done again. We believe in baptism, for we have seen it done. We believe in Divine Mercy, without wishing to take any of it. We think the Patriarchs were an honest and worthy lot, who have been shamefully misrepresented. We admire the wisdom of Solomon, and wish he had chosen to display it; and are amazed at the miracles of the Prophets, so little inferior to those of our own *prestidigitateurs,* and in some respects superior to the corresponding ones of their heathen predecessors and contemporaries. Of the four Evangelists, we have most confidence in John, because the Gospel bearing his name was written some hundreds of years after the others, and contains some facts which had not then occurred. And finally we believe that Jesus was the son of David, because two of the Evangelists trace the descent of His adopted father directly from that person. From this brief and imperfect statement of our theological position, our biographer will have no difficulty in classing us. A man who believes everything that anybody else does, can only be a Pagan. [14]

Cheerful Morbidity

[Bierce could not resist reporting on a variety of horrible crimes that occurred either locally or in other parts of the country. Suicides were particularly fascinating to him, and he reports these and other incidents with relish. The following passages are not for the faint of heart.]

A word to unfortunates: Razors are good in their way, but some knowledge of the location of the jugular vein must precede their use. Don't attempt to use more than one at a time, and go about it deliberately. Give yourself at least half an hour after business hours. Saw from left to right. A pistol is objectionable; it makes too much noise and wakes baby. If you must do it in this way, take a revolver, put the muzzle in your mouth (having previously removed the teeth), close the lips to deaden the sound, and fire five barrels. Wait two minutes by the watch, and if you don't feel sick, pull off the other barrel and hold your head in a tub of water. Shotguns are vulgar. Besides, they must be fired with the toe, which is liable to slip off the trigger and hurt one's corns. If used at all, it should be only in an aggravated case, such as the loss of office. Minor inconveniences, like conjugal perfidy, call for milder measures. Hanging will do on a stretch, and arsenic may be taken at a pinch. Strichnine is to be avoided; habit has rendered it innoxious to most of us. Jumping off Long Bridge is fashionable but dirty; Meiggs Wharf, when the tide is in, is preferable. Asphyxiation by blowing out the gas should not be thought of; it makes the corpse smell bad. We tender this advice gratis, in the interest of art; the bungling now so prevalent cannot be too strongly condemned. It is seldom necessary to leave letters behind, calling people names, but whenever it is deemed essential, blanks can be obtained at this office suitable for any occasion.[4] [15]

The other evening, as a man was proceeding quietly toward home, his hat blew off. His eccentric gestures in pursuit of it caused him to be arrested upon a charge of insanity, and in attempting to exculpate himself he became injudiciously vehement and burst a blood-vessel. Perceiving that he was bloody, the officer locked him up on a charge of murder, and went off to look for the victim. While he was gone the gentleman induced the jailor to enter his cell, when a shock of earthquake threw him against that functionary, who, imagining himself assaulted, beat the other's brains out with an iron bar. Death having entered a *nolle pros.*[5] there was no occasion for worrying the courts with the case, and the gentleman's remains were quietly chucked into a well, and the charge erased from the books. That is one reason the public has not before been made acquainted with these melancholy facts. Another reason is that the newspapers have not had sufficient enterprise to invent so consistent a story, and have frittered away their mendacity upon unimportant matters, while deeds of blood might just as well have been rife in their columns. [16]

We hold that genius in suicide is but indifferently appreciated: many cases are daily occurring in which the most splendid results are achieved with appliances seemingly inadequate to the production of even a temporary paralysis; and it is not uncommon for persons of little learning and no experience to make away with themselves after some ingenious fashion that mere talent and ripe scholarship might have sought in vain to devise. And yet these skillful operators receive no greater credit than the simple clod-pate who vulgarly disembowels himself with a grain sickle, or crushes out his soul under a steam hammer. This is all wrong, and tends to the discouragement of art. The question of the morality of suicide is not at all involved. It may be granted that this is a vice, without at all affecting the matter with which we are now concerned—the matter of method. Even murder is less repulsive when neatly and artistically committed, and there is no doubt but the slovenly practitioner who opens his victim's head with a knotty club gets it much better down below than the dainty gentleman who works deftly with a keen cleaver. But even a lack of genius and originality may be pardoned if accompanied with firm determination and unwavering persistence. The surgeon who amputated a patient's leg below the injury was an execrable bungler; when he severed it again immediately at the wound he became a tolerable operator; but when he finally cut the member off as high up as he could work, he rose to the dignity of a hero by virtue of that unyielding patience which will shed a lustre upon even the meanest acquirements. It is so with the kindred science of self-slaughter: if one do but adorn his awkwardness with the grace of persistence he merits a certain temperate meed of praise only less than that accorded to actual genius. For this reason we regard Mr. Michael Brannan, of Los Angeles, with feelings of unmixed admiration, and we clamor shrilly against the legal obtuseness that lodged him in jail. Mr. Brannan had tired of life's fitful fever, and sought to effect a cure with a pistol—a vulgar, hackneyed expedient justly deserving of emphatic disapproval. But mark the high qualities of this man! He emptied five barrels of that weapon at his head, each leaden pellet plowing its crimson groove through the Brannan scalp, but not ducking beneath the bone to the heroic brain within. The man who could look upon this marvelous attempt unmoved with admiration—nay, who could himself withhold a friendly shot, or deny the succor of the exterminating axe, is not to be lightly classed with Christian gentlemen. The scoundrel who could, and did, arrest and imprison Mr. Brannan can only be fitly characterized as a moral and social hog! [17]

Women's Rights

> [Bierce vehemently opposed all attempts at augmenting women's rights, in particular the right to vote. What he never mentioned, however, was that early in his career he actually wrote an essay in support of a woman's right to vote ("Female Suffrage," *Californian*, Dec. 7, 14, 21, and 28, 1867), and in it refuted many of the claims that Bierce put forth in the following passages and over the rest of his life.]

An ancient Eastern maiden, one Susan B. Anthony[6] by name, is coming to this city to deliver a series of lectures. This antique harridan is welcome. We long for her with a mighty longing; we yearn for the shrill cackle of her cracked larynx; we pant for the lively patter of her tireless tongue! How cheerfully we shall fall upon her skinny neck and weep—how lovingly encase her in our sinewy arms— how smilingly impale her upon our pen and roast her in the blaze of a righteous ridicule! The waters of anticipation drench our mouth with a delicious frigidity.

Come, Soozie, mavourneen; trot hitherward and unbuckle thy budget of peer-less platitudes—shake out thy wealth of wondrous words. Unfold thy tale! [18]

Miss Susan B. Anthony promises that if women shall be made voters they will accept the responsibility of war and take the field like men. There would be some advantage in this arrangement; there would be no necessity to go to any expense to furnish them with sabres and bayonets, nature having supplied them with a keener weapon, which they carry between their teeth. But we hope never to see woman go to the wars. We should shrink from encountering a lonely female vedette on a dark night, a mile away from our supports; and the heart flutters with terror at the thought of meeting a lady scout skirmishing about in the shades of some vast forest, where no human ear could hear the shrieks of her victim! And then to think of being placed at some solitary outpost, with only a female for a companion, and but one blanket for both! Yow, yow! it is perfectly depressing. We shall not enlist. [19]

The nasty women of the suffrage convention, last week, passed a resolution of which the following is as nearly intelligible a copy as can be made: "*Resolved,* That the present prevailing custom, which proscribes, degrades and socially ostracises women for unchaste conduct which is practically winked at and overlooked when practiced by men, subjecting his victims to a condition which renders their restoration to a modest and virtuous life not only difficult but practically impossible, is an indignity to womanhood, and will be continued till the same social penalties shall be imposed upon men for immoral conduct as are now visited upon women." We pause for breath and for divine grace to remark that we cordially concur in the belief that this custom will, as set forth, be continued until it shall be changed. We concur, also, in the opinion that it is an indignity to womanhood. But if these women wish to be unchaste, it is cowardly in them to refrain for a trifle like that. Now, high and mighty Dirtinesses, "screw up your courage to the sticking point,"[7] or *vice versa.* Don't stand there shivering on the brink, but take to the slums like a duck to the water. Strip your grimy souls of their chafing and ill-fitting reputations, and take a cleansing plunge into this angel-troubled Pool! We will guard your sweaty dimity, mesdames, while your limbs are poisoning the polluted waters by a brief bath. Now, Lemons, go in! [20]

A Cry from the Heart?

[How much of Bierce's misogyny was real and how much feigned? Is the first passage printed below a genuine cry from the heart (in spite of its wicked concluding twist) or another poke at womankind?]

The *Town Crier* is sick; he needs careful nursing and a multiplicity of medicines. His days are cheerless; he requires some one to sit up with him. His nights are feverish; he must have some one to lie—to him out of the *News Letter*. Males will not do; he is fatigued of them, and desires that they all travel in foreign countries—visit the Europeans or other distant tribes. What he wants is rhubarb, with a woman at the other end of the spoon. A very little rhubarb, a great quantity of woman, and a brief spoon. The rhubarb may be weak, but the woman should be strong enough to keep him from getting out of bed. Before assuming this Christian duty, the lady should understand that the *Town Crier* is twenty-eight years of age, powerfully constructed, very good looking, and—rather obviously—a bachelor. That is the nature of his disease. He is confident of his ability to cheer up and entertain an intelligent nurse through the silent watches of the night, by detailing his various symptoms, their probable cause, and the manner of their cure. Nothing will be said calculated to excite alarm in the bosom of the most fastidious. The best of references will be given, and none required if the applicant is handsome. All women are handsome. Some, however, are more handsome than others, and it is natural for the sick to prefer that kind. The mind weakened by suffering clings to beauty as a drowning sailor to a spar, and the body similarly affected likes to cling a little also. Salary is no object, and application may be made by photograph. Blondes will be gratefully rejected; the patient is himself a blonde, and that game will not impress. *Similia similibus non curantur.* LATER.— The *Town Crier* is convalescent, and will try to worry along without any assistance, thank you. [21]

Some time ago the *Town Crier* announced himself as an interesting invalid, and clamored for a dose of healing rhubarb with a woman at the other end of the spoon. He stated, as nearly as he can recollect, that as he was of a violent and irascible disposition, applications for the position of spoon-holder would better be made by photograph, to avoid unpleasant consequences from a possible disapproval of the personal appearance of the applicant. The only application received up to date comes from a young woman down East, and is accompanied by a "counterfeit presentment" of fascinating comeliness. The *T. C.* has gazed upon that portrait and allowed its beauty to sink into his soul like attar of roses into a bandanna handkerchief, or a stumbling child into a kettle of hot mush. The contour of that *chignon* has impressed itself upon his memory as indelibly as the hieroglyphics of the branding-iron upon the flank of a fat ox. The broad and ample beauty of that back will ever remain one of his most pleasing memories. The inspiring aspect of those shell-like ears, clinging to the head like twin pats of half-masticated gum pitched against the opposite sides of a country school house, shall be unto his mental eye an eternal source of ravishing delight. If the young woman has no face she may consider herself accepted. [22]

[Bierce could not resist poking fun at his own marriage on Christmas Day, 1871, and what implications it might carry in regard to
his already notorious misogyny. In a letter entitled "Female
Suffragers and the Town Crier," written under the pseudonym
"Almira Faircheek," Bierce's self-parodic skills are at their height.]

San Francisco, Dec. 29, 1871.

Mr. News Letter:—After the adjournment of the last meeting of the Woman Suffrage Association of this city, an executive session of the old maids of the society
was held, to consider a matter of some importance to the community, and it is
my privilege, as a reporter of the truth and a defender of the rights of maiden ladies, to give you an accurate report thereof. Miss Arabella Jones, a brunette, called
the meeting to order, and said: "Ladies—As soon as I read to you a short paragraph from a morning print, you will see the propriety of passing appropriate
resolutions and making such remarks as may seem proper. From the *Evening
Hypocrite* I read, 'MARRIED.—In this city, on Christmas Day, by Rev. Mr. Brains,
the Town Crier to ——.' Ladies, I cannot read the name of the unhappy (sobbing) person, who has been so (sobbing) unhappi- (sobbing) ly deceived." Why
did Miss Arabella Jones, a dashing brunette, sob, sir, as she read that, to me, unimportant announcement? Because the Town Crier is a blonde, and she madly
loved the brute. She was the only woman, sir, in the whole world, I believe, who
did ever love him, and she did it through sheer obstinacy and disappointment.
The other woman, who is now Mrs. Town C., and who may be surrounded, for
aught I know, in the future by a multitude of more degraded little Town Criers, I
believe to be a member of the International Society for the elevation of man, and
it fell by lot to her to raise this desolate being from the depths of skepticism and
distrust of our sex to the hight,[8] sir, of merely ordinary men—a dreadful task.
Well, sir, that announcement fell upon that executive session like an old Stilton
cheese. Every virtuous lady present turned up her nose, many sneered and some
groaned. Miss Turntoes said, that it was a blessing to married men, and an unhappy dispensation to the victim at the altar. Miss Eliza Stratelace said, she hoped
the newly married pair would live next to a meeting-house, and that the Lord
would exert His special providence for the saving of one eternal soul that had
been playing all his life hide-and-go-seek with the Devil, and been caught every
time. Miss Jane Squinteye rejoiced in her soul that the cause of immorality would
now lose one champion. Miss Medora Sawnose then believed she would not de-
tain the ladies with any extended remarks, but would offer the following resolutions, as expressing the sense of the meeting:

WHEREAS, By a dispensation of Providence (which could have been dispensed
with by Sawnose—*sotto voce*—who once had an eye out towards the T. C.), that
implacable reviler of women and scoffer of the marriage relation, the Town Crier,

has been caught in the pit which he himself digged, and has been yoked under the bitter yoke of matrimony,

Resolved, That the sympathies of this society and of the world are bestowed, without money and without price, upon the heroic woman who has offered herself a victim upon the altar of that dreadful being's desire to be received into decent society.

Resolved, That for her unsuspected, unheralded, and unsurpassed disinterestedness, she ought to be released at an early day from purgatory of such a married existence, into the heaven of widowhood and union with one worthy of her.

Resolved, That the *Town Crier* shall be tortured by having all his family affairs talked about by every member of this society, his wife aided by written candle lectures from each one of us, daily for one year, and herself sustained and soothed in her endeavors to keep him in nights, except when he is compelled to escort her to evening-parties, *soirées musicales,* and Wednesday evening prayer meetings.

Resolved, That he is no better than he should be.

Resolved, That it serves him right.

These resolutions were received with acclamations of delight and passed without a dissenting voice, and ordered spread in red ink upon the records of the society. The meeting then adjourned. Please stick a pin in there, and believe me,

Yours, yet hopeful,

Almira Faircheek. [23]

Some Famous Contemporaries

[Even in his early days as a journalist Bierce encountered several of the literary notables of his day, chiefly Mark Twain and Bret Harte, the latter of whom accepted several pieces by Bierce for the *Overland Monthly.*]

Mark Twain, who, whenever he has been long enough sober to permit an estimate, has been uniformly found to bear a spotless character, has got married.[9] It was not the act of a desperate man—it was not committed while laboring under temporary insanity; his insanity is not of that type, nor does he ever labor—it was the cool, methodical, cumulative culmination of human nature, working in the breast of an orphan hankering for some one with a fortune to love—some one with a bank account to caress. For years he has felt this matrimony coming on. Ever since he left California[10] there has been an undertone of despair running through all his letters like the subdued wail of a pig beneath a washtub. He felt that he was going, that no earthly power could save him, but as a concession to his weeping publishers he tried a change of climate by putting on a linen coat and writing letters from the West Indies. Then he tried rhubarb, and during his latter months he was almost constantly under the influence of this powerful drug. But rhubarb, while it may give a fitful glitter to the eye and a deceitful ruddiness to the gills, cannot long delay the pangs of approaching marriage. Rhubarb was not what Mark wanted. Well, that genial spirit has passed away; that long, bright smile will no more greet the early bar-keeper, nor the old familiar "chalk it down" delight his ear. Poor Mark! he was a good scheme, but he couldn't be made to work. [24]

It is announced that Mark Twain, being above want, will lecture no more. We didn't think that of Mark; we supposed that after marrying a rich girl he would have decency enough to make a show of working for a year or two anyhow. But it seems his native laziness has wrecked his finer feelings, and he has abandoned himself to his natural vice with the stolid indifference of a pig at his ablutions. We have our own private opinion of a man who will do this kind of thing; we regard him as an abandoned wretch. We should like to be abandoned in that way. [25]

Frank Bret Harte has been elected—what do you think?—"Professor of Recent Literature and Curator of the Library and Museum" of the University of California. The *Town Crier,* who, incredible as it may seem, happens to like Bret Harte, and believes in him, executes upon his larynx a difficult note of triumph. In plain language, he crows—throws back the top of his head and emits an inspiriting cock-a-doodle-doo! It has long been tolerably well known in literary circles that Mr. Harte could not afford to remain in California—where there is a conspicuous lack of the sense necessary to the appreciation of genius—unless he were bribed with a lucrative sinecure. The *T. C.* rejoices at a consummation devoutly to be hungered and thirsted after. Harte will stay with us along with our Golden Gate, and our Yosemite, and our Big Trees, and our mammoth vegetables, and our "finest climate in the world, sir." We've corraled him. [26]

A Lawsuit

> [It is remarkable that, through his entire stint as the Town Crier,
> Bierce was only once involved in a lawsuit for libel. The first two
> of the following paragraphs, written in 1870, are only a sampling of
> the vituperation Bierce heaped upon his victim; the third para-
> graph, written in 1872, notes the upshot of the legal action.]

The vacant-headed simpleton who has for some months misconducted a dramatic paper in this city, has been so persistently kicked by gentlemen across whose path he has had the temerity to crawl, that he has finally been compelled to purchase the luxury of sitting down without pain, by disposing of his interest. This ridiculous incarnation of inspissated idiocy, who, by a miraculous manifestation of morbid meanness in Mother Nature, was thrust upon a protesting world as a faultless specimen of the human hog, was a decent printer until his mirror suggested the aspiring monkey, which he straightway attempted to emulate in ambition as in face. His brief but brilliant career affords another illustration of the folly of attempting the *role* of a gentleman with the brain of a jackass. If it be not already clear that we allude to George T. Russell, we despair of describing a dunce by any ordinary method of delicate insinuation. [27]

We learn that Mr. George T. Russell has been telling about the town that he came on Friday of last week to the *News Letter* office, and so intimidated the entire concern that no attack was made upon him for his latest piece of damphoolerie. The facts are about these: Mr. Russell came to this office and said something about libels and his singular distaste for them. The editor happened at the moment to be deeply absorbed in the act of crucifying a blue-bottle fly in attendance upon Mr. Russell, and neglected to get the drift of the latter's remarks; but upon looking up, some moments afterward, and perceiving that gentleman, he requested him to be seated, which on account of some recent kickings was impossible with any kind of comfort. Mr. Russell was then blandly requested to betake himself to the street, and assured that in the forthcoming issue of the paper he would be roasted to a delicate nut brown. As he passed out of the office his bearing so forcibly suggested to the editorial mind the dignified demeanor of a chastened spaniel, that it became merely consistent to wallop our dog Jack, in which pleasing duty the flagellation due to the other puppy was wholly forgotten. It is hoped this paragraph may be accepted as sufficient reparation for an unintentional neglect. [28]

It is sad to stand and watch the laboring tumble-bug trying heroically to heave his unwieldy ball up a flight of stairs. The alternate hope and disappointment of Sisyphus were as nothing to the steady despair of this relentless worker. One pities him deeply, from the bottom of one's heart, and is tempted to step upon him to terminate his profitless travail. It is with compassion akin to this that we regard Mr. George T. Russell, who, having been jocularly alluded to by this paper a year ago in return courtesy for a long series of vicious newspaper attacks upon us, has ever since been following our trail with the grim vindictiveness of a lame pullet streaking it after a soaring grasshopper, and the fierce greed of a robin's callow nestling splitting its face to take in a passing cloud. Mr. Russell has spared neither time, money nor lack of talent, to work us a mighty woe. A fact not generally known, and not of overshadowing public importance, is that he moved heaven and earth to induce the late Grand Jury to find a true bill against the writer of the distasteful paragraph, who, by a singular coincidence, happens likewise to be also the writer of this one. His success was not encouraging: nobody was indicted, and it is stated that he was himself sharply rebuked for taking up the time of the Grand Jury with his imaginary grievance. If our memory be not at fault (some scoundrel has decamped with our tablets) Mr. Russell has still a civil suit with the proprietor of this paper, for fifteen thousand dollars damages to his precious character, pending in some one of our many Courts. As that is a matter in which the writer is not personally interested, he can only generally and comprehensively pray that Mr. Russell may always obtain strict justice. That he has not always obtained it heretofore, we are free to maintain; and in proof we point to the fact that his carcass is not at this moment poisoning the omnivorous buzzard or the reckless worm. [29]

During the past week, the *Town Crier*—who had already done something toward popularizing certain apt and cheerful forms of expression—has had the contentment of seeing several of his choicest modes of speech become household words. He has seen learned counsel wrangling before a perplexed Judge as to the exact meaning of the phrase, "peripatetic liar for a horse opera," and violently disagreeing with regard to the method of proving a man a "consistent sneak." These unfriendly expressions he some time ago applied to Mr. Geo. T. Russell, and in addition to these he called that person by what he confessed was a most odious epithet: he called him a George T. Russell! The *Chronicle*, only imperfectly comprehending the nature of these terms, incautiously copied them, and Mr. Russell promptly brought suit against that paper for libel. The publishers seeing they were "in for it," boldly maintained the truth of the charges, and proved them to the entire satisfaction of a jury, whom we will not slander by calling them Mr. Russell's peers. There were some doubts as to precisely what constitutes a "peripatetic liar," and some ingenious theories regarding the exact amount of harmony essential to the character and conduct of a sneak to entitle him to be considered "consistent;" but the jurymen did the best they could according to their light, and decided, practically, that if Mr. Russell was not a "peripatetic liar," nor "a consistent sneak," he was at least something quite as bad, and nobody ought to be punished for repeating these charming phrases, anyhow. The only thing the defendants did not prove is, that the plaintiff is a George T. Russell—a charge which is not susceptible of proof, without the testimony of some one who was present at his christening. Of course, the *Town Crier* cares nothing about the merits of this case, nor the justice of this verdict: he would have been as content to see Mr. Russell go forth from the Court-room vindicated as a gentleman, as he was to see him slink out branded as a "peripatetic liar" and "a consistent sneak;" but it is worth something to have enriched the vituperative vocabulary of mankind with these sweet, pungent and expressive terms. The press, the bar, the pulpit, the forum and the social circle need no longer complain of the poverty of our language in forms of disrespect. These two have now the sanction of law and the merit of popularity. They will be in common use long after the dainty buzzards have picked the meat from Mr. Russell's gibbeted bones. [30]

A Parting Shot

[In his final column for the *News Letter,* Bierce delivered a salvo that summed up his satiric purpose and encapsulated his cynical philosophy. It was, in essence, a philosophy to which he adhered for the remainder of his life.]

With this number of the *News Letter* the present writer's connection with it ceases for at least a brief season, be the same longer or shorter. Since December, 1868, he has, with but two weeks' intermission, contrived to spin out enough thought of one kind or another to fill this page of the paper. That he has always been entertaining he does not claim; that he has been uniformly good-natured is no further true than that he has refrained from actually killing anybody; that he has been "genial" is not true at all. It must be pretty evident that in penning some six or eight thousand paragraphs with the avowed design of being clever, he must have told a great number of harmless lies, and perpetrated divers cruel slanders. For the former he is responsible to his Maker, and shall offer no apologies; for the latter no apologies would avail, even if he were in the humor of making them—which he is not. He can only promise that California shall be his abiding place for some years, and he will always be "at home" to all sorts of people—creditors excepted. Now, there exist certain persons who, from envy, revenge, malice, honest stupidity, or what not, have been in the habit of attributing to the *Town Crier* an interested motive. There are persons who can see in satire nothing but the gleam of the highwayman's pistol, and in applied wit can hear only the robber's "stand and deliver!" These worthy blockheads—lineal descendants of the respectable Briton who dubbed Mr. *Punch* the "scurril jester," and raised against him the cry of "blackmail"—have not hesitated to disseminate their foolish falsehoods, somewhat to the injury of the *Town Crier*—and very much to his amusement. He has never thought it worth his while to deny their statements heretofore, but lest it should be said he did not dare, he will do it now; and will add that each and every man who has ever directly or indirectly countenanced this silly libel is a scoundrel and a liar, who will oblige by considering himself personally so addressed. To his friends, good and true—God bless them; their name is legion!—the writer bids a sincere farewell. May their lives be as bright before their feet as the memory of their goodness burns in the heart of him who has profited by their friendship and made but poor return. To his enemies he has but contempt—reserving the thorny chaplet of his actual hate for their betters, the enemies of mankind. One last word of explanation and we've done, in faith! The *Town Crier* does *not* "seek a wider field for his talents." The only talents that he has are a knack at hating hypocrisy, cant, and all sham, and a trick of expressing his hatred. What wider field than San Francisco does God's green earth present? Gentlemen—ah! and you, too, darlings, we came near overlooking you—a large, comprehensive and sincere farewell! Be as decent as you can. Don't believe without evidence. Treat things divine with marked respect—don't have anything to do with them. Do not trust humanity without collateral security; it will play you some scurvy trick. Remember that it hurts no one to be treated as an enemy entitled to respect until he shall prove himself a friend worthy of affection. Cultivate a taste for distasteful truths. And, finally, most important of all, endeavor to see things as they are, not as they ought to be." Then shall the *Town Crier* not have cried in vain; and if ever again he shall resume the whip of the satirist, it shall fall upon your shoulders as a snowflake settles against the rocky side of Mount Shasta. At present he resigns it to abler, and, he hopes, gentler hands. [31]

(1 8 7 2 – 1 8 7 5)

The English Jaunt

First Impressions of England

[One of the first things Bierce wrote in
England was a series of letters for the *Alta
California* (both daily and weekly editions)
recording his initial impressions of the people,
topography, and political and social conditions of what he believed would become his
adopted homeland. He reprinted these letters,
in highly truncated form, in *Nuggets and Dust*
(1873), but we have for the most part gone
back to the original letters in presenting the
following extracts. The section headings are
Bierce's own.]

Races and Race-Characteristics

England is winning laurels just now. Yesterday one of her
horses ("Cremorne," the winner of the Derby) carried off the
Grand Prix of Paris, 100,000 francs, and to-day she has
beaten the Americans in the great four-oared race on the
Thames. I shall speak of this latter contest further on.

The Ascot races are to come off this week and then this
horse-nonsense will be done for a year. The Ascot is the aris-
tocrat run of the season. The wealth, fashion, rank and

beauty go to Ascot yearly. Their Royal Highnesses, the Prince and Princess of Wales, are to be there, and I *may* go myself. After the racing season the town will begin to depopulate. People here are more or less crazy about this time of the year, and when they have a lucid interval they go out of town.

It is customary (I can't imagine how the fashion arose) to regard the British character as phlegmatic, unimpressible, staid, stolid, and the like of that. There never was a more absurd error, and what makes it the more ludicrous is that the British believe it themselves, and plume themselves upon it not a little. I regard myself as highly favored in being selected as the instrument for utterly over-throwing this antique mistake. Why, these people are volatile—they are mercu-rial. Put the liveliest Frenchman into London during the Derby week, and he seems, by comparison, a marvel of solemn respectability. People shun him as a man who has the canker-worm of remorse operating upon his vitals. His most emotional antics appear like studied coldness; his unrestrained outbursts of af-fection and esteem seem freezing politeness. Perhaps there *may* be another side to the English character, but it does not turn up at this season. The Academy of Sciences will be interested to know that my learned friend, Needlesight, attributes the vivacity of the British character to the quantities of that exhilarating bever-age, beer, which is consumed in England. My own observation is that English-men drink nothing but champagne, and drink that all the time. [1]

The Laboring Classes

You will be sorry to learn that Thomas Morgan has gone and committed suicide. Thomas was a bright lad of fourteen, residing at Joyford. The other day a neigh-bor found Tom down upon one knee in a hedgerow, and thinking he was there to frighten some one, went up to him and gave him a shake. This gentleman was the person Tom was there to frighten; and he did it nicely, for he was stark dead! He had twisted a handkerchief about his throat, tied one end to a branch and pulled on it till it choked him. No one can understand why he did it; for he worked in a coal mine for ten shillings a week, had been to school several months eight years ago, always had meat once a month, regularly, had frequently seen the outside of a church, and had clothes enough to almost cover a part of his body. Perhaps he was dissatisfied with his lodgings: he, his parents, and a few of his brothers and sisters occupying one apartment, which would have contained a bed had there been any bed, and had the apartment been large enough to contain it. Of course a suicide was denied burial by the Church of England; and so Thomas was taken out into the fields one rainy midnight and put under ground, without any ecclesiastical fooling, but in the presence of a large assemblage of his kind. It would be most unjust to instance the case of Thomas Morgan as a fair sample of what the laboring classes endure. His case is a most exceptional one: the others do not hang themselves.

I must say a word on the other side. Undoubtedly the condition of the

English laborers is a pretty bad one, but nine in ten of them deserve that it should be. What they might become in a few generations if they were not permitted to do any work, were furnished with nice houses and clothes, and fed on Sunday-school books, with Temperance tracts to sweeten their tea, it is impossible to say; at present they are a very brutal and undeserving lot, who repel sympathy as grease repels water. The best thing I know about them is that they are respectful, even obsequious, to those above them. A gentleman or a lady can safely thread a labyrinth of the drunkest and most uproarious of them. Some great hulking brute of a coal-heaver will take off his hat to you as you pass, or run to open the door of your cab for you, and then go off home and pound his wife with the fire-poker until she is of a beautiful steely blue. The latter diversion is his "national sport;" for thorough, consistent, and evenly sustained brutality to woman, I will hazard my ducats on the British workingman. Wife-beating is as common in London as base ball or euchre in San Francisco. It does not prevail, of course, in the middle and upper classes, but—well if lovely woman wishes to be idolized and made the most of, she may just as well save passage money by remaining in America; she can "play it" on the male of her species there as well as anywhere. I don't wish to imply that there is any open disrespect to woman here; perhaps I can best express my meaning in smallest compass by saying that she is never consulted. [2]

I don't know if I can give you any adequate idea of the condition of the labor market in England, without occupying too much of your space. In some of its aspects, it is truly alarming; and there is a well-defined uneasiness pervading all classes of society respecting it. It has for weeks formed the chief topic of discussion in the press, the views of which are as diverse and irreconcilable as if they had all been written by a single salaried Bohemian. Meagrely stated, the situation is something like this: Within the past twelve months the wages of nearly all classes of workmen have advanced very considerable. Those of some classes as much as a hundred per cent! though the average increase is, of course, much less. This advance has, in nearly every case, been brought about by strikes, and each advance is followed by a new demand and another strike. Of course the workmen have, in some instances, failed to carry their point, and in hardly any have they *wholly* succeeded; but the general result is an enormous advance in the price of labor, representing a proportionate, or rather an equal, increase in the cost of production. This exceptional and extraordinary tax upon production has borne its fruit of high prices, and the cost of living is immensely greater than ever before. As it was the high price of living that mainly provoked the original strikes, it is evident that these will continue; and it is equally evident that as long as they continue there will be a constant increase in their exciting cause. This is exactly the nature of the incline down which industrial England has begun to slide; and it is not wonderful that there is some anxiety as to *where* she is going to stop.

As a matter of course, the case, as I have stated it, is not the *whole* case: there are considerations of minor magnitude which materially alter the conditions, and complicate the operation of causes to the production of mixed effects. For example the agitation among the laborers is not wholly due to the cost of living: it is partly owing to a natural desire upon the part of the producer to participate in the recent extraordinary profits upon what he produces. For some years England has been enjoying a season of unexampled prosperity; and it is a general truth that a season of unexampled prosperity is commonly followed by a marked discontent among those who are only indirectly benefited by it—the working classes. Much, too, is undoubtedly due to the machinations of the International Society. Through this organization, with its central power and extended ramifications, a real or supposed grievance having its origin in one country, may be avenged in another, and so the labor market of England is sensitive, not only to local disturbance, but is susceptible to continental influences.

Nor has the increase in the cost of living its origin solely in the increased cost of production from the higher rate of wages. A good deal must be attributed to the decreased purchasing power of money, from the abundance of the precious metals caused by improved processes of mining, "absorption" from America, less consumption of them in French and German arts and manufactures, etc. Also, we must attribute a part of the high price of coals to their increased consumption in machinery, the world over, and a portion of the cost of meat to the rinderpest with which the cattle of nearly all Europe have, for some years, been afflicted. A dozen other factors to the problem suggest themselves, but I believe (against eminent authority, it must be confessed,) the causes are, in the main, as I have stated them. The accumulated discontent of generations has incited the working classes to demand a better compensation, and the obtaining it has saddled them with burdens more grievous than the ones against which they rebelled.

And so it has been clearly proven that, generally and broadly speaking, in all unnatural and extraordinary attempts to increase the price of labor, success is failure. The laborers must, or should, learn that, as a contemporary has clearly expressed it, "The more money he receives as a producer, the more he must pay as a consumer." There may be, temporarily, a balance in his favor—perhaps nearly enough to reimburse what he has expended while striking—but in the long run it is against him. This fact, which has long been well enough known to intelligent observers, has never before been subjected to a test by so wide a range of events as this year's industrial history of England has supplied. There is a lesson in all this which the American laborer would do well to heed, and which I observe he intends to wholly ignore. [3]

St. Paul's Cathedral

Did you ever actually *see* anybody who had been inside St. Paul's Cathedral? I ask because I believe one or two Americans have been to St. Paul's, and I'd like to know if they take on airs; for if it is proper, or customary, to do so, *I* mean to. Every American I meet over here asks me immediately he is introduced "if I have been in St. Paul's." My constant and undeviating reply has always been, Yes! The other day it occurred to me that all this lying was unnecessary; so I *went* to St. Paul's—and ever since, when the regular question has been put to me, I have answered No! St. Paul's was built by Sir Christopher Wren. It was begun *temp.* Charles II.; I don't remember if that party lived to see it completed, but I hope not. It took thirty-five years to build it, and it cost five millions, and seven and a-half millions, and ten millions of dollars; according to who happens to be your authority. It stands upon thirteen acres of ground, but doesn't cover it all. The top of the cross is ten thousand feet above the abdomen of Nelson, who lies directly under the centre of the dome, with Wellington at his heels, in a spacious and comfortable hall of the crypt. (Sir Christopher himself, a much better man than either, is stuck into the wall at one side.) The bell of St. Paul's is ten feet, and twelve feet, and fifteen feet in diameter. It weighs four tons, and six tons, and eight tons. It rings all the hours, but is never tolled except upon the occasion of a death in the royal family. I'd give anything to hear that bell tolled! The clock is eighteen feet across the face, and every American who goes in is expected to wind it up a little; about one turn of the crank is permitted to each American. It commonly gets wound up so tight by about eleven in the morning that it stops. So it is not regarded as a trustworthy timepiece after that hour, except upon Sundays, when Americans are excluded. My wife got hold of the crank of this clock and began to wind. I took the usher round to the other side of the machinery to have him show me the pendulum—which is twenty feet, and twenty-five feet, and thirty feet long, respectively. I kept him there until I had extorted from him a complete inventory of the Cathedral from top to bottom. Meantime, wife did not dare stop winding the clock, for fear the crank would fly back and hit her if she let up. So she then and there settled the business of that chronometer some three hours before the regular time; for we had gone early. It was painful to see the look of utter disappointment and distress upon the faces of the Americans as they came up the long stairs in squads to wind the clock. I never felt so sorry for anybody in my life. One of them said he would not serve his own mother such a trick. As soon as the stairs were clear I gathered up my wife and sneaked away, quite ashamed of myself; but the look of peaceful triumph has never departed from that innocent's face to this day.

The first feeling upon approaching St. Paul's is one of disappointment, as in all similar cases. It is only when you get some miles away, and see the dome lifting itself heavenward in the haze from the mass of buildings which cluster about it like ant-hills, that you begin to realize its real magnitude. The farther away you get, the higher it seems to rear itself, and when the surrounding architecture is merely an indistinguishable mass of points and shadows, the great cupola stands against the blue, seemingly larger than ever; and you look for the clouds to float themselves against its misty sides. And so it seems to grow and grow, until it is out of sight—for get it below the horizon you can't.

Upon entering St. Paul's you feel at first the same uncomfortable sense of disappointment; it is neither so wide nor so high as you had expected, and it is only after your eyes have somewhat adjusted their lenses to the unaccustomed distances, or perhaps your judgment has been sharpened by practice upon what the eyes report, that you begin to have any adequate conception of the immensity of the place. Then the walls begin to widen away, the ceiling to recede upward, and in a few hours you are oppressed with the vastness and loneliness of the interior; for the presence of a few thousands, more or less, is of no import here. Their contiguity is not companionship; the more there are of them the more alone each one seems. Their looks are unfamiliar; their voices startle; their footfalls wound. They speak below their breath, and seem to be talking to themselves. It is as if they were a part of the solitude; instead of dispelling they deepen it.

Let no one leave St. Paul's without mounting to the top. It is an arduous climb—one that no lady must think of undertaking—between the outer and the inner wall; but the compensation is full and ample. You are now directly over the centre of the dome, I don't dare to say how many feet above the floor. You lie down at full length, and peep through a hole the size of your face. The effect is indescribable; it is as if you were miles up in the air; so novel is your point of view that the judgment is utterly befooled by it. The people below you are black mites at the bottom of a blue mist; their movements are scarcely perceptible; their murmur wholly unheard. It is well for you if you do not happen to think of falling; if you do, your enjoyment of this extraordinary spectacle is gone forever—at least mine was.

I entered St. Paul's in the midst of a cracking thunder storm. The rain was plunging down in spouts, and the lightning cut the eyeballs like a knife. Some hundreds of clammy men and bedraggled women had already sought sanctuary in the church; most of them being huddled together under the dome, like frightened sheep; though a few kept up a show of indifference by the monstrous pretence of examining the execrable memorial statues of eminent boobies which deface the niches and walls. It is impossible to convey a notion of the effect of the storm, in here under the great gloomy concave. The lightning looked in through the painted windows as if the whole exterior world were on fire, while the thunder crashed, and rang, and jarred, in continuous echoes for nearly an hour. The peals could not be distinguished the one from another; it was one unceasing reverberation, mingled with the curious whisper of the rain outside. Down in the crypt, however, the storm was almost as inaudible to the living as to the dead.

I cannot close without giving a most exquisite little epitaph which I found cut in quaint old characters upon a lady's tombstone in this place. I have forgotten who the lady was, but whatever her name or station, she has had the finest tribute paid her that ever the dead received from the living. The lines seemed quite familiar as I read them, and doubtless many of your readers will be able to give the name of their author; for it is impossible that he should not be some well-known man of letters. Such a composition, simple as it is, could be the result of nothing less than years of close and conscientious intellectual culture.

> "Underneath this stone doth lie
>   As much virtue as could die;
> Which in its life did vigour give
>   To as much beauty as could live."

There! the human mind cannot get very far beyond the point at which it is possible to write lines like those. I will exchange my fame as a liar for the ability to write an epitaph half as good—provided I am supplied with a corpse that is suitable and deserving. [4]

Traveling

The first English soil that kisses the American foot is, almost from necessity, that of Liverpool—a mildly uninteresting commercial soil—a sordid earth, in which nothing but trade will flourish. Liverpool is the Purgatory through which the departed Yankee must pass to reach the Paradise of London; from which, also, he must purchase the release of his own soul at a ruinous price—more, in fact, than the article is worth. In this purgatory, indeed you are purged of nothing but your gold and your good patience. The tourist, if he be intelligent, will lose no time in exchanging the horrors of Liverpool for the delights of London—delights, however, from the full and satisfying enjoyment of which he is ever hindered by a haunting fever of impatience to go to Stratford-on-Avon. Until he shall have compassed the fulfilment of this wish, and attained to the true seventh heaven of his hope, the birth-and-burial-place of Shakspeare, the "educated American" is tormented with an inward flame, to which even the charms of the world's capital are but oil and resin.

For myself, I wrestled with my passion for months. It was easy enough to be amused in London during "the season," when I did not stop to think; the man whom London during the season would not somewhat amuse, must have something upon his conscience heavier than the worship of the great dead bard. But with the close of that charmed and charming period—when Westminster Palace had become "a dead silence walled about with cold stones"—when the Parks had become an habitation of the brooding philosopher and the aged single gentleman (those owls and bats of society)—when, in short, all but a paltry three millions of unimportant people had fled the town—then the fit came strong upon me, and I yielded—I fell. I fell to packing my trunk.

There are few experiences more delightful than traveling on one of the main lines of railway leading out of London; provided, of course, you go first class, and take along an easy conscience. The little cushioned apartment for six—it is ten to one you get it all to yourself and companion—is a wonder of cosy and comfortable privacy. And then the speed! Away you go, taking cities twenty leagues asunder at a single stride—reaching across the loveliest of spaces, and flashing past scores of big towns with never a slackening of the gait—gliding over green-sided rivers so quickly that the hues of bank and water are blended to the sight—sweeping along great parks, through which you catch dim glimpses of a modern palace or an ancient ruin—ever and anon leaping over a smoking manufacturing town—actually plunging house-high through its forest of tall chimneys, and wondering how it happens that your engine does not tumble them about like ten-pins! And all this without the endless click-click, the bump, thunder and dust, the moan and rattle and crash to which you have been educated by the railways of your youth. You do not thunder across the country; you glide along it with an easy swimming sense, and a gentle rocking motion which soothes like sleep. Shut your eyes and nothing shall persuade you that statute miles are being "payed out" astern at the rate of forty-five per hour.

A full-grown English railway is something of a marvel to a man of Western experience. It is, of course, a double track. It is practically without "joints," and "ballasted" like an asphalt pavement, for smoothness. The slopes are sodded from base to summit, and for long distances on either side the stations they are planted with flowers—sometimes. It is enclosed with a hedge, or handsome stone wall. No other railway, and no wagon-road—no foot-path, even—crosses it upon its own level; each has its bridge or its culvert of massive masonry; and the older ones are picturesque with clinging ivy. The way never lies through a town; it crosses above it on tall arches; and, as at the important stations, there must be scores of side-tracks, the structure is enormously wide, for their accommodation. In such cases the subjacent streets are long, dim tunnels, starred with perpetual gas-jets.

Should the engine-driver err, it will not be for lack of instruction. Planted alongside the metals, among the milestones, is all manner of information for his professional guidance—little boards inscribed with figures to indicate curves and their degree of curvature; other little boards to denote grades and their gradients; big boards telling him how fast to run and where to whistle. On long level reaches of air line, where there exists no necessity for these things, the monotony is pleasingly broken by other boards painted with the time of the day, quotations from the poets, and Scripture texts. In some places, where the country is *particularly* uninteresting, definitions from Johnson's Dictionary are posted up; but there is a good deal of complaint among passengers that the driver never conforms to them. All these devices—I mean the hour of the day, the poetical quotations, the Scriptural texts, and the dictionary extracts—would be of great assistance were it not that the train is driven so fast as to render them quite invisible. At least *I* never could see them. [5]

Stratford-on-Avon

I had expected to find Stratford-on-Avon a mean little village, shabby and shrunken with age, and painfully dull. It is in reality one of the most pleasing of villages, excellently clean, and with the grace of a tender charm lingering about it—a something indefinable, which addresses itself to some inner sense, and which may or may not depend upon the nature of the spectator and the feelings inspired by the town's associations. Leaving the railway station one needs not proceed far without a reminder of the Master. He has but to follow his nose, and lo—"The Shakspearean Iron and Brass Foundery." A little further on the laboring muse has delivered the following:

> "E. Beckett does live here,
>> Sweeps clean and not dear;
> If your chimney is on fire,
>> He'll put it out, if you require."

There is no mistaking the locality; you are in the very workshop of Poesy. The poetical spirit of the place is infectious. It took so strong a hold upon me that, having lunched badly and at a swindling price, at "The Shakspeare Hotel," I left the following effusion upon a page of the "Visitors' Book:"

> "It nothing boots exchanging 'saws'
>> With canting dunces who proclaim
> The lightness of the world's applause—
>> The worthlessness of human fame.
> Fame valueless? They'll have it so—
>> They still will teach and preach the same—
> Until by chance they undergo
>> The cheating done in Shakspeare's name.
> Perhaps they then will bow them down,
> And own there's profit in renown."

Soon after the above lines were discovered by the landlord I left "The Shakspeare Hotel."

I straightway sent off my little epigram to a widely-circulating London journal—which didn't print it—and then, by the merest accident, blundered into the famous "Red Horse Inn," immortalized by Washington Irving in the *Sketch Book*.[1] Mine host makes the most of this immortality, as you shall see. I took my meals in the "Irving Parlor," seated in the "Irving Chair," (duly labeled with a brass plate), stirred my fire with the "Irving Poker" ("Geoffrey Crayon's" sceptre), and gazed my fill at Irving in every style hanging against the papered walls. And, *mirabile dictu!* at the last I paid a most moderate bill for most comfortable and gentlemanly accommodations. It is not much to have sat in Irving's chair balancing Irving's poker; it is a mere trifle to have toasted my shins at the fire-place before which his were browned; to have slept in the bed which he occupied is barely worth mentioning; everybody visiting Stratford does some of these things. But, being an American and a stranger, to have shaken from my feet the dust of an English hotel without having previously shaken from my purse a double reckoning of sovereigns—to have got away without having been the victim of polite pillage and illimitable fraud, open and covert—this is an achievement upon which I reflect with some pride and a great deal of astonishment.

After the thousand-and-one descriptions of Shakspeare's birth-place and tomb (thousand-and-two, counting Joaquin Miller's) I am not hot to describe them myself. In the first place, I do not care to provoke a comparison between myself and Washington Irving; secondly, I was not sufficiently observant of the old half-timbered house in Henley-street, and the rather uninteresting church on Avonside, to qualify myself for the work. I did not much mark these things; I did not much care for them. I had eyes for nothing in its outer aspect, and a heart for but one thought.

Never for one waking moment was that thought absent from my mind; and in my sleep it haunted me like a sad-eyed spectre. Whether gazing my shilling's worth at the Shakspeare relics in the Henley-street cottage—or standing where stood the Shakspeare mulberry tree, (cut down by a vandal clergyman; may Heaven forgive his villain soul, as I do!)—or sauntering in the brown fields about Shottery—or tracking the late moon in the gleaming Avon—or bending with a full heart above the old tomb-stone with its terrible malediction—this saddest of reflections put up its piteous face in my soul, raised its solemn eyes and clasped its phantom hands in the agony of a dumb despair:

"Even he, alas! is dead! This Giant, from whose 'stupendous intellectual altitude' the difference between the highest and the lowest of *us* must have been imperceptible—who was higher above the highest than he above the lowest—in a world of men this first and only man—even he did die and rot; and here cowers his little heap of dust, guarded by his immortal curse!"

I am not exceptionally sentimental, nor, I think, very impressible. I have seen hundreds die, and forgot to grieve for them. I have stood at the graves of some of the world's greatest and best, and it never occurred to me to be sorry they were dead. It has seemed to me that Death, like the King, could do no wrong. But standing in the little old church on Avonside, with the ashes of that mighty brain beneath the soles of my feet, I could have wept for the dead man of two hundred and fifty years ago as for the grief "of an hour's age."[2]

I think this is not a general, but an individual experience. I have remarked the Poet's admirers, and even his lovers, furbishing up the dull platitude that he still lives in his works—lives for posterity and eternity. How pitiable was the failure of this bastard consolation when now, in the presence of the dumb dust, I first realized its utter shallowness and mockery—the sounding brass of this tinkling sentiment! And how bitter seemed the unconscious satire of this expression in my little guide-book: "The tomb of the immortal Bard!" A *tomb* for an *immortal!* Heaven help us to better sense!

I hope to never again see Stratford; the two days of my visit were the saddest of my life. There was no spot to which I could escape—no corner into which I could cower and shut out the dread sense of helplessness, inspired by the spot where pitiless Nature had reared her fairest son for the slaughter. In every street I heard, in fancy, his death-groan. In every field the wind whispered of his presence—and his absence. The very children playing by the wayside suggested unutterable things: thus had played their little ancestors when *he* passed—and passed away. A bald and bent old man whom I met in the churchyard roused my resentment like an insult. He seemed thrust upon my notice on purpose to recall the age at which death murdered my idol; the riper years accorded to the grosser clay were a shocking example of Nature's wicked partiality!

In the well-known "Chandos" portrait, representing what seems to me the handsomest of human faces, the world recognizes *its* Shakspeare; in the bad old bust set into the wall above the poet's tomb I recognize mine. As a work of art it is beneath contempt; as a likeness it is probably quite as faulty. For these demerits I am deeply thankful; they have preserved it to Stratford like a copyright; and outside of that town its similitude is seldom seen. It is, therefore, peculiarly sacred from its associations. It becomes mingled in memory with the birth-place, the tomb, and all the hallowed objects about which cling the affections of half a world. And so, while the better and truer image remains what it always has been—an image, merely—this other is invested with a sanctity which there can be no after experience to unsettle. It can never become so familiar to the sight as to generate indifference; and so it happens that he who has looked upon the poet's grave bears away with him a new and quickening conception of the poet's self—a mystery revealed only to the favored ones who have penetrated to the Holy of Holies, and in which the vulgar world can have no share.

I did not visit Charlecote, where Shakspeare stole the deer, nor did I extend my pilgrimage to the crab-tree under which Will and his guzzling companions lay drunk. For me it is sufficient that he *did* steal a deer, and that he *did* get drunk; and I say shame upon the canting morality which has been at such pains to disprove these gratifying facts—which would fain sever the only links connecting us with this higher type of being! None may claim kinship with him in intellect, but in human weaknesses, and in the sins of the flesh, God be praised, he was our brother!

This Shottery is a little village a mile from Stratford, and here it was that Ann Hathaway, aged twenty-five, wooed and won Will Shakspeare, aged eighteen; and in six months (another link, thank Heaven!) she bore him a daughter. Poor Ann sleeps unregarded alongside her lord, with a barbarous Latin inscription graven in brass above her breast. But all conscientious pilgrims walk across the fields to visit her old cottage, which seems about to sink into the ground under the weight of its thick thatch. Here they go to sit in the chimney corner where tradition politely says *Will* courted *her,* and to finger the product of her humble industry—an old patch-work bed-quilt, which she is positively known to have been supposed to make.

I cannot say I was much interested in Ann and her affairs. The visitors' book here was very much more to my mind; and therein, among a multitude of famous autographs I found those of General Sherman and Mark Twain.[3] I could not repress a smile as I read the name of the grim, heartless, and unimaginative warrior recorded at this shrine of pure sentiment—a sentiment, too, of the sicklier sort. From Mark something like this was to be expected. I had met him a few evenings before in London. We had dined together at one of the literary clubs, and in response to a toast Mark had given the company a touching narration of his sufferings in Central Africa in discovery of Dr. Livingstone! It was, therefore, not surprising that he should have penetrated as far as Shottery. He was probably looking for Sir John Franklin.[4] [6]

Warwick

I think it is about a hundred and ten miles from London to the little town of Warwick; and the little town of Warwick is about 1,800 years of age. I don't know if there is any relation between the age of the place and its distance from the metropolis; but the one is a reason why you should visit the village, and the other shows you where to find it. The route itself is not devoid of interest, if only for the reason that twenty miles out you dash past Windsor Castle—which seems only a stone's throw away, but is, in reality, a half-dozen miles. But, as you approach it, its piles of towers, and turrets, and battlements grow, visibly—they appear to heave slowly skyward; and, unable to at once realize their vast size, the judgment is cheated into a false estimate of distances. Before the mind can recover its powers, the giant structure has shrunk to a toy house, and is hidden by banks of green trees.

John Rous, the great antiquary—of whom I know nothing except that he died in 1491, and very few people know even that much (John is called a great antiquary from his great antiquity)—says Warwick was founded in the year of our Lord 1, by a British king named Gutheline, or Kimbeline, and was named after him, *Caer leon.* (You understand: "caer" means city, and the man who named it chose to pronounce Gutheline—"Leon.") It was afterward called *Caer-umber,* after Constantine. ("Caer"—city; and "umber"—Constantine.) Its modern name, Warwick, is only another way of pronouncing *Arthgal,* the name of the first Earl who lived in the vicinity. What we should do without antiquaries, I am sure I do not know.

Warwick is unquestionably a place of great age. The narrow, tortuous streets, the little old half-timbered houses, almost bumping their heads together across them; the remains of the old gateways, one on each side of the town, with a chapel perched atop of each; the various styles of architecture, from the early Norman to that of our own day; and, above all, the grand old castle, sufficiently attest the mature years of the quaint little town. It is from the castle that the place derives its only importance. This fine structure, about which cluster the memories of so much that is vital to the history of England—where the King-maker kept his court, and whence Piers Gaveston was led to the headsman's block—about whose strong towers the grass has often greened itself anew with fertilizing blood—in whose sunless dungeons may still be traced the carven prayers and piteous pleas-antries of men to whom daylight was a tradition, and the sounds of life were a vague half-memory—this stately pile, as which only the Tower of London "can boast so much of bloody fame," stands as for centuries it has stood, repelling the silent sapping of Time as grandly as it has so often beaten back the noisy storm-ing of the men-at-arms. Warwick Castle is not a ruin; it is good for another half-dozen centuries; barring the fires, of which it lately had a touch, and the "march of improvement," which has, so far, passed it by on the other side.

Mere words can give no idea of the curious, and rather stiff, magnificence with which this venerable building is furnished. The rooms to which the visitor is admitted are of great size and splendor, crowded, rather than adorned, with the rarest of paintings by Vandyck (portraits that visibly and audibly breathe), Rubens, Holbein, Da Vinci, Paul Veronese, Guido, Teniers, Salvator Rosa, Sir Joshua Reynolds, and Horace Greeley. I do not mean to say that Horace Greeley actually painted the Warwick pictures ascribed to him; I scorn to tell a lie, even in jest; they are only copies. There are statues by Praxiteles, Canova, Thorwalsden, Woolner, Powers, Mezzara, Michael Angelo and Michael Reese. There is an "ani-mated bust" by Sam Brannan. There are suits of armor by Kennedy & Monell—neat-fitting business suits, and evening suits with long tails. There are tables of bronze and lapis lazuli; vases of crystal; ornaments of ormolu; cabinets of buhl and marquetrie; things of pietra commessa; and other things of the other kind of pietra. There are more things in here than there are outside. There are a bed and a trunk which belonged to Queen Anne; and there is a table, composed entirely of stones, which belonged, I think, to Maria Antoinette. This latter bit is a little out of place among the really valuable articles with which it is surrounded; but since the fire there has been a lack of room, and while the repairs are going on, the kitchen furniture must be put *somewhere*. The table in question is valued at only fifty thousand dollars, and the servant who shows you round seems quite ashamed of it. The floors are inlaid in the most curious fashion with black and white marbles as hard as diamond and polished like mirrors. I believe there is not a carpet in the Castle, and I know there is not a stove. I think there is not a stove in England. It is to be wished there was not one in America, nor a carpet either. More people are killed by stoves, and by inhaling carpet-dust, than fall in battle. And they are better people, too.

The view from the windows of the main building is lovely beyond comparison. A hundred feet below, the smooth Avon washes the base of the south wall. Gigantic cedars of Lebanon spread out their flat palms below the spectator, as if inviting him to step out and take a walk upon them. The moss-veiled piers of the old bridge, destroyed by a flood in 1790 (in 1375 this bridge had become so old that tolls were levied to repair it) reach across to the other side like stepping stones laid by some giant, while away to the south and the west are wildernesses interminable of parks and lawns, and still villages and their delicate church spires shooting up sharply from beyond thick banks of foliage, shutting in the green fields from which they seem to have been crowded by pressure.

The main towers are Cæsar's and Guy's. (Every castle in England has a Cæsar's tower. One would suppose that during Cæsar's stay in Britain he did nothing but run about the country with a trowel and mortar laying corner-stones of towers. That is, one would suppose so if one did not know that not one of these things was erected within less than five hundred years after Cæsar's death.) The former is a noble structure, rearing its mural crown one hundred and fifty feet above the river at its base. It is of massive and irregular design and is extremely beautiful. Tradition, which has named it "Cæsar's," ascribes its erection to William the Conqueror. It was certainly erected in his time, and eight hundred years have been powerless upon it; the tireless ages have gone up unceasingly against it and have not prevailed. While in the town at its feet the degenerate architectural offspring of a later age are bowed and bent under their paltry decades, this gray veteran, declining even the gentle ministrations of the pitying ivy, bares his bald brow to the sun and the storm, shouldering his weight of centuries with never the failing of a joint.

Guy's tower was built by Thomas Lord Beauchamp, *temp.* Richard II. (about 1310.) It is a duodecagon, thirty feet in diameter, one hundred and twenty-eight feet in height and with walls ten feet in thickness. Its parapets are overhanging, open and supported upon huge brackets. (This arrangement enabled the garrison to entertain the besiegers with molten lead, boiling pitch, and other delicate attentions.) A massive embattled wall with a noble gateway connects the two towers and surrounds the castle proper on three sides, the other side being defended by a low-lying river and its own wall. In the gateway a strong wooden portcullis is still religiously let down at the approach of night, as if the dark were a marauding Baron with a thousand horsemen at his heels. A modest and rather neat arch usurps the place of the ancient draw-bridge, and what was once the moat is now a sunken walk.

If I have omitted to eulogise the objects of interest to be seen in this old stronghold, it is because there are too many of them, and not enough ALTA. The Great Vase from the Emperor Hadrian's villa; Cromwell's helmet; the bloody doublet taken from the body of Lord Brooke when that gentleman handed in his cheques at Litchfield, in 1643; the head of Stephen Massett—all these are very much admired. In the porter's lodge the visitor is shown the relics of the famous

Earl Guy; and as some people are base enough to assert that there never was any Earl Guy, I cannot do a more Christian thing than refute them by setting down a few of the articles shown: There is Guy's sword, weighing twenty pounds; his helmet, seven pounds; his breast-plate, fifty-two pounds; his dinner-pot, eight hundred pounds; and his table-fork, sixty-nine pounds. Many persons have pretended that the weight of the pot and fork is out of all reasonable proportion to that of the arms and armor; but I'd have them to know that this giant's appetite was out of all reasonable proportion to his valor. Anyhow, the same objection cannot be urged against the tusk of a wild boar he killed, and the rib of a cow he overthrew in single combat. These animals were evidently about the size of a rhinoceros and a whale, respectively. Everything about this hero seems to be on a stupendous scale, except his horse—the armor of which could not possibly have been got on an animal capable of carrying Mr. Guy. This can only be explained by supposing *him* to have carried the *horse*.

After the castle St. Mary's Church is the most interesting of Warwick's "lions." The most ancient part of the building is the choir, which was erected by the Earls of Warwick in the latter part of the fourteenth century; the main body of the present edifice dating only from the time of Queen Anne. But the "Ladye Chapelle" is the only portion specially worthy of attention. This was completed in 1464, and it bears its four centuries with a charming grace. It is one of the most perfect specimens of the pure Gothic in England. It is a little below the level of the nave—just enough to give it a touch of solemnity, as of a crypt. A noble painted window stains the still air a dim red. The ceiling springs from groined pillars at the sides, and displays the most delicate tracery. The floor is colored marbles, of lozenge pattern. About the walls are carved the cognizances of the Dudley's, the Riches, the Brooks, and the other noble families which, during the generations past, have supplied the world with Earls of Warwick and of Leicester. In the centre, the brazen effigy of Earl Richard, the Founder is stretched upon his altar-like tomb, clad in plate, with sword and dagger, the hands elevated as in prayer, the head wearing a coronet and reposing on a helmet. This image is very nearly perfect, and is said to be inferior only to that of Henry VII. in Westminster Abbey. The tomb itself is of Purbeck marble, but it would require a better knowledge of the curious science of heraldry than I possess to describe the devices wrought thereon. An inscription runs twice round the upper ledge, on brass plates. [7]

Kenilworth

It was on a bright Sunday morning that I ran down from Coventry to visit this famous place. I very well knew that on that day it would be impossible to obtain admission to the interior of the Castle, but, in addition to being a little ill of interiors and the everlasting guides who infest them, I craved a day's exemption from that "howling bore," the professional tourist. I knew Sunday wasn't his day out.

A brisk walk of five minutes from the station takes you in sight of this Castle.

The view is obtained from the summit of a hill three-quarters of a mile distant, and is extremely pleasing. The Ruin is a *ruin*—a very wreck. There is no swindling "habitableness" about it, as if it had gas clandestinely laid on, and Axminster carpets in the back kitchen, and cooking-ranges in the bed chambers, and inside blinds to pinch your fingers with, and shower-baths to take cold in, and places to fall downstairs, and all the modern improvements. It is one of the purest and completest ruins in England; though I believe there is one part of it just comfortable enough for a keeper to live in and swindle tourists, Heaven bless him!

The remains occupy a space of probably five acres. There are three "towers," each a castle in itself; and besides these there are numberless broken arches, crumbled walls, detached doorways and gateways, and the skeletons of pointed windows; big mounds of nothing in particular, and miscellaneous rubbish generally. But above all this chaos of architectural odds and ends rise great sides of strong wall, pierced with narrow, wicked-looking "loop-holes" for bowmen; clustering towers filled with masses of ivy; tall turrets; and ranks of battlements lifting their growth of green shrubbery to dizzy heights. About the desolate summits circle flights of tireless rooks, cawing, croaking, and clamouring, as if it were the business of their lives to do as much nothing as possible, and make more noise about it than the rooks of any other castle in England.

On one side of the Castle is a row of very old brick cottages, much out of joint, tenanted by farm laborers. On the other three sides extend low-lying meadows, once the bed of a lake, over which Queen Elizabeth passed on a bridge built specially for her, at the time of her celebrated visit to Leicester—when she considerately brought along thirty-one barons, a small army of women, and four hundred servants, all very hungry; with nine hundred horses to be watered and curried.

The present structure was begun in the time of Henry I., though there was a fortress here in Saxon times. Of course it has a "Cæsar's Tower"—no castle is complete without one. Henry II. gave it to Simon de Montfort, who, as was to have been expected, immediately rebelled, and was killed in 1265. (The historian from whom I have this, explains that he afterwards escaped to France, but this must have been a fresh Simon.) In 1286 there was a grand "chivalric festival" held here, in which a great number of ladies participated. One hundred knights took a hand in it, and a contribution was afterward taken up for the widows and orphans. Edward II. was confined here before being butchered at Berkeley Castle. It came afterward into the hands of John of Gaunt, who erected the portion still known as the "Lancaster Buildings." In the war of the Roses the partisans of Lancaster and York had a fine time thrashing one another about its walls. First one party held it, and then another; and owing to a lack of information, or absence of mind, the place was frequently attacked by the side that held it, and its unhappy defenders put to the sword by their friends. Queen Elizabeth gave it to Bob Dudley, and then made a friendly call on him, as aforesaid, stayed seventeen days, and cost him ten thousand pounds a day. The place, after a century or so, came into the possession of Charles I., from whom it and his head were taken by Cromwell. This is all: when anything came into Cromwell's possession its history terminated; there was nothing more to say, and nothing to say it about.

It was late in the afternoon when I slowly retraced my steps to the little cottage-crowned hill from which I had taken my first glance at noble old Kenilworth. My explorations had blessed me with a sharp appetite, and at a little inn I ordered the means wherewith to dull it. As I sat in my little ten-by-twelve parlour, looking upon the gigantic hot joint gracing my table, flanked with a jug of nut-brown ale, and then backward across the remnants of the old priory in the valley, to the solemn Ruin, the westering sun struggled from behind one of those mountains of tumbled cloud which I have never seen but in an English sky, and set the giant pile afire with a great glory. The light burned and flickered upon the angles like the flame of molten iron: broad banners of it seemed flung from every summit; it poured in jagged torrents through the rent sides, and shot in long straight beams through the narrow fissures, ribboning with gold the blue-black shadows darkening broadly about its base! Anon the glow crept athwart my own windows, streamed in, and gilded the brown joint upon the board with a radiance all its own.

To have seen Kenilworth Castle banked up against so glorious a sunset is to have added a precious jewel to memory's treasure; and I shall never recall its gracious image, and the gleaming pomp of its aspect, without a tender regret that I did not take another cut from the divine roast of which it was the humble prototype. [8]

Coventry

To go into Coventry is to step out of the nineteenth century into the fourteenth. Indeed, no small part of the architecture of the place bears a date no later, while several notable buildings can boast a much earlier one. Nothing can be stronger to one accustomed to the paint and varnish, and the somewhat tawdry gloss of new cities in the West, than this old country market-town in the heart of England. Its spa-breadth streets, nearly or quite shut in by the black-and-white half-timbered houses, with their overhanging storeys supported by clumsily-carved wooden brackets, and all awry with age; the roadways of pebbles with mere mathematical lines of sidewalk, laid down for eternity, I should say, for none but the most reckless would venture to tread upon them; the curiously peaked gables; the red tile roofs, sunken, misshapen, and crowned with clusters of eccentric chimney-stacks, no two alike; the reddish-gray old churches with their grotesque sculpture, their gargoyles grinning hideously from the cornices, their broken buttresses and worn angles; the picturesque remnants of the ancient defensive wall; the "business" signs in the erroneous orthography of Chaucer; the thousand-and-one oddities and whimsies of this very Rip Van Winkle of towns give rise to a peculiar sense in the observer's mind of having died and resumed some former existence in the person of a remote ancestor.

The most interesting of Coventry's buildings is St. Mary's Hall, a fine specimen of the fifteenth century architecture. It contains many valuable paintings among which I remember a full-length portrait of that good and great man whom Byron left in Heaven, "singing the one hundredth Psalm"[5]—His Majesty George III., by Sir Joshua Reynolds. A singular piece of tapestry is preserved here, thirty feet by ten, and crowded with nearly a hundred very life-like, figures. This piece of needlework was executed in 1450—and the colors are in excellent keeping. But I can't tell you who made it; and if I should you'd call it a puff. This singular city is as odd in its industry as in everything else. Its principal manufacture is book-marks—silken trifles to lay between the leaves of your Bible, to keep the place while you take a hand at whist. But it is mainly to the Lady Godiva that Coventry owes its fame. Presuming that everybody is thoroughly familiar with the story of this remarkable young woman, I will relate it. [9]

The Story of Lady Godiva

Cheops was King of Egypt; Leofric, who lived later, was "Earle" of Coventry. It is with the latter that we have here to do. Leofric was a great tyrant; he had an extravagant wife, and to keep her in pin-money he taxed his people in every iniquitous manner he could devise. He laid upon them every grinding impost except the income-tax—Leofric, wicked as he was, couldn't quite bring himself to *that*. His wife, the fair Godiva (noted for her shapely figure, of which she was extremely vain), tried to stop him, but she couldn't; the more she implored him to chain up the assessor, the more he let him loose, and gave him a deputy. It did not occur to Godiva to stop asking him for French boots, book-marks, and woollen blankets to make summer jackets of; but it *did* occur to her to promise that if it would reduce the rate of taxation she would ride through the streets on horseback, naked. Leofric, who had a nimble intellect, saw in a moment that it was just the thing—it was perfectly obvious that it would replenish the exchequer. So he gave gracious consent in these memorable words:

"You may ride to the devil if you like!"

So Godiva issued a proclamation to the people, stating when she would set out, and specifying the streets she intended to pass through; concluding by warning all men that *if they did not wish to see a naked woman* they must keep away from the windows. (The *italics* are hers.) At the appointed hour she clewed up her back hair, mounted her palfrey, spread her umbrella to prevent sunburn, and started nakedly out. It is stated that all her loyal subjects but one wrapped themselves in blankets and stowed their bodies away in dark cellars; and I believe it. It was bad for the one who didn't—a tailor named Tom. He ventured to go one eye upon her ladyship, and was stricken blind so quick it made his head spin. When the feat was accomplished, Leofric was so pleased with Godiva's heroism that, having just confiscated all the most valuable estates in the town, he remitted the taxes. Deeply touched by the gratitude of her subjects, Godiva afterward offered to repeat the performance in every town in the earldom, including the villages which were not taxed; but Leofric did not encourage her. [10]

Working for an Empress

[This essay first appeared as "How I Worked for an Empress" in the *Wasp* for December 23, 1882, and in revised form in "Bits of Autobiography." In one of his most engaging autobiographical pieces, Bierce recounts the circumstances behind the writing and publication of *The Lantern,* a journal that lasted only two issues in 1874 and of which Bierce wrote every word.]

In the spring of 1874 I was living in the pretty English town of Leamington, a place that will be remembered by most Americans who have visited the grave of Shakespeare at Stratford-on-Avon, or by personal inspection of the ruins of Kenilworth Castle have verified their knowledge of English history derived from Scott's incomparable romance.[6] I was at that time connected with several London newspapers, among them the *Figaro,* a small weekly publication, semi-humorous, semi-theatrical, with a remarkable aptitude for managing the political affairs of France in the interest of the Imperialists. This last peculiarity it owed to the personal sympathies of its editor and proprietor, Mr. James Mortimer, a gentleman who for some twenty years before the overthrow of the Empire had lived in Paris. Mr. Mortimer had been a personal friend of the Emperor and Empress, and on the flight of the latter to England had rendered her important service; and after the release of the Emperor from captivity among the Germans Mr. Mortimer was a frequent visitor to the imperial exiles at Chislehurst.[7]

One day at Leamington my London mail brought a letter from Mr. Mortimer, informing me that he intended to publish a new satirical journal, which he wished me to write. I was to do all the writing, he the editing; and it would not be necessary for me to come up to London; I could send manuscript by mail. The new journal was not to appear at stated periods, but "occasionally." Would I submit to him a list of suitable titles for it, from which he could make a selection?

With some surprise at what seemed to me the singularly whimsical and unbusiness-like features of the enterprise I wrote him earnestly advising him either to abandon it or materially to modify his plan. I represented to him that such a journal, so conducted, could not in my judgment succeed; but he was obdurate and after a good deal of correspondence I consented to do all the writing if he was willing to do all the losing money. I submitted a number of names which I thought suitable for the paper, but all were rejected, and he finally wrote that he had decided to call the new journal *The Lantern*. This decision elicited from me another energetic protest. The title was not original, but obviously borrowed from M. Rochefort's famous journal, *La Lanterne*.[8] True, that publication was dead, and its audacious editor deported to New Caledonia with his Communistic following; but the name could hardly be agreeable to Mr. Mortimer's Imperialist friends, particularly the Empress—the Emperor was then dead. To my surprise Mr. Mortimer not only adhered to his resolution but suggested the propriety of my taking M. Rochefort's late lamented journal as a model for our own. This I flatly declined to do and carried my point; I was delighted to promise, however, that the new paper should resemble the old in one particular: it should be irritatingly disrespectful of existing institutions and exalted personages.

On the 18th of May, 1874, there was published at the corner of St. Bride Street and Shoe Lane, E. C., London, the first number of "*The Lantern*—Appearing Occasionally. Illuminated by Faustin. Price, sixpence." It was a twelve-page paper with four pages of superb illustrations in six colors. I winced when I contemplated its artistic and mechanical excellence, for I knew at what a price that quality had been obtained. A gold mine would be required to maintain that journal, and that journal could by no means ever be itself a gold mine. A copy lies before me as I write and noting it critically I cannot help thinking that the illuminated title-page of this pioneer in the field of chromatic journalism is the finest thing of the kind that ever came from a press.

Of the literary contents I am less qualified for judgment, inasmuch as I wrote every line in the paper. It may perhaps be said without immodesty that the new "candidate for popular favor" was not distinguished by servile flattery of the British character and meek subservience to the British Government, as might perhaps be inferred from the following extract from an article on General Sir Garnet Wolseley, who had just received the thanks of his Sovereign and a munificent reward from Parliament for his successful plundering expedition through Ashantee:

> "We feel a comfortable sense of satisfaction in the thought that *The Lantern* will never fail to shed the light of its loyal approval upon any unworthy act by which our country shall secure an adequate and permanent advantage. When the great heart of England is stirred by quick cupidity to profitable crime, far be it from us to lift our palms in deprecation. In the wrangle for existence nations, equally with individuals, work by diverse means to a common end—the spoiling of the weak; and when by whatever of outrage we have pushed a feeble competitor to the wall, in Heaven's name let us pin him fast and relieve his pockets of the material good to which, in bestowing it upon him, the bountiful Lord has invited our thieving hand. But these Ashantee women were not worth garroting. Their fal-lals, precious to them, are worthless to us; the entire loot

fetched only £11,000—of which sum the man who brought home the trinkets took a little more than four halves. We submit that with practiced agents in every corner of the world and a watchful government at home this great commercial nation might dispose of its honor to better advantage."[9]

With the candor of repentance it may now be confessed that, however unscrupulous it may be abroad, a government which tolerates this kind of criticism cannot rightly be charged with tyranny at home.

By way (as I supposed) of gratitude to M. Rochefort for the use of the title of his defunct journal it had been suggested by Mr. Mortimer that he be given a little wholesome admonition here and there in the paper and I had cheerfully complied. M. Rochefort had escaped from New Caledonia some months before. A disagreeable cartoon was devised for his discomfort and he received a number of such delicate attentions as that following, which in the issue of July 15th greeted him on his arrival in England along with his distinguished compatriot, M. Pascal Grousset:

"M. Rochefort is a gentleman who has lost his standing. There have been greater falls than his. Kings before now have become servitors, honest men bandits, thieves communists. Insignificant in his fortunes as in his abilities, M. Rochefort, who was never very high, is not now very low—he has avoided the falsehood of extremes: never quite a count, he is now but half a convict. Having missed the eminence that would have given him calumniation, he is also denied the obscurity that would bring misconstruction. He is not even a *misérable;* he is a person. It is curious to note how persistently this man has perverted his gifts. With talents that might have corrupted panegyric, he preferred to refine detraction; fitted to disgrace the *salon,* he has elected to adorn the cell; the qualities that would have endeared him to a blackguard he has wasted upon Pascal Grousset.

"As we write, it is reported that this person is in England. It is further affirmed that it is his intention to proceed to Belgium or Switzerland to fight certain journalists who have not had the courtesy to suppress the truth about him, though he never told it of them. We presume, however, this rumor is false; M. Rochefort must retain enough of the knowledge he acquired when he was esteemed a gentleman to be aware that a meeting between him and a journalist is now impossible. This is the more to be regretted, because M. Paul de Cassagnac would have much pleasure in taking M. Rochefort's life and we in lamenting his fall.

"M. Rochefort, we believe, is already suffering from an unhealed wound. It is his mouth."[10]

There was a good deal of such "scurril jesting" in the paper, especially in a department called "Prattle." There were verses on all manner of subjects—mostly the nobility and their works and ways, from the viewpoint of disapproval—and epigrams, generally ill-humorous, like the following, headed *"Novum Organum"*:

> "In Bacon see the culminating prime
> Of British intellect and British crime.
> He died, and Nature, settling his affairs,
> Parted his powers among us, his heirs:
> To each a pinch of common-sense, for seed,
> And, to develop it, a pinch of greed.
> Each frugal heir, to make the gift suffice,
> Buries the talent to manure the vice."[11]

When the first issue of *The Lantern* appeared I wrote to Mr. Mortimer, again urging him to modify his plans and alter the character of the journal. He replied that it suited him as it was and he would let me know when to prepare "copy" for the second number. That eventually appeared on July 15th. I never was instructed to prepare any more copy, and there has been, I believe, no further issue of that interesting sheet as yet.

Taking a retrospective view of this singular venture in journalism, one day, the explanation of the whole matter came to my understanding in the light of a revelation, and was confirmed later by Mr. Mortimer.

In the days when Napoleon III was at the zenith of his glory and power there was a thorn in his side. It was the pen of M. Henri Rochefort, le Comte de Luçay, journalist and communard. Despite fines, "suppressions," and imprisonments, this gifted writer and unscrupulous blackguard had, as every one knows, made incessant war upon the Empire and all its *personnel*. The bitter and unfair attacks of his paper, *La Lanterne*, made life at the Tuilleries exceedingly uncomfortable. His rancor against the Empress was something horrible, and went to the length of denying the legitimacy of the Prince Imperial. His existence was a menace and a terror to the illustrious lady, even when she was in exile at Chislehurst and he in confinement on the distant island of New Caledonia. When the news of his escape from that penal colony arrived at Chislehurst the widowed Empress was in despair; and when, on his way to England, he announced his intention of reviving *La Lanterne* in London (of course he dared not cross the borders of France) she was utterly prostrated by the fear of his pitiless animosity. But what could she do? Not prevent the revival of his dreadful newspaper, certainly, but— well, she could send for Mr. Mortimer. That ingenious gentleman was not long at a loss for an expedient that would accomplish what was possible. He shut Rochefort out of London by forestalling him. At the very time when Mortimer was asking me to suggest a suitable name for the new satirical journal he had already registered at Stationers' Hall—that is to say, copyrighted—the title of *The Lantern*, a precaution which M. Rochefort's French friends had neglected to take, although they had expended thousands of pounds in a plant for their venture. Mr. Mortimer cruelly permitted them to go on with their costly preparations, and the first intimation they had that the field was occupied came from the newsdealers selling *The Lantern*. After some futile attempts at relief and redress, M. Rochefort took himself off and set up his paper in Belgium.

The expenses of *The Lantern*—including a generous *douceur* to myself—were all defrayed by the Empress. She was the sole owner of it and, I was gratified to learn, took so lively an interest in her venture that a special French edition was printed for her private reading. I was told that she especially enjoyed the articles on M. le Comte de Luçay, though I dare say some of the delicate subtleties of their literary style were lost in translation.

Being in London later in the year, I received through Mortimer an invitation to visit the poor lady, *en famille*, at Chislehurst; but as the iron rules of imperial etiquette, even in exile, required that the hospitable request be made in the form of a "command," my republican independence took alarm and I had the incivility to disobey; and I still think it a sufficient distinction to be probably the only American journalist who was ever employed by an Empress in so congenial a pursuit as the pursuit of another journalist.

The English Literati

[It did not take Bierce long to sum up both the literary and the personal characteristics of the English journalists of the day. The following accounts, taken from letters to Charles Warren Stoddard (another Californian on an English and European jaunt), attest to Bierce's acuity of observation. Other extracts provide rare glimpses of Bierce's family life, and are notable for being virtually the only mentions of Bierce's wife, Mollie, in the whole of his extant corpus of writing.]

I am doing just work enough over here to pay my current expenses at this somewhat expensive place. It does not require much of my time either. Have not attempted to get any permanent work, and don't suppose I shall; as my object in coming was to loaf and see something of the country—or as Walt Whitman expressed it when the paralysis had, as yet, invaded only his brain, to "Loaf and invite my soul."[12] [. . .]

We—wife and I and the lad—have been in Bath about a month. It is the most charming of all imaginable places. Every street has its history, every foot of the lovely country its tradition. Old Roman, and even Druidic, remains are plenty as green pease. You are aware that Bath was the stamping ground of Pope, Fielding, Smollett, Warburton, Malthus, Beau Nash, Ralph Allen—who "did good by stealth and blushed to find it fame"[13]—and a lot of worthies whose haunts I frequent, or whose graves I shed judicious drops above, and try to fancy myself like them. I don't succeed. The place is good for a dozen long magazine articles if I were not too lazy to write 'em. [1]

I am unexpectedly called away to Paris for a month, and you must try to forgive me for causing you the annoyance of coming out here. (If you have not dismissed your cab yet, don't pay the driver more than 3 shillings for driving you from the Station out here.) I wanted to see you badly, to tell you how to live, whom to know, whom *not* to know and how to get on generally. I daresay Miller[14] can tell you better than I, however, if you and he are still friends, as I hope you are. His address when I last saw him was 11 Museum-st.

I have told Tom Hood[15] to look after you. Now mark this: Tom is one of the very dearest fellows in the world, and an awful good friend to me. *But* he has the worst lot of associates I ever saw—men who (with one or two noble exceptions, whom you cannot readily pick out) are not worthy to untie his shoe latchet. He will introduce you to them *all.* Treat them well, of course, but (1) don't gush over them; (2) don't let them gush over you; (3) don't accept invitations from them; (4) don't get drunk with them; (5) don't let them in any way monopolise you; (6) don't let them shine by your reflected light. I have done all these things, and it is not a good plan, "for at the last it biteth like a serpent and stingeth like an adder."[16] *I* don't mind biting and stinging, but you would—particularly if done in the dark.

Remember this: London—literary London—is divided into innumerable cliques, which it will require some time to get the run of. Remember, also, that if you fall into the hands of one clique, all the others will give you the cold shoulder. Remember, also, that everybody will profess the most unbounded admiration for you, and not one of them can tell a line you have written. They will be very good, but upon the implied understanding that you are not to compete with them in their pitiful struggle for bread. The moment you do, God help you, if you are sensitive.

I speak, so far, only of the obscure journalistic nobodies—men with a merely local reputation or none at all. Let them alone. Make friends, if friends you must make—amongst the men whose work has delighted you in America; remembering, however, that an American reputation is easily made by a third rate Englishman. But the men at the top of the profession are at least above the necessity of being meanly jealous.

You will, by the way, be under a microscope here; your lightest word and most careless action noted down, and commented on by men who cannot understand

how a person of individuality in thought or conduct can be other than a very bad
man. Lord! how I have laid myself out inventing preposterous speech and demeanor just to set their silly tongues wagging. It is good fun for me—it would
ruin you. Walk, therefore, circumspectly, keep your own counsel, don't make
speeches at Clubs, avoid any appearance of eccentricity, don't admire anything,
and don't disparage anything; don't eat mustard on mutton!

I know all this will make you laugh. There is no reason why you should not
laugh; but you just "bet your boots", old man, I know these fellows, and their
ways. They think they know *me,* but they don't. I am hand-in-glove with some
hundreds of them, and they think they are my intimate friends. If any man says
so, or acts as if he were, avoid him; he is an impostor. When I come back, I'll tell
you the fellows you can tie to.

You will like the English when you get to know them; I do. I have not an enemy in London. There are a lot of fellows who would like to be my enemies, but I
won't permit it; I am cordial as a summer noon to them—the puppies. But, generally speaking, the English are good fellows, the Scotch are better, and the Irish
are a bad lot. You'll find this so; see if you don't. [2]

As to myself, I have another boy.[17] He is, I believe ["here insert the age of the
child".] It is either six weeks, two months, or something like it; I swear I do not
know, and Mrs. B. is not within call. He has had a hard struggle for life, and we
have only just begun to entertain hopes of saving him. Mrs. Day left for home a
couple of weeks or so ago. Do you know Belle Thomas of San Francisco? She is
in Paris, "training to howl". She just spent a couple of weeks with us. Then, too,
I have been, and am, up to my ears in work—grinding stuff for five publications: one semi-weekly, two weekly, one monthly, and one "occasional"—a
pizen thing of which I write every line.[18] If some of these don't die of me I shall
die of them. Perhaps *now* you'll forgive, or excuse, my neglect of your letter,
though *I* can't. [3]

Awfully glad you are back, and want to see you very much, for I am lonely, of
course, without the wife and babies.[19] The wife, by the way, told me before leaving that if you came back I'd better have you down here for a while. Perhaps
she thought you would keep me out of mischief. That's all very well, but I
wouldn't have you here for the world, although I have a whole house to myself.
First, I have no time to talk to you for I'm struggling with more work than I
can manage, and that is partly what has made me ill—for I am ill, though I keep
pegging away, somehow. Second, I live precariously and abominably. There is
only one decent place in the town to get a meal—a hotel which lives by swindling Americans, and which, having once swindled me, I do not enter. I am not
a good housekeeper, and my landlady, though honest for a wonder, has not the
advantage of knowing anything. So as soon as I feel well enough to travel I'm

coming to London till Mrs. B. returns, when I shall take a house somewhere in the scruburbs.

I have heard nothing from Mrs. B. since she left New York, but am expecting a letter every day from Salt Lake. She is probably at Pioche before this time.

I thank you very much for the kind interest you take in my health, but I am not so ill as you suppose. It is only a cursed sort of semi-lunacy, I think, from lack of sleep, hard work, and unchristian evoking. I shall throw over some of the work, take opiates, and come to London. [4]

That Ghost of Mine

[The following essay appeared in the *Argonaut* for April 6, 1878, and may be the earliest of Bierce's reminiscent pieces. It re- counts—perhaps with tongue in cheek—a peculiar incident in- volving one of Bierce's closest colleagues during his English stay, Thomas Hood the Younger.]

The incidents that I am about to relate are facts of my own experience, and hav- ing already been told not to exceed three or four times have probably not been colored or exaggerated by repetition; and it is partly in order that they may not undergo that process hereafter that I now fix them in print. Having had fre- quent occasion to observe in others, as well as in myself, how the senses fool one another—how, for example, sight is translated into sound, or sudden and strong mental impressions are mistaken for tactual ones—I indulge the hope that my narrative may have some small value in so far as it may bear upon that subject. The chief incident is, I am convinced, rightly capable of no other inter- pretation; though if it seem that a supernatural one is the more simple and rea- sonable I have no objection to that, inasmuch as I am not bound to accept it.

Some four years ago, while I was living in London, I occasionally passed a night at the house of a friend in Penge, a pretty suburb out beyond the Crystal Palace. Seeing no reason for a concealment that might beget distrust, I will ex- plain that the gentleman mentioned was the late Mr. Tom Hood, son of the late Thomas Hood, the poet. Tom (it is no affectation to so call him, for to the day of his death he believed himself to have been so christened—an error that has since been corrected in a memorial sketch by his sister) had an odd little house, full, and more than full, of odd things—rare books, objects of art, bric-a-brac, and curios. Back of his odd little house was his odd little garden, with odd plants and flowers; and here we were accustomed to burn our evening cigars, after which we commonly passed the entire night in a room up-stairs, sipping grog, pulling at our pipes, and talking on all manner of matters connected more or less remotely with this world and the next. We were neither of us very orthodox, I fear, but Tom had in him a vein of what in another I should have called superstition, but that it was so elusive in character and whimsical in manifestation that I could never rightly assign it a place, nor determine its metes and bounds. It may have been an undeveloped religion, a philosophical conviction, a sentiment—for aught I know, a joke. Whatever it was, it was at least suggestive and delightful, and like an intellectual will-o'-the-wisp led us many a merry dance into the "unsteadfast footing" of the unknowable, whence we were usually extricated and brought back to firm ground only by some such material-world necessity as the recharging of our glasses or pipes.

Naturally—Tom having recently lost a devoted wife—we talked much of death, immortality, and the possibility of spirits revisiting the earth; and, quite as naturally, we once made the usual pledge that whichever of us died first should, if possible, communicate with, or appear to, the survivor. This, I had reason to remember, was at the close of the last night we spent together, just before we retired for the day. Soon afterward I left London, and after living in various places, settled myself at Leamington, in Warwickshire.

At about this time Tom's health, never very good, began to fail rapidly, and his letters to me were full of half serious, half humorous presages of his approaching end. He knew he had to go, and I knew it; but I am ashamed to say we made the rather solemn necessity the subject of many a jest in prose and verse that would have seemed dreadfully heartless to others having advantage of access to this instructive literature.

One day I received a summons by telegraph, and hastened to London to find my worst fears confirmed—Tom was dying. I remained with him and saw him off, and during our last interview he assured me, "on the word of a dying man," that certain of my beliefs, or rather disbeliefs, regarding spiritual things, were erroneous. He spoke in an earnest, solemn manner that profoundly affected me, although, of course, it did not convince me, for I did not perceive then, nor do I believe now, that he had any new light. Compelled to return to Leamington, I could not attend the funeral, but poor Tom was followed to Nunhead Cemetery by some hundreds of the saddest hearts in the great literary world of London.

Some months later I was strolling, one evening, along an unfrequented street in the outskirts of Leamington, my attention occupied, as nearly as I can remember, with a sunset effect on the towers of Warwick Castle, pushing up through the trees some two miles away; I certainly was not taking thought of Tom Hood, or anything relating to him. A tall, dark man met me on the walk, his eyes fixed on mine with a familiar look of friendly recognition. It was Tom! It did not occur to me at the moment that he was dead, nor did I feel the faintest surprise at meeting him there, a hundred miles away from London. All seemed perfectly natural, and it was only when he had passed me without salutation, or even so much as seeming to see my outstretched hand, that I felt a sense of surprise. And it was only when in my surprise I turned about to recall him, and found myself utterly alone—the sole occupant of the street as far as I could see in either direction—it was only then that I remembered.

I need not attempt to describe my feelings; they were novel and not altogether agreeable. That I had met the spirit of my dead friend; that it had given me friendly recognition, yet not in the old way; that it had then vanished—of these things I had "the evidence of my senses." How strongly this impressed me the beating of my heart attested whenever, for many months afterward, that strange meeting came into my memory; but not being a believer in ghosts, and having no very strong faith in "the evidence of the senses," I declined to surrender, and resorted again and again to the same spot, at the same hour of the day, never seeing anything, but always coming away, somehow, with a weaker conviction that the dead are dead.

Once—it was many weeks after the apparition, and long since I had ceased looking for its reappearance—I was passing through the street by chance, at least without a conscious object. As I arrived at the well-known spot a gentle breeze stirred the shrubbery of a garden separated from the sidewalk by a wall or hedge, and on the instant I caught the peculiar odor of a certain plant—an odor singularly familiar. I do not know the name of this plant, and should probably not recognize it by sight; its scent I am unlikely ever to forget. I had previously seen it growing only in Tom Hood's odd little garden at Penge.

Having my ghost at a disadvantage, I now pressed him hard; he was soon resolved into some tall, brown-eyed, and portly resident of the place, on whom my nose-befooled eyes had set a face to which he had no title. But how account for his vanishing? Some twenty or thirty yards back of me, as I had met him, a narrow lane with high brick walls led off the street at a right angle from the side on which we had met. In my surprise at not receiving the salutation I had expected, I must have hesitated longer than I had thought before turning about, and in the mean time the stranger had turned into this lane, and was invisible.

This explanation is offered, not because it entirely satisfies me, but because it is less difficult to believe a familiar odor, with its train of associated recollections, could cheat the eyes a little than a good deal. In an actual face it might create a fancied resemblance; it could hardly evolve a full-grown image out of nothing. At the time of the apparition I was not conscious of any odor at all; but that it stole into my brain unperceived, and spoke the creative word to my vision, I have not the slightest doubt.

Of course I should like to believe that Tom Hood actually performed his promise to visit me from another world, though it would be agreeable to have, at the same time, some assurance that he will not do so any more.

Return to San Francisco

Some Self-Descriptions

[In several early columns in the *Argonaut*,
Bierce made no secret that his mission was to
attack the fools, rascals, and hypocrites whom
he saw flourishing in such abundance in both
his own city and in the world at large.]

Wanted for the local press—a writer who can be satirical
without giving offence, witty without saying anything uncommon, and scholarly without passing the comprehension
of the ignorant. He must have no prejudices, but must scru-
pulously respect all the prejudices of everybody else. He must
touch no subject upon which any two men differ, and ridicule no man who is not enamored of ridicule. If he have a
style he will be obscure to the illiterate; ideas will offend the
shallow. Within the four corners of profound respect for the
established order of things he may be as sarcastic as he can,
remembering ever that he lives in a world of fools, harlots
and rogues, who do not relish being knocked about the
mazzard with a bill-book. [1]

The writers with grievances have at last lost their tempers
and are making it very tropical indeed for poor me. One of

these unfortunates favors my eyes with as much damning as he can get into a half column of the *Mail,* his special cause of offense being that I did not write "The Dance of Death,"[1] that I say unkind things of my "brother" journalists and—heaven forgive me!—put my name to them. Suspicion ever haunts the guilty mind, and as to the last accusation I take the liberty to suspect that my good friend does not so much deprecate the appearance of my name in these columns as the appearance of his own. Anyhow, I do most humbly beg him to believe that I write under my own name, not wholly from vanity, though that virtue, I hope, is not without its just effect in determining such actions as I deign to perform. Dearly beloved fools and most enviable dunces, my name appears at the head of these columns, partly because I am generously paid to let it appear, but chiefly in order that when one of you, like him of the *Post,* bitterly accuses me of "stabbing in the dark," and at the same time prudently withholds his own name, he may seem, while indicting me, to convict himself. Thus for his greater glory do I persuade the modest ass to display his ears. [2]

When one of my paragraphs, writing itself, expires in a pun, I have always the disagreeable feeling of having met a fool and shaken hands with him. I don't like to be thought "stuck up," and I am not unsocial, but really I have an aversion to fools, and am choked by the atmosphere of the plane in which they move. As most of them are in the newspaper business, and many in my department of it, there would seem to be a certain fitness in our occasionally coming together on some common ground of fellowship. The field in which they cull their finest flowers of fancy—that of lying—I am dissuaded by shame from entering, and they never come near enough to the dividing line between it and the truth for me to even shake hands with them through the fence. I have not the skill and experience to collaborate with them in their immortal pictures of low life—can not relate a bout at carpet-beating, a hunt for a lost suspender button, a struggle with a stubborn bureau drawer, an attempt at compiling a stove-pipe, the decapillation of a hen-pecked husband, nor the overthrow of a dry goods salesman in a slangwhanging match with a vulgar beast of a she granger. Amongst the tubs and towels, soiled linen and soapy odors, of the literary scullery from which the "funny men" delight to draw their inspirations, "when fond recollection presents them to view,"[2] I should feel *de trop*. I am *not* proud; but pray, my good men, where are we to meet? There remains the pun. [3]

The Dance of Death

> [In the summer of 1877 a small book appeared under the title *The Dance of Death,* by William Herman. The book, which rapidly went through several printings, scandalized San Francisco. Under

the guise of condemning the growing practice of ballroom dancing as lewd and immoral, it portrayed the overheated emotions of the men and women who engaged in it in such frank terms as to be itself considered obscene. Only years later did Bierce admit that he had written it in conjunction with Thomas A. Harcourt; the book was financed by William Herman Rulofson. Although he maintained that the work was a joke—"condemning" a practice but describing it in enticingly lascivious terms—he quite likely did regard dancing as immoral, as the first quoted extract suggests.

Shortly after the publication of *The Dance of Death,* a pamphlet entitled *The Dance of Life,* by Mrs. J. Milton Bowers, appeared as an attempted refutation. Some Bierce scholars have believed the work to be Bierce's, but there actually was a Mrs. J. Milton Bowers living at the time in San Francisco. The likelihood is that she wrote the work without awareness that *The Dance of Death* was a hoax. Bierce took occasion to vilify that work just as much as he vilified his own.]

There is in this city a social club, comprising males and creatures of the opposing sex, which calls itself the "Glide," if we mistake not, and into the wide, wide ears of the same we beg to sing our mind. The "Glide," if perchance we have been accurately instructed in respect of its function, exists for a saltatory purpose, as its name witnesseth. Its membership of bald-headed bucks and gum-chewing misses (with a generous infusion of downy younglets of the upper gender and juiceless maids well stricken in years) convene at frequent hops to "chase the glowing hours with flying feet"[3]—which perspire. At these gentle orgies are enacted sundry fashionable indecencies of the minor sort—such, for example, as suggestive "hugs," the confusion of limbs, and the merging of identities withal; in brief, the "fancy dances" affected by the children of gaslight. Amongst these the "glide" is naturally in dominant favor, the frank grossness of its character commending it alike to the lecherous intelligence of the failing rake and the prying mind of the she simpleton, alert for lewd emotion. It may be urged that this shameless dance is held in no higher esteem by the club named in its honor than by society generally. Indeed, it may possibly be said in rebuttal of this our present growl that the he and she members of the "Glide" social club are no more indecent in their ballroom amours than the males and females who have the honor to belong to the better circles in which ourselves do move. Permit us to courteously inquire—Who has said they were? [4]

The literary critic of the *Evening Post* is avidly enamored of the new book that is fluttering the doves in that vast *columbarium,* the Palace Hotel, and elsewhere—*The Dance of Death,* by "William Herman." I have not that bold bad volume before me (the editor of this paper virtuously burned the office copy, after gloating over it during the whole of one day, to the dead neglect of everything, including the still small voice of duty and the still smaller voice of conscience) but if I had I could here quote from it a multitude of things unfit for publication. The book is a high-handed outrage, a criminal assault upon public modesty, an indecent exposure of the author's mind! From cover to cover it is one sustained orgasm of a fevered imagination—a long revel of intoxicated propensities. With superior indelicacy the author affirms the indelicacy of the waltz. To his perverted discernment this rather silly but harmless enough amusement is a seductive, naughty rite performed behind too thin a veil. Noble reformer! he snatches away the veil. To "the roses and raptures"[4] of the vice he denounces he adds the jewels of his learning, the charms and splendors of his fancy, the graces and vivacity of his style. And this is the book in which local critics find a satisfaction to their minds and hearts! This is the poisoned chalice they are gravely commending to the lips of good women and pure girls! Their asinine praises may perhaps have this good effect: "William Herman" may be tempted forth, to disclose his disputed identity and gather his glory. Then he can be shot. [5]

I am proud to have been deemed worthy to receive a book entitled *The Dance of Life,* by "Mrs. Dr. J. Milton Bowers." This engagingly vulgar title (that of the lady, not of the book) is a sufficient indication of the kind of brain-work the reader— if it have one—will find in the volume; but in my generous mood I am willing to exhaustively review all its distinctive peculiarities, by adding that the lady's pages are spattered with italics and reeded like an organ with notes of exclamation. It purports to be a reply—it is certainly not an answer—to "William Herman's" *Dance of Death,* and it is certainly the most resolute, hardened, and impenitent nonsense ever diffused by a daughter of the gods divinely dull. The prodigious feebleness of this tiresome volume, its penury of common sense, its colossal ignorance, and capable devices for subduing the reader with fatigue, mark it off from all other literature by a line of distinction as broad as a handsaw. It is a "smooth, solid monument of mental pain,"[5] as my lord Byron says—a monument, I venture to add, which seems to have been erected to the memory of the late English language, slain in its erection. [6]

From a published letter of Mr. T. A. Harcourt, it appears that the friends of "a certain Mr. Alstrom, a Swede," are very earnest in claiming for him the authorship of the *Dance of Death.* Mr. Alstrom himself, it is implied, is suspected of promulgating that view of the matter. Very good. Now let me ask that gentleman if he is prepared to return a deliberate and irrevocable affirmative to this question: Did you, of your own volition and without stress of necessity, write this passage on page 54th of the work mentioned? A pretty picture, is it not?—"the Grand Passion Preservative dragged into the blaze of gas to suffer pious indignities at the hands of worshipers who worship not wisely but too well! The true"—but it occurs to me that what one person could not decently write, another cannot decently quote. If Mr. Alstrom will acknowledge himself the author of that passage, his confession will strongly support his claim to the paternity of a certain other: "Thus I became abnormally developed in my debased nature." [7]

> [Years later the book briefly emerged from obscurity, impelling
> Bierce to expatiate once more upon it, although he still refused to
> specify his contribution to it.]

I have just come upon an allusion, in an Eastern paper, to a book entitled *The Dance of Death*. I had thought this once famous work forgotten; certainly it is no longer read. Yet it made a right pretty row in its day, only half a score or so of years ago, as not a few of my readers will remember—on being reminded. As the only person now living who had a hand in that piece of "admirable fooling," I am tempted to relate the entire incident—or, as our current slang would more graphically express it, "give the whole business away." Well, I will not—at least now; but a few particulars of the mischief I cannot forbear to state. In the first place, let me clear away a singular misconception affecting even many who read and some who approved the book, namely, that it was "a book against dancing." Nothing could be more erroneous: it was a book against certain kinds of dances fashionable at the time, which it denounced, and rightly denounced, as indecent. Of the manner of the denunciation I have nothing to say in defence, further than that it was rather intelligently adapted to the purpose. Of *what* that was there is now no record, except, possibly, certain private letters, some of which, I tremble to think, may be in my own handwriting. Suffice it that the purpose of the book was not moral reform, and all the commendation that it received on that ground was bestowed upon as unworthy a trinity of moral impostors as any that I ever blushed to belong to.

Where now are my collaborators in this monstrous joke? As dead as doornails, Heaven rest and forgive them! W. H. Rulofson (the "William Herman" of the title-page), who suggested the scheme and supplied the sinews of sin, himself executed a "dance of death" by walking off the roof of a high building. T. A. Harcourt, scholar and gentleman, went to the everlasting bad through domestic infelicity and foreign brandy, dying in poverty's last ditch as serenely as a king upon a golden couch.[6] As for me—God pity me!—I am living.

How we did fib about that book, to be sure! What misleading letters to the press about its authorship we wrote and caused to be written! How bitterly we assailed it in critiques as long as a man's leg! How well we dusted and peppered the eyes of the public, and those of our personal friends. And when Fred Somers started the *Californian* (now foolishly called the *Overland Monthly*) I wrote for it—partly from notes supplied by my most admired friends—a serial paper which was at once a history, philosophy and defense of dancing, a blazing censure of "William Herman's" book and, under cover of an attack on prudes, as detestable a piece of cynicism as ever deserved to be burned by the public hangman.[7] Altogether, there was a good deal more in the *"Dance of Death"* incident than the public was invited to know; and some of it will never be known, for, as one of Congreve's characters says of woman as a good person to keep a secret, "Although I am sure to tell it, yet nobody will believe it."[8] [8]

The Scourge of Poetasters

[Bierce quickly gained notoriety for the severity of criticism in regard to a particular breed of men and women: bad poets. There seems to have been no shortage of such in the San Francisco of the 1870s, and Bierce skewered them relentlessly and mercilessly. Such names as Hector A. Stuart, William D. Pollock, and Loring Pickering now live solely because of Bierce's invective; they are among the "black beetles in amber" whom he would likewise embalm in his verse.]

We have a letter from a gentleman who writes verses, complaining that, not content with breaking the bones of the local poets once or twice each, we persist with tiresome assiduity in breaking them over and over again. Perseverance is, indeed, reckoned amongst our virtues, but then it is also one of the vices of the local poets. Have they stopped writing? Have they once shut down the back windows of their souls and ceased for even a week to pour a deluge of bosh upon the earth? Is their assiduity less tiresome than ours? Who began this thing? as the steel-trap said to a struggling fox. Besides, when accused of persecuting any particular bard, we may reply in the words of Heine, when some one remonstrated with him for his repeated attacks upon Massmann: "Believe me, I am an aged man. I can no longer call up new fools at pleasure, but must be content to live upon the old. Massmann," he added, "is a profitable fool to me, and out of his folly I coin my revenue."[9] [9]

Concerning my epitaph, in last week's *Argonaut,* by Hector A. Stuart (who, to his honor be it said, is the only one of my favorite enemies that ever did or dared resent my censures over his own name), it is perhaps sufficient to say that I ought to be willing to have my name at the top of it if he is willing to have his at the bottom. As to Mr. Stuart's opinion that my work will be soon forgotten, I can assure him that that view of the matter is less gloomy to me than it ought to be to him. I do not care for fame, and he does; and his only earthly chance of being remembered is through his humble connection with what I write. True, I have, in the last two months, caused the sale of six copies of his poems,[10] whereas but three had ever been sold before; but I defy any man who reads that remarkable volume to afterward remember the author's name. He will do wonderfully well to remember his own. [10]

If local writers would have the goodness to understand that I know almost nothing about them personally, that in lack of appended names I cannot tell the work of one from another, and that it is to me a matter of sleeping indifference whether they are friends of mine or not, those of them who may chance to incur my feeble censure would spare themselves profitless conjecture as to my "motive," and, it may be, pervade the editorial rooms of this journal in smaller quantity as exhibiting cripples, holy martyrs and dead ducks. It is difficult for the local journalist (and altogether impossible for the local "poet," painter, or actor) to learn that one may mark the merit of him who is not a personal friend, and the folly of him who is not a personal enemy; the custom has been otherwise. I take the liberty to break the continuity of the practice, but if the "fools on fools," to me unknown, think it their duty to observe the tradition, while it would please them to take my literary scalp, I will see to it that they have each his justifying grievance as fast as they can be served; and as for opportunity the conductors of this paper will, I am sure, be only too glad to proffer their columns to fools of sense and discretion. But let there be no more uncovering of wounds and prating of motive. Motive, indeed! No doubt the dog of Alcibiades, yelling, tailless, through the streets of Athens, ascribed his bereavement to the jealous envy of a master to whom the gods had denied the dignity of a tail.[11] [11]

Mr. Sam Davis[12] says I make war on the verse-makers who contribute to this paper. Of course I cannot prevent the verse-makers upon whom I make war from contributing to the *Argonaut;* that is the editor's duty—which I am sorry to say he basely neglects. Mr. Davis' remark, however, affords me an opportunity to make, seriously, an explanation which I have long felt was due to the gentlemen whose rhymes have received the distinction of notice at my hands. To verse-makers, as verse-makers, I have no objection. (I make verses myself, and it is the unanimous testimony of others in the same line of literary business that they are very bad verses indeed.) It is only when the verse-maker fancies himself a poetry-maker that he becomes offensive to the cultivated and discriminating taste—my taste. It is important that the broad and sharp distinction between verse and poetry be as clearly perceived and sacredly respected by my brother rhymesters as it is by myself; and, God willing, I'll hold their noses to the mark until they see it. So far as my small reading goes, there is to-day west of the Rocky Mountains but one person who can write a line of poetry, and she no longer writes. There have been but three others. They shook the dust from their feet and went where every dunderhead who can do with difficulty what a born idiot would scorn to do with ease is not esteemed their peer. [12]

The trouble with you verse-carpenters is that you do not know the distinction between verse and poetry; if you did you would neither call your own lines poetry nor
mine attempts at poetry. I never attempted to write a line of poetry in all my life,
and when you call any of my work a "poem" I must either despise you for falsehood or commiserate you for ignorance.[13] Little as I think of your artistic sense I
cannot believe you such bunglers in censure as to willfully misrepresent. Surely you
know that the writer who cannot be severe without falsehood cannot be severe at
all; and therefore I am bound to believe that in your prose retorts to my good-
natured raillery you mean to be truthful but lack the sense to be discriminating. Personally I have little interest in the matter; it is agreeable to me to despise you, but
that satisfaction I have in reading your rhymes. I do not see that it would give me
any additional gratification to believe your equally bad workmanship in prose
caused by the error that falsehood is not a literary blemish, rather than by the folly
that poetry and prose are convertible terms. But if after this brief instruction you
call me "poet"—albeit a bad one—I must perforce regard you as distinguished by
deeper ignorance than that for which I have hitherto honored you. Gentlemen, you
are, for the present, dismissed. [13]

Mr. Hector A. Stuart, who calls himself Caliban, and who avers that he has been
called by others "The Bard of the South Seas," is to the fore with a blazing lam-
poon, of which the poetic merits transcend even those discovered (as himself informs us) in his other works by one hundred and eighty-two (182) editors of leading Mexican and South American periodicals. I have, unfortunately, no room for
the entire poem, but cannot forbear to quote the concluding stanza—which, like
the Pope's-nose of a chicken, is its most toothsome part. That I have the good
fortune to be the subject of these immortal lines is, I earnestly assure the reader,
a consideration of no weight in determining their reproduction here; I am singly
concerned to deliver from the oblivion of publication in a rival sheet this noble
specimen of Sardonic Stuartation:

> "If Mr. Bierce is as courageous
>   Physically as he professes
> To be scribically he can have
>   A chance to make that fact apparent."

The daintiness of the Calibanese meter is like the measured tinkle of a cow-
bell in the gloaming, but it must not lull the understanding to imperception of
more sterling merits—such, for example, as the author's formidable device (in
the metrically no less perfect lines following) for conveying, by use of plurals, the
disgusting impression that there are more than one of him:

> We are certainly his peers,
>   If not superiors,

In position, intellect,
    And financial standing;
He can therefore have no palli-
Ation on either of these grounds. [14]

A writer in a Nevada journal thinks I am not as nobly merciful as I could afford to be to the local poets, and comes near losing his head in resultless speculation as to the origin of my animosity. I really do not clearly apprehend the matter myself—am unable to determine the cause of my resentment, trace its progress, or assign a date to its perfection. The knowledge of their existence and the revelation of my contempt for them came to me so nearly together that I don't know if I read them before despising, or despised them before reading. If it is pretty much the same thing to them it certainly is to me, and they may profitably turn to the mending of their verses, and I to the manner of their mending. [15]

[Bierce also took occasion to ridicule the vapid songs that were published as separate sheet music and appeared in the Sunday editions of many newspapers.]

"Little Darling, Do You Remember?" "Save Your Kisses All for Me," "She's Just a Sweet Bouquet." These, beloved reader, are sample titles of songs which the music-sellers find it profitable to publish in this cultivated and critical community. Hunger is merciless—the stomach has no ears.[14] Entreaties are wasted on a starving composer; "Strike, but hear!" is the villain's motto, and you shall not win him to silence with a pick-handle. Serene and unalarmed upon the ridge of his own impudence this night-wailing assassin of sleep exalts his back, dilates his tail and sings you sick. The boot-jack of censure is flung in vain; all unregarded falls the beer-bottle of ridicule—the fiend hath his will of you, administering his devilish balladettes like audible emetics. "Darling, Let Me Wipe Your Nose" follows "Matching Gums by Moonlight," and is itself succeeded by "Who'll Chew Your Neck When Hubby's Dead?" And the next time you have the impatience to anticipate the delights of the lake of fire-and-brimstone by calling on a young woman she will scream these things into your understanding until you are beaded all over with red globules of agony. It amounts to this: the fellow who composes a ballad ought to be killed and mutilated. [16]

A Confrontation in the *Argonaut* Office

[One of the most striking incidents of Bierce's entire career as a journalist is related in the following passages.]

On Tuesday morning last a man named Widmer, the leader, I learn, of the Baldwin's Theatre orchestra, entered the *Argonaut* office, asking if my name was Bierce, and if I wrote a certain line in last week's issue. On being promptly assured that such was the case he as promptly struck at me with his fist or open hand—as the blow failed of its intent I can not say which. I do not enter into contests of that kind, and drew my pistol, when Mr. Widmer's friend, who had entered unperceived by me, and whose name I have not taken the trouble to ascertain, sprang upon me and seized the cocked weapon, Mr. Widmer closing with me at the same time. At this stage of a struggle rather dangerous for all concerned and all within pistol shot, Mr. Pixley,[15] knowing nothing of the cause of the contest nor who was the aggressor, emerged from his private office, seized Mr. Widmer and forced him into a corner. The "subsequent proceedings" consisted in a struggle between Mr. Widmer's friend and myself for the weapon, which eventually remained in possession of its owner. This necessarily terminated the contest, for it then appeared that the two gentlemen had had the singular indiscretion to come upon such an errand unarmed. Mr. Pixley and others now interceded for Mr. Widmer's life; to that gentleman's credit be it stated that he did not ask for it himself, nor appear to expect that it would be spared. Both gentlemen now left the building; the bravest men in the world could have done no more nor less.

It was a pretty enough quarrel, no cursing, nobody down, no blood; so far as I know not a blow received by any one—a struggle for a weapon the possession of which was decisive without merit in the victor or dishonor to the vanquished. A disinterested and impartial bookcase suffered the loss of a square of glass for which I think Mr. Widmer ought to pay.

These are "the short and simple annals" of this affair—this is the whole truth. In relating it I have this advantage over the reporters: no one who knows me can disbelieve me, whereas they, even though they write anonymously, are nevertheless not believed, owing to the bad reputation of their editors. They have lied so much that they can no longer deceive except by telling the truth, and conscientious scruples do not permit them. Such occasions as this are their harvest; it is then they gather their tar-weed sheaves of revenge, for it must be confessed that neither Mr. Pixley nor myself have been uniformly good to them. They can not meet us on the ground of truth; they have not wit—pray what would you have them do? I would not shoot an unarmed and defenseless man; is it to be supposed that I would carry on intellectual hostilities with the journalists of this town without giving them the odds of lying? It is a condition of the combat, and I am astonished at their moderation. What was to prevent them saying I had my hand in Mr. Widmer's pocket?

But the press reports have this serious aspect—they seem to have been inspired by Mr. Widmer. If they were, that altogether alters their significance; they no longer amuse, they insult. The most picturesque and imaginative narrative is given in what purports to be Mr. Widmer's language; but that is of course in the *Chronicle*.[16] It is impossible to believe that a man who in this matter bore himself like a man of courage with a grievance, when unsuccessful through an indiscretion accepted his life with dignity, and went away with the respect of his antagonist, is capable of the immatchable baseness of going about to newspaper and telegraph offices to retrieve his fortunes by a kind of victory for which even in excitement he could hardly be unaware that when cool he would despise himself. As a mere matter of common sense he could hardly desire that I should have the advantage of knowing that he suffered from self-contempt. Yet there are the reports, ostensibly his own version, certainly not mine, certainly emanating from no one in this office. They have not, to my knowledge, been disavowed. This, as I said, and beg Mr. Widmer to observe, is a serious matter. He must expect it to be so treated.

Mr. Widmer, under circumstances of grave provocation and supreme advantage I made to you a gift of your life, which morally you had forfeited, and in a sense legally, for had I taken it no jury in this country would have convicted me. Not one man in a hundred would have spared you; you did not expect to be spared. Because of this generosity I am described in the journals as a coward, and you are asserted to be their authority for the description. I do not ask you to confirm my version; I am satisfied to let that rest on my simple word, and the word of those who witnessed without taking a part in the quarrel. But, sir, if you are a gentleman you will disavow the version attributed to you. And this you will do not as a condition precedent to anything else, and wholly irrespective of any considerations other than those of truth and manliness. Reparation goes backward; it is the rule. He must not expect it who offends in his demand. Having disavowed the authorship of the falsehoods attributed to you, and not till then, it will be in order for you to demand a retraction of, or satisfaction for, the original offense—neither of which, I hardly need to remind you, you have yet obtained. [17]

Mr. Henry Widmer has not thought it expedient to act upon my studiously respectful suggestion that he disavow the insulting falsehoods published concerning me in his name. Moreover, I can prove him their author—that he devoted the life which I mercifully spared to systematic defamation of my character and misrepresentation of my conduct. I, therefore, take this opportunity to remind those who have the misfortune to know him, and inform those who have not, that he has the distinguished honor to be, not a man of principle, but a ruffian; not a man of truth, but a liar; not a man of courage, but a coward.

In order that there may be no mistake as to what member of the *canaille* I mean, I will state that I refer to Fiddler Widmer, the charming blackguard.

Concerning Fiddler Widmer's nameless friend (probably the Trombone or the Triangle), who did me the honor to call on me with him, witnessed all that occurred, and must have noted Mr. Widmer's accounts of the interview, I beg to remind him that he has not as yet addressed me a note repudiating Mr. Widmer. *Nous verrons.* [18]

On Coolies

[One of the most admirable of Bierce's stances was his bold and tireless defense of Chinese immigrants against the vicious prejudice and violence to which they were subject by native Californians throughout the latter decades of the nineteenth century.]

Some persons patriotically enterprising and thriftily philanthropic (philanthropy, my little dears, comes of two Greek words, and signifies peace on earth and good will to white men) have organized a company having two objects: 1. To prevent Chinamen from supplying us with rotten vegetables and unwholesome fruit. 2. To supply us with the same themselves. They propose to charge the same prices as the Chinamen, but they offer us the unspeakable advantage of purchasing "fruit and vegetables picked, sold, and delivered by white men." I note with satisfaction the significant omission of the word "grown;" it shows a conscientiousness that promises vegetables honestly rotten and equitably unwholesome. No righteous man who trades upon a popular sentiment by proffering a sentimental advantage will tell an unnecessary lie when the same purpose may be served by an easy evasion. The "American laundries," "anti-coolie shoe-shops," and "Caucasian duck-ranches" have hitherto proved inadequate to the employment of all the Chinese labor offering, and all good men who hold in heart the welfare of the Chinese workingman will unselfishly exult in the broadening of his field by addition of this new scheme. [19]

Mr. F. Langren addressed the members of a Scandinavian Club, the other evening, in their mother tongue, advising them to "roll up their sleeves and go for the Chinese." I am not enamored of the Chinese, and the Scandinavians are a very good class of citizens; but I do ardently hope that the first and each succeeding Scandinavian hand that is raised against the Chinese will be lopped off at the wrist. More than this, I hope that every tongue that threatens them in a foreign language, or with a foreign accent, may succumb to the dissuasion of paralysis. The foreigner, naturalized or not, who has come here to quarrel with the principles and traditions, the laws and treaties, under and by virtue of which he was himself admitted, would confer a favor by following the impertinent nose of him back to his own country with all possible expedition. America has issued a general invitation; that may have been judicious or not—it is not for those to say who have accepted it. If we keep open house we do not need, neither will we tolerate, an intimation from any guest that the company is not sufficiently select. That is the cast-iron sense of the matter, Mr. Kearney,[17] Irishman. That is the frosty truth of the business, Mr. William Wellock, Englishman. That is the bottom fact of the affair, Mr. M. F. Curier, Frenchman. That is the true inwardness of the situation, Mr. Langren, Swede. "Legal right?" Gentlemonkeys, I do not accuse you of a fault in law; you commit a crime in taste. [20]

Mr. Pickering[18] of the *Call* says he has "always claimed that, as the Chinese population in this city and State increased in numbers, they would become more exacting and aggressive." In proof of his prescience, he states that "now the Chinese demand common-school advantages, which means that they wish to learn the English language, so as to obtain larger wages and work their way into all the avenues of trade—so as to more completely compete with our own citizens." A wise enemy is a joy to the mind, but a foolish ally wrings the heart; and people who are honorably and intelligently working to restrict Chinese immigration will regard Mr. Pickering as a protagonist who puts weapons into the hands of the adversary and delivers battle with his back.

> John Chinaman, your race I hate,
> Because you "won't assimilate."
> You say you will? I know you will,
> And so, my lad, I'll hate you still.
> For what you will, or will not, do,
> I'll hate you, and for t'other too.
> Severely hold yourself aloof,
> Or eat of salt beneath my roof.
> A beggar be, or earn your bread
> By thieving, or by work instead.
> Bring Mrs. John and make a home;
> Or mateless o'er the country roam;
> Or, if your taste incline you, bring
> That other woman—horrid thing!—
> To learn our language and compete
> With ladies of the larger feet.
> Eat rat unspiced, or mutton spiced,
> And worship Joss, or Jesus Christ.
> (Man's creed depends, and much beside,
> On what he eats, and if it's fried;
> And heathens merely are a folk
> Their pig that purchase in a poke
> And cook it like John Rogers, one
> Of Persecution's overdone.)
> Our laws examine, with intent

To guilty plead, or innocent,
When haled before the magistrate
To justify your broken pate;
Or don't examine. All is one—
I'll hate you from the rise of sun
Until (also because) the seas
Allay his flame—until you please
To stand aside and make a ring
For Paddy when he's brandishing
His fair and lordly length of ear
In this contracted hemisphere.

I fear the foregoing lines are not as frigidly and rigidly anti-coolie in sentiment as they ought to be to make them suitable for this paper and agreeable to Mr. Pickering; but, like the wife (with nine small children and one at the breast) of the martyr John Rogers, whom, incidentally, they roast afresh, or at least warm over, I hate to see anything overdone; and this opposition to the Chinese is enduring the disadvantages of that process. Put a principle into the ear of a fool, and it will reappear at his mouth as a prejudice. Of ten men who write or speak against Chinese immigration, eight do the cause incalculable harm, for the unwisdom of their method makes it obvious to the observant that they are merely echoing local mobgabble, or voicing the reasonless antipathies of race. Of the other two, half the energies are wasted refuting the arguments provoked by the zeal and strengthened by the errors of these asses, who, flat on their sides in the arena, each with an Eastern editor sitting on his head disputing with the rest of us, can only bray into the dust and raise a cloud to darken counsel.

By the way, there is one argument which, aside from its weakness, suggesting as it does an analogy that makes against us we would do well to "abandon at sea," for we shall be "all at sea" as long as we trust it. I mean the mistake of assuming that we are better qualified to speak on this subject than the people of the East are. Now the evils of Chinese competition in the labor market, like all other evils of which that intricate and difficult science, political economy, makes account, are of so general a character, and are so modified by advantages in special directions—the mischiefs and benefits are so intertwined, overlapped, and trajected—that only omniscience could ravel the tangled web. They are not capable of demonstration, and must remain matters of opinion. Writers and speakers of the Atlantic States being better educated and less provincial than ours are better qualified in judgment. Having no present concern in the matter, they are more impartial. It is a proverbial, and all history proves it a political, truth that the looker-on sees most of the game. But over and above, though inclusive of, these considerations, actual contact with an alien and dissimilar civilization has not infected them with that horrible Race Antipathy—that mother of darkness, whose hideous touch lays upon the eyes of men's minds a blindness so black that not even clay and spittle could let in the miracle of light.

I said our favorite argument suggested a hostile analogy. Let me inquire of any man of observation and understanding, northern or southern: Who were right about the social and industrial phases of negro slavery?—those who had, or those who had not, the "light of experience?"—those whose interests were, or those whose interests were not, most affected by it?—those who knew the negro through life-long association and observation, or those who had but a literary acquaintance with him?—the practical insiders or the sentimental outsiders?—the players or the lookers-on? The parallel, so far as I have drawn it, is perfect. The moral is, that it is better to show wherein the Eastern Chinophile is wrong than to protest his inability to be right. The rascal has been so very right so exceedingly often that the fertility of the inner consciousness in which he grows his opinions ought to command our admiration and engage our civility.

It would be disingenuous and unprofessional of me to quit the subject without disclosing my own opinion upon it—an opinion the strength of which is, I hope, justified by exceptional advantages of investigation. I came to California in 1866 with a fair knowledge (since enlarged, I think) of political economy, and a cast-iron conviction about everything, from the self-evident to the unknowable, both inclusive. As a journalist I have naturally heard, read, spoken, and written a good deal on both sides of this *questio vexata*—hearing and reading chiefly for the gratification of others, speaking and writing mainly for my own instruction. And this I must be permitted to say: I have never stopped my ears with my bread-and-butter (seldom had enough to spare for the purpose) nor pulled my heart-strings to work my tongue. Well, the other day I saw walking before me a big, oleaginous, and saponaceous Chinaman, whose pig-tail, in some orgasm of the fancy, had amused itself by executing a contortion that made it exactly resemble a giant note of interrogation. I was at last face to face, as it were, with the Chinese Question in its most aggressive and alarming form. I considered it anew, marshaling to my aid all the heavy battalions of knowledge, observation, and experience that I had recruited and drilled, bore down upon it with the shrilling of pipes and the punishing of drums, shouted "Sick 'im!" to all my faculties. It was no use: and just as the unconscious propounder turned into an apparently impenetrable jungle of dank and dowdy habitations without waiting for an answer, I meekly and reverently gave it up. This tale has a rare and beautiful moral.

Rare and Beautiful Moral of This Tale.
All skill in hammering and all knowledge of nut-cracking will not enable you to crack a hard nut with a small hammer.

I don't know if I have made it sufficiently apparent in the foregoing paragraph that the Chinese Question, as presented by the fat Asian, was, according to my understanding of it, "Had you better kick me?" [21]

On Popular Government

[Bierce displayed equal boldness in challenging some of the most cherished American beliefs in regard to the theory and practice of government.]

I fear I have lately exhibited a spirit of most reprehensible levity with reference to some of the cherished principles and traditions of our American politics. In defense I can only plead that I never more than half understood, but did always wholly condemn, "government of the people, by the people, and for the people." I openly affirm, and can prove, the entire incapacity of our people, or any people, for self-government. I assert that no single proposition is supported by so formidable a series of historical facts as this. The chain of evidence is unbroken and indisseverable; the links that we are forging to-day for its hither end are as flawless as those which the early republics welded into the immeasurable sequence at the point where, beyond their desolation, all is dark. If democracy is not necessarily and inherently a failure—if an endurable republic is anything more than the splendid dream of a generous imagination—then the historical method of ascertaining truth is more worthless than the incantation of a thaumaturgist, and more misleading than the oracle of a pagan temple.[19]

The republic has the lowest aim of all forms of government; it proposes to accomplish only that modest Benthamite Utopia, "the greatest good to the greatest number;" and it is with reference to this unexacting standard that it must be judged—and judged to have failed. For the realization of that nobler aspiration, the greatest good to the greatest men, its competence is as that of a boa constrictor to wetnurse young lions. If I were dictator it is to the attainment of this latter object that I would direct all the energies of the State; nor would I too curiously consider the cost of success. Slavery is an ugly word; but if it seemed to me that the temple of the Greek civilization was reared upon a substructure of Helots' bones, I should not have the presumption cruelly to turn my back upon the practical significance of the fact. War is an unpleasant business; but if convinced that the lassitudes and cupidities of peace relaxed the national intellect and debauched the national conscience, I hope I should have the benevolence to make education by fire and sword compulsory. Poverty is a disadvantage, wealth a peril; but if hereditary leisure appeared a condition necessary to the growth of great minds, ought I dishonestly to refrain from heaping the coffers of the few with the earnings of the many?

I do not say I hold the opinion intimated above; what I do say is that I favor all such forms of dominion and subordination—all such codes and customs— all such relations of the individual to society—as tend to the rearing of broad-brained and great-hearted gentlemen. How dare we mediocre millions—males, females, and young—weigh our vulgar "welfare" and our purposeless "lives" against the precious possibility of a Shakspeare! Is it not matchless effrontery to measure and tally the tears, the sweat, the blood, that may be required of us to water the soil where Paul hath planted? Is humanity wiser or better for our lives; in pain when we suffer; and poorer when we die? What we need is the decent pride of the honest Irishman who boasted that the Duke of Wellington had spoken to him—saying, "Out o' the way, you blackguard, or I'll ride over you!"

Let us not deceive ourselves with cant—our solicitude and sympathy for mankind are quite as insincere as the affected distress concerning public affairs which Johnson rebuked in Boswell.[20] No one but Jesus Christ ever loved mankind. Our eyes are wiser than our tongues: every one has wept for the death of a man; no one ever wept for the death of a thousand. You may go into a cemetery and pass over a hundred graves of nobodies without so much as a sigh; you come upon that of a great man and are profoundly moved. The *Grosser Kurfurst* founders with three hundred sailors and marines; you pause midway in the dispatch to pare a nail. Suppose Bismarck had been on board! An entire army is destroyed in battle. Bah! that is what they might have expected. But it is different when Bryant[21] cracks his pate on a door-step.

As it is the regimental officers who are the regiment, the organization, so it is the world's great men—eminent and obscure—who are the world. These are they for whom governments should be "established among men." Their welfare is the justification of organized society. Is this hero-worship? I do not know—I never in all my life took three steps to see an eminent person with whom I had not personal acquaintance. Let me not be disingenuous; I once mounted a nail-keg to have a look at the Shah of Persia, and on another occasion climbed three pair of stairs to see Colonel Jackson[22] about an advertisement. [22]

The newspapers of this country appear to have settled it among themselves that the rigorous measures adopted by the Czar of Russia for the suppression of Nihilism will prove ineffectual, and that the iron hand of Bismarck will fail to crush the Socialists. I have a less accurate knowledge of the future than it is the happiness of my contemporaries to possess, but I will venture the conditional prediction that if such devil's-fire as Nihilism, Socialism, Communism, and Kearneyism be not quenched with blood it will not be quenched at all. It is idle, this half-sympathetic and wholly uninstructed babble about the vitality of ideas, the futility of force, and the rest of it. Those ideas have most vitality which most commend themselves to strong and resolute rulers. The people may think, and think, but the man with a million obedient bayonets needs not care what they think. The important thing is what *he* thinks.

In the Czar of Russia and the Chancellor of the German Empire lie the hopes of civilization, for they are in all Christendom the only strong men—the one by virtue of great governmental powers which his predecessors had not the folly to fritter away, the other through similar, though lesser, powers and colossal brains.

I firmly believe that if the despotic energies wielded by these two men fail of the purpose to which they are set the days of our civilization are numbered, and in the near future the continents of Europe and America will be devastated by barbarians from the Asian steppes, or infested with cut-throat savages sprung from our loins and wearing the skins of animals about their own.

In Russia and Germany the battle for existence must be fought for us all. Austria and Italy are blindly letting the days of opportunity slip irrevocably away, like pearls from a string. Spain is a thing of nothing. France, England, and the United States are without government—the people govern. Whom? Themselves. They govern themselves—by themselves they are governed. What monstrous nonsense! Who governs himself needs no government, has no governor, is not governed. If government has any meaning or function it means the restraint of the many by the few—the subordination of numbers to brains. It means the determined denial to the masses of the right to cut their own throats. It means the grasp and control of all the social forces and material enginery—a vigilant censorship of the press, a firm hand upon the church, keen supervision of public meetings and public amusements, command of the railroads, telegraphs, and all means of communication. It means, in short, the ability to make use of all the beneficent influences of enlightenment for the good of the people, and to array all the dreadful appliances of civilization against civilization's natural enemies—the people. Government like this has a thousand defects, but it has one merit: it is possible.

The Kearneyism "episode" is not an episode; it is a part of the general movement. Thousands—tens of thousands of armed men are drilling all over the United States to overthrow the government. As there is no government they will depose the functionaries. Do you suppose they will stop at that? I tell you the good god, Majority, means mischief. These people who outvoted you yesterday will have you by the throat to-morrow. The robber is at your casement, and you sleep. You have wedged your door with a school-book, and fastened your sash with a newspaper! The one has taught him his power, the other his wrongs. Where was your censor? I tell you, my countrymen, there is no magic in words. Liberty, Freedom, Progress, Destiny—these are noble names; they mean something. But they *do* nothing, and the People are buying guns.

Formerly the bearer of evil tidings was only slain; he is now ignored. Pharaoh brained his messengers; they had grieved him, but he spared them. The gods kept their secrets by telling them to Cassandra, whom no one would believe. My friends, I do not expect to be heeded. The crust of a volcano is electric, the fumes are narcotic; the combined sensation is delightful no end. Pray do me the favor to enjoy it. I have looked at the dial of civilization; I tell you the shadow is going back. That is of small importance to men of leisure, with wine-dipped wreaths upon their heads. They do not care to know the hour. I say to you there are signs and portents—whispers and cries in the air; stealthy tread of invisible feet along the ground; sudden clamor of startled fowls at night, and crimson dewdrops on the roadside grass of a morning. I think we shall have some weather shortly, but pray do not disturb yourselves. By the way, gentlemen, I hear that preparations are already making to celebrate the centennial of 1793. [23]

On California and the Press

[A French book on California was the occasion for Bierce's sardonic rumination on the California press's ingratiating praises of its native region.]

The California provincial vanity has been again tickled by the pen of a foreigner and smiles dollars. The tickler is a Frenchman, M. Leon Donnat, whose book, *L'Etat de Californie,* will be eagerly devoured, if translated, by the local patriot who fancies heaven bounded by his visible horizon when he is at home.[23] M. Donnat spent as much as several weeks in California, and being unable to understand a word of English must have made some valuable additions to his French. He devotes a laudatory chapter to the press, which is not ashamed to manifest its satisfaction and make payment in kind.

> If you love me, why, I love you,
> > And we love one another;
> If you didn't love me I wouldn't love you,
> > And your silly old book I'd smother!

Sing.

     With all due deference to M. Donnat's superior qualifications and opportunities, I venture to think I have observed one thing that he has had the politeness to overlook, and that is that the newspapers of this State, like most newspapers everywhere, manifest an unsleeping sycophancy—an alert and aggressive obsequiousness to their patrons that would be creditable in an English small shopkeeper, but neither creditable nor possible in an American one. There is no popular ignorance too deep and dark, no vulgar vanity or prejudice too unlovely, no local vice too base, for them to feed it with what it loves and scratch its back while it eats. If the people of California were proud of running at the nose, the catarrh editor of the *Morning Call* would compassionate the nasal aridity of "our Eastern brethren." If they believed stealing meritorious, the *Chronicle* would lay on a thief to teach the art. If they considered the Mechanics' Pavilion earth's foremost architectural gem, the *Bulletin* would labor to prove that Greece "proudly wears the Parthenon" in vain.[24]

These are extreme illustrations. It is not conceivable that we should boast of catarrh, but we boast of our "intense nervous energy," a worse disease. We do not think stealing honorable, but we justify murder by mobs. We are not proud of the Mechanics' Pavilion, but we perform raptures concerning "the beautiful city by the Golden Gate"—the ugliest and most forbidding town that chance, cupidity, and lack of taste ever conspired to produce, or benevolence and toleration ever yearned to demolish.

As to our climate—we have a thousand; that of this Peninsula is conspicuously the most detestable in the belt of civilization. But we all clear our throats of the fog and gravel to sing its praises, as if we had made it. Our soil is pretty good in spots, but take a map and trace off a space on the Atlantic sea-board, having the same area as that of California, and embraced by the same parallels of latitude. The nobler and richer variety of products in this area may be sufficiently indicated by explaining that you will have inclosed the whole of Virginia, Maryland, Delaware, North Carolina and South Carolina, nearly all of Pennsylvania, and parts of New Jersey and Georgia. There is some good climate in that region, too.

Of Pacific Slope art, literature, learning, and general culture, I prefer to say nothing at present, for the reason, among better ones, that there is as yet nothing to say about it.

With all our inferiority in the things that distinguish enlightened from barbarous peoples; with all our isolation, and that fatal narrowing of the intellectual horizon that isolation begets; with all our raw, crude, and ill-digested civilization, our impatience of law, our childish rage at criticism, our irrelevance of antiquity ablaze with its luminous lessons—knowledge that we scorn because we do not possess it, and will not acquire because we scorn it; with all these disadvantages and incapacities, and because of them, we are the most conceited sodality of insufferables for whom in the order and economy of nature it is appointed that the Adversary shall receipt to the Fool-killer.

It is herein that the press (*pace,* Mr. Pickering) is not an unmixed good; for we note the precession of penitence to reformation, conviction to penitence, and admonition to conviction. It is the necessary sequence. But if the journalist, perceiving our sin, will not exhort, but makes percussion of applauding palms instead, it is clear that whatever influence he may have (concerning the measure whereof let himself testify) is given against progress, and in confirmation of error. If the unlovely grub believe itself a gorgeous butterfly will it struggle to rend its hampering chrysalis? Having repeated assurance that it is a perfected frog, will the tadpole not resist the secession of its wayward tail?

As to the morality of flattering the people, there is no argument; it is immeasurably base. As a business method it is a mistake as crass as that of the man who should butter the pole he means to climb. It is an error having its origin in a misleading analogy and a misinterpretation of fact. The individual is enamored of adulation and impatient of rebuke; the community neither rewards the one nor resents the other, for no man draws his dividend of praise or pays his assessment of censure. Man is a fool, but men are not such fools as to make personal application of what is said about him. Successful journals are such, not because of their sycophancy to the public, although most of them are sycophant, nor in spite of it, although they commonly disgust. Success is a thing apart, and that writer has not duly considered its elements who subordinates the manner of his work to its matter.

The average local journalist knows this—that whereas his readers will not resent his psalms of praise, psalm he ever so ill, they will not endure to be preached at by dunces. He writes badly, but he makes honest confession by eschewing themes interdicted to bad writers. He has observed that the growl of a lion is more interesting than the hiss of a goose. He can not growl, he will not hiss, and so he cackles, and would have the public believe it has laid an egg.

Who writes well writes what he will; who writes ill writes what he must. It is the prerogative of genius to tell the truth, but dullness is condemned to falsehood—a life sentence. Talent bites in security the leg upon which mediocrity must fawn. Fancy De Young venturing,[25] with the regal impudence of a Sam Williams, to fasten upon the "shrunk shank" of Poesy,[26] in the trousers of Prince Hector Stuart, or imbed his teeth in the "fatted calf" of Military Power,[27] in the nether garment of General John McComb![28]

The remainder of my ideas on this subject I feel bound in honor to withhold for my forthcoming "Letters to an Infant Journalist," addressed to the alleged city editor of the *Evening Examiner,* but in conclusion of this present screed I can not forbear disclosing (to the profession) this important professional secret, expressed—in order that it may be the more palatable—in terms of advice; the public will have the goodness to politely avert its ear: Remember that in writing manner is everything, matter nothing. This will do you no good, for, whereas your subject is of choice, your style is appointed by nature. On no subject are you to write all you know, nor the half of it, and on every one be careful to omit (after making it obvious) some important consideration or controlling fact; I leave the reason to your sagacity—the public, I fear, is listening. Last but most important—do not try to please your reader. Destitute of art and style, you can not; having them, you need not. Indulge him in frequent dissent and occasional anger, but beware how you suffer him to once despise you. Pray why should you greed for his approbation, or make exaction of his esteem? Is it not enough that he reads? [24]

The Black Hills

Showdown with Shaler

> [Very soon after his arrival in Dakota, Bierce
> found the situation at the camp mired in con-
> fusion as a result of a standoff between two
> factions, with his assistant, Myron Willsie, on
> one side and Gen. Alexander Shaler (president
> of the company), Capt. Ichabod West (the
> company's superintendent), and B. G.
> Caulfield (a lawyer) on the other. Bierce's neat
> resolution of the impasse is pungently related
> in a letter to John McGinnis Jr. on July 15–16.]

Arriving in Deadwood on the 11th inst., I found matters in a
pretty bad condition. Willsie . . . angered by Shaler's defeat
of the arrangement proposed by himself . . . would make no
further advances to Shaler, who, on his part, would have
nothing to do with Willsie. . . . I at once undertook to make
peace, and during that day and the next visited the Overland
House six or eight times. In good faith and good temper I
tried every way I knew how in the first two or three interviews with Shaler, Iddings[1] and Caulfield to bring about an
understanding, assuring Shaler . . . that Willsie was acting

with my approval and by my advice—a statement received with indignation by
Shaler, and derision by Caulfield. I offered also to have Willsie produce full and
ample authority, and to do so myself, if Shaler would promise to meet and consult with us, in case our authority proved satisfactory. He would consent to nothing, and Caulfield berated the "intrusion" of Willsie and me, and my profession
of authority, with contempt and derision as long as I would permit him. I reminded him that if he was "counsel of the company" it was unbecoming in him
to ignore all the company excepting the president, for I really felt that, in the language of an eminent British statesman, I was entitled to at least as much consideration as the Ruler of the Universe might be expected to extend to a black beetle.
All to no purpose. . . .

Finding that nothing could be done with Shaler as long as Caulfield stuck to him
I prepared in my memory, and at my next interview deliberately but with as much
earnestness as I could command (and I *was* horribly in earnest) delivered a series of
accusations against Shaler covering the whole time of his stay in the Hills. I charged
him with devotion to West and treachery to the company—with deceit, cupidity
and systematic falsehood—I charged him with endeavoring to keep from my
knowledge and from yours various flagrant instances of West's misdemeanors and
mismanagement. I accused him of downright falsehood and mean innuendo to
break *me* down, knowing at the same time my confidential relations with his
confreres of the Executive Committee, and having received absolute proof of my
trust in him and my fairness to West, and of my lack of personal ambition and
fidelity to my instructions. He declared this last charge false, asserting that he had
never written or uttered a word of me that was not true, and *then* (may God and
Eaton forgive me!) I quoted from the latter—I am unfamiliar with the writings of
the former—to prove my assertions, and *did* prove them. . . . Well, the fellow lied,
and lied, and lied to my face. He lied knowing he was lying and knowing I knew it.
He lied for Caulfield's ears, to which ample organs all this was what it was intended
to be—a revelation. It succeeded; the bond between this precious pair was broken
at least temporarily—Caulfield, from self-interest, I think, visibly fell away from
Shaler and after I had next morning threatened to convene Willsie and formally depose Caulfield that luminary advised his client . . . to a better behavior. . . . I *do* know
that they gave us no further trouble, and Caulfield did good service. Shaler henceforth accepted every invitation to agree with us, and was the meekest of men since
Moses. Such he has since continued to be, though no doubt he considers himself a
martyr. He probably fights yet in his N.Y. letters, but he is a subjugated commonwealth here. Willsie and I will continue to consult him under the Board of Advisers
arrangement so long as you choose to continue that arrangement.

During one of my interviews with Shaler and Caulfield at the Overland West,
hearing his honored name taken in vain, burst into the room with his head tied
up in a rag, and looking like the lunatic he is, and began the most shocking imprecations of Willsie and pretty much everybody but Shaler. He was as pictur-

esque in this attitude as ever you saw Booth on the stage.[2] He was gently bundled out of the room, and five minutes later—after I had left—he was found, Caulfield told me, on the floor in an epileptic fit. . . . O, it has been a sweet and lovely time up in Deadwood, believe me!

. . . I am not sorry I repressed Shaler with "the strong hand," but *am* sorry it was necessary. I said to him: "You recognized neither my ability nor my power until I proved the one by making you feel the other." And yet I fear this infatuated man is, till this hour, trying to save some small scrap of respectability for himself and success for his owner from the hopeless shipwreck of that luckless mariner's venture. [1]

> [Shaler's departure from the camp shortly thereafter was heartily welcomed by Bierce.]

I confess I am glad that he is gone, for he has lately done little but object and dissent and decline to commit himself whenever his opinion was asked. There has been however no quarrel or exhibition of feeling; he, Willsie and I have treated one another—as far as I know—with civility and even apparent cordiality. In one interview with Shaler and Caulfield I said to Shaler all the unpleasant things that I had to say and never repeated them. The object of his going to New York I guess to be to set himself right and reinstate West. West delivered himself pretty fully on that point to several persons while here the other day and in Deadwood on the witness stand in his embezzlement case swore so Hale informs me that he was still Superintendent of this company and its authorized agent here.[3] That he will make a desperate effort to show himself the victim of conspiracy and misrepresentation I do not doubt, and that Shaler will back him up is pretty certain. There is nothing of it. These two men will tell any falsehood that they *dare* tell. . . .

The anxiety of the stockholders is natural; I hope to allay it and am assured by Mr. Willsie . . . that anything provided for in the contract can be done if not within the contract price at least considerably within that and the securities we hold. I am trying and I think Willsie is trying to save all of West's securities that we can—while he is going about saying we are thieves and—but really it does not much matter what he says. You did "make ample provision" for the building of our works certainly except in one respect. You did not provide a contractor of honesty and respectability. . . . How under the sun you gentlemen in New York took such a man up I do not know. As for his "reinstatement" it is enough to say that he has been physically and mentally incapable for a long time, & has been guilty of dishonesty and misconduct over and over again all of which can be proved before a court of law by testimony absolutely unimpeachable.

. . . *Don't* be discouraged; I have not the least doubt of restoring things to a good shape and making our mine *pay,* and pay *well.* [2]

The Derelictions of Capt. West

> [Shaler, returning to New York, had attempted to convince the
> company that it was Bierce and not West who had been respon-
> sible for much of the mismanagement at the mine, compelling
> Bierce to defend himself vigorously and also to specify his accusa-
> tions against West, which he did in the following letter to
> McGinnis on August 8.]

I could (and should it become necessary I will) establish by overwhelming evidence the following propositions:

> (1) Capt. West is a man of habitual falsehood and immoral life. (2) That
> the contract he got from this company was one of greater profit to him
> than a man who was a large stockholder and expected to be Superinten-
> dent had any moral right to secure. (3) That he sold a good deal of
> ground to the company as good ground that is absolutely worthless, and
> that he knows to be so. (4) That even had he obtained but a reasonable
> price for the work he contracted to do, the work was of needless and ob-
> viously needless magnitude and cost, in these respects, namely: The bed-
> rock dam should not have been built at all; it is wrongly placed, so as to
> greatly increase its cost. . . . The flume has double the capacity that it
> ought to have,[4] and besides the extra cost it must be partially empty a
> great portion of even the best seasons, subject therefore to rapid deterio-
> ration; a system of simple and inexpensive dams on the upper tributaries
> would have held surplus water and secured a more uniform supply of the
> same amount; there is for some miles of the line no conceivable necessity
> for a flume at all—it should have been a ditch, saving many thousand
> dollars in construction and repairs, and being in every respect superior,
> the character of the soil offering no difficulties whatever. . . . (5) That
> Capt. West could for the amount paid him for ground have brought
> large tracts of the richest gravel in the world, contiguous to Rockerville,
> nobly situated, easily supplied with water by a short extension of the
> present flume—sufficient to pay splendid dividends for a great many
> years, the same land being now more difficult to acquire by reason of the
> hopes of water inspired by the flume. (6) Capt. West by his personal un-
> popularity and bad treatment of others rendered the acquisition of ad-
> verse or desirable claims impossible. (7) He grossly imposed upon the
> President of this company, and the President's family, by introducing a
> public harlot to their house, and lodging them in the house of a public
> harlot during their stay here.[5] (8) He habitually neglected all his duties in
> connection with the work intrusted to him.

I hold myself ready, when necessary, to prove that in these several kinds of misconduct he was supported by Gen. Shaler, against repeated warnings and protestations of Gen. Shaler's friends. I hold myself ready to prove that Gen. Shaler would tolerate no suggestions, from officers or stockholders of this company, of any kind of mismanagement on the part of West and on many occasions resented the utterance of the most evident truths, respecting his incapacity.

Whether Capt. West obeyed or disobeyed his instructions obviously or violated his understandings with the Company, properly accounted for funds in his hands and advances made to him, and whether many of the foregoing charges against him, and against Shaler for earnestly supporting his policy, are true or false you know as well as I, and can as easily prove.

As to Gen. Shaler's assertions of my "lack of business experience," he probably means business *capacity,* inasmuch as he can hardly know anything about my life; and he is welcome to his opinion as to that, his own business capacity being a factor in his judgment, and that being at least debatable.

My best defence is, I think, contained in my private letters to you and Eaton. Statements I venture to believe could be copied from them which subsequent events came as near verifying as they did some of General Shaler's, and which show a not altogether vague and unintelligent notion of this business and the situation of affairs here.

. . . if there are any definite charges formulated against me I shall be glad to have them transmitted to me for answer. I fully appreciate your kindness in suggesting the letters of explanation and vindication, and if I could think it to either my advantage or yours to do more than I have already done, until I know just how my actions are to be assailed, I would cheerfully do so.

The Company has made a bad blunder and bad blunders in business have to be roundly paid for. The situation of affairs is mercilessly exacting and we must meet its demands. But let me here say that this if properly managed is not an enterprise of a day, but of a generation, maybe a century. It has had a bad start but it can have a splendid course. Let no man make the mistake of being disheartened now. [3]

Bierce Gets Mad—"All Over"

[West was indeed relieved of his duties shortly thereafter. But just when Bierce thought he was out of the woods, a new irritant—in the form of Marcus Walker, the corporation's treasurer—showed up at the mine, with several other individuals clearly intent on finding malfeasance on Bierce's part. Such a blow to his self-respect he was not about to take lightly, and he relates his wrath in a letter to S. B. Eaton on September 2.]

Well, here was a pretty turn of events. Walker, Girdler, Male, Alexander, Chambers[6]—all at once—and nobody had had the civility to say, "By your leave, Major Bierce, we shall on such a day sit upon you so and so." Mr. Walker had once already practically informed me that I was a liar by saying I had exaggerated the difficulties and labor of my position, and once that I was a coward, because I had insisted on his presence while issuing to the laborers, obligations which I had no assurance there would be money to meet, and of a kind of which those very men held many which I could not pay, although nearly a month overdue—insisted that he, as Treasurer, should assure the men they would be paid. Mr. Male had said ditto to Mr. Walker's opinion about "exaggeration." (I think that just at this writing Mr. Walker has had good reason to modify that opinion; he hasn't found this office a couch of roses.) Mr. Girdler, as I told him to-day—though he denied it—had from the first assumed toward me the attitude of an officer of the law to a convicted thief.

All these days I had courted investigation and held my temper, for I saw that if I objected to *anything* it would be construed as an objection to an investigation. This last disregard of official and social courtesy I would not endure. I got "mad"—all over mad—and I should now despise myself if I had *not* got mad. Taking Mr. Willsie and Mr. Walker apart . . . I told him I would no longer be treated as a criminal, and that if he insisted on taking possession of my office without mentioning their intentions, and doing things by secret methods, I should demand their authority or close the office; that if I was not treated with respect I should stop all business, refuse to sign another check, and start for New York with my accounts and vouchers to submit them to the Executive Committee, in person. I told Mr. Walker that if he made any more innuendoes about my lack of courage I would demonstrate it then and there. I told him that his remarks on my "exaggeration" were, under the circumstances, impudent, and I would have no more of them or his secret methods—nor will I. In short, I told him the wholesomest truths that probably he ever heard in all his life, and called him the "great white American question-asker," reminding him of the proverb that a fool can ask questions in a minute that a wise man cannot answer in a life time. I said (what I now repeat) that I had been required to perform impossibilities without the means of attempting them. He said my secretary was incompetent,[7] which is not true, nor approximately true and that my payment to him of $250.00 for last month's work was outrageous. It was simply *mean* of me to give him so little. . . . (Mr. Kaufman, by the way, is a gentleman . . . a thorough man of business who consented to serve me on my urgent solicitation, and without whom I could have done *nothing*. He has kept his accounts as I directed him to, until I could learn what books this same Mr. Walker required me to keep, get time to open them, and a man of ruler-and-red-ink to do that business. Mr. Kaufman does not "aspire" to be a mere book-keeper; he has had charge of the Company's money, made many of my payments in distant camps, and had worked literally half to death. I shall stand or fall with Mr. Kaufman.) He, Walker, objected to my employing Boone May[8] . . . who on Tuesday last had guarded us and our coming from Rapid; whom I need almost daily to protect the company's property and claims, and carry important papers, and *shall* need to carry gold and guard it. . . . Mr. May . . . is employed by me as a messenger in a kind of service in which I have not the time to risk my own life instead of his. Every mining company has to employ such men, and detectives besides. . . .

Well, Walker and Girdler, of course, disclaimed any intention of being offensive or uncivil; but they apologized, all the same, and then I *invited* (verbally and by letter) Mr. Girdler to assist Mr. Walker in the investigation and promised him every assistance from myself and all under my orders. . . . Mr. Walker . . . confessed, as he had good reason, that my position here was not exactly a bed of roses, and both he and Girdler have since treated me as if I were a human—very human—being. All the same, they are after my scalp, which they will undoubtedly get away with. Good enough—they are quite welcome.

I have told them to do anything they like in my office, and they may fill it with investigators of all sorts of kinds. But they have to treat me as a gentleman and an officer of this company as yet unconvicted of either incompetency or dishonesty. When I am no longer under fire you will receive my resignation of an office which seems to be without salary, and which no man can occupy without cutting his own throat. I've had enough of it.

I do not blame you or McGinnis—McGinnis I believe to have acted more handsomely than you, for he knows me less, and has, I think, had his confidence in me very much strained. You, I presume, have not, but you remember my promise in one of my long ago letters to step down and out when there was any lack of confidence among us three. That promise I shall fulfill, and God knows I shall breathe more freely when I am again free. . . .

To show the animus of the thing. When I informed Mr. Girdler in Mr. Walker's presence that in the absence of instructions, or even a verbal request from Mr. Walker, I doubted my authority to permit him, Girdler, to handle the company's money and assume official duties, he replied that he had decided beforehand *what to do in case of my refusal.* They had evidently contemplated such a possibility—perhaps thought it a probability—as my declining to be investigated at all; for I presume they thought their authority sufficient. What does it all mean? What has been reported in New York? Why have you kept me in the dark if anybody has been accusing me? I tell you these men came out here to, not investigate, but condemn. [4]

> [Walker now changed his tune, but Bierce was in the event right
> to suspect that Walker's shenanigans were not at an end. The
> following is from a letter to Eaton on September 6.]

Walker seems very friendly, but I suspect him of playing the hypocrite. That beast of a blackguard, Girdler, is sullen but civil, and keeps much out of my way, which he had better continue to do. Walker informed me that Girdler was here to see if things were all right and if so being a large stockholder he would advance money to help us out. Now, I suspect that all the stock he holds is the small block that he got for introducing West to his New York friends; and as for advancing money, it is thought here that he is pretty nearly flat broke. I have been inquiring today into his history (his character is obvious in his face and conversation) and it is not a good history at all. There is a man in Willsie's employ who knows all about him "from away back." He may be prejudiced but—I am too, I guess. . . .

If these gentlemen [Walker and Male] have any fault to find with me, I will answer their charges, and then quit if you and McGinnis think that course best for the company. But if they make no charges I must insist on my status being defined and assured so far as you can assure it. I don't propose to remain under fire very long, in a position which the circumstances of my own affairs have made peculiarly harrassing and disagreeable, nor to hold that position by so insecure a tenure that I dare not send for my wife and babies. I know you will do all you can but you must do it at once. Time presses, winter approaches and I mean to spend next winter with my family somewhere. *That* is the only thing that I am sure about. [5]

The Backstabbing of Walker

[Bierce's suspicions of Walker were all too readily confirmed when he learned that upon his return to New York, Walker had viciously attacked Bierce and accused him of the very crimes and blunders that Bierce had refuted to his face. Bierce's outrage is evident in his letter to Eaton on September 14.]

I certainly do not propose to submit to Walker's intrigues and falsehoods without giving you and Eaton a chance to justify me and your own judgment. Considering all that Shaler has done, and that he is to-day President of the Company, I think I have a right to at least a hearing, and this I demand. It is pretty hard, you will admit, that after working all this time at the most disagreeable and thankless duties that could have been required of me, now, just as the time comes for me to begin a more pleasing kind of duties, a kind to make directors and stockholders smile instead of frown, I am compelled to defend myself against the intrigues of such a man as Walker, who came out here with everything cut-and-dried for my overthrow. . . .

I know—learned to-day—that the management of this mine has been offered

to several persons in Deadwood, among others Mr. L. L. Alexander. . . . It was
offered, also, to Mr. Babcock,[9] who seems to have gone so far toward acceptance
as to try to engage Chambers for his secretary, but Chambers did not accept the
position. In short, since the arrival in the Hills of Walker, Male and Girdler, the
management of this mine has been "in the market."

I judge that the scheme includes a consolidation of our interests with those of
the Caulfield-Babcock party. Now these gentlemen neither have any money nor
any ground that is worth a dollar to us. The only ground they ever did have that
we wanted I jumped, and shall hold in spite of anything. . . .

Eaton writes me that perhaps the control of the enterprise *may* fall into the
hands of Walker. It looks like it, certainly—it looks as if it had already done so.
The reason of Eaton's apprehension is not very creditable to the rest of you—
namely, that Walker is the only man who can afford to devote his time to managing affairs at that end. There is not one of you, on the contrary, who can afford
not to do so. It is a good mine, and can be made a great one. It is not the scheme
of a year, but of a century. If you and Eaton let go, or have already let go, your
hold on its control you will, I am sure, bitterly regret it, for it will fall into the
hands of Walker, who has neither brains, nor honesty, nor truth. So far from
abandoning it you ought—one of you—to come here at once and see for yourselves. You send Shaler!! You send Walker!!! But you won't come yourselves. Are
sense and honesty to rely on the reports of incapables and rogues? This is all
wrong; it is unjust to yourselves and to me. In your last letter you express your
gratitude to me and say that money cannot repay me. Then keep your money and
repay me by coming here or sending Eaton. *That* would repay me. [6]

> [Realizing that he would probably not be given the opportunity to
> answer Walker's charges, Bierce felt the need to unburden himself
> in private to Eaton on September 24.]

I judge from the tenor of your letter of the 16th inst. that it is now too late to reply effectually to the charges of Mr. Walker therein contained; but having as yet
no notification of their having been acted on, I must treat them as if they certainly had not, and must beg the indulgence of being heard by the Directors, even
if I have already been removed *without* a hearing.

In the first place, I wish to protest against what I conceive to be the unfair advantage taken of me by Mr. Walker, who up to the time of his departure—after
he had gone through all my accounts, etc.,—professed, in unmistakable terms,
the satisfaction that he had at first not shown, thus throwing me off my guard,
and gaining nearly a week's time in which to present his accusations without my
knowledge of their nature or that they were to be made.

To the charge that I am nervous and irritable I shall only reply that I had much in Mr. Walker's manner to irritate me, and that at the time of his visit I was ill, and have been ever since, from over-work and loss of sleep. You will bear witness that I have repeatedly written you to the same effect, and to Mr. Walker, asking for relief.

"I am unskilled in dealing with men on business principles." That is a too vague accusation for either proof or disproof. I think I better know the character of Western men and miners than Mr. Walker does, and that the business principles familiar in New York are not adapted to the Black Hills.

That "I had no books open" is untrue, and in this connection I beg you to refer to my personal letter to you of the 14th inst. . . . and request that it be read to the Directors. That, I think, covers all Mr. Walker's charges relative to my accounts. . . .

My memoranda were "kept on a wire where they could be easily lost." As it is not asserted that they *were* lost it is unnecessary to further notice that statement.

That "there was no account regarding those important charges or disbursements which we may have to contest sometime in court against West." My cashbook shows every such charge and disbursement, and Mr. Walker knows it, for he made copious notes from it. It is open to inspection with reference to the truth or falsity of that statement by any expert that may be appointed to examine it. Indeed, Mr. Walker's own expert made up the statements alluded to above from that cash-book.

If my pay-rolls were "a mass of confusion" to Mr. Walker that is because Mr. Walker was unfamiliar with the cumbrous and involved system under which I was compelled to pay. They were not *my* pay rolls at all, but Mr. Pinney's,[10] whose debts I was paying, and whose system I had no right to alter, and could not arbitrarily have done so without giving him the right to say that I had impeded him in the execution of West's agreement with the company. The pay rolls are clear enough, and considering that they had frequently to be altered at the pay table, owing to the ignorance and carelessness of the foreman from whose inaccurate time-books they were made up, and that payments were commonly made at the camps at night, sometimes in a barroom filled with half-drunken and reasonless men, they are a marvel of lucidity. But I cannot, of course, hope to make the circumstances of my payments—particularly the first—understood in New York. . . . I did as I did with my eyes open, *knowing* that I laid myself open to such accusations, and knowing that they could be fatal if pressed, for it would be impossible to give the Directors any conception of the circumstances and exigencies of that time. I simply do not envy the man who takes advantage of such an opportunity, that is all.

Mr. Walker's judgment as to how I might have systematized my business, the proper office-hours etc., lacks the merit of being based on experience, however strongly it may be founded upon intuition. I venture to believe that I am as good a judge as he as to how I could best get through with my various duties, and economise my time. He came here when I had struggled through, and things were calm and comparatively well systematized. But *I* had done it.

If Mr. Walker learned that "the prominent men in the Black Hills are unanimous in the belief that I am not competent" I presume he furnished a list of their names, and showed that they were familiar with the workings of my office, and had devoted considerable time to the study and investigation of my affairs.

One of Mr. Walker's accusations has the accidental merit of truth—that I have "made some expensive mistakes." Even this, however, has not the merit of originality: I made the same statement myself, in a letter to Mr. McGinnis dated Aug. 17th, in one to you dated Aug. 24th, and at various other times. If Mr. Walker will have the fairness to specify *what* mistakes I have made I pledge myself to either refute his assertions or confess their truth. I have not professed to be infallible.

Regarding my secretary, he is not *only* a "gentleman" but a capable and experienced man of business. If Mr. Walker thinks I need a "book-keeper" I have only to reply that I tried every way I knew how to get one when I needed another besides Mr. Kaufman, with whose abilities in that way, however, I am entirely content. *If* I had no book-keeper, however, and *if* it is conceded that I tried hard to get one (and my letter book and telegrams will show that I did) how am I so severely censurable for the alleged informality of my accounts? Nobody, I hope, ever supposed *I* was a book-keeper.

The man whom Mr. Walker calls my "guard" he knows to be my "messenger." He never "sat about my office with a gun" at all. One day when Mr. Girdler assumed the duty of handling my money nearly all day, my messenger (who had guarded it in transit from Rapid, and guarded Mr. Walker, too) was in the office a good deal, whether from excess of zeal or suspicion of Mr. Girdler I really cannot say; I did not observe his presence until Mr. Walker mentioned it. . . . This man . . . has *never* acted as a guard except in escorting currency through a country infested with robbers and cutthroats. Mr. Walker was a little afraid of him, but he is really quite harmless if tenderly handled.

To sum up: I affirm of Mr. Walker's accusations that, in so far as they are not childishly vague and general, they are definitely and accurately false. [7]

> [In a separate letter to Eaton written on the same day, Bierce officially tendered his resignation.]

Rockerville, D. T.
Sept. 24th, 1880.

Major S. B. Eaton,
Dear Sir,

I hereby place in your hands, and authorize you to tender to the Board of Directors of the Black Hills Placer Mining Company, my resignation as General Agent of the Company in Dakota.

I am very truly yours,

A. G. Bierce.

This resignation to take effect immediately on presentation.

A. G. B. [8]

> [But of course this was not quite the end of the matter. Persuaded
> by Eaton's desperate appeals to remain at the mine until a succes-
> sor could be found, Bierce relented and hung on, in the face of
> lawsuits, increasingly bitter and potentially threatening complaints
> by workers, and a variety of other difficulties.
>
> The final blow came when the company, in deference to
> Walker, rejected the appointment of Daniel McLaughlin as the
> company's lawyer and reinstated Caulfield. This marked the end
> of the struggle for Bierce, as he outlines in a letter to Eaton on
> October 7.]

In employing McLaughlin I was acting with the full knowledge and approval of
the majority of the Executive Committee, and on a distinct understanding that
he was to be made the company's attorney. The understanding existed before I
was an officer of the company, and had been affirmed by legislation. The position of company's attorney was, in fact,—though not outwardly—a part of the
purchase price of the Oliver water-right, and the Committee's action is nothing
else than a bare and direct repudiation of a debt—an obligation all the more
binding because it was a kind of "debt of honor." McLaughlin parted with his
property on our repeated intimations that he was to receive the appointment.
Then we go back to him! If the company thinks it has either the advantages or
the skill to do that kind of thing with impunity in this country against a man like
McLaughlin, in favor of a man like Caulfield, it will make a costly mistake. Mr.
McLaughlin is a gentleman, wealthy and influential; Benney Caulfield is an impecunious fellow, commonly found in bar-rooms, has no social standing, and is
in all manner of schemes, every one of them adverse to this company's interest
or designed to "bleed" it.

Mr. McLaughlin has served us ever since about the 10th of last July, and has
sent no bill for his services, on the understanding that he was actually, and would
soon be avowedly, the attorney for the company in the sense that Caulfield now
is. Besides having been entrusted by me with the general business of the company, he has been regularly engaged in no fewer than five important cases now
pending in the First District Court. . . . He has all the papers, and has been by me
put in possession of many of the facts necessary to success, including all the information of such a nature that I will not impart it to Benney Caulfield. Neither
Walker nor Caulfield has the knowledge of the facts necessary to success in these
suits, and if I were still in a position to advise I should advise that they be settled

out of court, or that you let judgment go against you by default. It will be useless to incur the expense of contesting them. My present advice would be to immediately reverse your action in making Caulfield your attorney.

I shall at once withdraw my complaint against the First National Bank, and let the company recover its money in its own way.

As to Walker's "preference" for Caulfield. All the time he was here he gave me to understand that he favored McLaughlin. He said so a dozen times, and distinctly told me he approved my course in not consulting Caulfield. . . . The only bond of union or sympathy between Walker and Caulfield was their mutual disgust with Shaler, Walker in my presence saying to Caulfield that he thought Shaler a partner of West in the contract, and that he (Walker) would give anything for evidence to convict him. Caulfield confessed he had been deceived in and by Shaler. The next time I went to Deadwood Caulfield was "all for Shaler" again.

Can you not see from these things how you are being duped, and how you are about to be robbed? By Jove, it will almost serve you right for your retention of Shaler, your bad faith in McLaughlin, and your practical cooperation with Walker by giving him Caulfield.

I wash my hands of it all. [9]

A Final Defense

> [Bierce left Deadwood shortly thereafter and spent several months in New York, although the upshot of his meetings with company officials is not evident. Late in the year he was taken aback to find that a number of citizens of Deadwood had taken umbrage over what they believed to be Bierce's denigration of their region and sent a letter of protest to the company's directors. Bierce's sober reply was published in the *Black Hills Journal* on January 15, 1881.]

New York, Dec. 30, 1880.

To the Editor Black Hills Journal:

Sir:—My attention has been called to a letter addressed to the directors of the Black Hills Placer mining company, roundly abusing me and significantly praising a person named Walker. The letter, which purports to be written in refutation of my alleged "damaging reports" of the Rockerville district, is signed by some half-a-hundred residents and so-called residents of the district, only seventeen of those signing it being known to me by name; and fifteen of these having personal grievances of one kind and another, mostly my refusal as general agent of the company to pay Capt. West's private debts. In deference to the other two, and for the peace of mind of other Rockerville people who may have been similarly imposed on in the interest of those who, for their sins, have a wholesome but groundless fear of my return, permit me to say that I have never made any damaging reports of the Rockerville district. I have always considered and represented it as one of the richest I ever saw, and I am somewhat familiar with the mining camps of California, Montana, Nevada and Utah. Since leaving Rockerville, Oct. 16th last, I have made no report of any kind, nor had anything to do with the Black Hills Placer mining company, except to look on at an election in which I had no interest, and to advise one or two of the directors that, under circumstances obvious to me since arriving here, they had better sell their water. I had myself another plan, but as I was paid to serve the company, not the community, even that might in time have been forgiven me, in as much as it was "business." But I am not coming back; the community will get its water and keep its ground, and I sincerely congratulate it on its good luck. I have no further interest in the company, and shall always be pleased by the welfare of the citizens of Rockerville—who didn't sign that letter.

I am very truly yours,

A. G. Bierce. [10]

The Exploits of Boone May

[On one of the few occasions that Bierce spoke of his Black Hills experiences in subsequent years, he related a particularly stirring incident surrounding a bodyguard, Boone May, whom Bierce had hired to protect himself and the large amounts of money he occasionally had to carry in the course of his business. Bierce recast this passage in a section of "A Sole Survivor" (page 302-4).]

I observe that the Secretary of the American Express Company is but indifferently gifted with confidence in steel-clad express cars as a means of baffling the energetic and ingenious train-robber. There are facts warranting his unfaith. Some years ago, in the late '70's, the stage line between Sidney, Nebraska, and Deadwood, Dakota, in the Black Hills mining region, was infested by the bloodiest gang of robbers ever known in the West. They had no sense of moderation; they held up every coach. But for the bi-weekly treasure coach, taking bullion from the miners, their fondness had something of the intensity of the cat's love of cream. They took it in at every trip, either way, at several points along the route. They rode in it for miles and miles, swapped horses with the driver and shotguns with the messengers. Twice a month, in short, they relaxed the tension and austerity of their lives and went in for a good time. They even sent a respectful petition to the express company, praying that the treasure coach be run weekly, as a rough substitute for the Christian Sabbath, which their religion forbade them to observe.

The company put on an iron coach, loopholed for firing and carrying six messengers with repeating rifles. The gentlemen of the road were pained by this evidence of an unfriendly spirit, and for several trips morosely held themselves aloof while consignees in New York marveled at receiving consignments. It would be easy and artful at this point of the narrative to lead the reader to believe that this expedient was successful—then spring upon him a bloody battle, a taking of the coach by storm, a dramatic *finale* with red fire, and wickedness triumphing all along the line. But it is not for a moment to be supposed that anything of the kind occurred, for I scorn surprises. The road-agents got a cannon.

It is the pellucid truth—they brought in a small mountain howitzer, such as is used by the Army to astonish (and incidentally disrupt) the Red Man withal. This formidable firearm, charged with a solid shot, they planted conspicuously on a crest in the roadway, and to prevent the needless effusion of blood invited the stage driver's attention to the nature of it by a card upheld in a split stick just where, in rounding a turn, he would come within easy range. In consideration of their thoughtfulness in not provoking a breach of the peace the prisoners were released on parole and permitted to retain their clothing.

The *régime* of armored line-of-battle coaches was at an end. But that of stage-robbing was on its last legs, as well, for the express company played its last and winning card by raking the West with a comb for messengers who would fight and knew how to fight. They would fight against any odds that offered. They were, I think, but four or five in number, but they had been picked out of as many States and Territories—chosen from thousands for courage and skill with weapons. Singly or in pairs they repelled every attack upon the coaches, and he was a lucky road agent who got out of the affair with a ghastly wound and an instructed mind. They not only defended the stage, they pitched into the "bad men" wherever and under whatever circumstances found—shot them down in the streets and, trailing the survivors into adjoining States, brought them back to punishment or left them as coyote-meat by the wayside. The authorities having gone blind and deaf, the work was soon complete: not a scoundrel was left in the Black Hills—not a soul remained but sayers of the thing that is not and takers of the thing that is near.

I dare not relate many of the incredible feats of those daring and skillful men, but here is an instance of their characteristic "readiness." I had one of them, Boone May, in my employ at a mine, and one evening he and I set out from Deadwood to drive there, a matter of fifty miles through the mountains. We had a light, open wagon, and as our cargo was money preferred to travel by night, having taken care to keep our movements secret. A half-dozen miles out we were zig-zagging up a dark gulch alongside a bawling stream. It was raining and May, sitting by me as I drove, was nursing between his knees a cut-off rifle in a leathern case. Suddenly out of the noise of stream behind sounded a hoof-stroke and at the same instant a voice, sharp and imperative—"Throw up your hands!" Turning my head quickly as I reined in, I saw the dim figure of a horseman. Our sudden stop made his horse turn, and it was "side on" directly at the tail-board of the wagon. And Boone May, his body reaching horizontally backward over the seat, and breast uppermost, had the muzzle of his rifle within a yard of the rascal's mortal part! I estimate the time consumed in the conception and execution of these preparations for defense—the time, that is to say, intervening between the fellow's directions regarding the disposition of our hands and the ascension of his own—at three-tenths of a second.

Having said so much without exhausting the stress and mandate of my reminiscent mood, and being willing to cease from troubling the wicked for a week, by way of variety, I shall finish off Boone May. While in my service at the mine he had to have a leave of absence to go to Deadwood and stand a trial for murder; some fool grand jury had indicted him for abating a nuisance with a revolver. My Directors in New York heard of it, and some of them were inexpressibly shocked. The faction that happened at the time to be fighting me was, indeed, quite prostrated by the thought of having a murderer in their employ, and made a sturdy clamor about it. I thought it would be a graceful thing to do to make some formal recognition of their views, and this I did by an entry in my monthly salary account: "Boone May, murderer, $150 00." I am sorry to say this did not appease them.

When I last saw May he was organizing a buffalo hunt on an Indian reservation where he had no right to go. He offered me the command of it, but I was not ambitious and went to New York. A few weeks later the newspapers had accounts of the trouble: May and his party were fortified somewhere, standing off the circumjacent Red Man who was in great quantity, highly audible and appetent of gore. Then I missed the newspapers for a week or two and have never learned the extent of the disaster that befell those painted braves. But Boone May afterward went to Brazil and died there. May God be good to that intrepid soul! [11]

The *Wasp* Years

On His Enemies

[With the passing of years Bierce's frustration at the apparent ineffectiveness of his unrelenting campaign to reform his contemporaries by means of satire became increasingly evident. Particularly galling were accusations of bias, malice, and other features of what was scornfully labeled "personal journalism." It is scarcely surprising that, less than two years after beginning work for the *Wasp*, he wrote the tart poem "To My Liars" (published in the issue for November 11, 1882) and on other occasions defended the principles of his journalistic method.]

To My Liars

Attend, mine enemies of all degrees,
From sandlot orators and other fleas
To fallen gentlemen and rising louts
Who babble slander at your drinking bouts,
And, filled with unfamiliar wine, begin
Lies drowned, ere born, in more congenial gin.
But most attend, ye persons of the press

Who live (though why, yourselves alone can guess)
In hope deferred, ambitious still to shine
By hating me at half a cent a line—
Like drones among the bees of brighter wing,
Sunless to shine and impotent to sting.
To estimate in easy verse I'll try
The controversial value of a lie.
So lend your ears—God knows you have enough!—
I mean to teach, and if I can't I'll cuff.

A lie is wicked, so the priests declare;
But that to us is neither here nor there.
'Tis worse than wicked, it is vulgar too;
N'importe—with that we've nothing here to do.
If 'twere artistic I would lie till death,
And shape a falsehood with my latest breath,
Parrhasius never more did pity lack,
The while his model writhed upon the rack,
Than I should for my adversary's pain,
(Who, stabbed with fibs again and yet again,
Would vainly seek to move my stubborn heart)
If slander were, and wit were not, an art.
The ill-bred and illiterate can lie
As fast as you, and faster far than I.
Shall I compete, then, in a strife accurst
Where Allen Forman is an easy first,[1]
And where the second prize is rightly flung
To Charley Shortridge or to Mike de Young?[2]

In mental combat but a single end
Inspires the formidable to contend.
Not by the raw recruit's ambition fired,
By whom foul blows, though harmless, are admired;
Not by the coward's zeal, who, on his knee
Behind the bole of his protecting tree,
So curves his musket that the bark it fits,
And, firing, blows the weapon into bits;
But with the noble aim of one whose heart
Values his foeman for he loves his art
The veteran debater moves afield,
Untaught to libel as untaught to yield.
Dear foeman mine, I've but this end in view—

That to prevent which most you wish to do.
What, then, are you most eager to be at?
To hate me? Nay, I'll help you, sir, at that.
This only passion does your soul inspire:
You wish to scorn me. Sir, you shall admire.

'Tis not enough my neighbors that you school
In the belief that I'm a rogue or fool;
That small advantage you would gladly trade
For what one moment would *yourself* persuade.
Write, then, your largest and your longest lie:
You sha'n't believe it, howsoe'er you try.
No falsehood you can tell, no evil do,
Shall turn me from the truth to injure you,
So all your war is barren of effect;
I find my victory in your respect.
What profit have you if the world you set
Against me? For the world will soon forget
It thought me this or that; but I'll retain
A vivid picture of your moral stain,
And cherish till my memory expire
The sweet, soft consciousness that you're a liar.
It is *your* triumph, then, to prove that you
Will do the thing that I would scorn to do?
God grant that I forever be exempt
From such advantage as my foe's contempt. [1]

For many years in this town I have been performing sturdy service to Literature by calling all other writers dunces; to Honesty by pointing out the circumstance that all my neighbors are rogues; to Art by affirming that nobody but I knows anything about it; to Truth by asserting, after David, that all men—including the Psalmist—are liars. And what is the result? Why, whenever I go out for a solitary walk I don't feel satisfied that I am all there until I have taken out my pocket vocabulary of opprobrious epithets and called the roll.

It is amusing. In all this time I have never redressed a private wrong in print—have never censured or ridiculed a man *because* I had a personal grudge against him. It has not been necessary: my personal enemies are otherwise punished. Sooner or later they come always to grief. John S. Gray, whom I have hated for twelve years, stole fifty thousand dollars. Mike de Young, who started even with me in journalism, lives in a forty-thousand dollar house and is respected by Obadiah Livermore, who knows how he got it. The other day I saw where some heedless hand had chalked on a dead-wall, "W. H. L. Satan."[3]

One evening on a lonely road in Marin county I saw approaching a man against whom I had for years plotted ineffectual schemes of vengeance for a personal affront. My opportunity had come; I drew my pistol and awaited him. Suddenly he paused as if some invisible monitor had warned him of his peril. He stood a moment irresolute, then turned his face partially away, slightly bent his neck, raised his right hand and—blew his nose with his fingers! I was avenged—may he live a thousand years in the enjoyment of his no handkerchief.

If the malefactor last above mentioned see these remarks and discern their application to himself what will he do? Good reader, he will build a lie about me. It will be a staunch, sea-going deep-water lie—a long, low, black schooner of a lie, with raking masts and spreading a cloud of canvas—perhaps fitted with auxiliary steam power. He will complete it with diligence and expedition and launch it upon the ocean of conversation to cruise between all the ear-ports of his little social world. For the pleasure of ridiculing him, even without mention of his name, I shall incur the honest detestation of half a-hundred men and women whom I do not know. And it would be quite the same if the person derided were a notorious public misdemeanant. In short, the man who makes it his business to pull skunks out of their holes by the hind legs must expect to walk through this vale of tears very much alone.

It is all natural. When a rogue or other fool is attacked in print what can he do. He commonly has not wit and lacks the opportunity of type. It will hardly do to say, "This rascal attacks me with truth because he knows me a rogue or fool." He must find a bad motive, if he lies for it. Mendacity is his trustiest armor and his readiest weapon. And so he lies. He lies with due diligence and commendable industry. He lies openly by day and secretly by night. He lies all the time. He astonishes himself by the strength, splendor and vivacity of his talent. But finally he executes an example of so matchless mendacity that his senses are stunned by a thunder-clap of self-respect, and he lives ever thereafter cowering under the terrors of his own admiration.

These remarks are herein set down for the encouragement of the rising young satirist enamored of the truth regardless. May they lubricate the joints and energize the thews of his red right arm, making it supple, alert and strong to battle for the right in a world of wrong. May they cheer him like the blessing of a dead father and inspire his soul as by prayer. And when at the close of a loveless life he dies detested, may I be there to coo into the spathe of his drooping ear the consoling words "I told you so." [2]

The editor of a local journal called *The Ingleside* has experienced the singular misadventure of being Henry B. McDowell, and cherishes the ambition to "lop off a fungus." The fungus that enjoys the distinction of having lured his lopper is "personal journalism." For seventeen years in this town I have been noting with interest and approval the rise and progress of energetic young journalists affected with a similar zeal and purpose, but their names I have not now the happiness lucidly to recollect. They have not shared the immortality of the fungus which they assailed. In serviceable loyalty to his high design, this freshest enthusiast has deemed it expedient to become dissatisfied with the *Wasp,* and with me. This noble discontent—problematically profitable but indubitably blameless—he has thought might be most acceptably expressed in a defense of that hunted fawn, Mr. William Sharon. Many objections to my existence, some valid, some fallacious, have from time to time been urged in the local newspapers, but I observe that a significant number of them have been made coïncidentally in point of time with Mr. Sharon's manifested willingness to "fix the press." The junction of Mr. McDowell with this innumerable caravan of my dispiteous expostulants is regrettable, for I believe him to be an honest lad, with as much civility as is consistent with an ambition to be lampooned.

In lopping his fungus, Mr. McDowell ought, in my judgment, to be accorded the freest swing for his axe that is compatible with safety to the fungi that his circumspicious activities have overlooked. But as he is new to life and local journalism, I venture to remind him that in taking a hack at *me* it is commonly esteemed prudent to use the blade of truth. Upon what does he found the accusation against the *Wasp* of "graphically presenting all the loathsome details of the Hill-Sharon case"?[4] Can he mention a single one that has been so presented, or presented in such a way that it "stimulated and excited an appetite" for "dirty scandal"? "The loathsome details of the Hill-Sharon case" have never been presented in this paper, and have been mentioned only for censure and ridicule. The reasons for "attacking" Mr. Sharon were stated with intelligible particularity in these words:

> First, the conspicuous baseness of his political career; second, the detestable means by which he acquired his great fortune; third, the vulgar ostentation of his social life; and, fourth, the incredible depravity of his personal character, as disclosed through the lumination of its sombre depths by the testimony in this hateful trial.

If Mr. McDowell has a private system of morality to which these qualities are not offensive, his zeal as a fungus-lopper will, I fear, outrun his renown as a gentleman.

Here is a brief passage from my critic's criticism:

> Who is the man who guides the machinery of the *Wasp's* abuse? He generally signs himself "B." He is much more careful of his own name than he is of those he assails. It is Ambrose G. Bierce who is responsible for the character of the cartoons which appear in his paper.

In these four lines are five propositions—four direct and one implied. Each is distinctly false. I do not "guide the machinery of the *Wasp's* abuse"; my own work in it is all that I have anything to do with. I do not "generally" sign myself "B", nor anything. Always when I have the vanity to think my work of sufficient importance to provoke public resentment or private retaliation, I append my full name. I have never edited a newspaper without assuming the entire personal, and, so far as I could, legal, responsibility for everything that appeared in its columns, by whomsoever written, as all publishers, subordinate editors and contributors with whom I have had relations will affirm; and it is now a standing instruction at the *Wasp* office to give my name and address to any person who feels as a grievance anything from my pen. The cartoons in this journal are neither drawn nor suggested by me, nor is the *Wasp* in any sense *my* paper. If in the lines quoted there are other propositions than those specifically denied they also are untrue. Their writer may justly pride himself upon the immatchable terseness of his style—he can pack more falsehood into smaller space than any man I know.

Thanking Mr. McDowell for his neighborly service in "making a back" for my vaulting egotism to play at leap-frog, I beg him to accept, with his dismissal, the assurance of my distinguished consideration. [3]

Everywhere in civilized countries the earth's periphery is infested with broods of literary doves, and San Francisco is a vast columbarium. These harmless creatures are ambitious withal, and promise themselves no small fame in expounding the true principles of satire and illustrating the application in their work. Their faith is simple—they are opposed to "personal journalism." They do steadfastly believe that Juvenal and Pope and Swift and Junius, Voltaire and Byron, were in grievous error regarding the distinction between "legitimate criticism" and "abuse." They cherish the parlormaidenly theory that sin may be right sturdily assailed, but the sinner should enjoy a peaceful immunity from censure. In short, their notions have the merit of close conformity with those of every fool and rascal under the sun, and their practice engages the admiration and applause of all whose vices and follies they hopefully denounce.

They come and go, these amiable censors—whence and whither, who knows? Each takes his little hack at me, lamenting my blindness and predicting my speedy suppression; and then his gentle spirit, still intent upon the amenities, evanishes thence, and when I would ask if still he writes I have forgotten his name and all others his work. Troop after troop of these ambitious satirists have I seen "come like shadows, so depart,"[5] deplored by none but the savage rascalry above whose back they had cracked their whips in empty air. When by chance my own lash, idly falling on some naked scoundrel, draws blood, a previously unnoted chorus of these ephemeridæ springs forward to assist in the yelling and sobbing. . . .

Now mark you, rogues of all degrees and lettered fools with phosphorized teeth in mouths full of moonshine, I am among you to remain. While the public

buys my rebuking at twice the price your sycophancy earns—while I keep a conscience uncorrupted by religion, a judgment undimmed by politics and patriotism, a heart untainted by friendships and sentiment, unsoured by animosities—
while it pleases me to write, there will be personalities in journalism, personalities
of condemnation as well as commendation. The right to praise and flatter in the
public prints implies and is coterminous with the right—in the public prints and
by name—to blame and ridicule, and I mean heartily to exercise it, calling a
knave knave, but calling him also what he calls himself. Nothing can be fairer
than that—the name he got by his christening and the name he gets by his deeds;
between them the public can make choice of evils and all may be suited.

Let reformers spare themselves the disagreeable dampness of further
lacrymation: there is absolutely no hope of extending from local journalism personalities offensive to offenders, but by my removal to another—and, in deference to the prejudices of my enemies let us say, a warmer—world, where, no
doubt, I shall be a part of the apparatus. The thing is to be done *disponendo, non
mutando, me.*[6] [4]

The Failings of the Press

> [Bierce's criticism of the press for its manifold failings had been of
> long standing, but it emerged with particular vehemence and tart-
> ness in the *Wasp*. Political prejudice, slipshod writing, venality and
> corruption—all these things evoked Bierce's wrath and satire.]

The influence of some newspapers on republican government is discernibly good;
that of the enormous majority conspicuously bad. Conducted by rogues and
dunces for dunces and rogues, they are faithful to nothing but the follies and vices
of our system, strenuously opposing every intelligent attempt at their elimina-
tion. They fetter the feet of wisdom, and stiffen the prejudices of the ignorant.
They are sycophants to the mob, tyrants to the individual. They constitute a
monstrous menace to organized society—a formidable peril to government of
any kind; and if ever in America anarchy shall beg to introduce its dear friend
despotism, we shall have to thank our vaunted "freedom of the press" as the controlling spirit of the turbulent time and Lord of Misrule. We may then be grateful, too, that, like a meteor consumed by friction of the denser atmosphere which
its speed compressed, its brightest blaze will be its last. The despot whose path to
power it illumed will extinguish it with a dash of ink. [5]

. . . I have learned that it is hoped by the leading members of the Press Club to
make it in every way worthy of its name—an organization that shall not discredit, but honor journalism. It is intended that it shall be a helpful auxiliary to

the profession, with mutual improvement for one of its aims. If so, it will never have an unfriendly word from me. On the contrary, I am willing to dedicate my pen to its service by the most unsparing censure of its faults and failings; for mutual improvement is what I conceive to be the most imperative need of many of its members.

Incidentally I learn that the attitude of many reporters toward myself is singularly hostile. Their attitude toward me is not so important as their attitude toward literary art and the English language. Between them and me there is no other possible basis of reconciliation than a better sense on their part of the dignity of their calling and of the knowledge, honesty, social respectability and literary skill that are its requirements. Ignorance, insincerity, "Bohemianism" and slovenly work (I care not under what hard conditions performed) are not to be tolerated. I have never asked that they be tolerated in myself, nor will I condone them in others. [6]

I know no profession in which—in San Francisco—the standard of honor is so low as in my own. It is almost a disgrace to belong to it. That a newspaper man will lie; that he will defend his friends when he knows them unworthy; that he will avenge private wrongs by public censure; that he will praise for money or blame in the hope of extorting it—all this and much more is popularly held to be implied by the nature of his business. In the nature of the business there is nothing to justify this, but much in the characters of those who pursue it. Nine newspaper men in every ten are base enough habitually to do these things and the tenth has to suffer for their sins. His defense of his friends is supposed to have no reference to their worth, his censure is believed to have its inspiration in animosity or thrift or wanton cruelty. If he champion a corporation he is thought to be in its pay, if he attack it he is attempting extortion. Everybody censured is swift with a retaliatory falsehood concerning his motive. It can hardly be expected that a rascal will admit that he is attacked for his rascality.

It is a land of rascals. It is a city of all-mannered rogues. It is a paradise of imposture. Political ignorance, literary stupidity, social vulgarity have here their ripest and richest development. Of all our millionaires you cannot name two who came honestly by their wealth. Our public business is conducted by successive swarms of thieves and dunces. Our courts of law are not courts of justice, for bench and bar are but interchanging parts of a monstrous conspiracy against property. Our pulpits are fountains of ignorance watering pastures of hypocrisy. Whose hand is here denied to the unconvicted felon? Who turns his back when presented to the public officer who has betrayed his trust? Who refuses to exchange salutations with one whom he knows to have cheated a creditor or told a lie?

Sir, you mistake. Madam, I beg your pardon. These are not the random reproaches of a delinquent civility—the easy indictments of a general disaffection— the barren outcome of a deficient observation. They are utterances of a judgment deliberately formed by years of study of social phenomena. It is not denied that they are true in some degree of every community, European and American; but they are made after comparison and in full assurance of a local application that is exceptionally cogent and close. I am not concerned with exceptions. That San Francisco has gentlemen in all professions—even in journalism—and ladies in all respectable walks of life, goes without saying; and these are they who will be slowest to resent the censure which is unable to part them off by name.

But shall we foul our own nest? says the brainless writer, reverent of the fool's tradition that public sycophancy can charm dollars out of private pockets. He thinks that in some mysterious way—by its own inherent energy and independently of means—his ministrations to general conceit will advantage his private fortunes; that if he says the community is honest and intelligent, some member of it will be inspired by gratitude to advertise in his paper or, in hope of an iterated gratification, subscribe for it. It is of little importance to gentlemen if he is right or wrong: they do not accept the wage of servility; but in point of fact there is no profit in flattering thousands, naming none. The sycophant journalist simply does not know his business—wherein he is not singular. In all my life I never knew a dozen men who understood the business in which they were engaged.

Who does the fouling? Is it defilement to part the branches and expose the condition? Let me tell you, esteemed contemporaries, that for the faults and failings of Californian civilization no agency is so blamable as the press. Other newspapers in other lands are bad, but ours is vile. In every other country, in every other state, in every other city the people believe themselves to be the best and most progressive, and their journalists, themselves convinced, confirm them in this barbarous error of an imaginary superiority. Here local conceit has been reduced to a science and its encouragement is practiced as an art. In other places journalists are disingenuous. Here they are liars from principle. It is God's truth that among the self-taught editors and writers of this town it is considered professional to cheat in discussion and to lie for gain. There are men who would resent with a blow the name of liar and scorn to overreach in swapping jack-knives, who, nevertheless, in some sordid interest habitually write and print the most monstrous falsehoods with intent to mislead and defraud the men and women by whose favor they live. They will lie for a party advantage, lie in defense of a personal friend, lie to injure a rival journal, lie in praise of a stupid book or a scoundrel painting, lie to lure their readers into a worthless show or persuade to the purchase of a poisonous patent medicine. In good faith, and with a clear understanding of the breadth of the statement, I assure the readers of these lines that in the profession to which I have the honor to belong, a main part of the profit is got, and thought by its members to be rightly got, by the systematic deception and plunder of their patrons.

From whom, my friends, do you hear all this talk about the great good wrought by the press, its vigilant guardianship of the public interest, its conservation of the public morals? From the newspapers, and from those who accept their word without analysis. It is not so. There are honest publishers and writers who justly respect themselves, but the rule is otherwise—that journalists are not gentlemen—that they are ignorant, untruthful, dishonest and unthinkably servile. They are so destitute of common sense that in controversy they throw away the only advantage worth contending for, by permitting their opponents to despise them instead of compelling a reluctant respect. The duelist who should lower his guard and say, "Thrust here and here"—would he not be a fool? What folly, then, for the controversialist, by falsehood or disingenuousness, to invite and direct the contempt for his adversary—the one person in the world most eager to detest him. To despise my enemy and make him respect me—that is the whole battle.

Faith, I've done. Let the public, variously unworthy, be slimed, and swallowed, and vomited up, and reslimed, in endless alternation, by a press that is many kinds of a reptile. Let Stiggins bawl from the pulpit, and Bridlegoose deliver judgment with dice.[7] Let Crœsus gattle gold to the filling of his abominable belly and the construction of a palatial pain in his lap. Let Impecu invoke the thunders of dynamite on the Sandlot and Parvenu practice with dignity and *éclat* his unaccustomed paces, clothed with vulgarity as a garment. Let Latronus iterate discreditable platitudes in legislative halls, his gestures impaired by necessity of keeping both arms in the public treasure.[8] Let Education lock up her books, Morality be sentenced to the House of Corruption and Truth drown at the bottom of her well. Let the infernal show proceed. As for me, it is Sunday and I go a-fishing. [7]

In Defense of the Mormons

> [It may come as a surprise, considering Bierce's violent condemnation of orthodox religion, to find him a defender of the Mormon church; but his sense of fair play incited him to deprecate the violent prejudice to which the Mormons were subject throughout the latter part of the nineteenth century.]

The news comes blazing and thundering across the land that Garfield I is to "bust up" Mormonism; explode it so utterly that the long worn shirt of its highest dignitary shall be blown through space unwedded from its subjacent cuticle and the disunited hoop-skirt of the superior spouse form seven bangles on a septette of different pine-tops, the sister herself being decently though hastily interred in the stomachs of the coyotes who, like their political prototypes, await the pickings. Government—if we have a Government—can arrive at the solution of "the Mormon problem" in a quarter of the time that No Authority has already consumed in getting ready to prepare for taking thought whether to consider how to not act. Call off your parsons, your editors, and your pedagogues, make me dictator, and I'll engage to make Mormonism a very dim and tenebrous tradition indeed, and that, too, without troubling myself to inquire whether my measures have given to popular sympathies this turn or that. Should secular measures, however, be thought too barbarous for this rose-water age, I would cheerfully consent to employ only spiritual—say four squadrons of Episcopalian horse, six regiments of Methodist foot, and a battery of Presbyterian artillery.

This by way of illustration; it is right to explain that I have a sincere respect for the Mormons. Surviving one of the most hateful and sneaking aggressions that ever disgraced the generally straightforward and forthright course of religious persecution—an aggression that lacked alike the sanction of authority and the lustre of success—they dragged the feeble remnant of their dispirited body into the horrible wilderness, where, a thousand miles beyond the range of cupidity's most extravagant claim, they made a garden of abundance. There they reared the edible beast and the succulent vegetable, and to the feast came Famine from over the seas to line his ribs with firm white tallow, box-plaited and scalloped. Following his dusty toes thither, Nakedness was fearfully and wonderfully clad, yet warmly withal. There the stomach of Intemperance paled its ineffectual fires, and Immorality was fain to hide his diminished head. In short, Mormonism proved the greatest practical benefaction to the century. If it ruined any souls it had the right, for the starving carcasses of its converts had none until souls were created under their skeleton ribs by Mormon meats and herbs. And now we want to rout out the Mormons again, rapacity arming itself for the purpose with religion's exhausted mandates copied from the archives of Nauvoo and telegraphed out to Ogden.[9] [8]

I heartily wish that every "Mormon-hater" were given the clear-eyed intelligence to see himself and his holy zeal confrères as the mirror of history shows them to have always been. And then, still sickened by the hideous revelation, he ought, in some sudden frenzy of fair-mindedness, to read George Q. Cannon's paper, in the *North American Review,* on "Utah and Its People."[10] The article is dignified, gentlemanly and temperate. It is truthful, logical and graceful. Its periods are fluent, its sentences well balanced, its rhetoric, generally, pleasing and right. Yet I venture to think it disagreeable reading to the Mormon-hater, and particularly unpleasant to the brawling bawds of the Salt Lake *Tribune* and the pestilent ruck of book-making "Gentiles," male, female and asexual.

I have no religious convictions. I do not care a copper for the Mormons. But I care a good deal for truth, reason, and fair play; and whenever I cease to be indignant at the falsehood, stupidity and injustice that this harmless people have suffered at the hands of the brutal and brainless mob of scribblers and tonguesters who find profit in "denouncing" them I shall have had a longer life than I merited.

I know something of this singular sect of ignorant delusionaries. I have examined their religion and institutions as not one person in a thousand of those who have been in Utah, and not one in a million of those who have not, has thought it worth while to examine them. Not entirely without training as an observer, I have studied themselves. And this I say with honest conviction—that, excepting the Jews and Chinese, I know no worthier large class of people than they; and excepting our forefathers' treatment of the Jews, and our own of the Chinese, I know of no more shameful instance of concerted misbehavior than that of the American people toward the Mormons. And I beg to assure them that in me they have a friend who chiefly regrets his feebleness and obscurity because by these they are deprived of services which they would be grateful to receive and I to render.

Much, no doubt, can be urged against the Mormons; but they who undertake their indictment before the assizes of humanity labor under the disadvantage of compulsory plagiarism. The literature of religious persecution is a literature of accusations against the persecuted. In the first aggression of one faith against another all possible appeachments were exhausted, and each successive set of oppressors has to warm over the cold criminations of the set that preceded.

Every accusation against the Mormons in America I can parallel with an accusation against the Jews in Castile, the Parsees in Persia, the Waldenses in Piedmont, the Puritans in England and the Quakers in Massachusetts. The history of religions is a thesaurus of indictments, ready made to the hand of counsel for the persecution. [9]

The severely virtuous monogamist, contemplating his wreckage of miserable old maids, and satisfied with the goodness of his work, has got after the improper Mormon with another act of Congress. That malefactor is no longer to be permitted to run an unlimited wifery, except at considerable inconvenience, affecting his status as a citizen. And all because in the course and conduct of his domestic government he is jealously distrustful of the one-woman power.

No doubt polygamy has its disadvantages and demerits, but could not something have been done to mitigate them by compromise? The policy of mutual concession is a good one, generally speaking, and surely the Mormons would cheerfully give up most of their wives, if the Gentiles would only take them.

I speak with confidence in this matter, for I have been in Utah a good deal, and I don't remember that I ever asked a Mormon for his wife and was refused.

Polygamy goes too far; there is no doubt of that. It should not be lawful, for example, to marry more than one brunette, or one blonde, except, of course, in the case of twins. With a good pair of wives, one dark and the other fair, a man would be tolerably well guarded against the allurements of any outside symphony

in pink-and-white, or nocturne in spit-curls; and the favored two, relieved from
jealous assiduities and fears, could bend their whole energies to protecting him
from one another. [10]

On American Politics and Character

> [As Bierce surveyed the state of American politics and civilization, he
> found them increasingly wanting. The following extracts are among
> the sharpest rebukes he would ever deliver upon his own people.]

[T]he peerless and unspeakable corruption in our public life is only the natural
outcome of the American private character. My countrymen, we have the distinguished honor of possessing moral qualities that the devil would shame to share,
and the advantage of a kind of government ingeniously adapted to their culture
and display. Year by year we visibly grow in crime, and now the shadow of our
national enormities, flung blackly athwart the area of enlightenment, appals the
very dogs that had come out to bay the moonrise of civilization gilding the vestiges of original barbarism. If the general conscience of cleanly peoples be not
soon quickened for our extermination—if we are permitted to go reeking with
sin and bloating with conceit, there is another justice on earth, nor in heaven the
sense of expediency.

I am not unaware that Dr. Stebbins has given the sanction of his approval to
our form of government and its working. I do not say he is not a learned observer; I say he is an American. Comparing the world's religions, he has decided
in favor of the Christian, and is enamored of its results. He is himself a Christian. Should he train his impartial mind upon a comparison of the world's hats
he would accord the palm to the silken stovepipe. Doubtless he believes the No.
12 cowhide boot to be the crown and flower of the world's foot-gear. I mean no
disrespect to the reverend gentleman, personally; I take him as a convenient local type and exemplar of that mischievous blind egotism that sees in its own environment a higher, wiser and more beautiful utility than its tethered sense can
perceive outside the circle in which it strays—that intellectual provincialism that
asserts the superiority of the village pump, the peerless brevity of tail of the village yellow dog.

It is this class of talkers and writers, swarming about the country's ears as thick
as bees about Hymettus, lulling them with easy platitudes of conceit and set
phrases of saponaceous flattery, that prevents all reform by charming away the
sense of its necessity. The frosty truth of the situation is that we are a nation of
benighted and boasting vulgarians, in whom the moral sense is as dead as Queen
Anne at her deadest; that we are hopelessly floundering and helplessly founder-
ing in a sea of public and private corruption as offensive as that upon which the

Ancient Mariner saw the slimy things that "did crawl with legs;"[11] that we are a laughing-stock to Europe and a menace to civilization.

They will tell you, these observers with iridescent eyes, that we are no worse than other nations; that trickery and thieving are common to all political systems; that reformation which does not go to the length of reconstructing human nature is impossible and a dream. It is not true. To perceive how false it is we have but to compare England under Walpole with England under Beaconsfield or Gladstone[12]—the time when votes in Parliament were openly bought and sold, when battles were declined and sieges raised by the world's greatest soldier for so much money to him in hand paid, and when the civil service was a nest of unexampled thieves, with the time when bribery in Parliament is a thing unknown, when an English officer would as soon think of selling his heart's blood as his honor, and when not a dishonest penny soils the hand nor a shabby service the conscience of a man in any of the departments of the State.

Has English human nature undergone a radical reconstruction? Nonsense! The English people never *were* dishonest, never *did* condone theft, never *did* call robbery of themselves "smartness." A few ministers of brains and power secured now and then an alteration of the laws, in accordance with common sense and the public conscience, and the thing was done. It could be done here—with greater difficulty and less perfectly for our people are essentially dishonest. But it would be worth while to do even so much as would avert the sneers of Europe and the tears of the angels. [11]

Certain unannealed idiots whom I have the advantage of knowing have been pleased to be offended by my remarks last week on the essential dishonesty of the American character. Well, I don't say these remarks were not offensive; I only say they were true. It is one of my failings that I do not know any better than to write the truth. Somebody, however, might say this in my favor; that I have never insulted the intelligence of my readers by flattering them. Most journalists think it pays to do so; I think it does not. The moral difference between them and me, in this matter, is not a wide one, clearly, and I regard it as a highly creditable example of humility that I consent to be no better than they, but only wiser.

I remember that only a few years ago no less a man than Mr. James Russell Lowell had his confirmation as Minister Plenipotentiary to a foreign court bitterly opposed by my respected friends the idiots, on the ground that he was an enemy to his country.[13] He had written in the N.Y. *Nation* some acrid verses on the corruption of American politics.[14] How they gibbered, the good idiots!—how they slavered and drooled the ropy venom from their hanging lips upon the name of that great man—mopped the bloodsweat of silly indignation from their retreating foreheads, and gibbered again! And the poddy-bodied croakers of the press—how they ruffled up their lousy feathers and clattered their evil beaks at the man of letters who had dared to say the truth! May the devil be killed if, as a blazing martyr, I would not rather torch the tenebreous interspaces of the "patriot's" understanding than burn incense to his nostril.

However, I mean to reform, some day. But inasmuch as I must by the bent and manner of my capacities be censorious, I shall assault the follies of the non-subscribing Esquimau, and frown frostily upon the sins of the erring Ancient—who does not advertise. Yes, I shall make it warm for the Hyperborean and lively for the dead. But whether or no the proprietors of this journal will then balk my benevolence by removing the publication office to Greenland's icy mountains, with a branch in hell, I really cannot say. Being pretty good business men, I should suppose they would. [12]

The Assassination of Garfield and Its Aftermath

[Bierce's dire warnings on the corruption of American politics seemed vindicated when a mentally disturbed individual, Charles J. Guiteau, shot President James A. Garfield on July 2, 1881 (Garfield lingered on for several months, dying on September 19, 1881). But what disgusted Bierce even more than that event was its aftermath, with its outpouring of windy panegyric on a relatively undistinguished president.]

Since Man began his awful career upon the earth nothing has occurred more detestable than this assassination. A man of brain and character; a man with a past and a future—lord of a continent and ruler over fifty millions of people, ruling them wisely, too, and well; a great-hearted, clear-eyed gentleman, standing worthily upon his honors—such a man as that is suddenly brushed aside and effaced by the caprice of a smirking hoodlum! It is a colossal practical joke—an irritating and intolerable affront, reasonless and out of taste.

Unlike the murder of Lincoln, it has none of the dignity of the death-for-cause. The element of fitness, of proportion, the artistic element—all this is absent. The man's life and his death have nothing to say to one another. He might as well have died of the kick of a mule, or fallen down a cellar stair and broken his neck. This is not an event; there is nothing in it: a death without a cause and without an effect. Sorrow is sunk in disgust, and submission is not resignation; grin and bear it is the word. "The will of God," quotha'. O, go to the devil with your blasphemous platitude! It was the will of a blockhead.

Fancy God conspiring with Charley Guiteau—his accomplice! If so, He must likewise have had a "stand-in" with him to bilk landladies—must have stood by to see fair play when the fellow was beating his wife. Who are the hardiest blasphemers in the world? Always the Will-of-Godites. If God is a gentleman He had nothing to do with it.

Grant would have the Guiteau person hanged. The presidential nigger coachman wants to quarter him by stress of divergent horses. One of the most eminent barkeepers of this country cherishes a hope that he may be skinned alive. What! avenge a crime like *this* upon a man like *that!* Ought the sovereign commonwealth of Illinois to have pounded Mrs. O'Leary's cow? Nonsense! let the creature go. Give him a chew of tobacco or a consulship, and tell him to clear out. When one is snake-bitten unto death one does not bite back. [13]

I should like to know what purpose is furthered by the downright lying of our daily newspapers about the way in which the public was affected by the news of the President's death. What public interest did it serve, whose private pocket did it fill, to talk of strong men weeping in the streets; of women fainting with emotion; of vast crowds, pale with grief, discussing the sad event under their breath; of prominent politicians shocked into speechless silence by the tidings of the interviewer, who considerately waited for them to recover? Every man gifted with eyes and the faculty of observation knows there was nothing of all this, and could have been nothing. It is not even picturesque lying. It is open and forthright vilification.

If the human heart and head were constituted as these sugar-hearted sentimentalists would have us believe they are, life would be insupportable. If a general grief had the same crushing and unmanning intensity as a private bereavement we should all hasten to let out our bowels of compassion by hari-kari. As things are more wisely ordered, life is not altogether insufferable, and might even be enjoyable were it not for the exasperating bosh of the reporters calumniating human nature as hard as ever they can.

The Tuesday morning dispatches from the various interior towns, telling how the news was received, are examples of that intolerable "gush" that has made the American press a reproach and a by-word abroad. We were told that one town was "plunged in the deepest gloom;" another "reeled and staggered under the shock;" another was "shrouded in sorrow;" at another "a feeling of despondency pervaded all classes of the community;" at another the inhabitants were "stupefied with a sense of bereavement;" and so on, *ad nauseam*. The value of these telegrams is apparent when we reflect that in nearly all the interior towns the news was received after all the inhabitants were in bed, and its effect described in San Francisco before any of them were up.

I should like to say something, too, about the execrable style of the resolutions passed by various public bodies, notably by our Board of Supervisors; the turgid "fine writing" that burdened the wires in such dispatches as that which described the "moans of the restless ocean mingling with the sobs of the loved ones;" and, generally, the unutterable "stuff" whereby it was sought to show that the American people had offered up their common sense as a propitiatory sacrifice to the chastening gods; but I blush blind for my countrymen when I recall these evidences of their detestable taste.

Much is forgiven to a genuine sorrow; one does not criticize the incoherent extravagances of a broken heart above a coffin. But when men of sordid life and callous mind deliberately "pose" before the public, counterfeiting a degree of grief which they do not feel, by selecting the strongest terms in the vocabulary of woe and throwing them haphazardwise together to produce a kind of "general effect;" when, with one eye on our pocket and the other full of crocodile tears, they play disagreeable pranks of tongue and execute prodigious feats of pen, I submit that they are cheating, and the sable drapery of the stage upon which they perform shall not shield them from exposure. There is not an inch of sincerity in an ell of their abominable declamation. I hate them with a horrible antipathy. [14]

It is natural that the *Bulletin* writer who praises the effigy of Lincoln at the Lincoln School should find something to say in favor of the effigy of Garfield in the Golden Gate Park. He says it "recalls Garfield as he was, and that is the main point to be gained." I beg his pardon: that is *not* the main point; it is not a point at all. On the contrary, it is something to be avoided. The "main point" in all art is to give a noble and refined pleasure; the secondary point in a statue or portrait is to recall the person represented, not as he was, but as he was not—not with all the faults that he had, but with all the virtues and excellences with which the people's generous imagination has endowed him; and if it has endowed him with none, depend upon it, he is not worthy of a statue. Perfection in nature has not begun to exist, but art aims at perfection of effect. It tries to represent, not things, but conceptions. The popular conception of Garfield when this statue was begun was that he was a god.

He was not a god. He was not in any sense a great man. He surprised the country by the manner of his death and confused its judgment. It mistook the renown of his death for the nobleness of his life. Strong natures not affectible by the contagion of sudden, violent and evanescent public emotions, noted without comment the midsummer madness whose abatement they now remark without surprise. They know that our country's annual output of immortal names does not depend upon the death-rate in high place. They know that most of to-day's memorials will decorate to-morrow's rubbish-dump, and that those which will remain standing will be saved only by their intrinsic excellence as works of art. Let the worthy people whose minds and hearts are accessible to the sudden fervors of their environment, and who always when hot are promptly struck by the thrifty solicitor, look to it that no statue erected with their money shall too distinctly recall the man "in his habit as he lived;"[5] for assuredly if it do, posterity will serve it with a writ of *quo warranto,* on the ground that it does not resemble him; that is, if he happen to have been a really great man; for posterity will idealize his face till his own mother would not know him. If he was not really a great man (and the chances will be ten to one that he was not) his ugly image will find itself "broke o' the nose and cobwebbed all across," without inquiry. [15]

The Death of General Grant

[The death of Ulysses S. Grant on July 23, 1885, not only inspired
Bierce's noble poem "The Death of Grant" (*Wasp*, Aug. 1, 1885)
but also the following passages, in which Bierce's recollections of
his Civil War experiences come into play.]

There are signs that the brainless *claque* of *laudatores hominum* who have been
proning their unwholesome carcasses to slaver the dead feet of grand old Grant,
and doing their little best to affect all healthy souls with a wasting indisposition
of his name and fame, have had their day. Already the brazen serpent of truth
has been elevated (somewhat hesitatingly) in the midst of the multitude, and
many a sufferer, doubtless, lifting to its luster the despairing regard of a great disgust has felt the reptilian errors relax their constriction and fall away from his
understanding like cut cords. In the current number of the *Century* magazine
General James H. Wilson, a splendid soldier with a gentleman's head on his neck
and a gentleman's eyes in his head, ("the better to see with, my dear") has a paper of reminiscences of Grant, conceived in a spirit of honest and sane admiration.[16] General Wilson, however, points out what every man having knowledge
of the matter and brains to digest the knowledge with has all along known:
namely, that the great strategist was a poor tactician—which is to say that he did
not skillfully move his troops in actual battle. Doubtless General Wilson, for his
temerity, will have the entire pack of hero-worshipers yappeting and snatching
at his heels—the superpatriotic person, "hell-bent" (as Carlyle would say) on
having an American Napoleon but imperfectly informed as to the Corsican Napoleon; the simple soul with an iron faith that "the hour brings the man"; the
chap from Galena, who "knew him personally, sir"; the self-made man who is
proud of him as "a man of the people"; the moral monster for whom the truth as
an ingredient of history isn't good enough and the unclassible savage whose raw
sympathies and unsalted sentiments reek an audible incense round every kind of
distinction, mistaking it all for perfection of character and a flawless life. This
rabble, destitute alike of discernment and moderation, in whose mental perspec-
tive the fame which is nearest looks biggest, would be very unhappy if it could
return to earth some centuries hence and entering its Pantheon behold the ravages of time and truth.

It is pleasant, too, to know from General Wilson that Grant cherished personal resentments and "lay for" his private enemies till he got opportunity to pay
them off; and that Lincoln, had he not been assured immediately after the fall of
Vicksburg that Grant did not aspire to the Presidency,[17] was none too good to
have broken the back of him. Really the unnatural and impulsive whitewash of
these grand figures in our history begins to be tenderly tempered with a suffu-
sion of warm rosy light. In an age of manlier thought and freer judgment, it may

happen that they will escape the awful fate of Washington—that able person of amusing infirmities and surprising vices, who, as paragoned by sycophantic historians and biographers, affects the world, which otherwise might have loved him, with sentiments of reverence and aversion.

What a miserable business it is, this deification of the eminent. And to what a measureless length it is urged. Not a famous character but it has distorted out of all semblance to nature. The sycophants have added terrors to renown; their hateful existence bars the way to public service. The animosities, intrigues, envy, obloquy and falsehoods alurk along the paths of renown like rattlesnakes infesting a mountain trail may be lightly and gayly encountered; none but the maddest ambitionist, the hardiest philanthroper or the most insensible blockhead will incur public admiration and surrender himself naked to his eulogists. I would rather be a dead dog among buzzards than a dead hero among admirers. [16]

Americans Abroad

[Americans' sycophancy to European nobility when they went abroad is the subject of the following passage, which draws upon Bierce's own experiences in England.]

Mr. Pierre Lorillard owns a fast horse which won a race in England. Mr. Lorillard's wife is the sister of Mr. Stuart M. Taylor, of this city, now in England. These facts are deemed here to constitute a sufficient foundation for a steadfast faith in the accuracy of certain tales that seem to have drifted rudderless across the water—namely, that Mr. Taylor is the object of overwhelming attentions from English royalty and English nobility. If Mr. Taylor's friends think that by representing him in the attitude of a successful claimant to social honors because his brother-in-law owns a fast horse, they are doing him an acceptable service I suppose that compensates for the discredit they cast upon English hospitality. But Mr. Stuart is a gentleman, and I do not believe he would make that kind of claim to "horsepitality."

I don't know, though. It requires a pretty robust mental constitution in the American abroad to resist the infection of the midsummer madness that impels the patient to associate, or be thought to associate, with the tottering despots and bloated aristocrats of the Old World. Nine in ten of our countrymen in Europe spend one-half their time in trying to edge in amongst the royal and noble oppressors for whom they affected so lively a detestation on this side of the water, and the other half in putting their success on record in the home newspapers. I think I could create a good deal of local discomfort by recounting some instances of this detestable lion-hunting that came under my personal observation a few years ago; but I am not ungrateful, and I must confess that those who would be most pained by the disclosures have generously refrained from visiting upon my obscure head the contempt justly due to my own lamentable failures in the same competition.

During some years' residence in Europe I never dined with a prince or princess, and never enrolled any noblemen on the list of my personal friends; but it shall always be my proudest boast that I enjoyed on tolerably equal terms the companionship of many of my countrymen who habitually did, as I know from their own lips, and who yet were not too proud to speak to me—on that subject. Even so distinguished a compatriot as Steve Massett did not disdain to relate to me with considerable particularity the overtures made for his favor by the Prince of Wales and the Archbishop of Canterbury.

Mr. Massett had a pair of miniature boots which he slipped upon two fingers of his hand, and by covering the rest of the hand with a handkerchief, arranged as a skirt, and making the boots dance, he achieved a very creditable performance. "That interested Mr. Gladstone immensely," said Stephen.

In the blind and brutal scramble for social recognition in Europe the traveling American toady and impostor has many chances of success: he is commonly utterly unknown, even to ministers and consuls of his own country, and these complaisant gentlemen, rather than err on the wrong side, take him at his own valuation and push him in where, his obesity being again in his favor, he is treated with a friendly toleration and sometimes a genuine hospitality to which he has no shadow of right or title, and which, if he were a gentleman, he would not accept if it were voluntarily proffered. In relating his success he is naively unaware that he is uttering his own severest condemnation, and that it would be charitable to disbelieve him; for a lying boaster is, after all, a better man than a social impostor whose best credentials are the midnight obscurity of his name and the brazen effrontery of his methods. [17]

Soldiers and Civilians

> [Bierce's years as a soldier lent him a strong sense of the distinc-
> tion between soldiers and civilians, and he constantly rose to the
> defense of the army and its members against attacks from the press
> or from what he felt were pretenders like the state militia.]

The ravaging Apache is yearning for the tresses of the New-Mexican prospector, and his raucous war-whoop disturbs the deep serene of the San Francisco editor. For that worthy's ears have reached a rumor of the strife. Wherefore he loads his pen with a double charge of dark damnation and fires it at the officers and men of the United States Army. He has seen the regulars and militia parading the peaceful street in sections and platoons, and, with a mental grasp upon the weak points of the situation like the embrace of a starfish consuming a baby oyster, he infers that that is the way that soldiers fight the painted brave. But how the devil did he learn that it is not a good way?

It has not penetrated into the poor editorial brainbox that the officers of the Army, stationed for years on the troubled frontier, with no business but to study by practice the best methods of harrying the redskins, will naturally know better how to disconcert those sportsmen than he who in session on a stool fights fleas by the dim religious light of a dusty sanctum window. The notion that they don't march against them in solid column, with banners flung to the breeze, a brass band braying patriotic airs and a measureless extension of red wagons would unhorse his understanding from its hobby, as Saul was fired out of his saddle by the blinding beam of revelation.[18] The terrible censor of the newspaper office is, in short, a tolerably constant, consistent and indurated fool.

His folly is the bastard whelpage of that lying tradition which ascribes to the swashbuckler "frontiersman" and the vaporing "settler" a military prowess superior to that of a sheep. The red-shirted and war-weaponed "bad man" of the barrooms, with his fables of personal encounter and his mighty oaths; the claim-salting prospector, with long locks and a shot gun; the squaws-courting granger of the valley, and the whiskey-sodden horse-thief of the mountain—these are the material that the editor would fight Indians with. In publications of that eminent instructor, Mr. Beadle,[19] they are represented as good material. They are themselves of that opinion—tacitly when sober, vociferously when drunk. Fight nothing! There isn't one in a hundred of the disreputable rout of outlaws and vulgarians by whom our mining countries are settled that has the military virtues of a jackass rabbit. They will fight when it is fight or die; and then the angels in heaven surround the Throne and pray that it may be die anyhow.

Nobody fights Indians so intelligently, courageously and effectively as the United States soldier commanded by the United States officer; nobody so reluctantly, awkwardly and without result as the local "settler," under whatever name. It's hey, the blowsy braggart that he is! O, the insupportable preposterousness of his pretensions—O, the prodigious triviality of his performance! I have marked his terror-stricken hordes throng tumultuous into the forts before the delusive whoops of a dozen larking braves. I have observed his burly carcass scuttling to the rear of the soldiers he defames, and kicked back into position by the officers he insults. I have seen his scruffy scalp lifted by the hands of squaws, the while he pleaded for his worthless life, his undischarged weapon fallen from his trembling hand. And I have always coveted the privilege of a shot at him myself. Away with him to the headsman's block! [18]

Some gutter-blooded barbarian, whose acquaintance with military affairs probably consists in drawing a pension for injuries received during the late war in scampering across the Canadian border to escape the draft, is writing in the *Chronicle* in advocacy of closing that "nursery of favorites", the military academy at West Point. This dreg would also have the army officered by promotion from the ranks, and in various other ways give the private soldier "as fair a show" (by which the *residuum* means chance) "as the pampered officer." The hero of Cold Harbor, iconoclast of the Column Vendôme and formidable ally of the "gates of Hell" is also flinging his heels in the direction of West Point.[20] It is probably useless to point out to the dreg, as it has been already explained to the other person, that the life of an army officer commonly is, and always is likely to be, one of exceptional labor, self-denial and responsibility; that his services are more niggardly requited than those of the brainless hired man who does commercial desk-work; that military competency cannot be acquired in the ranks, a promoted private being almost invariably an inefficient officer; that all the successful commanders of armies in the civil war were graduates of the military academy at West Point, their abilities asserting themselves despite the most disheartening administrative discrimination and an ugly popular prejudice which the soiled and stagnant understandings of these scribbling twin relics do but dimly and imperfectly reflect. [19]

The Odious Mr. Wilde

[When Oscar Wilde's American tour of 1882 wound its way to San Francisco (he arrived on March 26 and remained in the area until April 8), it found in Bierce a violent opponent of the British dandy.]

That sovereign of insufferables, Oscar Wilde, has ensued with his opulence of twaddle and his penury of sense. He has mounted his hind legs and blown crass vapidities through the bowel of his neck, to the capital edification of circumjacent fools and foolesses, fooling with their foolers. He has tossed off the top of his head and uttered himself in copious overflows of ghastly bosh. The ineffable dunce has nothing to say and says it—says it with a liberal embellishment of bad delivery, embroidering it with reasonless vulgarities of attitude, gesture and attire. There was never an impostor so hateful, a blockhead so stupid, a crank so variously and offensively daft. Therefore is the she fool enamored of the feel of his tongue in her ear to tickle her understanding.

The limpid and spiritless vacuity of this intellectual jelly-fish is in ludicrous contrast with the rude but robust mental activities that he came to quicken and inspire. Not only has he no thoughts, but no thinker. His lecture is mere verbal ditch-water—meaningless, trite and without coherence. It lacks even the nastiness that exalts and refines his verse. Moreover, it is obviously his own; he had not even the energy and independence to steal it. And so, with a knowledge that would equip an idiot to dispute with a cast-iron dog, an eloquence to qualify him for the duties of caller on a hog-ranche, and an imagination adequate to the conception of a tom-cat, when fired by contemplation of a fiddle-string, this consummate and star-like youth, missing everywhere his heaven-appointed functions and offices, wanders about, posing as a statue of himself, and, like the sun-smitten image of Memnon, emitting meaningless murmurs in the blaze of women's eyes.[21] He makes me tired.

And this gawky gowk has the divine effrontery to link his name with those of Swinburne, Rossetti and Morris—this dunghill he-hen would fly with eagles. He dares to set his tongue to the honored name of Keats. He is the leader, quoth'a, of a *renaissance* in art, this man who cannot draw—of a revival in letters, this man who cannot write! This littlest and looniest of a brotherhood of simpletons, whom the wicked wits of London, haling him dazed from his obscurity, have crowned and crucified as King of the Cranks, has accepted the distinction in stupid good faith, and our foolish people take him at his word. Mr. Wilde is pinnacled upon a dazzling eminence but the earth still trembles to the dull thunder of the kicks that set him up. [20]

To the many aggrieved correspondents and the few lachrymose personal friends who have done me the honor to protest against my ungentle—or as some of them prefer to say, ungentlemanly—rhapsody on Oscar Wilde, and who have made the novel suggestion that abuse is not criticism, I beg to make answer thus: 1. This is not a journal of criticism. 2. In Mr. Wilde's lectures there is nothing to criticise, for there is nothing of his own. Every person familiar with the current literature of the last decade has read and re-read every one of his utterances a score of times; they are the current coin of the "decorative art" realm. The value of the mintage is not in question here, though I may remark that for some years we all rejected it with derision when offered by that famous æsthete, Dickens's Mr. Gradgrind.[22] The man who finds anything unfamiliar in Wilde's remarks may justly boast himself the possessor of a singularly superior quality of literary ignorance.

Of Mr. Wilde as a poet I did not write, and only do so now to assure those who think him a poet that I think him a joke. I am not myself a poet, but with some critical knowledge acquired by loving study of the laws and limitations of the poet's noble art (and without such study even the brightest natural intelligence can no more know what is poetry than without study it can know what is law) I affirm that Mr. Wilde's performances in that field have given him no right to be taken seriously. When he shall have written one considerable poem, original in conception and undebased by incredibly ludicrous faults of taste and sentiment, I shall consent gravely to prove that—it is not.

But Longfellow praised his verses, exclaim his worshippers.[23] In which of the works of this greatest of Americans is the judgment recorded, my good friends? It is perhaps to be found in the newspapers, or in a private letter. That is a different matter. The good-natured old man had in his later years a habit of praising every nincompoop—in letters. This he could do without risk, for, although the letter might descend to posterity, the nincompoop's work would certainly not. I have myself been shown by the tickled recipients a number of these letters, written in civil acknowledgment of books of verse, which I will swear he neither did nor could read. Moreover, I am not aware that this noble poet was ever held in very high esteem as a critic, except by those whom he loosely complimented, and by their following of delighted relatives and thoughtless friends.

Let us admit that Mr. Wilde's eccentricities in hair and innovations in attire are not in themselves displeasing. It remains true and cogent against him that men of brains do not deem it worth while to differ from their fellow men in these particulars, but only in point of superior mental or moral excellence. They do not compete for honors easily won by clowns and cranks. It follows that Mr. Wilde is not a man of brains; why should I concern myself with his work? I have read it and been unpleasantly affected by it. That is enough.

But, say his friends, there must be something in him, to arrest attention as he does. What kind of attention? Two nations have agreed to laugh at him, as they did at Sergeant Bates. Does that constitute a claim to patient consideration and serious refutation? Is there something in Guiteau? he has arrested more attention than Wilde. Cut from the scrap book of Wilde's fame all the pages of dispraise, and you have remaining—the covers, and a profound, searching, painstaking and exhaustive analysis of his work by that conscientious critic, Professor Ned Townsend, of the *Morning Call*.

One indignant lady assures me that Mr. Wilde's personal character is altogether irreproachable. That may be true, madam, but it is what I never take the liberty to say of man or woman; I have been too often and too rudely reminded that the public press has nothing to do with private character. I have learned my lesson: no opportunity shall tempt, no taunt shall provoke, no threat shall compel me to say that anybody's personal character is good, anybody's private life blameless, anybody's domestic relations clean and respectable.

After all, this disagreeable impostor has very little reason to complain. If he has failed to impress the understandings of American gentlemen, he has profoundly stirred the bosoms of American women and such eminent Irish patriots as Messrs. Bryant, Geary Buckley, Sullivan, Perry, Phelan and Paul Neumann, who implored him to deliver that lecture on the Poetry of Ireland. Mr. Neumann, it is understood, was in earnest worse than a hornet in this matter. Attired in green breeches and silk stockings clocked with shamrocks, topped with a sunflowery caubeen and twirling a she-lily, he called on Mr. Wilde, saying, "Arrah, now, me shtarlike gossoon, phwat is it you'd be at wid yer gammon of dadoes and fraizes? Give us a spaich on the bards of ould Erin, me broth of a b'y, or bedad—" Here Mr. Neumann's emotions overcame him, and delivering a sounding thwack upon the æsthetic head, he danced a barn-door jig upon the door-mat and retired, singing "The harp that once in Tara's halls." [21]

Dog!

[Ambrose Bierce is one of history's great dog haters. Those who admire "man's best friend" had best skip this section.]

I have been attentively considering a dog. He is looking in the sun on the sidewalk opposite, and is doubtless overdone, for he is the undisturbed incumbent of his bakery every sunny day. Pedestrians thoughtfully veer to the right or left lest they disturb him. He separates man and wife and breaks up families. He is fat and well-liking, comfortable, prosperous and without care. Yet he toils not, neither does he spin. The gifted owner of a superior bite, he will neither suppress the contiguous auctioneer nor allay the adjacent organ-winder. His life is without a purpose and without a plan. He a brother to the sunshine and a child of light—the holiest drone in all the hive of Nature. I should not like to be exactly that kind of dog.

And yet I do not know why the Dog should not proudly regard himself as "the roof and crown of things,"[24] the master work and ultimate excellence of creation. If Man thinks himself justified in accounting himself the highest type of animated nature and the peculiar care of God, with how much greater reason may Dog indulge the same pleasing fancy! Not one in a hundred of his race works for board and lodging; all are provided for by their intelligent handservant, Man—a little more intelligent than themselves, as having greater need, in order the more skillfully to administer to the canine wants. Precisely as it is unnecessary for Man to be able to pull a loaded wagon, having a horse to pull it instead, so intelligence is needless in the Dog, having Man to do his thinking. The only necessary quality in a dog's outfit is a measureless, immatchable and divine capacity for enjoyment. And this every mother's son of them takes good care to be born with.

It must seem to the Dog that the substances, methods and functions of nature are arranged with special reference to his needs, his capacities, his future. He can hardly help thinking himself gifted with peculiar advantages and inheriting the earth. Yet the rascal is an anachronism who exhausted his mandate ages and ages ago, and now lags superfluous on the stage. He is a "survival" who since the dawn of civilization has had no function and no meaning. Our love for him we have inherited along with many other instincts transmitted from our savage past. If there had never been a dog and one were created, we should fall foul of him with hard substances and a clamor of tongues. He would seem uglier than a reporter, and more hateful than a poet.

If the Dog regards himself as the peculiar care of God, it would seem to follow that he has formed some noble and exalted perceptions of so meritorious, so benevolent a Personage. Doubtless he pictures Him as somewhat resembling a dog. [22]

If I were dictator there would be no more dog shows, for there would be no more dogs. In the first few weeks of my reign the price of sausage would tumble to ten cents a yard on account of the abundance of raw material supplied by law. Of all anachronisms and survivals, the love of the dog is the most reasonless. Because, some thousands of years ago, when we wore other skins than our own and sat enthroned upon our haunches, tearing tangles of tendons from raw bones with our teeth, the dog ministered purveyorwise to our savage needs, we go on cherishing him to this day, when his only function is to lie sun-soaken on a door mat and insult us as we pass in and out, enamored of his fat superfluity. One dog in a thousand earns his bread—and takes beef-steak; the other nine hundred and ninety-nine we cheat the poor to maintain in the style suitable to their state. If ever there is a new and improved God His gospel will contain this passage: "Whoso giveth to a dog, from him shall be taken more than that which he giveth; yes, he shall lose his grip upon eternal life."

The dog is an encampment of fleas and a reservoir of sinful smells. He is prone to bad manners as the sparks fly upward. He has no discrimination; his loyalty is given to the person that feeds him, be the same a blackguard or a murderer's mother. He fights for his master without regard to the justice of the quarrel—wherein he is no better than a patriot or a paid soldier. There are men who are proud of a dog's love—and dogs love that kind of men. There are men who, having the privilege of loving women, insult them by loving dogs; and there are women who forgive and respect their canine rivals. There are dogs that submit to be kissed by women base enough to kiss them; but they have a secret, coarse revenge, sweeter than that of the waiter who spits in the soup. For the dog is a joker, withal, gifted with as much humor as is consistent with biting. [23]

The dog-worshipers are carrying their piety into literature: in the current number of *Harper's Magazine* one of them, named Hugh Dalziel, expounds his horrible religion through a dozen pages, with pictures representing a whole Olympus of his hideous gods.[25] He is frank with his flame—he loves dogs and doesn't care who knows it. The baseness of his taste is as refreshing to his soul as mud to a midsummer pig: he lies down and wallows in it. Before the shrine of his devotion this high priest of caniolatry performs postulations and genuflexions of so ignoble servility that a bunion-rumped baboon would blush blue to be seen executing them before the Ruler of the Universe. He begins the rites with an exposition of the "mutual liking" between Man and Dog, "which rests on the solid foundation of mutual interest," and shows how, through personal companionship, it "grows into something higher—into sentiments of esteem, involving on both sides sacrifices which strengthens the bond of union." As a reporter would say: The feeling ripened into a warmer attachment, which was consummated at the hymeneal altar, eventuating in the holy bonds of wedlock.

Mr. Dalziel's cyophile propensity inheres in his nature; it is not born of any such selfish consideration as "mutual interest" or even mutual esteem: he says we are "indebted" to the beast, not only for the good he does, but "even as the mere object upon which to lavish an exuberance of affection." Why, here's a person with more love than he knows what to do with; more than the New Testament enjoins; more than is good for his spiritual health. He is heaving and groaning with it: it rises in his throat till he can taste it, and sputters and sizzles in his pores like steam escaping from an ill-riveted boiler with a fat man on the safety-valve. If the suffering wretch must soil something with the slimes and oozes of his drop-sical heart why does he not experiment cautiously with his wife and children? If he has none, why not cultivate a taste for the wife and children of his neighbor? Nay, what is the matter with God?

This person's awful condition is neither here nor there—thank Heaven, it is at least not here—but in order fitly to set forth by warning example the extrava-gance and depravity begotten of the dog-habit I must crave leave to quote him further:

> "If I could persuade those who have a nervous dread of dogs to get a puppy and bring it up and educate it to good habits and proper behavior they would lose all fear of dogs in general, and find in their pet and scholar a rich return for the investment of that affection and sympathy with animal life, as a part of nature, which grows with exercise, and is its own reward."

Bones of Cæsar! a puppy—not a child, but an inchoate dog—a clammy-nosed, swell-fronted, Dutch-built, double-charged, flea-peopled, immodest epitome of all nastiness—whelp of a thousand infragrant sires, and itself smell-ing aloud! Reader, if you think, with the Dalziel person, that the care and com-panionship of an unripe dog would soften and humanize your nature and bring a holy peace into your soul, why—well, I think it would, too. But when the beast grows up don't forget which is the dog.

I have reserved the best of Mr. Dalziel's pious remarks to the last. He says he is earnestly desirous to inculcate by repetition and emphasis this lesson:

> "The man who makes a dog his own undertakes duties and responsibilities which he cannot discharge himself from except by performance, and that can only be done by intelligent study of the animal's nature and require-ments, and the adjustment of his [the man's] conduct to these."

This theory of man's duty to Dog—this conception of Dog as the controlling factor in human conduct—seems at first thought pretty radical, but I don't know. It goes far, certainly, but most of the people with whose dogs I have the honor to be acquainted are, I think, prepared to follow. If any man see madness in the proposition that he ought to live up to his dog and square his life to that creature's nature and requirements, it is to be feared that he has associated with only the lowest and basest curs. [24]

Belated Memories of the *Wasp*

[A few years after he left the magazine and was comfortably en-
sconced with the *San Francisco Examiner,* Bierce took the time to
reflect upon his years with the *Wasp.*]

I observe that Colonel Jackson has sold the *Wasp* and taken himself out of it. The gallant Colonel is marching upon the Custom-house, and expecting a pretty hard campaign, wisely disembarrasses himself of his *impedimenta.* The paper, I am told, was purchased by Messrs. Waldron and Dwyer, who have been connected with it for many years, and ought to be able to take it out of the gutter where it has been wallowing and floundering during the Jackson regime, unmarked of man. If Jackson were put in charge of the Book of Doom he would bring it into such public contempt that not an immortal soul would care to know if its own name were in it.

Apropos of the *Wasp,* I note a trifling error in last Sunday's EXAMINER. In an article on "Harry Dam in London" it is related that a few years ago, while Mr. Dam was still graciously shedding the light of his early genius upon this unworthy State, two of his friends "bought the *Wasp* for $5,000 and gave Harry the management of the paper." As I was the editor of the paper during the entire period of Mr. Dam's slight and brief connection with it, I can speak on this matter with a fair degree of knowledge. The paper was bought (from Korbell Bros.) with the money of Mr. Charles Webb Howard of the Spring Valley Water Company. The purchase was made in the names of Messrs. E. C. Macfarlane and Harry Dam, but very shortly afterward it was thought expedient that Mr. Dam's connection with the paper in the fictional character of proprietor should cease, and he was accordingly bought out. That is not quite accurate—he was bought off. He continued to write for it whenever we could find a chain strong enough to hold him to his desk, but he never at any time managed it nor had any kind or degree of editorial control. As an editor of weekly papers I have had in my time many valueless contributors, but in all the essential elements and measureless resources of unworth Harry Dam was a crowned king.

During Dam's incumbency of the throne of unusefulness occurred the Gubernatorial contest between Mr. Estee and General Stoneman.[26] The paper threw the awful weight of its influence in favor of Estee and Reform, but at the same time treated the cause of Stoneman and Reform with gentlemanly civility and fairness. On many occasions it warmly defended Stoneman's personal character and military record against the rancorous attacks of mean-spirited partisans, chief of whom was Colonel Jackson. Strange to say, despite our local opposition, Stoneman was elected. Soon after, to everybody's astonishment and our immedicable woe, he removed Dam from among us by appointing him, a white-hot Republican, to the position of Executive Secretary. I have been told—Heaven forgive us, reader, for listening if it is not true—that the appointment was procured by submitting to Stoneman a scrap-book containing all the articles which we had so generously published in his defense—articles, by the way, of which Dam had not written one line nor one word. His enterprise and thrift are related here as an example to American youth.

I afterward "soured" on Stoneman and filled the paper with abuse of him in prose and verse for his wholesale and indiscriminate pardoning of convicted felons. Such a godless lot of professional criminals as he turned loose from the penitentiary never before received "Executive clemency." Dam no doubt keenly felt this severity to his chief, but he did not say much. It was he who did it all. The stupid Governor charged with him the duty of reporting on all applications for pardons: he set up a brokerage and "Executive clemency" remained a purchasable commodity during his entire term of service. Years later, when he was in New York, the EXAMINER exposed him, and that is why last Sunday's article was headed "Harry Dam in *London*." The article mentions with commendation Mr. Dam's paper on prison management in the *North American Review*.[27] I concur in the praise: it was a good paper, although the subject has been exhaustively treated in the San Francisco *Bulletin* by Mr. William M. Neilson, *alias* McCann. Black Bart has not yet, I think, uttered his mind about it.[28]

While in the reminiscent mood I cannot forbear to state that Mr. Charles Webb Howard remained the owner of the *Wasp* for a long time. During the whole period an important part of its revenue was derived from advertisements (at good round rates) of the Spring Valley Water Company. They did not seem to be advertisements, but their publication must have put a very handsome sum into Mr. Howard's pocket. I violate no professional obligation in relating this, for I was kept in dead ignorance of Mr. Howard's ownership: it was rightly surmised that I would not work for him if I knew it. The way it "came out" is this. The Water Company had one of its customary quarrels with the people and threatened to shut off the water from the entire city. I told Mr. Macfarlane that I was going to take the side of the people. Then there was consternation, followed by persuasion. I was "labored with" worse than a sinner at a camp-meeting. As a last resort I was apprised of the true state of affairs. Angered by the deception so long practiced upon me, I was more obstinate than ever; and now when I remember the lofty scorn with which I met every overture of my employer I am filled with admiration and convinced afresh that I was born to be Rear-Admiral of a trades union. I straightway rewrote the article that I intended to publish, augmenting its asperity in every sentence.[29] I published it, too; but in the mean time Mr. Macfarlane had skirmished round and bought the paper—which never thereafter could count upon the Water Company as a source of unholy gains. Whether the company got back any of the money paid by President Howard to Journalist Howard I never learned, but suppose not. It was probably charged to the excessive use account.

Another amusing complication of this odd little comedy is seen in the fact that while Mr. Howard's paper was fighting the Railroad Company like a mad cat that concern and the Water Company were, speaking with literal accuracy, "as thick as two thieves." In the habitations of the hill-dwellers at the top of California street, where Mr. Howard's wicked editor was regarded with austere disesteem as a blackmailer, Mr. Howard himself was ever warmly welcome as a friend and ally; and (in justice let it be said) he sternly refrained from pocketing anything of value. His notions of hospitality permitted him to accept that of the men whom its paper was denouncing, and justly denouncing, as rogues and vulgarians, but he drew the line at silver spoons and remained a good man.

I hope the reader will pardon this camp-fire garrulity of a newspaper private who has seen service in two worlds. When I publish my great work, *The Confessions of an Impenitent Scribbler* (W. R. Hearst & Co., San Francisco), the narrative, I promise, shall be more coherent, and following Thackeray's advice I shall "promote my characters." They shall be all gentlemen of the spotless morals, scholars of golden attainments, *littérateurs* of wide and lurid fame beaconing the universe. Then for the first time shall the great Mr. De Young be word-painted as he is, the illustrious Mr. Pickering as he was, the pious Deacon Fitch[30] as he thinks himself to be and the gifted Mr. Pixley as, Devil helping him, he hopes to become. In that imperishable work posterity will find a monument to the virtues, and an enchanting record of the life, of every eminent journalist of this our heroic age who in passing through Mammon's dark domain leaves behind him a trail of light like the track of a wet match on a wall. If I do not affuse the memory of Dr. Bartlett[31] with the golden glow of a deathless fame it will be because the magic of my pen is inhibited by the magic of his own. [25]

(1 8 8 7 – 1 9 0 5)

The *Examiner* Years

A Thumb-Nail Sketch

["A Thumb-Nail Sketch," Bierce's alternately
tart and affectionate memoir of William
Randolph Hearst and his years of working for
Hearst's newspapers, appeared in Bierce's *Collected Works,* volume 12 (1912). In it Bierce
attempts to explain how he could work for
nearly twenty years on papers "with whose
policies I was not in agreement and whose
character I loathed."]

Many years ago I lived in Oakland, California. One day as I
lounged in my lodging there was a gentle, hesitating rap at
the door and, opening it, I found a young man, the youngest
young man, it seemed to me, that I had ever confronted. His
appearance, his attitude, his manner, his entire personality
suggested extreme indifference. I did not ask him in, instate
him in my better chair (I had two) and inquire how we could
serve each other. If my memory is not at fault I merely said:
"Well," and awaited the result.

"I am from the San Francisco *Examiner,*" he explained in
a voice like the fragrance of violets made audible, and backed
a little away.

"O," I said, "you come from Mr. Hearst."

Then that unearthly child lifted its blue eyes and cooed: "I am Mr. Hearst."

His father had given him a daily newspaper and he had come to hire me to write for it. Twenty years of what his newspapers call "wage slavery" ensued, and although I had many a fight with his editors for my right to my self-respect, I cannot say that I ever found Mr. Hearst's chain a very heavy burden, though indubitably I suffered somewhat in social repute for wearing it.

If ever two men were born to be enemies he and I are they. Each stands for everything that is most disagreeable to the other, yet we never clashed. I never had the honor of his friendship and confidence, never was "employed about his person," and seldom entered the editorial offices of his newspapers. He did not once direct nor request me to write an opinion that I did not hold, and only two or three times suggested that I refrain for a season from expressing opinions that I did hold, when they were antagonistic to the policy of the paper, as they commonly were. During several weeks of a great labor strike in California, when mobs of ruffians stopped all railway trains, held the state capital and burned, plundered and murdered at will, he "laid me off,"[1] continuing, of course, my salary; and some years later, when striking employees of street railways were devastating St. Louis,[2] pursuing women through the street and stripping them naked, he suggested that I "let up on that labor crowd." No other instances of "capitalistic arrogance" occur to memory. I do not know that any of his other writers enjoyed a similar liberty, or would have enjoyed it if they had had it. Most of them, indeed, seemed to think it honorable to write anything that they were expected to.

As to Mr. Hearst's own public writings, I fancy there are none: he could not write an advertisement for a lost dog. The articles that he signs and the speeches that he makes—well, if a man of brains is one who knows how to use the brains of others this amusing demagogue is nobody's dunce.

If asked to justify my long service to journals with whose policies I was not in agreement and whose character I loathed I should confess that possibly the easy nature of the service had something to do with it. As to the point of honor (as that is understood in the profession) the editors and managers always assured me that there was commercial profit in employing my rebellious pen; and I—O well, I persuaded myself that I could do most good by addressing those who had greatest need of me—the millions of readers to whom Mr. Hearst was a misleading light. Perhaps this was an erroneous view of the matter; anyhow I am not sorry that, discovering no preservative allowable under the pure food law that would enable him to keep his word overnight, I withdrew, and can now, without impropriety, speak my mind of him as freely as his generosity, sagacity or indifference once enabled me to do of his political and industrial doctrines, in his own papers.

In illustration of some of the better features of this man's strange and complex character let this incident suffice. Soon after the assassination of Governor Goebel of Kentucky[3]—which seemed to me a particularly perilous "precedent" if unpunished—I wrote for one of Mr. Hearst's New York newspapers the following prophetic lines:

> The bullet that pierced Goebel's breast
> Can not be found in all the West.
> Good reason: it is speeding here
> To stretch McKinley on the bier.[4]

The lines took no attention, naturally, but twenty months afterward the President was shot by Czolgosz.[5] Every one remembers what happened then to Mr. Hearst and his newspapers. His political enemies and business competitors were alert to their opportunity. The verses, variously garbled but mostly made into an editorial, or a news dispatch with a Washington date-line but usually no date, were published all over the country as evidence of Mr. Hearst's complicity in the crime. As such they adorned the editorial columns of the New York *Sun* and blazed upon a bill-board in front of Tammany Hall. So fierce was the popular flame to which they were the main fuel that thousands of copies of the Hearst papers were torn from the hands of newsboys and burned in the streets. Much of their advertising was withdrawn from them. Emissaries of the *Sun* overran the entire country persuading clubs, libraries and other patriot bodies to exclude them from the files. There was even an attempt made to induce Czolgosz to testify that he had been incited to his crime by reading them—ten thousand dollars for his family to be his reward; but this cheerful scheme was blocked by the trial judge, who had been informed of it. During all this carnival of sin I lay ill in Washington, unaware of it; and my name, although appended to all that I wrote, including the verses, was not, I am told, once mentioned. As to Mr. Hearst, I dare say he first saw the lines when all this hullabaloo directed his attention to them.

With the occurrences here related the incident was not exhausted. When Mr. Hearst was making his grotesque canvass for the Governorship of New York the Roosevelt Administration sent Secretary Root into the state to beat him.[6] This high-minded gentleman incorporated one of the garbled prose versions of my prophecy into his speeches with notable effect and great satisfaction to his conscience. Still, I am steadfast in the conviction that God sees him; and if any one thinks that Mr. Root will not go to the devil it must be the devil himself, in whom, doubtless, the wish is father to the thought.

Hearst's newspapers had always been so unjust that no injustice could be done to them, and had been incredibly rancorous toward McKinley, but no doubt it was my luckless prophecy that cost him tens of thousands of dollars and a growing political prestige. For anything that I know (or care) they may have cost him his election. I have never mentioned the matter to him, nor—and this is what I have been coming to—has he ever mentioned it to me. I fancy there must be a human side to a man like that, even if he is a mischievous demagogue.

In matters of "industrial discontent" it has always been a standing order in the editorial offices of the Hearst newspapers to "take the side of the strikers" without inquiry or delay. Until the great publicist was bitten by political ambition and began to figure as a crazy candidate for office not a word of warning or rebuke to murderous mobs ever appeared in any column of his papers except my own. A typical instance of the falsification of news to serve a foul purpose may be cited here. In Pennsylvania, a ferocious mob of foreign miners armed with bludgeons marched upon the property of their employers, to destroy it, incidentally chasing out of their houses all the English-speaking residents along the way and clubbing all that they could catch. Arriving at the "works," they were confronted by a squad of deputy marshals, and while engaged in murdering the sheriff, who had stepped forward to read the riot act, were fired on and a couple of dozen of them killed. Naturally the deputy marshals were put on trial for their lives. Mr. Hearst sent my good friend Julius Chambers to report the court proceedings. Day after day he reported at great length the testimony (translated) of the saints and angels who had suffered the mischance "while peacefully parading on a public road." Then Mr. Chambers was ordered away and not a word of testimony for the defense (all in English) ever appeared in the paper.[7] Instances of such fair-mindedness as this could be multiplied by the thousand, but all, I charitably trust, have been recorded Elsewhere in a more notable Book than mine.

Never just, Mr. Hearst is always generous. He is not swift to redress a grievance of one of his employees against another, but he is likely to give the complainant a cottage, a steam launch, or a roll of bank notes, if that person happens to be the kind of man to accept it, and he commonly is. As to discharging anybody for inefficiency or dishonesty—no, indeed, not so long as there is a higher place for him. His notion of removal is promotion.

He once really did dismiss a managing editor, but in a few months the fellow was back in his old place. I ventured to express surprise. "Oh, that's all right," Mr. Hearst explained. "I have a new understanding with him. He is to steal only small sums hereafter; the large ones are to come to me."

In that incident we observe two dominant features in his character—his indifference to money and his marvelous sense of humor. He who should apprehend danger to public property from Mr. Hearst's elevation to high office would err. The money to which he is indifferent includes that of others, and he smiles at his own expense.

If there is a capable working newspaper man in this country who has not, *malgre lui,* a kindly feeling for Mr. Hearst, he needs the light. I do not know how it is elsewhere, but in San Francisco and New York Mr. Hearst's habit of having the cleverest (not, alas, the most conscientious) obtainable men, no matter what he had to pay them, advanced the salaries of all such men more than fifty percent. Possibly these have receded, and possibly the high average ability of his men has receded too—I don't know; but indubitably he did get the brightest men.

Some of them, I grieve to say, were imperfectly appreciative of their employer's gentle sway. At one time on the *Examiner* it was customary, when a reporter had a disagreeable assignment, for him to go away for a few days, then return and plead intoxication. That excused him. They used to tell of one clever fellow in whose behalf this plea was entered while he was still absent from duty. An hour afterward Mr. Hearst met him and, seeing that he was cold sober, reproved him for deceit. On the scamp's assurance that he had honestly intended to be drunk, but lacked the price, Mr. Hearst gave him enough money to re-establish his character for veracity and passed on.

I fancy things have changed a bit now, and that Mr. Hearst has changed with them. He is older and graver, is no longer immune to ambition, and may have discovered that good fellowship with his subordinates and gratification of his lone humor are not profitable in business and politics. Doubtless too, he has learned from observation of his entourage of sycophants and self-seekers that generosity and gratitude are virtues that have not a speaking acquaintance. It is worth something to learn that, and it costs something.

With many amiable and alluring qualities, among which is, or used to be, a personal modesty amounting to bashfulness, the man has not a friend in the world. Nor does he merit one, for, either congenitally or by induced perversity, he is inaccessible to the conception of an unselfish attachment or a disinterested motive. Silent and smiling, he moves among men, the loneliest man. Nobody but God loves him and he knows it; and God's love he values only in so far as he fancies that it may promote his amusing ambition to darken the door of the White House. As to that, I think that he would be about the kind of President that the country—daft with democracy and sick with sin—is beginning to deserve.

Some Philosophical First Principles

[Bierce never expounded his philosophy of life systematically, and
one must infer its various aspects from random remarks made
over the course of his life. The following paragraph perhaps en-
capsulates his misanthropy as compactly as any.]

I am in receipt of a kind invitation to join the Theosophical Society,[8] whose main object, it appears, is "the practical realization of Universal Brotherhood." I must be excused—that is about the last thing that I could wish to bring about. Universal brotherhood, if it means anything, means (for me) a closer relation between me and the rest of the race. As a considerable majority of the rest of the race happens to be made up of knaves, dunces and savages, I am not seeking that kind of relations with it. The Society may tickle its ears with fantastic phrases babbled in gorgeous dreams until it is drunken with words, but I shall not join the debauch. The universal brother, as I know him, has ever manifest in the manner of him an invitation to be slapped on the back and addressed as "old feller"—to the which love-feast I am deeply disinclined. In the circumstance that many of us are descended from the same species of apes, I find a sufficiently near approach to universal brotherhood to satisfy my highest and holiest aspirations for spiritual gregariousness. If I believed that the gabble of Theosophy had the slenderest relation to facts of nature or anything worth knowing I should concede it a certain efficacy of inspiration: it would inspire me with a fervid zeal for universal smotherhood. [1]

> [Given Bierce's cynicism and his hostility toward organized religion, it is perhaps a surprise to find him recommending the following mode of ethical behavior.]

A man named Tiffany has discovered, up in the mountains near Truckee, a baking powder mine. The ore consists of "soda, an acid resembling cream of tartar, and traces of alum." I hope it can be easily and cheaply got out of the market and kick their quarreling proprietors into the latter half of the twentieth century. I should not like to have anything evil occur to Mrs. Sarah B. Cooper, who is a good woman and ought to be given plenty of time to repent. For more than twenty years I have been fighting her battles in my rough, rude way (not a bad way when it comes to fighting) and have not now the heart to wish her any ill, even when she sells her honored name to "puff" a tradesman's wares. I am aware that in doing so she is following the example of Mme. Adalina Patti and the late Henry Ward Beecher,[9] who found a certain kind of soap efficacious for washing the conscience; but I beg to submit that she is *not* following the example of Jesus Christ. I do not mean merely that Christ did not sell the use of his name as an advertisement, but that his doing so, or having done so, is an unthinkable proposition.

That is my ultimate and determining test of right—"What, under the circumstances, would Christ have done?"—the Christ of the New Testament, not the Christ of the commentators, theologians, priests and parsons. The test is perhaps not infallible, but it is excellently simple and gives as good practical results as any. I am not a Christian, but so far as I know, the best and truest and sweetest character in literature is that of Jesus Christ. He taught nothing new in goodness, for all goodness was ages old before he came; but with an intuition that never failed he applied to life and conduct the entire law of righteousness. I have before described him as a lightning moral calculator: to his luminous intelligence the statement of the problem conveyed the solution—he could not hesitate, he could not err. That he founded a religion which in a debased form persists and even spreads to this day is mere attestation of his marvelous gift: adoration is a mode of recognition.

It seems a pity that this wonderful man had not a longer life under more complex conditions—conditions more nearly identical with those of the modern world and the future. One would like to be able to see, through the eyes of his biographers, his genius applied to more and more difficult questions. Yet one can hardly go wrong in inference of his thought and act. In many of the complexities and entanglements of affairs it is no easy matter to find an answer off-hand to the question, "What is it right to do?" But put it in another way: "What would Christ have done?" and lo! there is light! Doubt spreads her bat-like wings and is away; the sun of truth springs into the sky, splendoring the path of right and marking that of error with a deeper shade. Then if you want a nice cool walk you know which way to go. [2]

The Art of Newspaper Controversy

[Given that the *Examiner* had a far wider circulation, even in the 1880s, than any other periodical for which Bierce wrote, it is not surprising that his tart opinions would embroil him in any number of disputes and controversies. Early in his *Examiner* period he laid down some guidelines for the conduct of such disputes.]

Having been engaged in newspaper controversies during a great part of my life, it occurs to me that it may not be uninstructive to younger and less experienced disputants to say something of the strategy and tactics of that kind of warfare. So if my good friend, the gentleman answered in the foregoing paragraph, will absolve me from any intention of paining him I will expound a few of the principles. In a newspaper controversy it is important to remember that the public, in most cases, neither cares for the outcome of the fray, nor will remember its incidents. The controversialist should therefore confine his efforts and powers to accomplishment of two main purposes: 1—entertainment of the reader; 2—personal gratification. For the first of these objects no rules can be given; the good writer will entertain and the bad one will not, no matter what is the subject. The second is accomplishable (1) by guarding your self-respect; (2) by destroying your adversary's self-respect; (3) by making him respect you against his will as much as you respect yourself; (4) by betraying him into the blunder of permitting you to despise him. It follows from this that any falsification, prevarication, dodging, misrepresenting or other cheating on the part of one antagonist is, in so far, a distinct advantage to the other, and by him devoutly to be wished. The public cares nothing for it, and if deceived will forget the deception; but *he* never forgets. I would no more willingly let my opponent find a flaw in my truth, honesty and frankness than in fencing I would let him beat down my guard. Of that part of victory which consists in respecting yourself and making your adversary respect you you can be always sure if you are worthy of respect; of that part which consists in despising him and making him despise himself you are not sure; that depends on his skill. He may be a very despicable person yet so cunning of fence—that is to say, so frank and honest in writing—that you will not find out his unworth. Remember that what you want is not so much to disclose his meanness to the reader (who cares nothing about it) as to make him disclose it to your private discernment. That, my young friends, is the whole gospel of controversial strategy.

You are one of two gladiators in the arena: Your first duty is to amuse the multitude. But as the multitude is not going to remember, after leaving the show, who was victorious, it is not worth while to take any hurts for a merely visible advantage. So fight as to prove to yourself that you are the abler swordsman—that is, the more honorable man. Victory in that is important, for it is lasting, and is enjoyed ever afterward whenever you see or think of the vanquished. If in the battle I get a foul stroke, that is a distinct advantage for I never by any possibility forget that the man who delivered it is a foul man. That is what I wanted to think him, and the very thing which he should most strenuously have striven to prevent my knowing. I may meet him in the street, at the club, at my home—not at his—anywhere and under whatever circumstances he becomes present to my consciousness I find a fresh delight in recalling my moral superiority and in despising him anew. Is it not strange then that ninety-nine disputants in a hundred deliberately and in cold blood concede to their antagonists this supreme and decisive advantage in pursuit of one which is merely illusory? Their faults are, first, of course, lack of character; second, destitution of brains. They are like an enraged mob engaged in hostilities without having taken the trouble to know something of the art of war. Happily for them, if they are defeated they do not know it: they have not even the sense to ascribe their sufferings to their wounds. [3]

I expounded last week some of the elementary principles of the strategy of newspaper controversy; I should like now to say a few words on newspaper "attacks." And, first, what is an "attack"? It may be defined as mention without commendation. I am entirely serious: nine men in ten, finding their names (unaccompanied by the most sickening flattery) in those columns of a newspaper in which they have not been taught to look for them, will conceive themselves "attacked" and "raise the song." It matters not how good naturedly they are mentioned: they are bound to discover a "hidden meaning," a covert sneer, a breach of civility. If their ingenuity can find nothing of that kind they will take offense at being mentioned at all. I can speak with some knowledge herein, for of all the victims of this kind of irreclaimable stupidity he is most subject to it who has a reputation for saying disagreeable things, however justly. Such a writer may spare himself the trouble of saying an occasional good natured one; its subject will consider it only a weaker kind of "attack"—particularly if he is, or suddenly chooses to think himself, a personal friend. That he will at once assign a mean and malicious motive, inventing one for the occasion, goes without saying. When I wish to rid myself of a tiresome friendship I write something pleasant about the man who professes it.

Endure my confidences, gentle, because as yet unmentioned, general reader, and I will lead you to the borderland of a domain of human stupidity which is to you an undiscovered country. There are men in this odd world who seem really to think that *because* a certain writer does not like them they should have immunity from his censure. Nay, that is not the half of it; there are editors—but let me put it this way. A is a professional writer. Naturally he has at various times professional relations with B, C and D, editors. These relations are subject to the law of change. At one time he writes for B. There is a disagreement and the connection terminates. Naturally, you would say, this restores their original irrelation: A the writer and B the editor are thereafter upon the same footing as before the connection. Would it surprise you to know that B is not likely so to regard it?— that he actually expects immunity from criticism and censure from his former employee, and is consumed with indignation if he gets them? Why? I leave it to you to figure out. You think you have had a look-in on the very bottom of level of the inexhaustible mine of human idiocy. O, no; below that lowest deep there is, as Milton hath it, a lower deep.[10] *Attendez-vous:* I knew a writer (it was not I) who once submitted a valuable manuscript to Editor X, who rejected it, as was his right, and destroyed it, as was not. The writer afterward "sailed into" him and his paper, as he had often, without giving special offense, done before. Editor X now raised the duse's own delight, pointed out the blackness of the villain's vengeful motive and eventually got him discharged. Quite unconsciously, and with such honesty as Heaven deems it safe to entrust to a fool, X acted on this view of the situation: Because I injured this man he wants a vengeance; vengeance is mine, saith the Lord; therefore, this man must let me alone. If this is valid logic the prudent newspaper writer will write for no newspaper, lest he be discharged and his freedom of censure abridged, and himself driven eventually to a life of shame—that is to say, to the awful career of a rattling good fellow! [4]

> [Bierce was not slow in instantiating his principles. When a reviewer had unjustly criticized one of his short stories (see page 251), Bierce defended himself; but that very act brought down another criticism upon him, to which he responded as follows.]

Another anonymous blockhead, nearer home, affects a holy glee in his discovery that I, whose trade is censure, wince when criticised—and the smirking wretch will no doubt construe my recognition of his needless existence as another wince. He and his myopic sort have never observed that personal controversy is a labor I delight in, ever grateful for invasion of my den by the masticable dunce with his

club. If a writer cared to order his conduct with reference to the nebulous notions of these cattle he would have a perplexing time of it, truly. Suppose him to
have been "attacked." Does he fondly imagine, good easy man, that he can keep
silence? Not so—that course is not open to him: he can remain "silenced." Does
he think he can reply? How vain the hope!—he can only "writhe." Either way
(and they point out no middle course) the chorus of asses celebrate their advantage with a stentorian acclaim.

In making a back for my vaulting egotism to play at leap-frog withal, this
amusing and useful being does me a real service. By thoughtfully presenting himself in the nick of my wish, this animated pretext has put me under an obligation
of magnitude. Partially to discharge it I will give him the happiness of seeing himself quoted for the first time in his life:

> To criticise and be criticised are as different as fire and ice. Ambrose can
> now realize a little how it seems to be cremated as he has cremated others'
> ideas that did not quite gibe with his own herculean efforts, etc.

Now, a New York writer "criticised" me by lying. My criticism of him was to
tell the truth in showing that he lied. Despite this plain distinction, this other fellow coolly affirms my roasting *as I roast others.* And in this statement I think him
entirely honest. It is altogether unlikely that concerning anybody's censure of
anybody else, he has ever thought whether it was true or false, just or unjust; or
has ever felt such distinctions to be sufficiently important and fundamental to affect the essential identity of all kinds of censorious writing. Nor do I think that in
this blind inattention and brute inaccessibility to knowledge of the difference between good and evil in "newspaper attacks" he is at all exceptional; if he were it
would not be worth while to say anything about him. His value for my present
purpose is the same as that of a dead criminal to a demonstrator of anatomy.
There is instruction in even the smell of him.

I said the other day that I never had been engaged in a newspaper controversy
in which my opponent did not willfully lie in statement and cheat in inference
and argument. No newspaper man, nor any man or woman writing in a newspaper, has ever to my recollection attacked me, or made a defense against my attack, without a lie to do the fighting with. That I have been exceptionally fortunate in that respect (for he who is permitted to despise his antagonist is victor) I
see no reason to believe: undoubtedly the lie is the favorite arm of imprecision.
The public is therefore not greatly to blame for assuming that its use, being general, is universal; and it does so assume. Moreover, the great body of the public is
honestly incapable of recognizing at the back of habitually satirical or censorious
writing any other motive than a wanton desire to wound, injure and defame. It is
this spice of "malice" which the "general reader" supposes himself to be enjoying
as he reads. To him the employment of even the wittiest of personalities comes

through his consciousness of some presumably worthy man suddenly grassed by a scapegrace enemy tripping him up as he goes his way, thinking no evil. That the gentleman incurring the mischance is a fool or a rogue, honestly, openly and righteously knocked down in the public interest—that is a view which the general reader does not bethink him to entertain, and which would seriously impair his joy in the performance. [5]

> [One of Bierce's most exhaustive comments on, and instantiations of, newspaper controversy occurred when John Bonner, a writer in the *Wave,* chose to chortle over attacks on Bierce by Greer Harrison and Arthur McEwen. In the course of his remarks, Bierce takes up the issue of whether he is uniformly misanthropic.]

Whether Greer Harrison can or cannot write a play, he has proved that he can conduct a controversy. His reply to Mr. Bierce is almost as crushing as McEwen's was.[11] It is a pity that one who has so many vulnerable points as Ambrose Bierce should be so insatiate for war. He is a consummate master of the language; he has a nimble fancy and a keen wit; his Prattle is always delightful reading; there is no sign (Mr. Harrison to the contrary notwithstanding) of any decay in his powers; but he is like the Irishman who never saw a head without wanting to hit it, and he seems imbued with the delusion that he is the guardian of letters on this Coast. To writers who may not be his equals in literary force, he denies the right not only to use the pen, but to exist. With savage insistence he stamps upon them when they venture to show their faces, and spits their mangled forms with his poisoned lance for the amusement of the public. On the grave of another such misanthrope ran the words:

> Here lie I, Timon, who alive all living men did hate.
> Pass by, and curse thy fill, but pass, and stay not here thy gate.[12]
> —John Bonner in "The Wave."

John Bonner, you are a good writer, and I love good writing. You are a scholar, and I admire learning. You are an old man, and I respect age. I am told that your private life is irreproachable, and that an irreproachable private life is an excellent thing in man or woman. Nevertheless, if when I shall have done with you you are not soundly ashamed of yourself you are not the thoughtless gentleman that I take you to be, but the unworthy fellow that your hasty championship of a conscious literary impostor makes you seem. By one who so rarely is censured by a writer meriting a serious reply, an opportunity like this is not to be lightly ignored, and I mean to "improve the occasion" with gratitude to the dear God who inspired you to go forth and catch a Tartar. To a man of so wide and varied knowledge as you, John Bonner, it is needless to point out the origin of that colloquial phrase and expound its application to the matter in hand. Only let me assure you that you have a merciful and considerate prisoner, who will restore you to your comrades a wiser and a better man.

John Bonner, how do you know that the Greer Harrison person "can conduct a controversy"?—that is to say, as you obviously mean, conduct it effectively? Have you sufficiently examined all his statements and the facts upon which they bear to know that he has not confirmed his opponent's ill opinion of him? How do you know that he has not by falsehoods permitted me to despise him? That were poor conduct of a controversy, were it not? That were disastrous and irreparable defeat, were it not, John Bonner? In war it is a maxim to prevent the enemy from doing what he most desires to do. In unfriendly controversy my strongest wish, naturally, is to despise my opponent; is he skillful if he permits me—nay, compels me? And if he lies can I respect him? Are you prepared by investigation to vouch for the truth of all that Mr. Harrison says? Remember, he says many things; if any are false he knows not how to "conduct a controversy." With reference to one or two, having already delivered judgment, perhaps you are willing to hear counsel.

John Bonner, I beg you to observe that this enchanted idiot, Harrison, desirous, after the fashion of rascals generally, to enlist the churches on his side, says that I made a "sacrilegious attack upon the Lord's Prayer," but offers nothing in evidence. There is no evidence: it is a pure invention. Had you conviction of its truth by revelation, or how? Again he says: "Once Bierce dared to say 'Poor old God!'" In some verses written four or five years ago for a midsummer Jinks of the Bohemian Club (Dr. J. D. Arnold, Sire) I quoted those words from a famous monologue of an old and respected member of the Club.[13] Why did you believe the Enchanted Idiot without evidence? Surely, John Bonner, you would not have commended his manner of conducting a controversy if you had known that he lied. I do not permit myself to think that you regard falsehood as commendable.

John Bonner, I will give one more instance, which ought to take attention as a flawless example of the method that you stand pledged to admire. It relates to one of the most amusing episodes of a somewhat stormy controversial career of more than a quarter of a century. The distinguished discoverer of the jayness of the metropolis that wouldn't have his play and the degeneracy of the critic that wouldn't have his presumption mentions my "brutal assault upon one of the most charming and brilliant women of our country." In this solemn indictment he had been anticipated by Arthur McEwen, as honest a gentleman as ever garbled letters, falsified telegrams and instigated murder, and who wears a wide hat to shelter himself from the tears of all the angels. Indeed, this grave accusation has for many moons burned in the mouths and boiled on the pens of all my favorite enemies. It has this much of truth. Writing in these columns on the lack of necessary relation between an author's literary work and his personal character, I said in illustration: "One of the sweetest poets that I know is a drunkard, a malicious liar and a generally disreputable woman." There was absolutely nothing in the context to identify the person alluded to. I know several sweet poets, and nobody but I can say who they all are, nor where they live. I never have at any time, in speech or writing or by intimation, signified whom I had in mind. Yet it is a ludicrous fact that a certain lady whom for a score of years I had been sedulously persuading this ignorant and indifferent public to accept as a sweet poet rose in her place and in a storm of tears pointed herself out as the object of my "attack."[14] Not only so, but she personally sought out such of my friends as were accessible and strove to persuade them of the reality of her wound—by what arguments I am not advised. That is not all by much: her own friends (from whom may she be delivered) ran to her banner and the long array drew itself across the land, uttering its mind of me in various keys, every manjack of the funny outfit personating her Knight Champion and execrating the creator of the role. Never was such a hullabaloo heard along the slopes of Parnassus—never had the Phocian cats so hearty a laugh!

John Bonner, is it, then, true that a scholar and gentleman holds his approval so cheap that it goes without hesitancy to whomsoever can by stupid falsehoods be "almost as crushing" as to him who by the same method is but a little more "crushing" than he? As one somewhat accustomed to be crushed, I venture to remind you that an artist in compression—one really skilled in administering the peine forte et dure, wastes no time by loading his penal apparatus with so light a substance as untruth. What anybody can do is not worth doing, and therefore not worth commending. Are you not sorry, sir, that you permitted this fatuous falsifier to take your good opinion by surprise?

John Bonner, apart from the fibs, your hero's "reply" consisted in affirming and feebly reaffirming the decay of my mental power. This controversial method is not quite so original as each successive sorehead is proud to think it. It came into fashion twenty years ago, and has never gone out. Of my collection of more than one hundred "crushing replies" in which it is used, more than one-half bear dates earlier than 1875. In contemplating these evidences of distinction I cannot repress a natural pride in a decline that for smooth, unbroken uniformity is unique, and, in my judgment, the perfection of art. But you, John Bonner, have the hardihood to declare that I am not decaying—you who cannot, as yet, stand forth and say: "He struck me here and here!" But if I am not "decaying"—if the corroborating testimony of a hundred estimable and soreheaded gentlemen is to go for nothing, how am I "crushed" when the disability is reaffirmed by the latest two of that long illustrious line? And if I am much of what you are kind enough to say I am, wherein am I "vulnerable"? It almost looks, sir, as if in the matter of reasoning you are merely human; and I feel it my solemn duty to invite the attention of my good friend Johara[15] to the truly awful state of his apparently brilliant contributor.

John Bonner, how do I seem "imbued with the delusion" that I am "the guardian of letters on this Coast"? I write of the things that interest me, knowing that only so can a writer interest his readers. You do pretty much the same, do you not? It happens that the work of other writers interests me. Naturally, I speak my mind of them, as you, John Bonner, speak yours of me. Is your right of criticism superior to mine?—your authority greater?—your mandate from a higher power? Why, sir, I know, and you know, men who write of nothing else than the work of other writers. We call them "critics" or "reviewers," and their vocation has commonly been esteemed legitimate and honorable. Mr. George Hamlin Fitch of the "Chronicle" is such a man; is he in the same delusion? That which is arrogant presumption and hardy usurpation in me—how can it be right and reasonable in him? Mr. Hazeltine of the New York "Sun" is such a man; can it justly be said of him, with no other evidence than his weekly work, that he thinks himself the guardian of letters on the Atlantic Coast? Some of the greatest work in literature of the world has been done, and done avowedly, as criticism of writing. Carlyle, Macaulay, Taine, De Stael[16]—were they afflicted with a delusion as to the extent of their rights and privileges? In citing the practice of the masters (to what other authority can one appeal) I present you, John Bonner, with an opportunity to make the Harrisonian and McEwenese retort that I "compare" myself with Carlyle, Macaulay, etc. But perhaps you are a cut or two above that. O, well, I only want to know this: on what do you ground your belief that I seem to think myself the guardian of letters on this Coast and your feeling that you do not seem to think yourself the guardian of criticism on this Coast? On your moderation and my severity? Let us appeal again to the masters. Was not Pope more severe than I have the skill to be? Might not his victims of "The Dunciad" have accused him of "savage truculence"? Really, he was very hard upon the poor devils, and had not the faintest compunction about plainly pointing them out as impostors and pretenders. Doubtless you would describe them more mildly as "not his equals in literary force"; but would you wish to expunge from English literature the delightful "Dunciad"? Would you efface a single line of it out of tenderness to the memory of some luckless dunce who lives only in Pope's work, as the Harrison person will live only in mine if I have the good fortune to live in yours? In "English Bards and Scotch Reviewers" Byron is commonly felt to have "spitted their mangled forms with his poisoned lance for the amusement of the public." Could we spare that admirable work, albeit the author lashed no vice but the vicious, not folly but the fools?

Fools are my theme, let satire be my song.[17]

True, while arranging for a reissue and carefully revising the proofs, he uttered solemn deprecations of his own performance, but the world's scholars are now in fair agreement that with the light he had he did well. Since when, indeed, has it been considered wicked to lash the money changers and those who sell doves, out of the temple of letters?

John Bonner, when you say, "To writers who may not be his equals in literary force he denies the right not only to use the pen but to exist," you give the impression, unwittingly, I hope, that I deny those rights to all such writers. When we were students of logic we were taught, you remember, to give that sort of thing the ugly name of suggestio falsi. "Omission of the partitive makes"—you know the rest, John. If you had cared to give your accusation the accuracy which, as Mill said, it is the best purpose of scholarship to impart, you would have framed it this way: "To some writers who may not be his equals in literary force he denies the right to use the pen, though not for that reason." Do you not think it rather loose to say that I deny to any writer unconvicted of murder the right to exist? Let that pass, but I should like to say that if all the living writers who, at a time when I considered them, and they considered themselves, inferior to me in literary force, owed their first encouragement and assistance to me—if all these were to point out your error by letter it would materially augment your mail. Do not be alarmed: I have never known any of them to come forward in my defence. Doubtless it seems to them that I am able to defend myself. How does it seem to you, John Bonner?

John Bonner, you are pleased to compare me with Timon of Athens, and to call me "misanthrope"—a hater of mankind. Do you think it philosophical to judge of one's attitude toward the race by one's attitude toward a few scores of individuals whom rightly or wrongly one regards as unworthy of respect?—and this without a knowledge of one's life associations or friendships? For the betterment of your understanding, J. B., I might wish to introduce you to the members of my little social circle, but I fear they would stare at you. They are a picked lot and a trifle exclusive—they would perhaps not approve you. I know, for I have been told, of your goodness, your gentleness, and all the virtues that adorn your character, but they would have to judge you by your work, some peculiarities of which I have been at the pains herein to point out. I know not what they would think of you; they might not assent to your notion of how to conduct a controversy—and your manner of beginning one. That would be very sad.

John Bonner, does it really seem to you that contempt for the bad is incompatible with respect for the good?—that hatred of rogues and fools does not imply love of bright and honest folk? Can you really not understand that what is unworthy in life or letters can be known only by comparison with what is known to be worthy? He who bitterly hates the wrong is he who intensely loves the right; indifference to one is indifference to the other thing. Those who like everything love nothing; a heart of indiscriminate hospitality becomes a boozing ken of tramps and thieves. Where the sentimentalist's love leaves off the cynic's may begin. You have lived and written to little purpose if you have yet to learn why the good do not make the bad behave themselves.

John Bonner, is it unknown to you that this California of ours is one of the world's moral dark corners—that it is a happy hunting ground of rogues and dunces and such small deer, and that they are everywhere and always obstreperous, conspicuous, unscrupulous, dominant? Does it surprise and pain you that I find every year several scores of such, whom I deem deserving of the treatment that you describe in so lively metaphor? Can you not understand that the satisfaction I find in making enemies of them is a harmless satisfaction? And what excellent enemies they are! They never tire, they never sleep; never for a moment anywhere do they forget. No scheme of revenge is too base for them, no lie too monstrous to set going and keep going. And how sedulously they cloak the scars upon their backs, which would betray their motive!—how soberly they disclaim animosity, even affirm goodwill and admiration! Are you altogether sure, John Bonner, that you are not yourself affected by exposure to the insidious infections of this diligent and versatile malevolence? Are you quite persuaded that your study and investigation and taking of testimony about me have been such as to assure you that your views of my life-work and character have not been colored by the false lights thrown upon them from so many sides? Are there no historical instances of men concerning whom public opinion— that is to say the voice of the average man—that is to say the judgment of mediocrity, has been reversed? Out of your knowledge of history I think you can evoke instance after instance. He who tells truth of fellow men (John Bonner) will get lies a bellyful in return. I do not complain that this is so; I only say that it is not otherwise.

John Bonner, that is not the whole story; there is another side to it—a side that concerns you not, yet might enlighten. It has to do with loyal and steadfast friends; with words of cheer and encouragement; with sympathetic letters from all over the world, signed with great names and names unfamiliar in the mouths of men—letters, too, of gratitude from victims of injustice and imposture, and sometimes from young writers "not my equals in literary force." O, believe me, John Bonner, this black business of mine has its gleams of light—its compensations and consolations—even its rich rewards. That among them I am unable to name your approval is a privation that I must endure as Heaven may send me the strength to do. That my enemies do not love me is a lighter affliction; it is not apparent why they should. Still, they might be fair, and not resort to cremation when dead, thereby denying me the harmless gratification of standing at their graves, a tear in the right eye and in the left. And now, John Bonner, in turning to other and lighter themes, I thank you for the loan of your back from which to speak to the people. It is a good back—broad, flat, firm underfoot. Done with you, John Bonner. [6]

On Politics

[During the election of 1888—in which the Republican Benjamin
Harrison defeated the incumbent President Grover Cleveland—
Bierce felt impelled to lay down some principles of his own politi-
cal philosophy.]

In the struggle of interests which we call politics, I—having no interests to be hurt
or helped—have never thought it worth while to engage. Make me a manufacturer of something which can be produced more cheaply abroad and I will be a
Protectionist—with a mental reservation regarding my raw material if I have to
import it. Give me a wheat ranch and I will be a Free Trader. As soon as I own a
silver mine I shall go in for the double standard, with silver an unlimited legal
tender and the Government compelled to purchase as much as it can get of it—
preferably from me. When I get my cigar factory going my antipathy to Chinese
immigration will undergo a profound and radical modification. Pending the accomplishment of some of these great, and I venture to think beneficial, changes,
or others similarly necessary to the public welfare, I propose to care for such affairs as I have, which are wholly intellectual. I carry my entire possessions in my
skull and mean to keep them from the service of my neighbor's pocket.

It is useless to tell me that a political campaign is a contest of principles—that
Candidate Tom and Candidate Dick and Candidate Harry "represent" anything
but certain policies which certain considerable classes of their more intelligent
countrymen are persuaded will advance their own material pecuniary interests.
If I am for Free Trade it is because I find that for nearly everything which I buy I
am compelled to pay more under Protection than I could get it for if the small
class of my countrymen who make it were not protected; while the one thing that
I sell—my thought—has to compete on even terms with the better thoughts of
better men, which the Government permits my customer-class to purchase wherever it can be most cheaply got. This is unfair. If I am compelled to purchase of
my own countrymen they ought to be compelled to purchase of me. The work of
every foreign-born writer should be taxed at least 50 per cent *ad valorem*. The
professional writer, paid by salary or "space," who advocates Protection is either
some kind of a fool or a mean-spirited creature who would rather lie than starve.

My neighbors, you are minded madwise all. The quadrennial insanity is now
upon you, and you fling froth. You are about to make the customary spectacular
extravaganza of this country for the grieving of the judicious. One-half of you are
already accusing the other half of cherishing the basest designs against the peace
and welfare of the only thing that you all know enough to respect and love—albeit with a blind esteem: your country. And the accused half "hurls back the alle-
gation" with an energetic sincerity divinely idiotic. When your welfare is accom-

plished the under dog will remount his chewed legs, free his beslubbered pelt of
the dust of conflict and trot cheerfully away, to polish his abundant daily bone,
certain that the licking which he has incurred is the only evil that will befall him
for a period of four years, and wondering why the devil he was at the pains to
incur it.

Do you really expect me, my friends, to engage in this squabble? Would you
like to see your devoted Prattler making a triumphal progress of himself, headed
by a brass band to convince the erring, his mouth venting an upeast draft of
hoarse noises in sets of three? Would you wish to see him in the character of an
army with banners, gunpowdering and far-barreling and Roman-candling his
political faith? Would he look well balancing himself upon his legs on the "rostrum," exerting his agitable chin and dealing damnation upon the chaps whom
he cannot persuade to his way of thinking that he thinks? If the security and welfare of this country depend upon the performance and execution of these rites,
do you, my friends, perform them. For myself, I am in doubt whether their cel-
ebration is a duty or a privilege. When I have resolved that doubt I shall ask you
to perform them again.

In the mean time let us all turn prophet. It is not enough that you vote for the
man of your choice—as with a fine, frosty humor you call your action at the poll-
ing place; you must also prophesy his success. You have observed that in various
feats of rivalry confidence assists to win, and you think that it will somehow enhance the weight of your ballots—the vote of a turkey-cocking sovereign elector
considerably more than overcoming that of a timorous and despondent soul who
thinks there are more men of your sort than of his. As a matter of fact, the
unhopeful one is denied the advantage of existence: in the scheme of creation he
was overlooked and his place given to the Hepsidamian whangdoodle. Every man
Jack of the lot of you honestly and calmly believes that the election is going his
way. He is incapable of the conception of so worthy a man as he in a minority; he
could as soon think of an archangel caught in a quail trap; and when the ugly fact
is borne in upon the consciousness of him he feels as if he had fallen out of a clear
sky and struck astride of his own neck.

No, mamn—excuse the profanity. I am unafflicted with a desire to catch the
contagion of politics to the irreparable wrecking of my heart and mind. It is a
pitch that defiles, a tope that endrunkens, a poison that penetrates the bones and
gets into the hair. You may eat my leg off if I know a man zealous in politics
whose judgment in any political matter I would prefer to that of a last year's pine-
cone, or whose word I would believe if I were myself under oath—the editor of
this political journal alone (and only partly) excepted. Which has the honor to
be why I am not a politician. I can afford to live under any kind of government
which a majority of my countrymen is likely to afflict me with, but I cannot afford to have a muddled brain and an evil heart. I want those organs clear and
clean: I need them in my business.

Nevertheless I have my preferences and can give reasons for them. Four years ago I was a Mugwump because I thought Mr. Blaine no better than a thief.[18] Since then he has reformed, and I've gone Democratic, partly because the Republicans, while protecting so many industries don't show any disposition to protect mine, partly because I am opposed to rotation in office except for cause and partly because the Republicans have insulted my intelligence by nominating two obscure men. In this there would be but one intent—to cheat. In nominating a man "against whom nothing can be said" you nominate one against whom it may be said that he is a candidate of rogues. Had not the Republican party men enough of brains and honesty and fair renown but it must go into the backwoods of Hoop-hole county, Indiana, and hale out this cave-dweller, this man without a history, this second Hayes,[19] this "person," this distinguished obscurian? What! shall I vote for the candidate of a party which fears to accept the country's judgment on its known leaders?—a party which asks of me so profound a belief in hereditary transmission of character that it will serve in place of knowledge? I am not prepared to say that Mr. Harrison is the mental and moral image of his grandfather; the chances are that he is not. And I don't think the elder Harrison was much of a man anyhow. As to the Morton person,[20] it is admitted that he is rich and the son of a preacher. They are commonly good lads, I understand.

On the whole, I am for Cleveland and Thurman[21]—not because of their eminent services but because of their eminence, which enables us to judge. There was no secret sneaking into the darkness to drag out a man whom nobody could say he would not make a good President. The men at St. Louis knew what they were about and whom they wanted. They had the honesty to give us men concerning whose opinions, principles and works there are abundant and accessible data. That goes for much with voters who do not relish being tricked and cajoled. There are still a few of such, and if they do not support Cleveland and Thurman they ought not to get one postoffice to a dozen of them. [7]

An ingenious reader of this paper has made the discovery that in all my "caviling at the Republican party and its methods" during this "campaign" I have never made a distinct and definitive declaration of my own "political faith." This very observant man is correct. I have refrained for two reasons. First, I have not the vanity to suppose that my political convictions are of interest or importance to any one but myself. Second, they are not in issue in this canvass. They are not expressed in any platform nor professed by any candidate—except, of course, in so far as all the platforms express, and all the candidates profess, those beliefs and sentiments common to every civilized and more or less enlightened human being. I am neither Democrat nor Republican. I never was. What my correspondent is pleased to term my caviling at his party and its methods is due to the fact that I find much to cavil at—a thousand times more than I have said anything about. That I do not cavil at the other party and its methods may justly enough be attributed to the fact that this is a Democratic paper. True, the editor (with either commendable generosity or a most reprehensible indifference to what I say or think) has never limited my liberty in any direction, and if he saw me taking a firm clutch upon the scalplock of Mr. Cleveland would probably make no attempt to prevent a breach of the peace; but there is a decent etiquette in such matters, and it is never any trouble to me not to do something if I can as well do something equally agreeable. I may add that what I most dearly love to do is to refrain from doing anything; but in the faulty organization of the newspaper business (as compared with the profession of law, wherein one may accept a retainer *not* to appear) that is incompatible with receipt of an income.

For various reasons I really do not care a straw which party wins in this contest; and two of these reasons I have no objection to making known. First, I have no important personal interests that in my judgment will be either materially furthered or materially injured by the result of the coming election, while one that is very precious to me—the clarity of my understanding, such as it is— would be imperiled by taking either side. Second, I have so profound a reverence for the wisdom and goodness of my countrymen that I am forbidden to entertain a doubt of their deciding all questions at issue in a way that will be good enough for me and them. In a republic no man's abstention from politics can prevent the others from having as good government as they merit. Do they want better?

Some scores of worthy gentlemen are bracing themselves to hurl at my head this familiar "crusher": "What if we *all* abstained?" That, my friends, is what is called in the terminology of discussion a "hypothetical question"—which nobody is bound to answer. There is no obligation on me to consider a state of affairs which exists only in somebody's imagination; when confronted with that emergency as an actual condition—for which, as I do not recommend it, I should not be held accountable, and of which there is no discernible prospect—my views upon it might be more pertinently asked. Nevertheless, it is easily answered. Suppose you all did abstain—what would ensue? Anarchy, doubtless. But of what would you then have the right to complain? Of my abstention? That gave you greater power in the management and direction of affairs. Of the consequences of your own abstention? Those you foresaw. You observe, gentlemen, that you have not a leg to stand upon.

This eternal harping upon the sin of "incivism" is incivility. Let us examine the matter another way. A is that kind of a sinner; B is not. Now, B is either a Democrat or a Republican, or a Prohibitionist, or an "American," or something—let us say a Democrat. He says to A: "I need your assisting intelligence." "Very good," says B—"but I am a Republican. You are bound to believe, do believe and constantly assert the perversion of my intelligence and the pernicious character of my assistance." May I ask what B could say to that? What a man really means when he accuses another of not voting is not that it is a sin to abstain from voting, but that it is a sin not to vote as *he* votes. If A does not vote at all, and B votes one way and C another, B is logically bound to consider A less mischievous than C is, while C is logically bound to think him a better citizen than B is. And, in point of fact, we never complain of incivism in the other party, but do all we can to encourage it. It is easy to say: "I like a man who votes according to his light, right or wrong." As to that, I beg leave to say that this is not a question of who is the more lovable man. And if it were it should be submitted for decision to a woman, upon the competent, relevant and material evidence of personal acquaintance.

I like to fancy—perhaps erroneously—that my position as a looker-on enables me to see more of the game than the players do; that my indifference to the result makes me a better critic of the moves; that my freedom from political sympathies and antipathies gives my judgment an intrinsic worth superior to its current value. But (it may be urged) if it has any current value at all it ought to go into circulation for the general good. As to that, anybody is welcome to my political views, on seasonable occasions. Concerning this present contest, for example, I think both parties notably wrong, as, after the election has occurred and reason resumed its empire, I shall endeavor to show. But of the two the Democrats seem to me the most nearly right. With regard to methods there is simply no comparison. It is the misfortune of the Republican party to have secured the allegiance of most of those men who believe their great wealth to be a creation of the laws—men who believe they would not prosper as well, if the Government did not supply them with customers by compelling other men to purchase their wares. These men know that their tenure of at least a part of their prosperity is extremely precarious: the law giveth and the law taketh away—blessed be the name of the law so long as it giveth. That fortunes erected upon a schedule of import duties have a sandy and shifting foundation is a truth ever present to their apprehension, and they see in the Democratic demand for lower duties an encroaching tide menacing the stability of their several structures. They look forward with something like terror to the time when this advancing wave, like that which angered Browning's Caliban, shall have "lolled out its large tongue" and "licked the whole labor flat."[22] What could we expect them to do? What, in their situation, would we probably do ourselves?

These men are strong in numbers, in wealth, in organization, in brains. They are skillful in all the direct, and in all the devious, ways of influencing public opinion and controlling legislation: so they acquired their fortunes, so they must guard them. They cannot afford to keep a conscience; they are as unscrupulous as the devil, and as ingenious. They have made this the corruptest campaign ever known in a country of corrupt campaigns. No favoring falsehood is too monstrous for them to set afoot, no expense too great to incur in endowing it with vitality and endurance. They have ransacked all the arsenals of deceit and leveled all the defenses of credulity. Their energy is tireless, their activity unsleeping, their vigilance invincible alike to the admonitions of nature and the persuasions of indulgence. They have confused the march of mind with a rearward cloud by day, an inconstant pillar of fire by night. From all the mazes of interest they have removed the clews of conscience. The paths of moral and intellectual rectitude they have sophisticated with lying guide-posts and branching by-ways leading from the light. With the hands of Esau but the voice of Jacob they beseech a blessing from a paternal Government by themselves made blind.

Doubtless this is highly figurative speech, but it reports a phenomenon of so extraordinary sort and magnitude that history does not relate its equal. So vulgar, so sordid, so impudent, so intelligent, intrepid and formidable a conspiracy to defraud is conceivable only by an imagination instructed by the fact itself. In every quadrennial agitation of our political sea, among the many marine creatures dashed upon the strand is some particularly hideous monster of a type not previously seen—a child of the time, serving to give shape and character to our memory of the storm. Its mnemonic mission accomplished, it staggers back into its generating environment, and if ever cast up again is unmarked in the fresher splendor of its more intolerable successor. The awful water-brute herein feebly described is the distinguishing largess of this present political tempest, a horrible gift of the Oceanides to the science of immoral zoölogy. May the devil take the thing, with all and singular of those who deem it fine and fair! I'd rather be the humblest stowaway in the hold of the Ship of State than tread her quarter deck while sailing such a sea.

I say I have no political antipathies. But swindling is not politics; hatred of it is not a political antipathy. The most fair-minded and even-handed no-politician in the world may consistently detest a rascal wherever he finds him. The robbers and thieves whose dominance is disgracing the Republican party in this campaign, and may be disgracing the Democratic in the next, are no more an essential element of the Republican party than fleas are an essential element of a dog. Just as the fleas prefer the fattest dog that enjoys the advantage of their acquaintance, these Knights of the Slender Hand attach themselves to whichever party they can persuade to go in for wide pockets. That the Republicans have not sense enough to shake them off should excite our compassion rather than our anger. Nature's bounties and benefactions are various. She gives to one man brains, to another the capacity to follow Andrew Carnegie[23] to the polls and vote for General Harrison. As there can be no envy, let there be no bickering, but each enjoy his gift in thankfulness, the one passively content to be no Carnegie, the other actively happy in the consciousness of his own identity and delighted to be just as God made him, as the butcher said of the skinned lamb.

It was my intention to uncover a little more of my "political faith," but already this Plaint of an Impenitent Incivilian is insufferably long and as full of eyes as the tail of a peacock. If I say any more may I be roasted whole at a Protectionist barbecue and given to the political poor! [8]

God and the Constitution

[In a discussion concerning the role of religion in the Constitution, which is highly relevant to present-day concerns, Bierce found an opportunity to attack his nemesis, Frank Pixley of the *Argonaut*, who had refused to rehire him upon his return from the Black Hills.]

As a coquette surviving her charms becomes a prude; as a rake shorn of his powers sets up as a moralist; so the *Argonaut*, outlasting its Pixley, has experienced religion. It is making a fight for the "recognition of God in the Constitution"; but after reading what it has to say in the matter, God will, I think, regret that He has obtained recognition in the *Argonaut*.

The quality of the logic employed by the infinite ass conducting God's case in the *Argonaut* may be judged by the following sentence with which he concludes his latest, and let us hope his last, plea for the Petitioner:

> While we do not believe that it was necessary to raise this question at all, yet now that it is raised, we hold that to *exclude God from the constitution,* by refusing to recognize him there, would be unconstitutional, inasmuch as it would be giving a constitutional and governmental recognition and pre-eminence to the no-God religion of the atheists.

Let us analyze this. Acts of individuals are neither constitutional nor unconstitutional; nor can one "refuse" to do what he has not the power to do. We must assume, then, that this extraordinary writer means that it would be unconstitutional for Congress and the State Legislatures (I shall speak of them for convenience as the Amending Power) to refuse so to amend the Constitution as to recognize God. But until the Amending Power is asked to amend it cannot "refuse"; that is to say, until an Amendment is introduced and rejected the Constitution as it stands is constitutional. But not afterward: the rejection being unconstitutional, the Constitution, lacking the unconstitutionally rejected Amendment, would be unconstitutional!

The refusal to amend, being unconstitutional, would be void, invalid, inoperative; therefore the rejected Amendment would be a part of the Constitution! By following the *Argonaut* person's logic to its legitimate conclusion we come to this interesting proposition: whenever the recognizing Amendment shall be formally submitted to the Amending Power, whatever action that Power may take or not take is affirmative and adopts the Amendment; or, rather, submission and adoption are the same act and the Amending Power has nothing to do with it. Yet this measureless idiot, thinking that way and partly conscious that he so thinks, regrets the raising of the question! This is abnegation itself, but is it not also a hardy and indign betrayal of his Client?

I cannot willingly let go my hold of this uncommon animal—this *rhinaugh-tycurio innominatus:* he seems all tail. Observe: The reason that it would be unconstitutional to refuse to "recognize God in the Constitution," if asked to, is that the refusal would favor "the no-God religion of the atheists." As no one can have a religion who does not believe in a God, there can be no such thing as a "no-God religion" to be favored. The refusal, therefore, would be unconstitutional because it would give "a constitutional and governmental recognition of and pre-eminence to"—something which has not the advantage to exist!

It is the peculiar distinction of atheism to be nothing at all. The atheist, as such, has no belief. To say he believes there is no God is inaccurate; he merely does *not* believe there is a God. Atheism is a word without a corresponding thing; to object to its recognition and pre-eminence is the same thing as to be jealous of a vacuum.

Subjected to logical analysis, every particular argument employed by the *Argonaut's* miserable intellectual pauper is seen to be no less devoid of sense and meaning than the one which I have selected. On the whole, I think the *Argonaut's* "success in piety" is not sufficiently marked to justify it in departing from the paths of sin, and the sooner Mr. Pixley steers its toes back into those pleasant by-ways the better we shall all feel about it. The asses that have been turned loose in its editorial columns bray no more acceptably for having been supplied with prayer-cushions.

The expediency of "recognizing God in the Constitution" is a matter which I do not care to discuss on its merits, and the questions at issue between religious people and atheists do not interest me: I have other (and better preserved) fish to fry. I have taken up this unthinkable dunce's remarks because they seem fairly to represent the degree of intelligence that concerns itself with controversy in our newspapers. In saying that nine in ten of all the arguments which I find in the press are as clearly devoid of sense and logic as the one under examination, I am conscious of understating the proportion. It is almost invariably obvious that the writer is unacquainted with the nature of a syllogism—does not know logic as a science—does not know that it is a science. Most people understand that a foreign language cannot be acquired without study, and the few who have acquired their own know that the same is true of that. Not many expect to play the violin really well at the first attempt. Almost anybody will admit that first-class work in civil engineering requires some small knowledge of at least mathematics. But an immense majority of men and women think it possible to write good verse with no knowledge of prosody, and to reason like an angel without an acquaintance with logic. I have known men of no small distinction as writers and speakers—some of them distinguished in an especial way as debaters—whose arguments were never arguments except by chance—whose writings and speeches so swarm with bastard brats of conclusion in no way related to their premises as to resemble an asylum for foundlings. [9]

The Morality of Suicide

[Whereas in earlier years Bierce had merely poked fun at the
bizarre suicides that occurred in his vicinity or that had come to
his attention, he now began seriously pondering the moral issues
of the matter, wrestling with many of the issues we face today.]

Out at the Pest-house is a Chinaman afflicted with that form of leprosy known as
elephantiasis. He is miserable, incurable, hopeless—a horror to himself, a burden
to the public, a constant and emphatic negative to doctrines held most precious by
all the churches. The existence of this loathsome and suffering creature screams an
emphatic "no" to every affirmation of an omnipotent and benevolent Deity—chal-
lenges the very fundamental faiths of all mankind. His death is demanded by every
racial, national and individual interest directly or indirectly concerned. The world
would be better off without him, the loss of his remnant of life and body would be a
distinct advantage to himself. Why not put him to death?

I ask this in no flippant spirit, but in all seriousness; for in all seriousness I
believe that the mercy which we extend to dumb animals, "putting them out of
misery" when unable to relieve it, we are barbarians to withhold from our own
kind. If it is kind and right to preserve as long as possible the life of a human being stricken with an agonizing and incurable disorder it is wrong and cruel to
shoot a horse having a broken leg. Scores of times it has been my unhappy lot to
deny the piteous appeals of helpless fellow creatures, comrades of the battle field,
for that supreme and precious gift by which a simple movement of the arm I was
able and willing to bestow—the simple gift of death.[24] Every physician has had
the same experience, and many (may blessings attend them!) have secretly given
the relief implored. The Government has the right of intervention in this matter
between a blameless citizen and an undeserved fate: if it has the right to take life
at all it has the right to determine when and why. If it has the right to take a life
that is perilous to the community it has the right to take one that is already a disaster to the individual. That it is immediately expedient to set up a reform which
public opinion has not demanded, and which the noisy declamation of cranks
which passes for an utterance of public feeling may howl down, may well be
doubted. Our present need is a discussion of the matter, by cranks and all, in a
manner that is free (why should it be otherwise?) and fearless—there is nothing
to fear. With a view to its proper debating, permit me to formulate the proposition in practical shape:

> *Resolved,* That immediate death is a natural civil right of the citizen
> painfully and incurably afflicted.

I know the first move that will be made by the great body of those holding the negative: they will plant their controversial feet upon religious grounds: we are "placed" here and have no right to leave until taken away—even if that be done piecemeal. On this point I will only say that the world has for many centuries been trying to conform its laws, not to its own needs, but to the supposed wishes of some Power not affected by their action; to those observers who believe the result to have been satisfactory I have no argument in reply. Though you should bray them in a mortar yet would they not cease to do most of the braying.

It has been urged—for this question is as old as the Pyramids—that by putting the sufferer to death we cut off a part of the time in which he would otherwise prepare his soul for the other world. It is amazing how the pious disparage their Gods: to me it seems that a Deity of the ordinary intelligence would naturally make the appropriate allowance in favor of the deceased, crediting him with whatever sum and degree of penitence he would have felt if he had not been deprived of a part of his opportunity. A Deity who would not do that would hardly be fit for adoration. [10]

A correspondent who is kind enough to profess an interest in my remarks on suicide in the last "Sunday Examiner" asks me to name some instances in which I think it courageous to commit suicide. It is always courageous. We call it courage in a soldier merely to face death—say to lead a forlorn hope—although he has a chance of life and a certainty of "glory." But the suicide does more than face death; he incurs it, and with a certainty, not of glory, but of reproach. If that is not courage we must reform our vocabulary.

True, there may be a higher courage in living than in dying—a moral courage greater than physical. The courage of the suicide, like that of the pirate, is not incompatible with a selfish disregard of the rights and interests of others—a cruel recreancy to duty and decency. My correspondent asks: "Do you not think it cowardly when a man leaves his family unprovided for, to end his life, because he is dissatisfied with life in general?" No, I do not; I think it selfish and cruel. Is not that enough to say of it? Must we distort words from their true meaning in order more effectually to damn the act and cover its author with a greater infamy? A word means something; despite the maunderings of lexicographers it does not mean whatever you want it to mean. "Cowardice" means the fear of danger, not the shirking of duty. The writer who allows himself as much liberty in the use of words as he is allowed by the dictionary-maker and by popular consent is a bad writer. He can make no impression on his reader, and would do better service at the ribbon counter.

But I have not complied with my correspondent's request. The ethics of suicide is not a simple matter; one cannot lay down laws of universal application, but each case is to be judged, if judged at all, with a full knowledge of all the circumstances, including the mental and moral make-up of the person taking his own life—an impossible qualification for judgment. One's time, race and religion has much to do with it. Some peoples, like the ancient Romans and the modern Japanese, have considered suicide in certain circumstances honorable and obligatory; among ourselves it is held in disfavor. A man of sense will not give much attention to considerations of that kind, excepting in so far as they affect others, but in judging weak offenders they are to be taken into the account. Speaking generally, then, I should say that in our time and country the following persons (and some others) are justified in removing themselves, and that to some of them it is a duty:

One afflicted with a painful or loathsome incurable disease.

One who is a heavy burden upon his friends, with no prospect of their relief.

One threatened with permanent insanity.

One irreclaimably addicted to drunkenness or some similarly destructive or offensive habit.

One without friends, property, employment or hope.

One who has disgraced himself.

All the men I hate. [11]

Women in the Press, Politics, and Business

[During the 1890s Bierce's hostility to women's increasing demands for access to literary, political, and economic opportunities made him notorious as a misogynist. On the issue Bierce was both unrelenting and unrepentant.]

The Pacific Coast Women's Press Association—I know not what meat it feeds upon, that it is grown so great—shows distinct signs of aggression, and I for one, as its unworthiest critic, confess the necessity and obligation of saying something in defence of God for permitting me to exist. It is not possible to take the Association quite as seriously as it takes itself, but I promise to take it as seriously as I can. On Sunday last Miss (or Mrs.—I really do not know, and shall deny her the benefit of the doubt) Eliza D. Keith[25] published in this paper a disputatious exposition of the Association's character and purpose, in somewhat ailing English, but with that peculiar sincerity of intention with which Controversial Woman commonly attests by disingenuousness of method. As Miss Keith is said to be one of the Association's officers I take her utterance to be an authoritative expression of her fellow-members' views on these high themes, and so entitled to more consideration than might be due to its intrinsic weight and worth. For Miss Keith has generously refrained from unveiling her full splendor: in the manner of her sex, she leaves something to be desired. It is candor, I am sorry to say.

Let us note a few of the statements, beginning with her protestations against the "malicious discourtesy" of certain wicked males who have had the hardihood to laugh. "We welcome criticism," she says, rather clumsily, "deprecate being burlesqued, and resist being misrepresented." That is a very proper spirit, but every male critic knows that the kind of criticism which women welcome has not been invented. It is not as yet given to the daughters of Eve to apprehend the distinction between "criticism" and "misrepresentation"—"burlesque" and "malicious discourtesy." Only very earnest women band themselves together for even so high and holy purpose—germane to letters withal—as encouragement of "the planting of ornamental trees to break the dust along the country roads" and "the construction of permanent highways;" and very earnest women are not commonly distinguished for either the discretion to remain at peace with the windmills, nor for the humor to accept without offence men's dissuasion from the fray. It is the fate and function of women's associations to amuse; for those which exist for any other purpose than to amuse their members amuse all the rest of the world.

The statement that the Women's Press Association has been treated with malicious discourtesy, or discourtesy of any kind, is, naturally, untrue. It is made in obvious ignorance of literature and the literary laws limiting the liberty of censure, as deduced from the practice of the masters in all ages. The study of such matters is probably not worthy of attention from lettered ladies who plant ornamental trees, make permanent highways, kiss Adolph Sutro[26] and place themselves "in touch with the vital interests of the country generally." They have been told some wholesome truths, and more pleasant fun had been made of them, doubtless, than they have the sense of humor to comprehend. It is destitution of the sense of humor that makes people ridiculous. Whoso is without that saving grace is unable to discern the line between dignity and absurdity, and is as likely to be upon the wrong side of it as the right, wondering, like the man with dragging suspenders, what people are laughing at. There are women who have the sense of humor, but its general absence in the sex constitutes the hardest of all the conditions under which they must guide their own activities. I dare say not a half-dozen members of the Women's Press Association see anything ludicrous in their function of tickling "local pride" that it may laugh schoolhouses and roadways. In their character of Board of Public Works these good ladies probably find a solemn satisfaction that serves them in place of the hope in Heaven which they have commuted into newspaper notoriety.

"One of the most important canons" of the Association, according to Miss Keith, authorizes it "to entertain people of note who come to this coast." I wonder if the Association ever heard the common American practice of "entertaining people of note" called a vulgar and discreditable practice. It is so regarded in Europe in the best literary and art circles, and by none is it held in lighter esteem—nay, in opener contempt—than by many of those who have been "entertained." The reason is not far to seek. "People of note" are entertained by such "*mi todita*"[27] organizations as the Bohemian Club of this city for the advantage, not of the entertained, but of the entertainers. They wish to shine by his light, link their name with his name in the newspapers, gratify a vulgar curiosity and give themselves the right to claim his personal acquaintance. (I refer, of course, to strangers from afar, in whose entertainment there is no element of personal friendship.) Commonly these base motives are entirely clear to the "guest of the evening," who, like Kipling and a score of others more just than well-bred, tranquilly enjoys the food, patiently endures the oratory and then, putting his sycophant entertainers upon the literary spit, does them to a delicate brown and serves them in their own gravy. The ladies of the Women's Press Association will probably escape this unhappy fate: their "guests of the evening" will be mostly American women, and American women do not know how to cook—not even one another.

It is disingenuous of any member of the Women's Press Association to profess ignorance of why they are spoken of with levity. They cannot, of course, understand the smiles that come of a tickled sense of humor in the Tyrant Man— as when, for example, Miss Keith gravely writes: "The literary work of many a man too ill to write has been performed by his wife, unknown to his editors, who have complimented him upon the improvement noticeable in his work, to be attributed, no doubt, to his freedom from office duties and the privilege of writing at home"! But it has been repeatedly pointed out to them that their offence consists largely in the solemn pretense that they are members of the press. It will not do to talk in generalities about the surprising amount and variety of newspaper work performed by women; newspaper *men* happen to know a good deal about all that. There are but few of us, indeed, who do not know that of the one hundred and fifty members of the Association not a dozen are also members of the press, as that term is rightly understood. There are not on the Pacific Coast twenty women who earn their living by newspaper work, nor fifty whom any newspaper has ever paid a cent the second time. There is a practicable decency in matters of this kind, and since the lawyers and the physicians have been held up to us uncivil critics as models of mannerly behavior, I too will use them to point a moral. I venture to remind the learned ladies of the P. C. W. P. A. that it is unusual for a Bar Association to increase and multiply by admitting litigants to membership, and a Medical Society does not mainly consist of those who *take* medicine, or even sometimes, like good mothers, administer simple household poisons to children.

Nothing worth saying is true of all women, nor even of all women who write, but it is true in a general way, and with rare exceptions, that women who write are destitute, not only of common sense, but of the sense of right and wrong— they are moral idiots. A woman may live out half her life, a bright, pleasing, conscientious and companionable creature, then take to writing for the newspapers and become a sore trial to the spirit of every one who loves her—offensive to every taste that she formerly gratified and breaking in succession all the moral laws that can be broken with a pen and ink. I hold an opinion as to the cause of this, but am unwilling to disclose it. Perhaps Mrs. Atherton,[28] whose terrible truths of her own sex appear to be uttered *con amore* in the joy of discovery, might be more frank and intrepid, but I have my scalp to look after and content myself with a statement of the fact observed. For more than a score of years it has been my lot to be in controversy most of the time. Among my male opponents I have found those who scorned the unfair advantage of a falsehood or a dishonest argument, but never have I known a female antagonist who did not lie and cheat with as little concern, and apparently as little consciousness of wrong, as a pig with a mouthful of young larks. *Apropos de rien*, the champion of the Women's Press Association coolly assumes throughout a long paragraph that certain members have been harshly dealt with because they publish verses in the newspapers. She is, of course, entirely aware that they are ridiculed, not because they publish verses in the newspapers—as do also those who ridicule them—but because the verses which they publish in the newspapers are considered silly verses. I know a male controversialist—hardened veteran of a thousand intellectual combats—who would go gray and blush like an aurora borealis if caught at such "misrepresentation" as that; but if I see any ruddy glow in the sky out Miss Keith's way to-night I shall know that there is a fire.

We are told that "the association is not formed to boom private interests." If this means what it seems to mean how does it come about that since its formation the names of its three most active members have been so often in the newspapers—and seldom without credentials of reasonless and unauthenticated eulogium—that their owners, if not stark drunken with the vapid *vin du pays* of local notoriety, would curse their christeners? Of neither their work nor their character is anything known to account for the cackle. I may as well explain that I refer to Mesdames Stetson, Parkhurst[29] and Keith. Of the first I know nothing discreditable except that she is a show and permits herself to be fêted—lunched, for example, by the fashionable women of Oakland, who have a national reputation for lunching impostors and being lunched upon by them. It does not follow that Mrs. Stetson is an impostor. I do not say that she is not a worthy and clever woman; I only say that her *claque* is working the oracle in her service with more diligence than discretion.

Of Mrs. Parkhurst it seems to me sufficient to say that a few months ago she was promoting the publication and sale of a volume of incredible drivel—known by her to be drivel—to assist the fortunes of its senile author, who, by the way (although the fact is irrelevant), was a very worthy man and had done the State some service. That there is anything discreditable in a woman of letters subordinating the interests of letters to the interests of benevolence is a truth of which no consciousness has probably penetrated Mrs. Parkhurst's indurated understanding. It is characteristic of the female writer to defile her art in the service of any fad engaging her favor, from religion to spatter-work. Benevolence is a good fad, but the writer who would not rather see fifty old men die than assist one bad book to live has a natural and remediless incapacity to write.

As to Miss Keith—who can do with difficulty what another would scorn to do with ease—who has neither thought, wit nor style, but only a mean industry which never has produced, and never can produce, a line worthy of attention— she has sought to provide herself with a ready-made fame in the pen-name "Di Vernon."[30] She lately had the amusing effrontery to protest against being called by her own name when she had labored so hard (her co-laborer, Sir Walter Scott, was not mentioned) to make the other one famous! God knows where and when this industrious young woman performed her part of the labor; nobody ever heard of her except in connection with the Women's Press Association. Doubt- less she will in time lay off her stolen plumage, and like the good little jackdawess that she probably is, learn to admire her own simple and sable suit. She has fledged herself in rather gaudy colors but her heart, I am sure, is true black.

"There is no sex in brain," says this acute observer. I beg her pardon; in no respect do men and women differ so widely, so conspicuously, so essentially, as in mind. They think after altogether different methods; their mental processes are to a competent and comprehensive observation absolutely without resemblance. So different is the mental constitution of the two sexes that whereas we see not mainly with the eye, but with the judgment, the understanding, even the outer aspect of things is, I am persuaded, not the same to a woman that it is to a man. I have taken some trouble to test this theory, with results of the most interesting character, which I purpose giving to the world some day. It is my conviction that if a man who had lived all his life in San Francisco were to become a woman while passing along Kearney street she would be unable to find her way home without inquiry. [12]

> [As the movement toward female suffrage gained momentum,
> Bierce's anger bordered upon mania.]

The Daughters of Thunder are urging their demand for the ballot with a new ve- hemence, and Tyrant Man is apparently about to smile a sort of sickly smile and curl up on the floor, like the Stanislaus scientist experiencing his chunk of old red sandstone. The Republican "platform" of this much bewomaned common- wealth concedes their right to participation in the villainy of politics, the Popu- lists are committed to the same policy, and doubtless the Unterrified Democracy will fawn upon the female farthingale in due season. Lively Woman is indeed, as Carlyle would put it, "hell-bent" on purification of politics by adding herself as an ingredient. It is unlikely that the injection of her personality into the conten- tion (and politics is essentially contention) will allay any animosities, sweeten any tempers, elevate any motives. The strifes of women are distinctly meaner than those of men—which are out of reason mean; their methods of overcoming op-

ponents distinctly more unscrupulous. That their participation in politics will
notably alter the conditions of the game is not to be denied; that, unfortunately,
is obvious; but that it will make the players less malignant and the playing more
honorable is a proposition in support of which one can utter a deal of gorgeous
tommy rot, with a less insupportable sense of its unfitness than in the service of
any other delusion.

The frosty truth is that, except in the home, the influence of women is not el-
evating, but debasing. When they stoop to uplift men who need uplifting they are
themselves pulled down, and that is all that is accomplished. Wherever they come
into familiar contact with men who are not their relatives they impart nothing,
they receive all; they do not affect us with their notions of morality; we infect
them with ours. In the last quarter-century, in this country, they have entered a
hundred avenues of activity from which they were previously debarred by an unwritten law. They are found in the offices, the shops, the factories. Like Charles
Lamb's fugitive pigs, they have run up all manner of streets.[31] Does any one think
that there has in the last quarter-century been an advance in professional, commercial and industrial morality? Are lawyers more scrupulous, tradesmen more
honest? When one has been served by a "saleslady" does one leave the shop with
a feebler sense of injury than was formerly inspired by a transaction at the
counter—a duller consciousness of being oneself the commodity that has
changed hands? Have actresses elevated the stage to a moral altitude congenial to
the colder virtues? In studios of the artists is the voice of revelry by night invariably a deep masculine bass? In literature are the immoral books—the books
"dealing" with questionable "questions"—always, or even commonly, written by
men? It is admitted that the Pacific Coast Women's Press Association is virtuous—why not?

There is one direction in which "emancipation of woman" and enlargement
of her "sphere" have wrought a reform: they have elevated the *personnel* of the
little dinner party in the "private room." Formerly, as any veteran man-about-
town can testify if he will, the female contingent of the party was composed of
persons altogether unspeakable. That element now remains upon its reservation;
among the superior advantages enjoyed by the man-about-town of to-day is that
of the companionship, at his dinner *in camera*, of ladies having an honorable vocation. In the corridors of the "French restaurant" the swish of Pseudonyma's
skirt is no longer heard: she has been superseded by the Princess Tap-tap (with
Truckle & Cinch), by my lady Snip-snip (from the "emporium" of Boltwhack &
Co.), by Miss Chink-chink, who sits at the receipt of custom in that severely
unFrench restaurant, the Maison Hash. That the man-about-town has been morally elevated by this Emancipation of Girl from the seclusion of home to that of
the private room is too obvious for denial. Nothing so uplifts the Tyrant Man as
the table talk of good young women who earn their own living.

I do not wish to be altogether ironical about this rather serious matter—not so much so as to forfeit anything of lucidity. Let me state, then, in all earnestness and sobriety and simplicity of speech, what is known to every worldlywise male dweller in cities—to every scamp and scapegrace of the clubs—to every reformed sentimentalist and every observer with a straight eye, namely, that in all the various classes of young women in our cities who support, or partly support, themselves in vocations which bring them into personal contact with men, female chastity is a vanishing tradition. In the lives of the "main and general" of these, all those *considerata* which have their origin in personal purity, and cluster about it, and are its signs and safeguards, have almost ceased to cut a figure. It is needless to remind me that there are exceptions—I know that. With some of them I have personal acquaintance, or think I have, and for them a respect withheld from any woman of the rostrum who points to their misfortune and calls it emancipation—to their need and calls it a spirit of independence. It is not from these good girls that you will hear the flippant boast of an unfettered life, with "freedom to develop"; nor is it they who will be foremost and furious in denial and resentment of my statements regarding the morals of their class. They do not know the whole truth, thank Heaven, but they know enough for a deprecation too deep to find relief in a cheap championship of the purity of their sex—which is, and always has been, the creature of Seclusion.

What Woman's invasion is doing for the "business" world it will do for the political. This is not mere prediction, nor mere reasoning from analogy: the statement is grounded upon abundant fact, unfortunately. In the great Government departments in Washington the effect of women's participancy, as clerks and otherwise, is—not seen, certainly, but thoroughly well known to all observers excepting the myopic and fatiguing optimist. The kind of "influence" that obtains a clerkship in Washington depends upon the sex of the applicant. There are no statistics to which to appeal, but it is the judgment of those best qualified to hold an opinion in the matter that a majority of the great army of women clerks at the national capital would hardly like to name their original claims to preferment. If they did so there would be consternation in high places, and the divorce courts would suffer from congestion of the calendar.

Once in two years the Legislature of California convenes in Sacramento. It has "in its gift" a few dozen clerkships, most of which are useless, and their bestowal with a salary is a misappropriation of public money. The "term" is limited to the life of the session, which is but two months, and the pay will average some four or five dollars a day. For these paltry positions there is a grand scramble among several hundred persons of both sexes, mostly young women, who eventually secure the greater number of them. How? In some instances by honest, open persecution of the members, with recommendations, petitions and oral cadging; in most by proffers and promises that cannot be named here. So open, notorious and naked is this biennial scandal that no one is suffered to remain in ignorance of it; not a newspaper but relates the hideous incident with natural but unregarded indignation. The shadow of the shame reaches to the remotest hamlet of the State, darkening the land like an eclipse. At the capital no man escapes: Senators, Assemblymen, all the State officials—all men in any way prominent or influential are subject to these disgraceful solicitations. I am writing now from personal observation of a horrible week during which, as a newspaper man with a not altogether unfamiliar name, I was glad to be able to affirm with a fair approach to the truth as it is in newspaper men that I was absolutely destitute of influence.

It may possibly be thought odd that so many disreputable women should go to Sacramento in quest of clerkships of committees and other small sinecures. Why, as to that, not many do go—but a goodly number come away at the close of the session. In the moral atmosphere of the political world it does not require a very glittering prize nor a very long pursuit of it to make the average woman disreputable. But whether the loss of her purity of character is the eternal gain of politics this deponent is unable to state; I have never met a politician to whom any of it seemed to have been imparted. So far as any one knows, the biennial irruption of Woman into affairs of state at Sacramento has never discernibly elevated politics nor uplifted Brute Man out of his environing mud. The wretch is still grunting with a fat and fatuous content in his congenial matrix, happy in the consciousness of defiling all that touches him.

With a suitable School Director on the rack, it would, I fancy, be possible to extend those instances and examples into the domain of popular education. Ugly rumors are abroad concerning some of the more notoriously incompetent women teachers, and how they obtained and hold their places in the department. To some of them, I am persuaded, these tales do grave injustice: the price of their positions was paid in good honest money. During the time when God and Mr. Buckley were a majority in the municipal government of San Francisco a woman holding a teacher's certificate asked my assistance in obtaining a position in the city schools. She explained that she was well aware that it would have to be purchased: she had even taken the pains to ascertain the price, which, with never the suggestion of a blush, she said she was prepared to pay. This woman was entirely respectable, middle-aged and plain enough to know it herself. She was under no illusion as to the kind of payment that would be expected of *her*. On learning that I thought a more suitable position for her would be that of convict in the State penitentiary she was unaffectedly surprised and I fear pained. The incident has no great significance: the woman's conscience was racial; the only thing especially characteristic of her sex was her appalling incaution—which is not a profitable quality in practical politics. With such ministers of his will as she, how could even so great and wise a statesman as Col. Burns[32] effect the secret combinations necessary to good government by the sovereign people?

But the fitness of women for political activity is not in present question; I am considering the fitness of political activity for women. For women as men say they are, wish them to be and try to think them, it is unfit altogether—as unfit as anything else that "mixes them up" with us, compelling a communication and association that is not social. If we wish to have women who are different from ourselves in knowledge, character, accomplishments, manners, as different mentally as physically—and in these and all other expressible differences reside all the charms that they have for us—we must keep them, or they must keep themselves, in an environment unlike our own. One would think that obvious to the meanest capacity, and might even hope that it would be understood by the Daughters of Thunder. (If Col. Stetson's discovery of Herbert Spencer is not too recent she has probably read something of the effect of environment in promoting differentiation.) Possibly the Advanced One, hospitably accepting her karma, is not concerned to be charming to "the likes o' we"—would prefer the companionship of her blue gingham umbrella, her corkscrew curls, her epicene audiences and her name in the newspapers. Perhaps she is content with the comfort of her raucous voice. Therein she is unwise, for self-interest is the first law, and highest duty beautifulest sentiment. When we no longer find women charming we may find a way to make them more useful—more truly useful, even, than the speechladies would have them make themselves by competition. Really, there is nothing in the world between them and slavery but their power of interesting us; and that has its origin in the very differences which the Colonels are striving to abolish. God has made no law of miracles, and none of his laws are going to be suspended in deference to woman's desire to achieve familiarity without contempt. If she wants to please she must retain some scrap of novelty; if she desires our respect she must not be always in evidence, disclosing the baser side of her character, as in competition with us she must do (as we do to one another) or lamentably fail. I have sought to show in foregoing paragraphs that she is not at all backward in disclosing it; and in *The New Review* Mrs. Edmund Gosse, like "Ouida,"[33] Mrs. Atherton and all other women of brains, declares that the taking of unfair advantages—the lack of magnanimity—is a leading characteristic of her sex. Mrs. Gosse adds, with reference to men's passive acquiescence in this monstrous folly of "emancipation," that possibly our quiet may be merely the calm before the storm;[34] and she utters this warning—which also, more strongly, "Ouida" has uttered in *The North American Review*:[35] "How would it be with us if the men should suddenly rise *en masse* and throw the whole surging lot of us into convents and harems?"

It is not likely that man will "rise *en masse*" to undo the mischief wrought by noisy protagonists of Woman Suffrage working like beavers to rear their airy fad upon the sandy foundation of masculine tolerance and inattention. No rising will be needed. All that is required for the wreck of their hopes is for a wave of reason to slide a little farther up the sands of time, "loll out its large tongue and lick the whole labor flat."[36] The work has prospered so far only because nobody but its promoters has taken it seriously. It has not engaged attention from those having

the knowledge and the insight to discern beneath its cap-and-bells and the mot-
ley that is its only wear a serious menace to all that civilized men hold precious
in women. It is of the nature of men—themselves cheerful polygamists with no
penitent intentions—to set a high value upon chastity in woman. We need not
inquire why they do so; those to whom the reasons are not clear can profitably
remain in the valley of the shadow of ignorance. Valuing it, they purpose having
it, or some considerable numerical presumption of it. As soon as they perceive
that in a general way women are virtuous in proportion to the remoteness of their
lives and interests from the lives and interests of men—their seclusion from the
influences of which men's own vices are a main part—an easy and peaceful
means will doubtless be found for the repression of the shouters: the Cady
Stantons, Susan Anthonys, Sarah Grands, Col. Charlotte Stetsons[37] and the long
haired he ones of the pack. It is unlikely that they will fight—even Mrs. Foltz is a
man of peace.[38]

These remarks, in the course of which I have had to say much that it would
have been more agreeable to me to have left unsaid, have been made with a view
to the shifting of the discussion to new ground, where it has all along belonged.
Nobody, apparently, has cared to incur the consequences of pointing out what I
know many men and women of brains and courage clearly to have perceived,
namely, that if we are to have woman suffrage and all that it implies and entails
we must be prepared to surrender our immemorial notions of female chastity,
and accept a new deal in morals. [13]

> [We have seen Bierce put forth the argument that women, by en-
> tering the workforce, will take jobs away from men. In the follow-
> ing extract he adopts a different course of reasoning to justify his
> desire to exclude women from employment.]

A correspondent having the hardihood to dissent from certain political and industrial doctrines of the Henarchists asks me to make exposition here of the shadow-
side of women's competition with men in many of the employments recently
"opened" to them. The subject has already been given attention in these columns,
and repetition is not the life of trade; but there is never a lack of something overlooked by the Daughters of Hope. Indeed, they have not yet given evidence of ap-
prehending the simple elementary consideration (and its application to the matter
at hand) that an advantage to one of them is not necessarily an advantage to all, and
may even be purchased at a price that the others have to pay. "Opening to women a
new avenue of support" may mean depriving of support the women dependent on
men previously occupying that avenue. For opening it to women means closing it
to men.—The Sister-in-Evidence will please be seated; the fact that in all "avenues"
recently "opened to women" the Needless Male is still to be found in a considerable
quantity is irrelevant. I did not say that opening them to some women closed them

to all men; they are closed to men in the degree in which they are opened to women; and the she Sister will be good enough to take a seat alongside yonder he one, and not draw the shillelah until this coat-tail is in actual transmigration across the Path of Progress.

Indubitably a woman is under no obligation to sacrifice herself to the good of her sex by refusing needed employment in the hope that it may fall to a man gifted with dependent women. Nevertheless our congratulations are more intelligent when bestowed upon her individual head than when sifted into the hair of all Eve's daughters. This is a world of complexities, in which the lines of interest are so intertangled as frequently to transgress that of sex; and one ambitious to help but half the race may profitably know that every effort to that end provokes a counterbalancing mischief. The "enlargement of woman's opportunities" has aided individual women. It has not aided the sex as a whole, and has distinctly damaged the race. The mind that cannot discern a score of great and irreparable general evils distinctly traceable to "emancipation of woman" is as impregnable to the light as a toad in a rock.

A marked demerit of the new order of things—the regime of female commercial service—is that its main advantage accrues, not to the race, not to the sex, not to the class, not to the individual woman, but to the person of least need and worth—the male employer. (Female employers in any considerable number there will not be, but those that we have could give the male ones profitable instructions in grinding the faces of their employees.) This constant increase of the army of labor—always and everywhere too large for the work in sight—by accession of a new contingent of natural oppressibles makes the very teeth of old Munniglut thrill with a too poignant delight. It brings in that situation known as two laborers seeking one job—and one of them a person whose bones he can easily grind to make his bread. And Munniglut is a miller of skill and experience, dusted all over with the evidence of his useful craft. When Heaven has assisted the Daughters of Hope to open to women a new "avenue of opportunities" the first to enter and walk therein, like God in the Garden of Eden, is the good Mr. Munniglut, contentedly smoothing the folds out of the superior slope of his paunch, exuding the peculiar aroma of his oleaginous personality and larding the new roadway with the overflow of a righteousness secreted by some spiritual gland stimulated to action by relish of his own identity. And ever thereafter the subtle suggestion of a fat Philistinism lingers along that path of progress, like an assertion of a possessory right.

It is God's own crystal truth that in dealing with women unfortunate enough to be compelled to earn their own living and fortunate enough to have wrested from Fate an opportunity to do so, men of business and affairs treat them with about the same delicate consideration that they show to dogs and horses of the inferior breeds. It does not commonly occur to the wealthy "professional man," or "prominent merchant," to be ashamed to add to his yearly thousands a part of the salary justly due to his female bookkeeper or typewriter, who sits before him all day with an empty belly in order to have a tolerable back. He has a vague, hazy notion that the law of supply and demand is mandatory, and that in submitting himself to it by paying her a half of what he would have to pay a man of inferior efficiency he is supplying the world with a noble example of obedience. I must take the liberty to remind him that the law of supply and demand is not imperative; it is not a statute, but a phenomenon. He may reply: "It is imperative; the penalty for disobedience is failure. If I pay more in salaries and wages than I need to, my competitor will not; and with that advantage he will drive me from the field." Then, dear sir, you are not here addressed. If your margin of profit is so small that you must eke it out by coining the sweat of your workwomen into nickels I've nothing to say to you. Adopt in peace the motto "I cheat to eat." I do not know why you should eat, but Nature, who has provided sustenance for the worming sparrow, the sparrowing owl and the owling eagle, approves the needy man of prey, and makes a place for him at table. But here, sir, you are irrelevant. You walk these ways of pleasantness and paths of peace a trespasser. You are "matter out of place"—dirt. I wash my hands of you.

The gentleman whose attention I beg leave to call to the circumstance that he has his hand in a woman's pocket and is absently taking the means whereby she lives is the chap who, while employing her at a wage determined by a congress of professors of the law of supply and demand and pirates of the Spanish Main, is making a few tens of thousands yearly in his business or profession. I know this fellow: in my social environment he is one of the commonest phenomena; and the easy cordiality with which he takes my hand (with that hand which is familiar in the mouth of the woman's pocket) is to me a matter of delight and pride. At such times as I venture to look so great and good and rich a man straight in the eye of him I fancy he blushes a bit; but I suppose it is really nothing more serious than a touch of apoplexy. From that great convulsion of nature, the blush of a girl-driver, may Heaven in mercy save us!

Human nature is pretty well balanced; for every lacking virtue there is a rough substitute that will serve at a pinch—as cunning is the wisdom of the unwise and ferocity the courage of the coward. Nobody is altogether bad; the scoundrel who has grown rich by underpaying the workmen in his factory will sometimes endow an asylum for indigent seamen. To oppress one's own workmen and look out for the workmen of a neighbor—to skin those in charge of one's own interests, while cottoning and oiling the output of another's skinnery—that is not very good benevolence, nor very good sense, but it serves in place of both. The man who eats *pate de foie gras* in the sweat of his girl cashier's face, or wears purple and fine linen in order that his typewriter may have an eocene gown and a pliocene hat, seems a tolerably satisfactory specimen of the genus thief, but let us not forget that in his own home—a fairly good one—he may enjoy and merit that highest and most honorable title of the hierarchy of woman's favor, "a Good Provider." One having a just claim to that glittering distinction should enjoy a sacred immunity from the coarse and troublesome question: "From whose backs and bellies do you provide?"

If any honest wife of a Good Provider would know the answer to that question; if she cares to learn how she herself is provided for, let her undertake to collect from some "prominent lawyer," or "leading merchant," or "eminent banker," or "distinguished manufacturer"—in short from some "man of affairs"—another woman's bill for work duly ordered, faithfully performed and honestly charged. The bill should be for not less than one hundred dollars, and the woman must be thought to be the one who did the work. It will be an enlightening experience to the Good Providee: it will give her a new and revised notion of man's nobility.

What will occur? This: She will be promptly and firmly directed to "cut down" that bill. Probably it will not be intimated that the work is not satisfactory, nor that the rate is higher than the current one; that play is not at all necessary to the game. The ground upon which the reduction is frankly demanded is that the amount is excessive—that is, it is more than the man wishes to pay to a woman. And before that bill is paid it will be "cut down." In short, when the Good Provider is providing the Devil is very happy indeed. I do not say, madam, that every man of affairs is of that species of animals; I only say that there is a tremendously strong numerical presumption that the man is who does business next door to your husband's place. Fail not, fair and well nourished dame, to thank Heaven mightily that you are not his wife, but the wife of the honest gentleman doing business next door to his place.

Let us make an end of the subject—upon which I have a guilty consciousness of having written with more diligence than discretion. If any one of my dear friends among men of affairs, and especially among the Rich (who, it has been pointed out, are also the Good and Wise), has the faintest fancy that any part of this preachment is intended for personal application to himself, I trust that in the kindly and charitable spirit of the season he will give me the benefit of the doubt by a final decision that it indubitably is. [14]

The Evils and Errors of Literary Biography

> [Bierce's hostility to the practice of literary biography was unremitting; perhaps this is why he rarely wrote about his own work, even in private correspondence. A general statement of his views, written in 1898, is followed by two earlier instances of comical errors in regard to the basic facts of Bierce's literary career.]

It is commonly said, and doubtless believed, that biography is a great help to the

understanding of literature—that one may profitably go to an author's life for
light upon his work. This is one of those popular errors which certain low intelligences sedulously promote; for they thrive by writing about writers and find their
account in dignifying a vulgar and impudent curiosity regarding an author's personal affairs as an enlightened interest in literature. The truth is that nothing is
more false and misleading than biography—except autobiography. When the
"subject" is an author it operates to prevent, or rather to postpone, a clear judgment of his work and rank. As a rule there is no relation between the character
and the work of a man strong enough and wise enough to write what is worth
considering: the apparent relation is almost wholly the work of the biographers,
who, knowing little of the character (and who really does know much of the character of another?), base their account of it upon what they find, or think they find,
in the work. As to an author's own account of himself, it is like anybody's account
of himself—altogether untrustworthy, with an added incredibility from his
knowledge of the credulity of his readers, who from a distinguished author will
accept anything with the unquestioning faith of a pet pig at the feeding trough.

Among the several reasons why in literary matters the judgment of posterity
is better than that of an author's contemporaries, the chief is that posterity
knows less about his life and character, and is in a position to consider his work
on its merits without prepossession or prejudice, just as if it had fallen down
from the clouds, or grown up from the ground, without human agency. And
that is the way that all must eventually be judged, excepting those few unfortunates whose biographies (or autobiographies) are themselves works of permanent literary vitality. It is not likely that Dr. Johnson will ever be granted the
justice of a hearing before his judges without that smirking Boswell being
present to darken counsel. [15]

I have been looking through Mark Twain's new *Library of Humor*[39] and find that
it justifies its title. Possibly I am a trifle prejudiced in its favor, for the very funni-
est thing in it, according to my notion of humor, is a brief biography of myself. It
is as follows—barring the bracketed words—

> Ambrose Bierce, author of "Bierce's Fables" [I am not], was born in
> Akron, O. [I was not], in 1843 [I was not]. He served as a soldier in the war,
> and in 1865 went to San Francisco [I did not], where he was engaged in
> newspaper work until 1872. Then he went to London, where he had great
> success [I had not], and published "Bierceiana" [I did not]. With the
> younger Tom Hood he founded London *Fun* [I did not]. He returned to
> California in 1877 [I did not] and is now an editor of the San Francisco
> EXAMINER [I am not].

That is just like Mark Twain: he will not publish another fellow's work without tacking on something of his own so confoundedly amusing that the other chap's reads, in the shadow of it, like a call to the unconverted, or a pen-picture of a dead Emperor in an advanced state of decomposition. I wish I had written my own biography and he the extracts from my work. [16]

And that reminds me of a New York syndicate letter about me that is "going the rounds," and I rise to a question of privilege to explain that the writer not infrequently "says the thing that is not." For example, this, of my early work in San Francisco:

> He sent certain contributions anonymously to the *News Letter* and they fell under the genial eye of James T. Watkins, now of the New York *Sun*, who has always been a warm friend of Mr. Bierce. Mr. Watkins was so pleased with the articles that he hunted out the writer and made him an associate of his own on the *News Letter*, etc.

Mr. Watkins, who was never a warm friend of anybody but Mr. Watkins, did nothing of the kind: I superseded him on the *News Letter*—a bad arrangement, I have always thought, for he is a better writer than I. But he is not so good a man by the breadth of a selfishness that is truly continental.

Here is a gem from the same article:

> He is a scoffer and a scorner, and he wrote his tales of horror [*Tales of Soldiers and Civilians*] with a sort of fiendish delight at the effect that they would produce on the nerves of the unsuspecting and the innocent, not because he himself had let his mind go astray in imagining them.

Well, it is something not to be accounted insane, but how this ingenious writer came to know my secretest motives I am unable to guess. I venture to tell him, however, that I wrote my "tales of horror" without reference to the nerves, or even the existence, of the innocent, and in the belief that they are good and true art—a belief in which I have the obstinacy to remain.

My motives may seem a matter of opinion and legitimate discussion, but here we come to matters of fact:

> About seven years ago Mr. Bierce came to New York and tried to begin a career as a writer in his peculiar vein, and the pieces of various sorts which he offered to *Life*, the daily papers and the book and magazine publishers were exceedingly clever, as everyone acknowledged; but nobody would think of printing them. An attempt was made to syndicate his "Prattle," but only a San Francisco paper could be found so indiscreet as to print such atrocious personalities.

"Lord! how this world is given to"—erring![40] I have not been in New York for twelve years, and was then there on business connected with mining, and on that only. In all my life I have submitted but one little piece of my work to an editor of any New York newspaper; and that was accepted and printed—in the *World*.[41] No other Eastern publication, daily, weekly or monthly, has, to my knowledge, ever had a line of my manuscript; and if ever an attempt was made to "syndicate" my "Prattle" I did not know it, and the syndicator was attempting to sell goods that he could not have delivered. Whether the publication of my "atrocious personalities" is an indiscretion or not I really do not know; but if I cared to know, or thought it any of my business, I should ask the editor of the EXAMINER: he has probably had a good deal of counsel on that point.

One more quotation and I've done, i' faith!

> Mr. Bierce personally is one of the gentlest of men. He has doubtless been embittered by his failures, but he is ready to forgive any individual who will show him sympathy.

Without inquiring in what my failures have consisted, nor by what inspiration my biographer knows what it is that I am trying to accomplish in this little life, I will let that stand without comment; and carrying in my soul this touching picture of a heart-broken cynic, glittering with tears in the consciousness that nobody but God loves him, yet smiling through his hair as he feels upon his chine the plash of other tears than his'n, I back away from that sacred scene, and bidding myself a silent farewell, fall first upon my knees, and then upon my fools. [17]

The Principles of Literary Art

> [During his *Examiner* years Bierce was given the space to ruminate at length upon the nature and function of literature, and to comment upon the literature of his own day. The following remarks on magazine fiction continue the attacks upon William Dean Howells and other Eastern literati that had emerged in his *Wasp* period. This extract was later incorporated into the essay "The Short Story."]

The art of writing stories for the magazines of the period cannot, I think, be acquired. Success depends upon a kind of idiocy that must be "born into" one—it does not come at call. The torch must be passed down the line by the thumbless hands of an illustrious line of prognathous ancestors unacquainted with fire. For the torch has neither light nor heat, and is, in truth, fire-proof. It radiates darkness, and all shadows fall toward it. The magazine story must relate nothing: like Dr. Hern's "holes" in the luminiferous ether,[42] it is something in which nothing can occur. True, if the thing is written in a "dialect" so abominable that no one of sense will read, and so unintelligible that none who reads will understand, it may relate something that only the writer's kindred spirits care to know; but if told in any human tongue action and incidents are fatal to it. It must provoke neither a thought nor an emotion; it must only stir up from the shallows of its reader's understandings the sediment which they are pleased to miscall sentiment, murking all their mental pool and effacing the reflected images of their natural environment.

The master of this detestable school of literature is Mr. Howells. Absolutely destitute of that supreme and sufficient literary endowment, imagination, he does, not what he would, but what he can—takes note with his eyes and ears and "writes them up" as does any other reporter. He can tell nothing that he has not seen or heard, and in his personal progress through the rectangular streets and between the trim hedges of Philistia, with the lettered old maids of his acquaintance curtseying from the door-ways, he has seen and heard nothing worth telling. Yet tell it he must, and having told, defend. For years this diligent insufferable has been conducting a department of criticism in *Harper's Magazine* with the sole purpose of expounding (at the expense of his employers) the after-thought theories and principles which are the offspring of his own limitations. He has now shifted his smug personality and his factory of little wooden men and women on wheels to the *Cosmopolitan*,[43] and his following of fibrous virgins, fat matrons and oleaginous clergymen has probably gone with him, to cheer and direct him in pulling down that periodical to the level of inanity from which his successor will have to try to pull up the other.

I want to be fair: Mr. Howells has considerable abilities. He is an Insufferable only in fiction and when, in criticism, he is making fiction's laws with one eye upon his paper and the other upon a catalogue of his own novels. When not carrying that heavy load, himself, he has a manly enough mental stride. He is not upon very intimate terms with the English language, but on many subjects, and when you least expect it of him, he thinks with such precision as momentarily to subdue a disobedient vocabulary and keep out the wrong word. Now and then he catches an accidental glimpse of his subject in a side-light, and tells with capital vivacity what it is not. The one thing that he never sees is the question that he has raised by inadvertence, to decide against his convictions by implication. If Mr. Howells had never written fiction his criticism of novels would entertain, but the imagination which can conceive him as writing a good novel under any circumstances would be a precious literary possession, enabling its owner to write a better one.

The influence of this unique enemy to distinction as a quality in literature— this dead-leveler to the grade of dullness absolute—has apparently outlasted him in the place that has shaken his dust from its feet. In the May *Harper* the fiction is, first, an installment of a novel by Mr. Howells himself, and that needs no description: his worshipers and his scoffers are agreed as to what and how he writes; they are at variance in their estimate of its interest and value only. There is, next, a short story by a wretch named McLennan—in the most abominable "dialect" yet, and tolerable only because mostly unintelligible. Another by a malefactress named Stuart is all about niggers and nearly all in the Niggerese tongue. It smells. The place of dishonor is given to a serial by that dreadful Philistienne, Mary E. Wilkins.[44] Of course I have not read it. I do not need to: the artist who illustrated it tells what it is. Naturally an artist selects with nearly unfailing instinct the most picturesque and striking situation for illustration. Following are the title-lines (from the text) to Mr. Smedley's pictures: "She took the child's little hand" (frontispiece); "I wish you wouldn't be in such a hurry"; "Mrs. Field stood by the front gate, looking down the road"; "They stood looking at the young girl"; "She watched her mother out of sight." Those being, presumably, the most striking situations which the writer's imagination has been good enough to give us in this month's installment of her story, it may easily be conjectured what the rest of it is. And fancy, O thou who in reward of a God-fearing life hast not seen them, what the pictures are!

I have mentioned *Harper's* because it happens to lie before me as I write, but it is neither worse nor better than the other illustrated magazines; in point of fiction they are as like as one vacuum to another, and every month they are the same as they were the month before, excepting that in their holiday numbers at the last of the year their vacuity is a trifle intensified by that essence of all idiocy, the "Christmas story." To so infamous a stupidity has popular fiction fallen—to so low a taste is it addressed, that I verily believe it is read by those who write it!

As certain editors of newspapers appear to think that a trivial incident has an investiture of dignity and importance by being telegraphed across the continent, so these storywriters of the Reporter School hold that what is not interesting in life becomes interesting in letters—the acts, thoughts, feelings of commonplace people, the lives and loves of noodles, nobodies, ignoramuses and millionaires; of the village vulgarian, the rural maiden whose spiritual grace is not incompatible with a habit of falling over her own feet, the somnolent nigger, the snuff-rubbing clay-eating "cracker" of the North Carolinian hills, the society person and the inhabitant of Missouri. Even when the writers commit infractions of their own literary Decalogue by making their abominable creations and abominabler creationesses do something picturesque, or say something worth while, they becloud the miracle with such a multitude of insupportable descriptive details that the reader, like a tourist visiting an artificial waterfall at a New England place of last resort, pays through the nose at every step of his way to the Seventh Wonder. Are we given dialogue? It is not enough to report what was said, but the record must be authenticated by enumeration of the inanimate objects—commonly articles of furniture—which were privileged to be present at the conversation. And each dialogian (*pace, Henrice Jacobe!*)[45] must make certain or uncertain movements of the limbs or eyes before and after saying his say. All this in such prodigal excess of the slender allusions required, when required at all, for *vraisemblance* as abundantly to prove its insertion for its own sake. Yet the inanimate surroundings are precisely like those whose presence bores us our whole lives through, and the movements are those which every human being makes every moment in which he has the misfortune to be awake and at the mercy of the story teller. One would suppose that to these gentry and ladry everything in the world except what is really remarkable is "rich and strange." They only think themselves able to make it so by the sea change that it will suffer by being thrown into the duckpond of an artificial imagination and thrown out again.

Amongst the laws which Cato Howells has given his little Senate, and which his little Senators would impose upon the rest of us, is an inhibitory statute against a breach of "probability"—and to them nothing is probable that is outside the narrow domain of the commonplace man's most commonplace experience. It is not known to them that all men and women sometimes, many men and women frequently, and some men and women habitually, act from motives absolutely impenetrable, and in a way that is consonant with nothing in their lives, characters and conditions. It is known to them that "truth is stranger than fiction," but not that this has any practical application in letters. It is to him of widest knowledge, of deepest feeling, of sharpest observation and insight, that life is most crowded with figures of heroic stature, with spirits of purest fire, with demons of the pit, with graves that yawn in pathways leading to the light, with existences not of earth, both malign and benign—ministers of grace and ministers of doom. The truest eye is that which discerns the shadow and the portent, the dead hands reaching everywhere, the light that is the heart of the darkness, the sky "with dreadful faces thronged and fiery arms."[46] The truest ear is that which hears

> Celestial voices to the midnight air,
> Sole, or responsive each to the other's note,
> Singing—[47]

not "their great Creator," but not a nigger plantation melody, either, nor the latest favorite of the drawing-room. In short, he to whom life is not picturesque, enchanting, terrible, astonishing, is denied the gift and faculty divine, and being no poet can write no prose. He can tell nothing because he knows nothing. He has not a speaking acquaintance with Nature (by which he means in a vague general way, the vegetable kingdom) and can no more find

Her secret meaning in her deeds[48]

than he or any other strolling idiot can discern and expound the immutable law underlying coincidence.

Let us suppose that I have written a novel—which God forbid that I should do! In the last chapter my assistant hero learns that the hero-in-chief has supplanted him in the affections of the shero. He roams, aimless, about the deserted streets of the sleeping city, and follows his toes into a silent public square. There, after appropriate meditation, he resolves in the nobility of his soul to remove himself forever from a world where his presence cannot fail to be disagreeable to the lady's conscience. He flings his hands upward in mad disquietude and rushes down to the bay, where there is water enough to drown a million such. Does he throw himself in? Not he—no, indeed. He finds a tug lying there with steam up, and going aboard descends to the fire-hold. Opening one of the iron doors of the furnace, which discloses an aperture just wide enough to admit him, he wiggles in upon the glowing coals, turns his body sidewise so that it shall be no easy matter to hook it out, and there, with never a cry, dies a cherry-red death of unquestionable ingenuity. With that the story ends and the critics begin.

It is easy to imagine what they say: "This is too much"; "it insults the reader's intelligence"; "it is hardly more shocking for its atrocity than disgusting for its cold-blooded and unnatural defiance of probability"; "art should have some traceable relation to the facts of human experience." "Let us arise, O brethren, and drive this literary malefactor forth, corticated with tar and fledged birdwise!"

Well, the readers of this newspaper know that that is exactly what occurred a few days ago in the stoke-room of a tug at one of our wharves. *Only* the man had not been disappointed in love, nor disappointed at all. He was a cheerful sort of person, indubitably sane, ceremoniously civil and considerate enough (evidence of a good heart) to spare whom it might concern any back talk in writing, defining his deed as a "rash act."

Probability? Nothing is so improbable as what is true. It is the unexpected that occurs; but that is not saying enough; it is also the unlikely—one might almost say the impossible. John, for example, meets and marries Jane. John was born in Bombay, of poor but detestable parents, Jane, the daughter of a gorgeous hidalgo, on a ship bound for Buenos Ayres. Will some gentleman who has written a realistic novel in which something so nearly out of the common as a wedding was permitted to occur have the goodness to figure out what, at their birth, were the chances that my John would meet and marry my Jane? Not one in a thousand—not one in a million—not one in a million million! Considered from a view point a little anterior in time, it was almost infinitely unlikely that any event which has occurred would occur—any event worth telling in a story. Everything being so unearthly improbable, I wonder that writers of the Howells kidney have the audacity to relate anything at all. And right heartily do I wish they had not.

Fiction has nothing to say to probability: the capable writer gives it not a moment's attention, except to make what is related *seem* probable in the reading—*seem* true. Suppose he relates the impossible; what then? Why, he has but passed over the line into the realm of romance, the kingdom of Scott, Defoe, Hawthorne, Beckford and the authors of the *Arabian Nights*—the land of the poets, the home of all that is good and lasting in the literature of imagination. Do these little fellows, the so-called realists, ever think of the goodly company which they deny themselves by confining themselves to their clumsy feet and pursuing their stupid noses through the barren hitherland, while just beyond the Delectable Mountains lies in light the Valley of Dreams, with its tall immortals, poppy-crowned? Why, the society of the historians alone would be a distinction and a glory! [18]

To Train a Writer

[The essay entitled "To Train a Writer" began as an excerpt from an *Examiner* column of 1899. In it Bierce offers wry advice on the instruction of literary apprentices—instruction that Bierce himself has clearly followed in his own work.]

I observe that Mr. W. C. Morrow, the author of "The Ape, the Idiot and Other People,"[49] a book of admirable stories, is setting up a school to teach the art of writing. If he can teach his pupils to write half as well as he can write himself he may be called successful. There is a good deal of popular ignorance about writing; it is commonly thought that good writing comes of a natural gift and that without the gift the trick cannot be learned. That is true of great writing, but not of good. Any one with good natural intelligence and a fair education can be taught to write well, as well as he can be taught to draw well, or play billiards well, or shoot a rifle well, and so forth; to do any of these things greatly is another matter. If one cannot do great work it is worth while to do good work and think it great.

I have had some small experience in teaching English composition, and some of my pupils are good enough to permit me to be rather proud of them.[50] Some I have been able only to encourage, and a few will recall my efforts to profit them by dissuasion without hampering them with gratitude. I should not now think it worth while to undertake to teach a pupil to write merely well, but given one capable of writing greatly, and five years in which to train him, I should not permit him to put pen to paper for at least two of them—except to make notes. Those two years should be given to broadening and strengthening his mind, teaching him how to think and giving him something to think about—to sharpening his faculties of observation, dispelling his illusions and destroying his ideals. That would hurt; he would sometimes rebel, doubtless, and have to be subdued by a diet of bread and water and a poem on the return of our heroes from Manila.

If I caught him reading a newly published book, save by way of penance, it would go hard with him. Of our modern education he should have enough to read the ancients: Plato, Aristotle, Marcus Aurelius, Seneca and that lot—custodians of most of what is worth knowing. He might retain what he could of the higher mathematics if he had been so prodigal of his time as to acquire any, and might acquire enough of science to make him prefer poetry; but to learn from Euclid that the three angles of a triangle are equal to two right angles, and not to learn from Epictetus how to be a worthy guest at the table of the gods would be accounted a breach of contract.

But chiefly this fortunate youth with the brilliant future should learn to take comprehensive views, hold large convictions and make wide generalizations. He should, for example, forget that he was an American and remember that he was a Man. He should be neither Christian, nor Jew, nor Buddhist, nor Mahometan, nor Snake Worshiper. To local standards of right and wrong he should be civilly indifferent. In the virtues, so-called, he should discern only the rough notes of a general expediency, and in fixed moral principles only time-saving predecisions of cases not yet before the court of conscience. Happiness should disclose itself to his enlarging intelligence as the end and purpose of life, and love as the only means to happiness. He should free himself of all doctrines, theories, etiquettes, politics, simplifying his life and mind, attaining clarity with breadth and unity with height. To him a continent should not seem wide, nor a century long. And it would be needful that he know and have an ever present consciousness that this is a world of fools and rogues, blind with superstition, tormented with envy, consumed with vanity, selfish, false, cruel, cursed with illusions—frothing mad!

We learn in suffering what we teach in song—and prose. I should pray that my young pupil would occasionally go wrong, experiencing the educational advantages of remorse; that he would dally with some of the more biting vices. I should be greatly obliged if Fortune would lay upon him, now and then, a light affliction. A bereavement or two would be welcome, although I should not care to have a hand in the killing. He must have joy, too—O, a measureless exuberance of joy; and hate, and fear, hope, despair and love—love inexhaustible, a permanent provision. He must be a sinner and in turn a saint, a hero, a wretch. Experiences and emotions—these are necessaries of the literary life. To the great writer they are as indispensable as sun and air to the rose, or good, fat, edible vapors to toads. When my pupil had had two years of all this I should let him try his 'prentice hand in a pig-story in words of one syllable. And I should think it very kind and friendly if Mr. de Young would consent to be the pig. [19]

Wit and Humor

[On two occasions Bierce analyzed the critical distinction between
wit and humor, maintaining that American readers were markedly
deficient in perceiving the former quality, into which most of his
own work fell.]

"Americans are distinguished for a subtle sense of humor and a quick appreciation of the humorous," says a contemporary—an American contemporary. I am
of the same opinion, somewhat modified by doubt, but suspect that I was deprived, by some pre-natal blundering or other untoward fate, of my rightful share
of this common heritage. Heaven forbid that I should in cold blood and unprovoked deliberately set about the business of being humorous. I know of no
gloomier reading than results from a man "taking his pen in hand" with an iron
intention to be funny. The fact that our countrymen do find amusement in work
of that kind—that all they require to make them laugh is perception of a humorous intention—proves, if it proves anything, a lack, not a possession, of the sense
of humor. As a writer in "The Bookman" pointedly says: "Nothing so fatally
classifies a man as the things he laughs at." I have seen an entire audience "con-
vulsed with laughter" by one actor whacking another all over the stage with a
stuffed club. What, in my loneliness and gravity, had I to deplore but the stingi-
ness of nature in my mental endowment?

As a public writer whose work—done, albeit, with a serious purpose—is not
marked by that inflexible solemnity distinguishing our useful fellow-creature
the ass, I have naturally many opportunities of observation; and I have no hesitancy in saying that the average American "general reader" knows a joke as far
as he can read the label. Unfortunately he is myopic. In illustration I will relate
a typical incident, one of ten thousand. Some months ago, while the Spanish
war was raging, a question arose as to the correct pronunciation of a Spanish
name. Asked for a decision, I gravely explained that I was "too patriotic to know
the Spanish language" and requested some "traitor to his country" to assist.[51] I
got about a score of letters solemnly denouncing my narrowness and bigotry
and protesting in all good faith that an American's knowledge of Spanish was
no evidence of treason. One good gentleman went so deeply into the subject as
to point out that one's Spanish must have been acquired before the declaration
of war.

Apropos of this matter of humor, the only instance of my arrest for libel was
for writing of a man that he had been discharged from the editorship of a magazine and had brought an action "for restitution of marital rights."[52] After some
"proceedings" the action was dismissed on motion of the District Attorney.
That was years ago, and it has only just occurred to my mind that not a soul

connected with the case on either side knew that the offending statement was merely my humorous way of saying that the complaining witness had sued the proprietor of the magazine for reinstatement as editor. I feel sure now that I should not have been molested if my little joke had been understood, though some of the complainant's evil feelings toward me may have had their origin in the fact of my having carelessly added to it, for his encouragement, that another opening for him was supplied by the portal of the state penitentiary. [20]

If one could acquire a thorough knowledge of literature, the ART of literature, without having the faculty of observation one would be astonished to learn "by report divine" how few professional writers know how to distinguish between one kind of writing and another. The difference between description and narration, that between a thought and a feeling, between poetry and verse, and so forth—all this is commonly imperfectly understood, even by most of those who work fairly well by intuition. The ignorance of this sort that is most general is that of the distinction between wit and humor. Now, it will be found that, as a rule, a shoemaker knows calfskin from sole leather and a blacksmith can tell you wherein forging a clevis differs from shoeing a horse. Equally and manifestly it is a writer's business to know the difference between one kind of writing and any other kind, but to writers generally that advantage seems to be denied: they deny it to themselves.

I was once asked by a rather famous author why we laugh at wit. I replied: "We don't—at least those of us who understand it do not." Wit may make us smile, or make us wince, but laughter—that is the cheaper price we pay for an inferior entertainment, namely humor. There are persons who will laugh at anything at which they think they are expected to laugh. Having been taught that anything funny is witty, these benighted persons naturally think that anything witty is funny.

Who but a clown would laugh at the maxims of Rochefoucauld, which are as witty as anything written? Take, for example, this familiar epigram: "There is something in the misfortunes of our friends which we find not entirely displeasing"[53]—I translate from memory. It is an indictment of the whole human race; not altogether true and, therefore, not altogether dull, with just enough of audacity to startle and just enough of paradox to charm, profoundly wise, as bleak as steel—a piece of ideal wit, as admirable as a well-cut grave or the precision of stroke of the public headsman, and about as funny.

Take Rabelais' saying that an empty stomach has no ears.[54] How pitilessly it displays the primitive beast alurk in us all and moved to activity by our elemental disorders, such as the daily stress of hunger! Who could laugh at the horrible disclosure, yet who forbear to smile approval of the deftness with which the animal is unveiled?

In a matter of this kind it is easier to illustrate than to define. Humor (which is not inconsistent with pathos, so nearly allied are laughter and tears) is Charles

Dickens, wit is Alexander Pope. Humor is Dogberry, wit is Mercutio.[55] Humor is Artemus Ward, John Phoenix, Josh Billings, Bill Nye, Mark Twain[56]—their name is legion; for wit we must brave the perils of the deep; it is "made in France" and hardly bears transportation. All Americans are humorous; if any are born witty, Heaven help them to emigrate! You shall not meet an American and talk with him two minutes but he will say something humorous; in ten days he will say nothing witty; and if he did your own, O most witty of all possible readers, would be the only ear that would give it recognition. Humor is tolerant, tender; its ridicule caresses; wit stabs, begs pardon—and turns the weapon in the wound. Humor is a sweet wine, wit a dry; we know which is preferred by the connoisseur.

They may be mixed, forming an acceptable blend. Even Dickens could on rare occasions do this, as when he says of some solemn ass that his ears have reached a rumor. Lovely! [21]

Defending *Tales of Soldiers and Civilians*

[The publication of *Tales of Soldiers and Civilians* in late 1891 or early 1892, and the many reviews it received in newspapers and magazines across the country, compelled Bierce on several occasions to defend both the aesthetic and literal veracity of some of his Civil War stories. These passages represent virtually the only instances in which he discusses at length the tales upon which his reputation now rests.]

Having in the beginning of this screed made certain strolling comments on the Author as I know him, I am minded fairwise to say something of the Critic; for the two go together, like hare and hound, author a little ahead. The immemorial quarrel between them is comparable to nothing but the permanent misunderstanding between the driver of a stage-coach and the off wheeler. The driver has really nothing against that animal; its only sin is accessibility to the lash. And the driver is himself not at all bad; he is severely addicted to the whip-habit, and the awful imprecations accompanying his blows are produced by some kind of reflex action, without his connivance. The book reviewer, too, is commonly a very good fellow and would not willingly hurt a fly; and if he pile his immediate circumference with tumuli of dead the fault is attributable rather to opportunity than to a bad heart. Who is proof against opportunity?—it tempts us and we fall as fall the early pious in the bud and promise of their bloom. But as there are honest publishers, there are wicked critics—critics whose hearts are nests of naughtinesses, and who but open their minds to let out and in the evil beasts infesting them. Such a one I know, and I have it in purpose to expose the

wretch to public reprobation and deprive him even of his own esteem as an un-
detected rogue.[57]

The fellow reviews books in the New York *Sun*. That journal is said to be regarded as "high authority" in matters literary, mainly because of this chap's
works. I'm told that his name is Hazeltine, but of that I'm not sure. A few months
ago I had the hardihood to utter upon an unoffending world a book of tales,
which the critics generally received with surprising favor. But this *Sun*-dog!—he
got hold of it (it was not sent him) and chewed it into small wads. As he was not
invited to the feast I won't have things left in that condition without exerting the
flexors and extensors of my red right leg—no, indeed. He says:

> The opening tale, 'A Horseman' in the sky is the worst in the book so far
> as illusion is concerned. We will venture to say that no such erroneous
> impression could have been produced in the Federal army, or in any por-
> tion of it, as the author here alleges. We are certain that the horseman in
> the sky was never mistaken for a repetition of the Apocalyptical vision, but
> was only regarded as a Confederate General and his horse descending a
> precipice in obedience to the laws of gravitation, as the facts warranted.

Now, the author alleged nothing of the kind—yes, something of the kind,
but mark the difference in degree. The only "Federal army" or "portion of it"
that saw the horseman in the sky was a single man, who saw him for one instant and for that instant half believed it an Apocalyptic vision. The exact words
of the yarn are:

> Filled with amazement and terror by this apparition of a horseman in
> the sky—half-believing himself the chosen scribe of some new Apocalypse,
> the officer was overcome by the intensity of his emotions.

A moment afterward he was searching for the "vision's" body, among the
trees. If the critic's comments on that insignificant passage do not rise to the dignity of virtual lying of a pretty lofty sort there are no pigs.

He goes on to say:

> Nor does there seem to us to be the appearance of truth or reason in
> some of the other tales. * * * If the San Francisco physicians had got an
> ordinary undertaker to sit up with their dead man matters would have
> gone on with the utmost felicity; and if the officer in charge of the battery
> at Coulter's Notch had publicly explained the circumstances, we feel quite
> sure that he could have avoided the unpleasant duty of shooting cannon
> balls at his wife and child.[58]

O what a thing it is to be an ass! No doubt the undertaker might do a number of things "with the utmost felicity," but my story was about a man unaccustomed to the society of the dead, who heard the corpse walking softly toward him in the darkness. If his death from fright lacks "the appearance of truth and reason," it can hardly be because an undertaker might have been braver. I will cheerfully confess that if my story had been different from what it was it might have been worse than it is. Regarding the officer at Coulter's Notch, I will confess, too, the probable efficacy of a "public explanation," whatever that might be in an army, though military subordination is not favorable to it. Unfortunately, though, for the relevancy of the suggestion I had chosen to write of an officer whose pride and sense of duty forbade him to explain. On the whole, I am of the conviction that my critic was at his best at first; he shines with a brighter splendor as a liar than as a fool, though in either character I should suppose he might cause a good deal of trouble to the fire department. [22]

Among examples of "literary criticism" which I joy to collect for no better reason than that they relate to my books are some in which I cannot fail to discern the hand of a frowning Providence put forth to humble my proud spirit. Beneath the following, from "Life,"[59] I bend my corrigible neck like a rose detected in an attempt to associate with cabbages:

> "The younger American writers are doing some very artistic killing in their stories. Stephen Crane, Robert W. Chambers, Ambrose Bierce, E. W. Thomson, Owen Wister and Richard Harding Davis have all tried their hands at blood-spilling with the accessories of war. They are clever young men who never smelt powder burnt in battle, but they have a certain realistic faculty of making the reader see what they have only imagined. Whether Kipling started them on their career of revolution and slaughter, or whether it was something in the air that struck them all about the same time, is not quite clear." Etc.

To which I venture to add, in corroboration, the facts following: (1) I am an older man than any young man in America. (2) The fragrance of "powder burnt in battle" has many times reminded me of my preference for that of roasted critic. (3) The stories that this gentleman had in mind were published (and reviewed in more than four hundred of the magazines and newspapers of this country and Europe) before Mr. Kipling had been heard of outside the editorial rooms of "The Mulligachutney Bango." If my esteemed reviewer will add these facts to his esteemed review he will enhance its value by as much as two cents.

By the way, it commonly occurs that in my poor little battle-yarns the incidents that come in for special reprobation by the critics as "improbable" and even "impossible" are transcripts from memory—things that actually occurred before my eyes. In mentioning a certain story of mine the curio that "censures letters" in "Life" supplies an added instance:

> "It is a great thing to watch the 'Son of the Gods' ride out to his sure death like a stage hero. It is magnificent, but it is not war."

Well, I saw that thing done, just as related. True, the "Son" escaped whole, but he "rode out" all right, and if matters had been as we all believed them to be, and as he thought them himself, he would have been shot to rags.

Let me not be unfair. My critic's civilian training has led him into the lamentable error of censuring me, but with reference to the other story-tellers whom he names his reprehension is singularly intelligent—he could not have overdamned them if he had tried. This admission, I take it, is commendably just. 'Egad, it is magnanimous! [23]

Defending "The Damned Thing"

[The publication of Bierce's collection of supernatural tales, *Can Such Things Be?* (1893), impelled the following defense of one of its most striking stories.]

A person who, for aught I know, may represent a considerable class of readers fiercely accuses me of having, in a story entitled "The Damned Thing," plagiarized from a story by Fitz-James O'Brien entitled "What Was It?"[60] If I know anything of the unwritten laws of literature my accuser is as wrong in matter as in manner; anyhow I should not like to be thought unwilling to give all possible publicity to the charge. I will waive whatever advantage may accrue from affirming that in writing my story I did not even think of O'Brien's (for that I cannot prove) and proceed to point out what I deem essential differences in the sole incident upon which the charge is based. In O'Brien's story a man is attacked by, and overcomes, a supernatural and impossible being, invisible because transparent; in mine a man is attacked and killed by a wild animal that cannot be seen because, although opaque, like other animals, it is of an invisible color. The one story is devoid of basis in life or fact—though none the worse for that; the other is such a transcript from nature as no prior play of another's imagination can deprive one of the right to make. That there are colors invisible to the human eye is a fact attested by science; that there are animals and other things having them, wholly or in part, I have the strongest reasons to believe, and do believe. Indeed, my story was suggested by a rather disquieting personal experience while gun-

ning. I am convinced that in daylight and on an open plain I stood in the immediate presence of a wild beast invisible to me but sufficiently conspicuous to my
dog, and sufficiently formidable, to frighten it exceedingly.

"Invisible" is, of course, hardly the word to use of an opaque body, which
must necessarily obscure, or blot out, its background, and, that being favorable,
and the body at rest, reveal its outline to the eye. The color only is really invisible, but we have no word for the strange effect. In my story the obscuration of
the animal's background is several times distinctly pointed out. In order that any
curious reader may judge for himself I may add that my story appeared in the
last Christmas number of the New York *Town Topics*, and that I wish it were as
good as the tale with which it is ignorantly "paralleled."

If my critic were not, through his ignorance and ill-manners, so impossible
a controversialist I should like to ask him this: Suppose I write a yarn about a
lunatic or somnambulist with a stony stare and a long white robe, which may
be a bedgown. Now *ghosts* of that sort have walked the ways of literature from
the dawn of letters. Am I therefore a plagiarist? Nay, of the hundreds of authors
who have used the lithoptic spook, noctivagant in a white habiliment, are all
thieves but the long-dead and let us hope well-damned first? If not, *why* not?
His conception was original and very striking; if the second man had no title to
it, by what title is it held by the chap at the hither end of the long illustrious
line? How frequently must a theft be committed before the thing stolen belongs
to everybody? Not all these doubts are relevant to the case at bar; their purpose
here is to show that questions raised by literary resemblances are not necessarily distinguished by that admirable simplicity which alone should commend
them to the stamping critic

> endowed
> With a chest-note loud
> And a special kind of ear.

If it is really desirable to charge me with plagiarism why does not some ingenious gentleman state that the title of my latest book of stories, "Can Such
Things Be?"—published last autumn by the Cassell Publishing Co., New
York—is identical with that of a romance by Mr. Keith Fleming, published by
Geo. Routledge & Sons, London, in 1889? When that accusation is definitively
made in print by some one of sufficient note or civility to command consideration I may have something to say in explanation. In the mean time it strikes
me as rather hard that my enemies are so ignorant or slothful that I am compelled to point out my own depravity. As Col. John P. Irish, P. O. S.,[61] is now
enjoying a felicitous distinction as an authority in letters, I beg leave to invite
his attention to the coat-tail that I am dragging within a pace of his toes. [24]

Bierce vs. Huntington

[Bierce's greatest triumph as a journalist occurred in 1896, when
Hearst sent him to Washington to help defeat a funding bill
whereby Collis P. Huntington, owner of the Southern Pacific Railroad, was seeking to receive an enormous extension of the time
limit for repayment of debts. Between February and May, Bierce
wrote more than sixty articles. Few of them exhibited the "objec-
tivity" that we like to think is a hallmark of our own journalism,
but they were effective. His first column, boldly entitled "Bierce on
the Funding Bill," is given below.]

It is painful to observe that in his methods of affirming his right to the property
of others, Mr. Huntington employs means not always justified by the end.

For a week past his daily contributions to the "Post" of this city have appeared
in that honest journal as special telegrams from San Francisco, each duly dated
the day before publication. Yet for three days or more of this week the dromedary
head of Mr. Huntington, with its tandem bumps of cupidity and self-esteem
overshadowing like twin peaks the organ that he is good with, in the valley between, has been more or less visible in the town. Indeed, the "Post's" distinguished special correspondent, with one leg in the grave, one arm in the Treasury and one eye on the police, has lighted the air with a dusky glimmer in all the
dark corners of the Capitol, the dog-star of apprehension to all honest men and
the sun of hope to Grove Johnson.

We have it on the best of authority that a man cannot be in two places at once
unless he is a bird; so we are compelled to accept the painful conclusion from
these premises that our friends, the telegraph companies, are none the richer for
Mr. Huntington's connection with journalism. Indubitably he composes his San
Franciscan dispatches in the shadow of the Capitol, already famous as the birth-
place of Mr. Fleet Strother.[62]

This inference is supported by other evidence that amounts to proof. There is
in Washington, as elsewhere on this side of the continent, an acute public apathy
regarding Mr. Huntington's methods, his aims, his accomplices and his cries for
credit. The history of the crimes committed by him and his partners is almost
unknown. Few persons one meets have a very definite knowledge of the Pacific
Railroads, the enormous robberies connected with building and operating them,
or the still greater robberies now in contemplation. To the general public here
the various funding schemes now in discussion by a packed committee of the
House are absolutely devoid of interest.

That a Washington newspaper should think it worth while to give columns of
its space to the daily consideration of these matters for the entertainment or instruction of its readers is not conceivable without a mighty effort at making be-

lieve. The utmost concession that one can make with regard to the editor's good faith is that he prints the stuff at cut rates in deference to the poverty of a corporation that has yet much to steal.

There is also a significant similarity of literary style in the utterances of the thrifty Californian gentlemen quoted in these amazing works of the half human mind. It is as if some cunning hand had written the railroad's entire "case" on a continuous slip of paper, which had then been cut into lengths and each piece fitted with the name of some prominent citizen with a thoughtful pocket known to entertain kindly sentiments toward theft. This may not be the plan that was pursued, but certainly there is a charming uniformity of expression among these gentlemen who believe that a corporation which for thirty years has defaulted in the payment of interest and is about to default in the payment of principal because it has chosen to steal both principal and interest can henceforth be trusted to pay both.

These beads of personal opinion are strung upon a thread of editorial commentary satisfactorily strung in time to hold them from spilling. Some of these statements have a hardy audacity that makes a Californian gasp, though the majority of the House Committee on Pacific Railroads, to whom they are specially if not tacitly addressed, read and repeat them with lungs undisturbed. Here are a few of these pearls of thought, selected almost at random:

"THE OPINION IN FINANCIAL AND COMMERCIAL CIRCLES IN SAN FRANCISCO IS OVER-WHELMINGLY AGAINST THE GOVERNMENT TAKING THE PACIFIC ROADS AND OPERATING THEM."

"THE FINANCIAL AND COMMERCIAL COMMUNITY OF SAN FRANCISCO IS SOMEWHAT ALARMED LEST CONGRESS SHOULD THINK THAT THE JUDGMENT OF THIS CITY IS IN FAVOR OF GOVERNMENT OWNERSHIP OF THE CENTRAL PACIFIC RAILROAD."

"THE EFFORT TO REVIVE THE RULE OF THE SANDLOT IS A DISMAL FAILURE."

"OUTSIDE OF A FEW DISAPPOINTED AGITATORS, THE PEOPLE FAVOR AN EXTENSION OF THE DEBT AT A FAIR RATE OF INTEREST."

"THERE ARE BUT A FEW PEOPLE IN THE CITY OUTSIDE OF THE SANDLOTTERS WHO ARE IN FAVOR OF GOVERNMENT OWNERSHIP AND OPERATION OF THE PACIFIC RAILROADS."

"THE OPINION OF ALL CLASSES HERE IS LARGELY IN FAVOR OF THE CENTRAL PACIFIC FUNDING BILL."

All these monstrous statements, be it not forgotten, are made of San Francisco, whence these so-called telegrams profess to be sent. That they seem credible and true to those who have not special knowledge of the matter there is no reason to doubt. Their falsehood has been exposed in the committee by Representatives Bowers, Maguire[63] and others, and will be exposed on the floors of both houses if ever the matter comes to a debate; but in the mean time it is having its natural effect elsewhere, despite the amusing fact that the other day an incorruptible linotype machine in the printing office of the "Post" dropped the honest words "Ad Pacific Railroads" in shooting capitals into the middle of one of Mr. Huntington's articles. [25]

My prediction that Mr. Huntington would not again appear before the Senate Committee on Pacific Railroads unless summoned has gone the way of most predictions, as, like all of them, it richly deserved to do. To-day he not only appeared, but took his hand out of all manner of pockets long enough to hold it up and be sworn. He was not asked if he knew the nature of an oath; it was assumed that he did.

Mr. Huntington was a disappointment; even Grove Johnson,[64] who dropped in to give him moral support and encouragement, must have felt that much. Those who had come to scoff remained to pity. All felt that the show did not meet the just expectations of the audience. He was nervous and in a visible tremor. His manner was distinctly apologetic, he had the air of one begging pardon for his existence and permission to prolong it. His speech, if such it may be called, was type-written and apparently unfamiliar. Frequently he got "stalled" in the middle of a sentence and had to make repeated rushes at what was ahead of him before he could have his way with it. Once he attacked a word five times before overcoming it. At times he was almost inaudible.

Some of the committee appeared to think these failures were due to the infirmities of age; and doubtless that belief was useful to him in securing him somewhat more consideration than the nature of his purpose and the matter of his discourse merited. For after all he merely sought to promote plunder by perjury.

Perjury is an ugly word, but it is to be remembered that Mr. Huntington was under oath. He had sworn to tell the truth, yet his address consisted largely in affirmation of the honor and generosity of himself and his associates in the construction and operation of his railroads—ungenerous and dishonorable men, as anybody can prove.

The spectacle of this old man standing on the brink of eternity, his pockets loaded with dishonest gold which he knows neither how to enjoy nor to whom to bequeath, swearing it is the fruit of wholesome labor and homely thrift and beseeching an opportunity to multiply the store, was one of the most pitiable it has been my lot to observe. He knows himself an outmate of every penal institution in the world; he deserves to hang from every branch of every tree of every State and Territory penetrated by his railroads, with the sole exception of Nevada, which has no trees. Yet this notorious old man stood there before a committee of the highest legislative body of his country and made oath that he was an honest and unselfish citizen. [26]

For three hours the great bulk of Mr. Huntington confronted the light frail figure of Senator Morgan,[65] with only the width of a table between. For three hours the Senator plied the railroad man with questions that he answered most reluctantly and with every evasion of which his faulty intelligence was capable, with every falsehood that he dared when evasion was no longer possible, and with every outward and visible sign of an inner torment that the flesh could denote.

Hardly another member of the committee than Mr. Huntington spoke a word. When one did it was a comfort to Mr. Huntington—a question calculated to break the force of some terrible admission that Morgan had wrung out of him.

The situation was dramatic, the bad old man pathetically defending his claim to the right of adding to his useless millions, shuffling, falsifying, cowering under the pitiless gaze of his persecutor, mortified by admissions already made and trembling under apprehension of ones to come, the tranquil earnest manner of his great antagonist patiently but steadily holding him to the matter in hand or bringing him back to it when he thought it successfully evaded and forgotten; the breathless attention of the spectators, who hardly breathed for fear of missing a word—all this was interesting to the end.

The strain upon Mr. Huntington must have been tremendous. I should not have been surprised at any stage of the proceeding to see him break down and go all to pieces. One thing has been demonstrated beyond the shadow of a doubt by to-day's events: Mr. Huntington is not the moral pachyderm that we Californians have always believed him to be.

He feels the disgrace and discredit as keenly as anybody that cannot make up his mind not to deserve them. He sets as high a value on the respect and esteem of the reputable as he can afford to do. He has more frank cynicism than he needs in his public business. No man need henceforth fear sharp words of censure will be wasted on this malefactor; they will not reform him, certainly, but they will hurt him. If not deterrent they will be punitive. The tradition of his invincible callousness is henceforth (to me at least) faded fiction.

I wish every boy in the land could have been in that committee-room to-day and seen what it may cost to be dishonestly rich. As an awful example to American youth Mr. Huntington, sweating beads of blood in the heat of exposure, would have done something to repair the moral ravage caused by public honors to his sainted accomplice of Palo Alto. [27]

After the adjournment of the Senate Committee on Pacific Railroads to-day I had a conversation with Senator Morgan. He asked me to assure the people of California that he is maturing a plan for their relief, which he hopes will satisfy all their reasonable demands and just expectations.

This I understand to foreshadow a minority report and a bill in place of the Frye[66] bill which, with trifling modification, will almost certainly be favorably reported by the majority.

Nor have I much doubt that the Frye bill would pass both houses were it not for the Republican managers' wholesome fear of losing the Pacific States in the Presidential election. That may not prove an absolute deterrent, but the best service that can be done to California by Californians is to impress Speaker Reed[67] and his assistant men of destiny with the "imminence and dread" of that penalty.

Whatever may be the fate of a Pacific Railroads bill introduced by Senator

Morgan, the people of California may confidently assume that it will embody the honest convictions of the clearest intellect and most righteous heart in the Fifty-fourth Congress. His assurance that he is evolving a plan is ground of hope. With such a message from such a man despair would be a blunder and a crime. [28]

> [When Huntington, clearly stung by Bierce's torrent of abuse,
> attempted to suggest that his paper's animosity was a result of
> Huntington's withdrawal of financial support to the *Examiner*,
> Bierce wrote the following open letter to Huntington, published in
> the *Washington Star* and reprinted in the *Examiner*.]

To the Editor of the "Evening Star": On Friday of last week, immediately after the House Committee on Pacific Railroads concluded its session, C. P. Huntington was asked by Representative Johnson of California to confirm the statement made to him (Mr. Johnson), namely, that on becoming President of the Southern Pacific Company he had cut off the company's annual payment of $12,000 to "The Examiner." In the presence and hearing of three members of the committee Huntington said that it was true. The statement appears to have been made in explanation of "The Examiner's" hostility to him and his scheme for funding the debts of the Pacific railroads.

I have reason to think that Huntington will be given an opportunity to prove in court his accusation that "The Examiner" was once on the payroll of his company. In the mean time, if he will prove it to the satisfaction of three gentlemen— one to be named by him, one by me, and one by the two others—I hereby pledge myself to retire permanently from the service of "The Examiner." As he has frequently signified his earnest disapproval of my work on that paper, he should think my retirement desirable and advantageous.

I promise, moreover, that if he makes his accusation good I will take him by the hand, which recently I have twice refused when he offered it—once in presence of three members of the press in the corridor of the Capitol, and again in the room of the Senate Committee on Pacific Railroads in the presence of the committee and many gentlemen attending one of its meetings. As to this latter promise I exact but one condition: Mr. Huntington is not to object to my glove. I am, Mr. Editor,

Very respectfully yours,

AMBROSE BIERCE.

Hotel Page, March 20, 1896. [29]

[Clearly, Huntington did not take up Bierce's challenge, for the
latter's articles continued to appear without cessation.]

As the time approaches for Congressional action on the Powers[68] funding bill
there is a gathering of the railroad clans from all points of the compass.

Never before in the history of Congress has been observed so powerful and
shameless a lobby as Mr. Huntington has summoned to his assistance in this crisis of his fortunes, for never before has the game of "influencing legislation" been
played for so enormous a stake. The perpetual net earnings of the Union and
Central Pacific railroads, subject only to an annual deduction of two and a frac-
tion per cent for ninety years, constitutes a glittering prize for which it is not
strange that gentleman of indurated consciences can be persuaded to contend.

A distinguished member of the House said to-day that he had noted no fewer
than twenty-six of Huntington's retainers infesting the corridors of the Capitol,
and it is hardly likely that all are known to him or to any one but their employer.
It is not the habit of this secret soul's emissaries to set the trumpet to their lips
and blow their mandate into the public ear. Like him whom in everything else he
least resembles he "moves in a mysterious way,"[69] and his "unfathomed gulfs of
guile"[70] are among the seven wonders of the world.

Among the known twenty-six is that benevolent old gentleman of New
Hampshire whose famous bill apportioning $100,000,000 of the States in the ra-
tio of their illiteracy once caused an inextinguishable laughter to overrun the
country like a prairie fire. Mr. Blair's ambition ought now to be in course of
gratification; through no talent and with no effort he seems to be rising from the
lowly estate of clown to the proud distinction of scamp.

Senator Morgan has at last succeeded in getting his minority report on
Pacific railroads before the Senate, if not the country. By what suasion the heart
of his colleague, Mr. Pugh,[71] was changed is not known, but that gentleman to-
day reintroduced the report which yesterday he withdrew. He read a letter from
Morgan explaining briefly its character and asking that it be printed in the
record.

Opposition was made by "the Gang," however, and his wish was disallowed.
He has been taken to the country to-day and carries with him the sympathy of
every honest heart and its hopes for his recovery. But Mr. Huntington is understood to be very well content to let nature take her course in that matter.

The opposition to the railroad bill is taking heart. A few weeks ago expressions
of apprehension and dejection were upon every lip, whereas now nearly every anti-
funding member with whom I talk manifests a cheerful disposition toward sunny
views. They seem, indeed, rather to "court a fight." This, I believe, is fairly attributable to the circumstance that every member of Congress, every head of a Government department and every distinguished man in the service here is in daily receipt
of "The Examiner." It is reasonable to presume, then, when a man gets a newspaper

every day he will sometimes read it, and it is hardly possible that one who even occasionally reads "The Examiner" can fail to get some degree of light on the railroad
question, dark as may have been his previous mental condition.

As a single example Speaker Reed, who has a tenderness for the gentle art of
caricature (which also has a leaning toward him) has the walls of one of his rooms
profusely decorated with "Examiner" cartoons, and in their silent influence
grows unconsciously a wiser and a better man.

Nor is he altogether inaccessible to the infection of the letter press, as the following incident will serve to show. The other day a member of the Californian
delegation was in the Speaker's room at the Capitol when a member of the House
Committee on Pacific Railroads entered and laid before the great man a copy of
the issue of April 1st, containing a two-column editorial exposition of the loss that
would be incurred by the Government in borrowing money at $3\frac{1}{2}$ per cent and
loaning it to the Huntington financiers at 2. The showing made in that article
gave them deep concern. They would not explain away those afflicting figures, so
after much scratching of heads they sent for Mr. Powers, the Chairman of the
committee and putative father of the present Funding bill.

Mr. Powers, a man of vast intellectual resource, was equal to the crisis; he read
the article with gravity to the bitter end and scratched his head as hard as the two
of them together. But the devil a word uttered he, and the consultation solemnly
adjourned. [30]

> [What really seemed to turn the tide of public—and Congres-
> sional—opinion against Huntington was another scheme uncon-
> nected with the funding bill, as related by Bierce in an article in
> the *New York Journal* in early May.]

The men interested in the Pacific Railroads Funding bill find promotion of that
giant iniquity an inadequate field for expansion of their powers and satisfaction
of their greed. For several sessions of Congress they have been pushing on the
Western coast of the continent a scheme that is even more frankly naked and un-
ashamed in its rascality than the other, though the immediate profits that it
promises are considerably smaller. This is the construction by the Government
of a private and proprietary harbor near the village of Santa Monica, in Southern
California. The so-called harbor at Santa Monica is a shallow, open roadshed, the
only advantage of which is that Mr. C. P. Huntington and his plundering Kentucky corporation, the Southern Pacific Company, own the only railroad that can
approach it and most of the land surrounding it. At San Pedro, on the contrary,
is a very good harbor, which has been used by ships from the earliest occupation
of the country, and which a small expenditure will make a safe and commodious
anchorage for deep-water vessels.

San Pedro is the natural port of Los Angeles, twenty-two miles inland, the metropolis of Southern California. The disadvantages of San Pedro are that Mr. Huntington has not and cannot secure a monopoly of its railway approaches; that it has permanent docks and wharves, constructed by the people of Los Angeles and an environing country that Mr. Huntington does not own. Both California's Senators and six of her seven Representatives oppose the expenditure of public money on the roadshed of Santa Monica and favor the improvement of the harbor of San Pedro. Two boards of Government engineers, after careful examination, have reported against the former and in favor of the latter, whereas the only report favorable to the former was made by a railroad "expert" in the service of Mr. Huntington.

A few weeks ago, in compliance with a hot popular demand from California, a committee of the House of Representatives struck out of the Rivers and Harbors bill a clause that had been "sneaked" in, carrying an appropriation of $2,800,000 for Santa Monica. The Senate Commerce Committee has not only restored it, but increased the sum to $3,098,000. An interesting and characteristic incident is that Mr. Elkins,[72] who, as Secretary of War, condemned the Santa Monica swindle, is, as Senator, a loud and leading advocate of it. By what suasion this gentleman's change of heart was wrought is imperfectly known here below, but doubtless it is of record in the supremest court.

At the time when the people of Los Angeles were holding indignation meetings and inundating the House Rivers and Harbors Committee with protests and petitions Mr. Huntington was not idle; he had counter meetings, composed of the very scum of the earth, with a small contingent of Santa Monican brought into Los Angeles free by special trains. Brakebeam statesmen and jailbird petitioners swarmed the telegraph offices and divided the attention of the committee. Affidavits are now being published showing that hundreds of these petitioners had not even the small distinction of existence. One man swears that he signed 150 fictitious names; another contented himself with 100 labor unions, having telegraphed to Washington more than a hundred names of workingmen, not one of which was known as that of a man belonging to any labor organization. These frauds, it appears, were engineered by a "railway editor"—a type not peculiar to California, but more numerous and infamous there than elsewhere—and have come to light in the usual way, namely, through a quarrel between him and his chief assistant over an allotment of the spoil.

But "worse remains behind."[73] In the printed report of the proceedings of the Senate Commerce Committee is a petition signed by 200 citizens of Los Angeles advocating "Santa Monica." This surprising phenomenon is easily accounted for: somebody dallied with the telegram, and cheerfully substituted that name for "San Pedro." The real author of this felonious act has not been discovered, but it would not be difficult to name him. These facts are bad enough in themselves, but their larger significance is found in the circumstance that the hopeful beneficiaries of them are the same excellent persons whose interest lies in the success of the Pacific Railroads Funding bill, which has been promoted by the same methods. That is a greater theft, but none is great enough wholly to engage the exuberant activities of these unthinkable thieves. [31]

The news that the Sacramento Republican Convention has passed an anti-funding resolution is glad tidings to our side. It is merely what we had a right to expect, and is perhaps not so significant as would have been the failure of the convention to pass any resolution at all.

A pro-funding resolution was, of course, out of the question, but non-action in the matter would have something of the effect of one. It would have meant that the railroad was in control and that the anti-funding resolution, which was sure to have been offered, was rejected. Indeed, it was reported here to-day that such was the case. Even last evening some of Huntington's forehanded followers were declaring, with a joyousness pretty hard to bear, that such was the fact; and if I rightly understood Tom Geary, he was intolerably happy about it.

The effect of the convention's action cannot be otherwise than beneficial. It is a plain intimation to Speaker Reed and to Messrs. Gear,[74] Powers and Frye that the Funding bill is a perilous toy. If their party is hurt by it they will now be unable to plead that they didn't know it was loaded. The resolution distinctly foreshadows the loss of California's electoral vote for the Republican candidate if a Republican Congress ventures to pass that bill—and California's electoral vote is thought by the party to be a precious possession which they hold in fee simple.

"The action of the California Republican Convention is certainly a great blow to the railroads," said Representative Hilborn,[75] when shown a dispatch containing the news of the adoption of the anti-funding resolution. "It controverts the effect of the repeated assertions of Mr. Huntington that there were not more than a hundred people in California opposed to a funding bill. It is the first time in twenty years that the railroad has been thrown down hard in a Republican convention in California. The action of the convention will be of inestimable aid to the opponents of the Funding bill in fighting this measure in the House. If they had taken no action it would have given the friends of the bill an opportunity to say that there was no sentiment in California in opposition to it.

"This convention being called merely to select delegates to the National Convention to nominate a President was not called upon to express an opinion as to any matter pending before Congress, and the fact that it did so emphasizes the truth that all Californians realize that the railroad question is a live and vital issue, and near to the heart of the people of the State."

"That's bully," said Judge Barham, when informed of the resolution. "With such an indorsement of our course in this matter we can push the fight against the Funding bill with renewed vigor and almost a surety that we will be able to defeat it."

"General" Huntington was holding a council of war at the Normandie upon the Santa Monica swindle, with his friend Senator Jones,[76] and a number of lesser lights who compose his active corps of lobbyists here, when the news was conveyed to him that the California convention had adopted anti-funding resolutions.

He immediately complained of a faint feeling and announced to his friends that he believed he would retire in order to get a good night's sleep and be on the ground early to-morrow to hear what Senator White had to say about the Santa Monica appropriation.

From the excited manner of his lieutenants, however, it is evident that the President of the Southern Pacific received a very unwelcome piece of news to-night. [32]

[Bierce's farewell article is rightfully, but discreetly, self-congratu-latory.]

The close of the session is in sight, and, in all probability, Huntington will be unable to get his Funding bill up in either house, even if he had the hardihood to attempt it. His hundreds of thousands of dollars paid to half-a-hundred high-priced lobbyists has been absolutely wasted. These conscienceless malefactors have fed him fully of false hopes to the last moment, being naturally reluctant to let go their hold upon him as long as he could be made to believe in their power to gather figs from thistles and grapes from thorns. But the end of their power to derive otherwise than by telling the truth—than which they would rather fall—has come at last. The scales have fallen from the eyes of their wretched master; he has retired to the Cave of Adullam to gnaw his gold-worn fingers in impotent rage and curse mankind. He "drags at each remove a lengthening chain"[77] of bitter memories.

In all that he has attempted during the session he has been beaten; and if he renew the struggle next winter, he must do so with broken prestige, his pretensions discredited, himself despised by those who once sought his alliance, entreated his favor and ran with glad feet in the pathway of his will. He could not now secure consideration for his villain bill if he dared. If he could and did, it would not pass the House. If it passed the House a half dozen men could talk it to death in the Senate. If it passed both houses it would incur the Presidential veto. Mr. Cleveland has his vices, but a forgiving disposition is not among them, and I happen to know that the treacherous attempt to take out of his hands the power to appoint the board of engineers in the San Pedro–Santa Monica matter has incensed him. Huntington is now as powerless at the White House as at the Capitol.

What new combinations and alliances he may make during the recess, none can conjecture, but this meanest of all mean men in life or history—this indefatigable seeker for unfair advantages—this promoted peasant with a low love of labor and an unslakable thirst for gain, being already so rich that he stinks—this Huntington person is dead until December.

> Step lightly, stranger, where soe'er you tread;
> All spots are sacred, save where he lies dead.

My work here is at an end. To friends, co-workers, well-wishers and readers, greeting and benediction. [33]

> [The degree to which Bierce's and the *Examiner*'s efforts were ap-
> preciated can be inferred by reading the resolution passed at a
> meeting at Metropolitan Hall a month after the event: "RESOLVED,
> That the thanks of this meeting and of the people of the entire
> Pacific Coast are due to 'The Examiner' and its Washington corre-
> spondent, Mr. Ambrose Bierce, for their faithful publication of all
> the information concerning, and invaluable services against, the
> funding infamy."][78]

The United States and Imperialism

> [In 1898 the onset of the Spanish-American War caused Bierce to
> ponder deeply the role of the United States in international affairs,
> especially in regard to the nation's apparent quest to become an
> imperial power.]

Whatever may be the future position of the United States in international politics; whether we shall adhere to our traditional policy of self-sufficient isolation,
non-intervention in the affairs of the Old World and unquestionable dominance in those of the New; whether we are to remain content with continental
possessions, or join in the general scramble for colonial expansion by treaty,
purchase and conquest; however these momentous questions may be answered
by events impossible to foresee, it is clear enough that we are conducting this
war, if not with a view, yet in a way, to promote the larger scheme. We have,
indeed, already made a distinct departure from the narrower policy and have
put difficulties in the way of a return to it. The Philippine islands are not ours
as yet. They stretch over an enormous area, their geography is largely conjec-
tural and even their number is unknown; but of some of them at least, and these
the most important, we shall probably take possession, and may ever thereafter
find it less difficult and perilous to hold on than to let go. That permanent occupation of Manila will entail annexation of Hawaii goes without saying. It is
to be hoped that even in Congress there is no American who is fool enough to
favor retention of the Philippines and rejection of Hawaii—rejection, that is, of
the indispensable means to an acceptable end. Occupation of Porto Rico presents problems less difficult, and mainly military. It commits us less imperiously

to an abandonment of the Monroe doctrine. Permanent occupation of the Philippines, with such other of Spain's belongings in the Old World as we may find it necessary, expedient or agreeable to take, does so commit us, for it will be futile for us to cry "Hands off!" in the Western Hemisphere while in the Eastern we consecrate property to our uses by the laying on of hands.

This is not a purely military war: like most wars it is partly political and sentimental. It is not conducted as it would be by one whose trade is war alone, and to whom defeat of the enemy in the shortest time and at the least expense of blood and treasure is the sole purpose of action. With such a one at the head of affairs and such a purpose in hand we should not have needed to call for a single volunteer soldier: our little Regular Army was more than strong enough to meet the emergency. This would have been a purely sea war. Our ships would have been ordered to find, pursue, engage and destroy the ships of Spain. They, wherever they might be, would have been the objective points upon which to move. As long as one of them was afloat Havana would have been unmolested, Cienfuegos ignored, San Juan at peace. The rural batteries along the Cuban coast would have been quiet places in which to meditate on the vanity of human life and the mule of Matanzas now be leisurely accomplishing a green old age. None of these places would run away, and the sea power of Spain once broken they would surrender without firing a gun (having nothing to fire it at) on the mere threat of a blockade with nothing afloat to break it. What else could they do?

In such a war Dewey, having destroyed the fleet at Manila,[79] would have left the city unmolested and returned to Hongkong, whence he would have pointed his prows to the Strait of Magellan or to that of Gibraltar, according to his confidence in Sampson and Schley.[80] That is to say, he would have joined the hunt for the rest of the Spanish Navy, knowing that with its effacement the Philippines, like Cuba, Porto Rico and whatever else we might need in our business, would come to us as naturally as ripe fruit falls from a shaken tree.

Why is it that instead of this simple and soldierly programme we have a complicated and enormously costly regime of invasion, requiring more than two hundred thousand volunteer troops? Through what necessity have we violated one of the primal rules of strategy by permitting the enemy to take the initiative and cut out our work for us, absolutely paralyzing us in every effort that we make to carry out our multiplex intent? That is not easy to answer. Mr. McKinley, who was never much of a soldier, may be holding the peculiarly civilian view that effective fighting consists in striking whenever, wherever, however and whatever you can, and that the way to obtain a thing by force is to lay hold of it and hang on, instead of trouncing the owner until he will go get it for you. It is more likely, though, that the policy of invasion is really a policy of retention. We are sending soldiers to the Philippines, and shall be sending them to Porto Rico as soon as the Spanish fleet will let us, not because they are needed there now, but because they will be when the war is over and European powers are disposed to have a hand in the allotment of its fruits. With these islands already held by armies of occupation we can more confidently affirm our right to them than we could if that rested on the assent of a beaten and powerless enemy. Possession is even more points of the law that he shall take who has the power and he shall keep who can than it is of any other law.

The case of Cuba is different. There, as obviously as elsewhere, not a soldier is needed to take the island, and none will be needed to hold it, for we do not mean to hold it. Nor is there any apprehension of its seizure by any other power. As political considerations dictate invasion of the Philippines, so sentimental ones urge invasion of Cuba. Rightly or wrongly, sincerely or disingenuously, we have made the ribby reconcentrado our peculiar care: he is an issue in this case and an exhibit for the prosecution. We have bound ourselves to promote his longevity and soften his crow-bait lot. He has a right to expect that we will take such action as will detach his belly from his back, instead of cementing the union by continued blockade. In his interest we must invade his fatherland whether we need to or not, for he may be still partly alive.

Doubtless it is such considerations as these that have determined the character of the war. If so we are already committed by our action in the Philippines, and our proposed action in Porto Rico, to that new and larger national policy which will give us high rank among the robber powers engaged in partition of the world. [34]

We are taking the Philippine islands from Spain because we have the right. They are spoils of the victor and a victor's rights are coterminous with his power. We are taking them from the Filipinos because we want them. Our action has no other character than purveyance to our own desires. Why should we not candidly say so, and free ourselves from the charge of sniveling hypocrisy? All this talk about our new responsibilities, thrust upon us by the fortunes of war, and so forth, is fool talk. For what we do or don't over there we are responsible to nobody. We could let go if we chose, and if other nations chose to take hold, and should come to blows over what we left, that would be their own affair, not ours. Nothing has been thrust upon us; we had not been pitchforked into the van of the landgrabbers; we have deliberately entered into the squabble and elbowed our way to the front. If we are really concerned about the fate of Great Britain, France, Germany and Russia—if we fear that in precipitating themselves headlong upon what we leave they may crack their precious skulls, and in their greed to grab it scratch one another's hands, we can do as we propose to do in Cuba—give the natives self-government under our protection. It does not greatly matter what we do, but it greatly matters how we do it. If we want the Philippines let us hold them, but let us do so with dignity and self-respect, giving no reasons or true ones. It is well enough understood that national magnanimity is a lie; that nations act from no higher motives than the desire to promote their own interest;

that the basis of international relations is selfishness tempered by mistrust. The entire business of being a nation is as innocent of morality as that of a thief or a pirate. Diplomacy is the art of getting what you can in exchange for what you cannot.

These things being so, and generally known to be so, what is the good of gilding our honest greed with glittering platitudes that deceive nobody, not even ourselves. To the Spaniards we owe no explanation; to the Filipinos we can make none; but to ourselves, in the privacy of the newspapers, we might with moral advantage admit that when the savage Philippine islands came running after us to bite us we could have got away from them if we had tried. [35]

Bierce Is Hit Hard

[Personal disasters were by no means absent from Bierce's life during his *Examiner* period, but few receive mention even in private correspondence. He separated from his wife in 1888; in 1889 his eldest son, seventeen-year-old Day, died in a duel over a girl; and in 1901 his second son, Leigh, died of pneumonia. The last event is noted only briefly in a few letters of the period.]

I thank you for your sympathy and offer of service. There is nothing that you can do.

As to the funeral, I do not yet know when it will be. I would rather see you here than there. Being a little broken in body and mind I don't want to take any chances of making an idiot of myself before my friends. [36]

Maybe I owe you a lot of letters. I don't know—my correspondence is all in arrears and I've not the heart to take it up.

Thank you for your kind words of sympathy. I'm hit harder than any one can guess from the known facts—am a bit broken and gone gray of it all. [37]

(1905–1913)

The End

Troubles at *Cosmopolitan*

[Almost from the start, Bierce's tenure on
Cosmopolitan was soured by disagreements
with the editorial staff—a situation not
helped by the fact that editors on the magazine came and went with bewildering rapidity. To Bailey Millard, editor in 1905–6, Bierce
defends his practice of writing "tragic" stories
rather than those with conventionally happy
endings.]

All right—we'll write stories for each other some day.
Meantime, my stories for the magazine are made on the
lines of Mr. Hearst's preference if I rightly understand him.
But I've other reasons—one of which is that I consider tragedy not only a higher order of thing than comedy, but a
thing which takes a stronger grip on attention and has a
more lasting vogue—*teste* the continued fame of it in the
instance of such men as Poe, and the wide contemporary
"popularity" in the instance of such as de Maupassant. Of
which their works does one think first (and last) when
thinking of Shakspeare, Goethe, Keats and all

"The dead but sceptred sovereigns who still rule
Our spirits from their urns"?[1]

—I mean those who have done work in both manners.

For me to write a yarn with none of the tragic in it would hardly be what you call "breaking out in a new place". In my first story-book are a few that haven't any of it, and in my second a half-dozen or more. [1]

[Bierce also expressed frustration at being hamstrung by Hearst's
stipulation that Bierce write a column of commentary on current
events, "The Passing Show."]

I have all along found that department the most difficult and unsatisfactory work that I have ever done, as I have repeatedly pointed out to Mr. Millard, who, I think, understands. The reason is this: The title, "The Passing Show," compels the stuff to be topical, to deal with passing events, things going on. But to write of passing events that which cannot be published until the events are a month-and-a-half dead is a thing that it is impossible to do intelligently. This I foresaw from the first, and ventured to give my stuff another (though not a good) title, although the title now used was suggested by Mr. Hearst. He requested that I use the title that he had chosen, and I have done so, but it mastered me—handicapped me. The work has been bad except where I have departed from the topical character that it implies.

Mr. Hearst, doubtless, has so many other and larger affairs engaging his attention that he has not thought much about this small one. I hope, at least, that he has not thought as much about it as I have; to me it has been a veritable nightmare. It is like the consciousness of being a dealer in stale champagne.

Of course I like to work for the magazine, and I have no objection to a "department." My notion is that some such work as that in the August number[2] (with a better head) is what I can do best and is best for the mag, but I'm hospitable to suggestion. Will you kindly let me know if my proposal meets with your approval? Perhaps, if the matter seems to you of sufficient importance, you will submit it to Mr. Hearst. [2]

[The first of Bierce's several resignations—most of them very
short lived—occurred in late spring of 1906.]

I'm off Mr. Hearst's payroll—by voluntary resignation. Couldn't stand the monkeying of his editors with my stuff, and had tired of appealing to him. He always decided in my favor, but never enforced his decisions by "appropriate penalties".

So I'm now without an income, but retain my self-respect, which is not a bad substitute. Anything that comes so high ought to be good. [3]

My emancipation from Mr. Hearst's service was, alas, brief. He did not want it that way, and I can't resist him, for he has been, on the whole, mighty good to me. He promises redress of my grievance, though I'm convinced that after a little while things will go wrong in the same old way. The trouble is, he lets his editors "run" him; and they are the scurviest lot living. He is starting a new magazine, "America", and wants my help. Maybe when he has magazines enough I can cut his newspapers altogether. [4]

> [Bierce did indeed "cut" his work for the Hearst newspapers, writ-
> ing nothing for them after July 1906. But troubles at *Cosmopolitan*
> persisted, especially in regard to a new editor named Maxwell.]

You say that "two contributions by one author in the same number is, I think, something that no good editor will endure." The traditions of every business are the creation of the small men in it—they being in an overwhelming majority. They sometimes make small successes. The great successes are made by men great enough to disregard them and their traditions. I have succeeded in some things myself (editing, among others) but never did so in any other way. That is the "secret" of Mr. Hearst's success—in business. It is the secret of every man's success. That is a matter for you to decide, however; it is none of my affair. But I understood Mr. Hearst to want more of my work in the magazine, and you told me that he did. How can he get it under that rule? We agreed on a department. That, of course, will go in every month, and it will bear my name. You have told me that you want stories too, and I know that Mr. Hearst wants them, for *he* told me so. Your rule excludes them. (I have one already written and was about to make another, but of course I shall not send any now.) Pardon me, but you seem a little inconsistent.

The title "Matters of Fact" will hardly do for my department, for much of the work will have nothing to do with fact. Some of that which you have is not related to fact at all; much of it being imaginary and much being opinion. "Matters of Fact" was a subhead for the first paragraphs only. My preference for a title is "Small Contributions."

I shall expect it to go as written, the verses, the epigrams, the dialogue and all. You assured me that I should have "absolute liberty"; the work would have no charm for me if I had not.

I sincerely hope that we shall not have irreconcilable views about my place in the scheme of the magazine. It is not to my interest to have any place in it, but if I have one it must suit me. It suits me to do as little as you think Mr. Hearst will stand, but none will be anonymous (I wish the law permitted *nobody* to write anonymously) and you must not take the cream and throw away the milk, or what you consider the milk. That *I* would not stand. [5]

> [Matters dragged on unsatisfactorily until the summer of 1907, when Bierce's patience was exhausted and he felt compelled to resign again. This time he wrote directly to Hearst.]

Since coming East I have not been allowed a free hand in your papers. You have yourself (as was your right) limited my liberty of attacking the men whom *I* think the worst enemies of the country. Your editors have gone much further in a policy of repression. I could not even write book-reviews unless I conformed to *their* views. (For examples, I wrote one on the work of Upton Sinclair and another on that of Maxim Gorky, considered *merely as literature.* Both were turned down because these gentlemen were "going to" do something for the paper— which they didn't do. In a few weeks the paper was abusing Gorky as if he had been a thief!) So I retired to the Cosmopolitan. It was my last ditch. I tried to earn my salary on it, but Mr. Maxwell would not let me. I was willing to write the whole magazine, covers and all, but more than half my stuff was thrown out, and they have now on hand three "ghost stories" of mine and a review of a poem. (Maybe Chamberlain[3] will run them; he says he will, but it was on account of him that I quit your newspapers.) All this time the magazine has found plenty of room to run a story by Mr. Block *every month.*[4]

In brief, I have wasted eight years trying in your papers to make the same reputation here that you permitted me to make in California, and I have given it up. But if I cannot fight the men whom I think public enemies I will not fight anybody. I don't like the job of chained bulldog, to be let loose only to tear the panties off the boys who throw rocks at *you.* You wouldn't like it yourself in my place. Henceforth I won't *bite anybody;* a nice quiet life for mine. I'm going to be a literary gent, thank you—it is nicer, and there is nobody that can say me nay.

From what I have said it follows you have a right to my resignation from your service. It is hereby tendered, and on its acceptance I will be "heard to cease."[5] Please notify me by wire and say that you don't mind. [6]

From the tenor of your telegrams to Ihmsen[6] I judge that you have been dissatisfied with the amount of my work—not with its quality, I hope. You could not be any more dissatisfied than I was, as I explained in my other letter. You will recall, I think, that in my last conversation with you I told you that I could no longer work for your paper, and as I was allowed only a little space in the magazine I suggested a change in my salary. Your reply was that you were not shrieking. Of course, then, it was not up to me to shriek. Still I felt that you ought to have more work for your money. Your editor seemed to think differently, limited my department to three pages and, on the foolish ground that he did not want my name *twice* in the table of contents, would run nothing else of mine. I enclose carbon copies of two of my letters about this matter, in order that you may see that I did all that I could to earn my salary from the magazine.

Chamberlain is now showing a disposition to give me a square deal—or rather give you one—by running the stuff that Maxwell would not.

I never knew anything about the ownership of the magazine, or which of your publications paid my salary. I supposed that was merely a matter of book-keeping.

No, I cannot again work for your newspapers under the kind of men that run them. They know that I detest them—most of them—and in gratification of their revenge they do not hesitate to sacrifice your interests along with mine when the two are mixed. Even your express wishes, communicated to me and to them, count for nothing with them. It was not so in California, and there I did great work for you; but it has always been so here and always would be so.

The purpose of this note is simply to clear me of any suspicion that you may possibly have entertained that I took your money without *trying* to earn it. The delinquency, I think you will admit, was not mine. [7]

> [A new proposal by yet another editor, S. S. Chamberlain, in the summer of 1908 met with Bierce's emphatic disapproval, as re-corded in another series of letters to Hearst.]

You have larger affairs on your hands than the simple matter of *me*. Don't bother about me at all. I don't care to work for your newspapers: the combination of Chamberlain, Brisbane[7] and Block is too many for me. For that matter I don't care to work for any newspaper.

As to Chamberlain's proposal, it is altogether absurd and insincere. If he would not use my stories (for example) when he got them for nothing—I being on salary—is it likely that he would use "six a year at $200 a story?" He makes me weary. He may, as editor, blue-pencil and waste-basket me into oblivion, but that he should have power to starve me in addition is out of the question. When he is my editor I must of course correspond with him occasionally, but *negotiate* with him or accept any terms of payment that he will have the power to affect—nay, nay.

If you want me to work for your magazine I shall be pleased to do so for any salary that you may name, and I will perform an equivalent service, as I have always done. But *you* will have to see that you get the worth of your money; the Chamberlains, Maxwells and Blocks of your entourage will not let you get it if by cheating *you* they think they can worry *me*. If you don't really care for my work the matter is very simple. I have remained on the magazine because you did not accept my resignation and I supposed that you *wanted* me to remain—

despite my unwillingness to be a man-of-all-work (which I never undertook to be) and despite your persistent misunderstanding of my jocularity as sarcasm and my chaffing as serious accusation. But if you do not care for my work you have only to accept the resignation which I beg you to consider that you have always in hand. (I am working on my memoirs and need a whole lot of time anyhow.)[8]

I have never believed you cognizant of the annoyances to which I have been subjected, for you have tried to stop those that I have brought to your attention—thereby incensing their authors and making my last state worse than my first—but have always felt that you had somehow the notion that I entertained a personal dislike of you—which is so far from the truth that my personal regard for you is all that has kept me in your service, "in daily contact with the things" (mostly Chamberlains and Blocks) "I loathe."

You promise to consult with Chamberlain about me. Good, but how would it do to consult with *me?* If you will give me some idle half hour I can tell you some things that you will find interesting and profitable to know. Not about my compensation—that does not need any talking over with me or anybody. Fix it to suit yourself and you will suit me—if it does not depend on your editors' "acceptance" of my stuff. [8]

I am sorry that in a matter more nearly affecting my interests than Chamberlain's you declined to consult me as well as him. That was neither friendly nor just. You say that there is no one about the Cosmopolitan office who is the least bit unfriendly to me. How can you know that? You have of course nothing but somebody's word for it, whereas you have had repeated proofs of Mr. Chamberlain's unfriendliness extending over a period of years. I have submitted them myself and you have acted on them by "reversing" him. If he is unfriendly to me is it to be supposed that he would tell you so? Surely you know human nature better than that. Well, I will submit more evidence. Since he came to the magazine my name has been carefully left out of the list of contributors, in the advertisements. I think it has not appeared once, whereas the others have been persistently "boomed," even the poorest of them. This is not a complaint, for I care nothing about it; it is mentioned as evidence of unfairness, and is not subject to any other interpretation.

Mr. Chamberlain tells you that he "cannot use a great amount of any one person's contributions without depriving the magazine of variety"—and you apparently accept that as true. Now it so happens that I am the only contributor whose work has been *various.* I have written nearly all the kinds of stuff that I used to write for your newspapers. I could write them no better, for whether I am writing for a newspaper, a magazine, or a book I cannot help writing as well as I know how. No good writer *can* help it, and no honest man would if he could. But Chamberlain has, persistently and without consulting me, cut out of my department all but one kind of stuff—this stickler for "variety"! If you looked at the slaughtered stuff that I sent you know that this is true. But I fear you find it more trouble to be just than to take somebody's word for it—somebody's else than mine.

Chamberlain finds no difficulty in using "a great amount of one person's contributions" in the cases of his much beboomed contributors, Lewis[9] and Block. One of them has a story every month and the other has had dozens—enough to make a large book. I have succeeded in getting in *two* (not counting three or four little ones of a page or so each.) If I had as much in the magazine as either of these two favorites would you not have thought that I earned my salary. If not your appraisement of the value of my work differs from that of the editors who are always asking me for stories. Only one of my two stories was run by Chamberlain, yet he promised to use as many as I cared to write.

Are Lewis's and Block's yarns distinguished for "variety"? One writes of nothing but cowboys, the other of nothing but Jews—one story just like another. I don't say that their work is not better than mine; I scorn to say anything about it; but they have no variety, and Chamberlain's reason for excluding me is an obvious lie. No, not an obvious one, or you would have seen its falsehood, but a lie all the same.

Now, I have told you that I would accept for the magazine work any salary that you choose to name. I stand to that. But it must be a *salary,* guaranteed by *you* and not dependent on Chamberlain's or anybody else's good will to me or my work, or anybody's treatment of it. I would not write for you for a dollar a word if any part of my money depended on any of your present editors' "acceptances" of the work. I've had a bellyful of that in my time.

If you figure my pay on the basis of Chamberlain's proposal, as to rate and amount of work, you will find that (assuming him to act in good faith) it about cuts my present salary in half. That is all right if I get the half, and may, as you say, write for other magazines and the weekly papers, or your papers. (But if I do write for your papers I shall set my own price on the articles and your editors can take them or leave them.)

So—I am willing to do the work that Chamberlain outlines (if that is what you want) for a salary of $2500 a year, so long as I am not subjected to any of the ten thousand kinds of annoyance that editors know how to use against contributors whom they personally dislike; some of which you know have been used against me, for on my complaint you have put a stop to them—temporarily. But I warn you that your stuffed Machiavelli will again resort to them when your back is turned.

It is a little amusing, the "fear" of me that you say pervades that neck o' woods. Perhaps that was why you refused to see me, though truly I should not have trampled you with my hoofs nor gored you with my horns. I should have

been restrained by what has kept me working for you all these years: certain
pleasant memories of the lovable Will Hearst of the old Merchant Street days—
in the Hon. William Randolph Hearst I never took much interest.

O well, I am sixty-six, but I still cherish the hope that you may, before I peg
out, meet a gentleman who personally knows me. Meantime, I shall await your
answer to that part of this letter that is relevant to yours. The other parts are just
"thrown in" for the joy of battle, and because I have a habit of proving my assertions. No part of it is confidential: I am entirely willing that Chamberlain should
know what I think of him. It is honey and sugar compared with what posterity
will think of him when I've done with him. [9]

> [Bierce's continued dissatisfaction led to another plea to Hearst in
> the spring of 1909 to exercise greater control over his editors.]

I thank you for your good opinion of my story.[10] And it amused me to observe
that you are not without a vestigial influence in the magazine; for both Mr. von
Utassy and Mr. Norcross[11] have suddenly discovered that I am a great writer. Such
an awakening!

Now, seriously, the story is no better than others that I have written for the
mag. nor nearly so good as "The Moonlit Road," January, 1907; yet that and most
of the others met with even more contemptuous treatment than *it* did—lying in
the office for months unpublished, against my protestations. Indeed, nearly all
my work has been treated in the same way. There is, or should be, pages of it in
the office now.

In the three months since you and I had a distinct and definite agreement
(which was immediately, and on two other occasions, "ratified" by Mr. Norcross)
nothing has been done to carry it out, except to give me Horace Taylor to illustrate the "Little Johnny" stuff.

Mr. Norcross, when here a month ago, said the trouble was caused by Mr.
Casamajor's disobedience of his orders, and he would discharge him—which I
did not suggest. But Mr. Casamajor (who once, in the presence of the whole
office force, told me that I should have but three pages in any issue) is still "disobedient" and still "undischarged". As long as that worthy Jew peasant and anar-
chist of the Brisben Walker régime[12] is within a mile of the office there will be
trouble about my work. I venture to suggest that you promote him to The
Evening Journal and replace him with a human being. You are wrong, though,
in the inference that I whacked him for what he did to my last story. I simply
stopped sending stories. Excepting my last letter to Chamberlain, I have never
written about my work to any of the gang otherwise than in the most civil and
conciliatory way. All to no purpose.

You have always said you liked my work, and I suppose you do or you would not employ me. But have you ever seen it commended ("featured," I think they call it) in the magazine's advertisements and announcements? Tom, Dick and Harry have been crowed over (ineffectually, of course) as the greatest writers of the age, but Ambrose Bierce is never deemed worthy of more than mention by name, and seldom by so much as that. I am pretty tired of playing second fiddle, or no fiddle at all, to the nobodies whom your yellow journalist editors choose to think great. Do you wonder if I am not an enthusiastic contributor?

You will call this a roast of *you.* Not at all: I don't believe that you know how the men that serve *you* serve *me.* The matter seems hopeless. There can be no peace and good work until I am treated up there with at least as much consideration as is due from the Creator of the Suns to a scullery maid polishing a new tin pan.

Our agreement was that I was to have for my department of "Small Contributions" an irreducible minimum of five (5) pages, and was to do one article per issue (which might be a story), in addition—and I'm willing to throw in a "Little Johnny". Please look over the magazine of the last three months and see if that agreement has been kept. If not, I suggest that you demand an explanation. Of course I cannot, in making an agreement, deal with editors whom you change every foggy morning. I can only negotiate with you, for you only are permanent.

When Mr. Norcross was here he said that I should virtually edit my own department. Nothing came of the promise, and I have no more knowledge of what is going into it than the man from Mars. If *you* are willing that I shall edit my own department, and can rid yourself of the notion, sedulously implanted by your Chamberlains, that I would wreck your magazine, I will at my own expense go to New York and do so, every month. I don't hanker for the job, but foresee that it will pretty soon have to be that or nothing. But, anyhow, if the agreement that we made still suits you please see that your wishes are respected. Then you will get all the stories that you can want. I have carried out my part of our understanding by sending oceans of copy and giving you a monopoly of my work.

I am going to New York to-morrow to see what those fellows have done, or are going to do, with my stuff, though I have repeatedly done this before, at no expense to you. I shall probably be for a few days at the Navarre hotel, and shall be glad to call on you if for any reason you should care to see me. [10]

[Nothing came of this, however, and Bierce resigned shortly thereafter. His last contribution to *Cosmopolitan* was published in May 1909.]

The San Francisco Earthquake

[The cataclysmic earthquake and fire in San Francisco on April 17, 1906, found Bierce a distant, helpless, but keenly concerned by-

stander. His first wish was to hear of the fate of his friends, to
whom he later lent considerable assistance. Later he ruminated on
whether he could ever endure to visit the city that had been his
residence for nearly three decades.]

I write in the hope that you are alive and the fear that you are wrecked.

Please let me know if I can help—I need not say how glad I shall be to do so.
"Help" would go with this were I sure about you and the post-office.

It's a mighty bad business and one does not need to own property out there
to be "hit hard" by it. One needs only to have friends there.

We are helpless here, so far as the telegraph is concerned—shall not be able
to get anything on the wires for many days, all private dispatches being refused.

Pray God you and yours may be all right. Of course anything that you may be
able to tell me of my friends will be gratefully received. [11]

But here I am forgetting (momentarily) that awful wiping out of San Francisco.
It "hit" me pretty hard in many ways—mostly indirectly, through my friends. I
had rather hoped to have to "put up" for you and your gang, and am a trifle disappointed to know that you are all right—except the chimneys. I'm glad that tidal
wave did not come, but don't you think you'd better have a canoe ready?[13] You
could keep it on your veranda stacked with provisions and whiskey.

My letter from Ursus[14] (written during the conflagration) expresses a keen solicitude for the Farallones, as the fire was working westward. [12]

It was indeed a rough deal you San Franciscans got. I had always expected to go
back to the good old town some day, but I have no desire to see the new town, if
there is to be one. I fear the fire consumed even the ghosts that used to meet me
at every street corner—ghosts of dear dead friends, oh, so many of them! [13]

Writing Off Old Friends

[As Bierce aged, he appeared to become increasingly intolerant of
the foibles of those he once considered his friends. The following
letters to Herman Scheffauer—a poet whom Bierce had assisted
for more than a decade—are typical of the habit he adopted late in
life of dismissing old friends from his favor.]

The friends that warned you against the precarious nature of my friendship were
right. To hold my regard one must fulfil hard conditions—hard if one is not what
one should be; easy if one is. I have, indeed, a habit of calmly considering the character of a man with whom I have fallen into any intimacy and, whether I have any

grievance against him or not, informing him by letter that I no longer desire his acquaintance. This I do after deciding that he is not truthful, candid, without conceit, and so forth—in brief, honorable. If any one is conscious that he is not in all respects worthy of my friendship he would better not cultivate it, for assuredly no one can long conceal his true character from an observant student of it. Yes, my friendship is a precarious possession. It grows more so the longer I live, and the less I feel the need of a multitude of friends. So, if in your heart you are conscious of being any of the things which you accuse *me* of being, or anything else equally objectionable (to *me*) I can only advise you to drop me before I drop you.

Certainly you have an undoubted right to your opinion of my ability, my attainments and my standing. If you choose to publish a censorious judgment of these matters do so by all means: I don't think I ever cared a cent for what was printed about me, except as it supplied me with welcome material for my pen. One may presumably have a "sense of duty to the public", and the like. But convincing one person (one at a time) of one's friend's deficiencies is hardly worth while, and is to be judged differently. It comes under another rule. Particularly is this so when the person enlightened is the publisher of the person under consideration, and there are pending between the two delicate negotiations affectible by the conversation.

Maybe, as you say, my work lacks "soul," but my life does not, and a man's life is the man. Personally, I hold that sentiment has a place in the world, and that loyalty to a friend is not inferior as a characteristic to correctness of literary judgment. If there is a heaven I think it is more valued there. If Mr. Neale[15] (your publisher as well as mine) had considered you a Homer, a Goethe or a Shakspeare a team of horses could not have drawn from me the expression of a lower estimate. And let me tell you that if you are going through life as a mere thinking machine, ignoring the generous promptings of the heart, sacrificing it to the brain, you will have a hard row to hoe, and the outcome, when you survey it from the vantage ground of age, will not please you. You seem to be beginning rather badly, as regards both your fortunes and your peace of mind. . . .

I must commend your candor in one thing. You confirm Neale's words in saying that you commented on "my seeming lack of sympathy with certain modern masters," which you attribute to my not having read them. That is a conclusion to which a low order of mind in sympathy with the "modern masters" naturally jumps, but it is hardly worthy of a man of your brains. It is like your former lofty assumption that I had not read some ten or twelve philosophers, naming them, nearly all of whom I had read, and laughed at before you were born. In fact, one of your most conspicuous characteristics is the assumption that what a man who does not care to "talk shop" does not speak of, and vaunt his knowledge of, he does not know. I once thought this a boyish fault, but you are no longer a boy. Your "modern masters" are Ibsen and Shaw, with both of whose works and ways

I am thoroughly familiar, and both of whom I think very small men—pets of the drawing-room and gods of the hour. No, I am not an "up to date" critic, thank God. I am not a literary critic at all, and never, or very seldom, have gone into that field except in pursuance of a personal object—to help a good writer (who is commonly a friend)—maybe you can recall such instances—or laugh at a fool. Surely you do not consider my work in the Cosmopolitan, (mere badinage and chaff, the only kind of stuff that the magazine wants from me, or will print) essays in literary criticism. It has never occurred to me to look upon myself as a literary critic; if you *must* prick my bubble please to observe that it contains more of your breath than of mine. Yet you have sometimes seemed to value, I thought, some of my notions about even poetry. Still it must be very comfortable to feel that it is purely "by your own efforts" that you have risen. I am very glad indeed that you do not suffer from the sense of obligation which some minds find it a delight to feel. . . .

I bear you no ill will, shall watch your career in letters with friendly solicitude—have, in fact, just sent in to the Cosmopolitan a most appreciative paragraph about your book,[16] which may or may not commend itself to the editor; most of what I write does not. I hope to do a little, now and then to further your success in letters. I wish you were different (and that is the harshest criticism that I ever uttered of you except to yourself) and wish it for your sake more than for mine. I am older than you and probably more "acquainted with grief"[17]—the grief of disappointment and disillusion. If in the future you are convinced that you have *become* different, and I am still living, my welcoming hand awaits you. And when I forgive I forgive all over, even the new offence. [14]

[Thereafter there seems to have been a temporary reconciliation, but a final break came in early 1909.]

If our "falling out" is "incomprehensible" to you I suggest that you read our recent correspondence in the matter.

I would further suggest that if there is a way to my favor open to you it lies (as noted in that correspondence) through the region of repentance, confession and reform. My objection to you is your character, as illustrated in every phase and incident of our acquaintance—in your letters, in what all who know you tell me of you, and, more clearly than all, in what you have told me of others. As to that last I will recall to your memory a few characteristic instances. For the purpose, apparently, of establishing your reputation as a lady-killer you did not hesitate to slander George Sterling's sister.[18] On the way to Saybrook you told me a particularly foul story, explaining that Shatsie told it to you. That needed no refutation. What it called for was something that (the more shame to me) I did not administer. When we were last in New York you told me that a lady whom it is needless to name had complained of the conduct of Dr. Franklin, whom I had taken to her house. That I found to be false, and I hardly think you will reaffirm it. Generally speaking, you have villified pretty nearly everybody that you and I have known, and I do not doubt that you have performed, or will perform, the same office for me.

Even in this letter before me, asking a reconciliation, the same ruling passion is manifest, first, in abuse of Mr. Neale, morally, socially and intellectually your superior, and, second, in a singularly dastardly attempt to set me against my friend Ed. Clough by as puerile and transparent a device as could be found in all the history of secret stabbing. I might forgive the stroke, for like all your assassin methods it is ineffective, but your low opinion of my discernment is unpardonable.

Do you care for further light upon your personal character? Of course you know it as well as I; the trouble is that you think it unknown to others; you are such an intellectual babe as to believe that one's character is a thing that can be hidden. You believe, doubtless, that your faithless and ungenerous nature did not show when in the famous controversy over George's poem—when your two friends were being foully assailed by the vicious and ignorant—you stood aside and made mouths.[19] You probably think that I am unaware of your ingratitude in withholding any public acknowledgment of my years of service to you—a niggardliness which you accounted for with a lie derogatory to our dead friend Dr. Doyle.[20] You did not know that I had the disproof of that falsehood in what I suppose to be the last letter that he ever wrote. Has it ever occurred to you to contrast yourself in this matter with that generous soul, George Sterling? I fancy it has. I fancy it was the consciousness of the difference that prompted your impudent attempt to minify my friendly help of others, even in letters to *me.* The attempt was to convince yourself. You would feel better if you could do that— your mind is that kind of mind: the sense of obligation is painful to it. "Every little distinction I have ever achieved has been through hard work, and purely by my own efforts." *This* to *me!*

I can easily conceive your state of mind on reading this letter. Even a friendly controversy is inconceivable to you; a difference of opinion is to you an opportunity for insult, and it is nothing else; and when you are cornered you are like a rattlesnake pegged down by the tail—you strike at everything in sight. But let me warn you: I have now struck at you, for as an honest man I have the right; but if ever again you strike at me I shall punish you.

I have kept these things to myself. The men and women that you have slandered do not know that you have slandered them. The fact that some of them maintain friendly relations with you should show you that. I hope for your success in literature, and shall probably do something (in a different way from the old way) to promote it,—an attitude that I do not expect you to comprehend. But our personal relations are at an end. If you have no more self-respect than to

reply to this letter, that will be most unwise. Continue in that "serenity" of which
you boast, but let me alone now and henceforth. [15]

The Collected Works

[In the spring of 1908 the young publisher Walter Neale proposed
the issuance of an edition of Bierce's collected works in ten volumes (later expanded to twelve). The project would occupy much
of Bierce's time during the years 1908–12. Presented below are
vignettes of Bierce's work on the series—selection and arrangement, proofreading, and numberless other details—derived
mostly from Bierce's voluminous letters to Neale.]

I am glad that your project still seems practicable to you—that is, that you think
not only that you can come out without a loss, but with a profit. I should be better
pleased to drop it than to fear that you'd lose by it; and if at any time hereafter you
have reason to fear a loss please do not hesitate to say so and we will abandon it.

There is one part of your plan that I'm doubtful about—the size of the volumes.
Your notion is to have them 400 or more pages octavo. I have been hard at work
getting the stuff that I have into shape and planning for the ten volumes. I can't find
4,000 octavo pages of my *best* work, unless I use too much of one kind. I have
enough (of all sorts) to make 10,000 or 20,000, but I want to be severely critical, admitting nothing but what I think my best work. And I figure out about 3,000 pages
instead of 4,000—that is the volumes to be of 300 pages, or thereabout. Your first
"Can Such Things Be?" is a fattish book, but it has only 320 pages.[21] The London
edition of "In the Midst of Life" is about the same size, with only 244.[22]

We will talk of this when we meet. I go to New York (to dinner) tomorrow,
but expect to be back in time to take luncheon with you here on the 6th May. I
hope you can come out to the house, for I want to show you my "program" and
what I have for the books. I've a tentative plan for each volume. [16]

To the early issue of so elaborate a prospectus[23] as you have in mind there are
even more difficulties than you mention. I am thinking hard how to overcome
most of them, but the one about the table of contents of each volume is, I fear,
insuperable. Of even the volumes that I have virtually made up I cannot make
tables, for I'm unable to say if I shall not have to add to, or subtract from, them
when you have computed their bulk. With reference to those still to be made up
the difficulty is worse. One or two of the books, as now existing, contain as many
as 240 titles, some of which will be dropped, others added.

Within a few weeks I shall be able to make a *general* table of contents (some-

thing like the merely experimental one enclosed) with an account of the character of each volume.[24] [17]

[Enclosure:]
Vol. I.	Ashes of the Beacon
	The Land beyond the Blow
	For the Ahkoond
	John Smith, Liberator
Vol. II.	In the Midst of Life
Vol. III.	Can Such Things Be?
Vol. IV.	Shapes of Clay
Vol. V.	Black Beetles in Amber
Vol. VI.	The Devil's Dictionary
	Epigrams+
	Apocryphal Dialogues+
Vol. VII.	Grotesque and Humorous Tales+
	Little Johnny+
Vol. VIII.	The Monk and the Hangman's Daughter
	Fantastic Fables
Vol. IX.	The Howes Stuff—title undetermined+[25]
Vol. X.	Essays in Little+
	Miscellaneous+

+Unpublished in Book Form.

As to my "Collected Works". Vol. I is long out, and Vol. II is now due from
the press. Of course I know little of Neale's manner of putting it on the market,
except that it is a subscription work and that he says he will not take orders (and
pay commissions) through dealers. He told me that you had been apprised of
that. As to the expediency of that policy, I am of course unable to judge, but
am sorry if it deprives anybody of the book who wanted it. It is very beautiful
and he (Neale) says so expensive to him as to leave no margin for commissions.
I'm hoping that he'll not decide that he cannot afford to pay royalties either.
[18]

> [By the spring of 1911 Neale, having achieved sufficient success on
> the sale of the first ten volumes, decided to add two more, one of
> them being largely a reprint of *The Shadow on the Dial*. Bierce
> plunged into the work of compilation immediately.]

I shall proceed to make Vols. XI and XII at once. This will enable us to use the
omitted copy that your printers have on hand—the "overplus". Some of it is al-

ready in type—all the "Apocryphal Dialogues" and a part of the "Little Johnny." I suggest that it be all set up at once and proofs sent to me, so that I can see how to "bestow" it. Some of it will have to go in Vol. X, and I think that for congruity a part of it should go in Vol. VIII—I can tell better when I see it.

I have turned up a lot of stuff that I had prepared before going to California, laid away and forgotten about. We shall have plenty from the twelve volumes without "Write It Right"[26]—which probably ought not to be included anyhow.

We have the *legal* right to use much (not all) the contents of the Howes book, but it will be better to have his written consent, which he will doubtless cheerfully give. I am writing him about it. [19]

> [As early as the fall of 1908, Bierce was excoriating Neale's printers.
> The issue would cause considerable disaffection between the two
> over the next several years.]

If you control the printers please, O *please,* forbid *close* punctuation.[27] In Vol. I I did not chase out the needless commas in the copy—so I didn't feel at liberty to get after them in the proofs. The result is pretty bad—not infrequently it is awful! In reading it I feel as if walking over freshly plowed ground, or the ties of a railway.

Printers go by hard-and-fast rules, but a writer's punctuation is an important part of his style, expressing many subtle things, and cannot be reduced to rule except in a general way. I've looked after that in all the volumes (except the first) that you have, and shall in the others, but fear the "intelligent compositor" will beat me. His upsetting sin and particular lunacy are profusion of commas. [20]

I'll read and return the proofs as soon as possible—have gone over them already to see if corrections have been made. My temper suffered. I don't see how you get your work done by such printers. I've had to do with printers all my life, and yours are the absolute worst that I ever knew. Almost always (for example) in taking out a line to correct one error they make a worse one, transposing the letters in the most awful way. And your editor does not know how to mark proof sheets—that is, does not know the alphabet of the trade. Yesterday I got into such a state of mind over these matters that I had to quit work and was, I fear, rude and unmannerly in the presence of Miss Christiansen.[28] As she cannot be here to assist me further, I'm expecting this volume to be full of damnation. [21]

Vol. VIII came yesterday. I'm ashamed to be worrying you with further complaints of the awful work done by your printing house, and would not do so only in the hope of betterment before the whole edition is run off (since you say, to my bewilderment, that books are not "printed".) Look at p. 291. The second half of the foot-note beginning on the page preceding is put at the *top* of the page. On page 317 a foot-note is put immediately *after* the part of the text to which it relates—not at the *bottom of the page,* where God would have put it.

That's why I'm taking medicine for nervous prostration and have stopped work on Vol. XI.

What further disclosures are in store for me I dare not conjecture. But this I will say that the firm of printers you now employ is the absolute worst that I ever had anything to do with. Their work is disgraceful all through and all over.

Dammum! [22]

[When the entire set finally appeared, Bierce delivered his most exhaustive complaint about Neale's printers.]

We *seem* to be making a mountain out of a molehill, with all this correspondence about the printing in the "C. W.," but I really must notice some things in your letter of the 21st. First, though, let me say that you err in supposing that I "take no pleasure" in this culmination of my life's work in literature because of such defects in the printing as I have pointed out for possible correction in the far future. They do not worry me at all. I think them more numerous and more important than you do, but if I am right, a good deal more injurious to you than to me. I am entirely cheerful about it, but wish that you were a little less sensitive to criticism of that merely mechanical part of your work that you do not do yourself.

I can not agree with you that it is difficult to say what is a "typographical error"; it seems to me a very simple matter, and very easily avoidable. The question of "a publisher's accountability for the imperfections of his authors" seems to me not to enter into the matter at all. I don't hold you in any degree accountable for mine; my having marked some of them means nothing of the kind. As explained in a previous letter, I marked them only in the hope that they might be corrected in some future edition. My notion was that sometime you or your successors *might* want to make a new edition from new plates—that is, set up again the entire work. In that case my mistakes could be as well corrected as yours, or rather your printers'. I had no thought of your making any changes in *these* plates that could not be made easily and without expense, or with *little* expense.

But here is a graver matter. You imply that two of your "expert proof-readers" declined to go on with the work because I was hard to get on with. If either, or any, of them told you that he lied. In the first place, no expert proof-reader (in *any* sense of the term) has had anything to do with them. I *know* the work of an expert in proof-reading as infallibly as I know the degree of scholarship of a man whom I talk with. The expert marks a proof differently from another man— marks it according to a code which I know. I sometimes do not know whether (for one example of many) small caps should be substituted for large or large caps from another font; I am not an expert in type; but I know the technical mark for every error that a printer can make. No proof-reader that has had to do with the "C. W." has had this knowledge. Their markings have been intelligible mostly, but frequently clumsy and awkward—amateurish, so to say. I doubt not that you believe your proof-readers expert, but you must try to pardon me if I believe my own eyes.

In the first two or three volumes the proofs were marked by one whom I understood to be your editor—I think his name was Mac-something, perhaps MacQueen. I had several little controversies with him, always conducted politely and, as I supposed, without feeling. He began them. Several times he marked supposed errors by me and called my attention to them; so I explained to him that they were not errors. Once, or oftener, he "corrected" my Latin without knowing anything of Latin. I patiently and good humoredly cited authorities, though as to those particular expressions I was myself an authority. Once he pointed out my error in writing of the "stock" of a rifle—which I might be supposed as a soldier to know about. He thought the word meant the "butt" of the rifle. There were many other instances, which I'll not bore you with. If he "quit" it was probably because he did not care further to disclose his ignorance—which is dark, profound and general. There was never anything between us that you are, or he is, justified in calling a "dispute". Nor with any other of your editors or mechanics. You might as reasonably call *this* correspondence a "dispute" between you and me.

As to your second man, I know nothing about him; I had no correspondence with any other; and if you care to look over the proofs (in case they still exist) you will not find a single mark of mine on them that is in any degree uncivil, or that implies censure or temper. I "cussed" them to you only, and you cussed them too, as you habitually and not altogether unjustly, cuss all printers. The savage things that you have written and said to me about your workmen would make a small volume of delightful reading. But lo! all at once they are saints all, and I am apparently a very testy and impossible person! Well, I "aint".

You say you are "held accountable" for my "arbitrary ruling on the division of words at the ends of lines". Held by whom, to whom? And you add: "I know of no power that could force you to write down your art as you know it." This I do not understand, if it means anything. As to "the division of words at the ends of lines," no power is needful to force me to expound so simple a thing as that: my principle is merely not to divide a syllable. If all the editors, foremen, printers, and even publishers in the world ignored (as I think they mostly do) or disputed the correctness of that principle (as many of them do, or would) it would not move me. And I venture to say that if you would adopt it, and insist on it, it would commend your books to those who know and love the English language.

Your memory is at fault: you never "told" me that the proof-reading would be left to me and Miss Christiansen, and if you "wrote" me so I did not receive the letter—at least I have no recollection of it, and can not find it in any of your letters. I fear that if I had received a communication of that kind, either oral or written, I should not have gone on with the work—might even have fallen dead! Anyhow, it was *not* left to me and Miss Christiansen, for all proofs were marked by somebody else, both before and after we had them.

Of course I shall be glad if you will refer me to a letter of yours from which I would have reason to think that Miss C. and I were to be the *only* proof-readers, and will promptly confess that your memory is better than mine—as in some things I know it to be. I shall not ask her about it, for I don't want to draw her into this amusing controversy; she has trifles enough of her own to look after. And some day (age having removed me from the field of your resentment) you might waylay and murder her, which would make me turn in my grave and— smile at your error in assassinating the wrong person.

You did not need to show me that you are not the only publisher issuing books typographically imperfect; I read books, and have eyes. What I "would have otherwise" is your apparent conviction that what I called a near approach to perfection is unattainable and your apparent near approach to indifference about it. We disagree as to the importance of it, that is all—except what appears to me your needless "touchiness" and your rather headlong determination to make me see black as white. I guess you see it so, as a mother thinks her child altogether beautiful; but, as I said, I must use my own eyes.

I *hope* you have read this screed in a comfortable mood. The reception accorded to a letter depends altogether on the mood of the receiver. If one is grouchy, and imagines his correspondent writing with a frown, the letter will seem objectionable—impolite, unfriendly; if he imagines him writing with a smile it will seem pleasant and amiable. Please understand that this is written in my most rollicking and playful frame of mind. I have, in fact, taken two drinks of uncommonly good Jamaican rum since beginning it. [23]

> [Reviews of the volumes as they appeared were decidedly mixed;
> Bierce felt that some uncharitable reviews were written by old en-
> emies seeking revenge.]

As to that London chap,[29] *he* sees nothing humorous apparently in a condemnation of me by one who confesses that he does not know if I am "living or dead," nor where I "was born", nor if anything of mine has been published in *his* country—nay, one who confesses that he has "read little" of me, yet pronounces my stories as "probably" my best work. How does he know? Suppose the claim made in my behalf were (as in fact it often is) that my best quality is versatility—how would a reader of only one small section of it be competent to refute *that*?

Dear Neale, I hope that by this time you retain no vestige of the superstition that "literary criticism" in England is any different from what it is here—that it has any value or importance in either country. Really, I shall have to labor in that field again, just to show (by precept and example) the childish futility of the whole business. It may be interesting or amusing—that depends on who writes it; but its futility is fundamental, immutable and eternal. [24]

Lord, what a liar that "Current Literature" fellow is![30] Fancy my being a leading spirit of the Bohemian Club—to which I have not belonged for more than thirty years, and in which I never did take much interest. And did you observe how, in order to convict me of imitating Poe, he attributes to Poe a work that Poe never did—"a grotesque satirical tale" depicting "the downfall of the American republic."[31] Do you know of any such tale by Poe? If I had left the tragic and supernatural out of my stories I would still have been an "imitator of Poe," for they would still have been stories; so what's the use? For your entertainment I'm enclosing the Hildegarde Hawthorne and the Harrison Gray Otis "reviews".[32] Otis is ungrateful: when he was generally accused of cowardice for resigning his commission in the midst of the Philippine war I defended him by pointing out that it required the highest kind of courage to leave the battlefield and come home to face his wife's poetry.

As to Hildegarde, somebody probably told her that she was witty and could pee against the wind. You may return these things when you've had your smile. They trouble me not. [25]

Bierce and Ezra Pound

[In early 1910 Ezra Pound's father sent Bierce some of his son's poetry. Bierce expressed guarded approval of the work—an opinion not shared by his pupil George Sterling.]

I'm enclosing something that will tickle you I hope—"The Ballade of the Goodly Fere".[33] The author's father, who is something in the Mint in Philadelphia, sent me several of his son's poems that were not good; but at last came this—in manuscript, like the others. Before I could do anything with it—meanwhile wearing out the paper and the patience of my friends by reading it at them—the old man asked it back rather peremptorily. I reluctantly sent it, with a letter of high praise. The author had "placed" it in London, where it has made a heap of talk.

It has plenty of faults besides the monotonous rhyme scheme; but tell me what you think of it. [26]

I don't think you rightly value "The Goodly Fere." Of course no ballad written to-day can be entirely good, for it must be an imitation; it is now an unnatural form, whereas it was once a natural one. We are no longer a primitive people, and a primitive people's forms and methods are not ours. Nevertheless, this seems to me an admirable ballad, as it is given a modern to write ballads. And I think you overlook the best line: "The hounds of the crimson sky gave tongue."

The poem is complete as I sent it, and I think it stops right where and as it should—

> "I ha' seen him eat o' the honey comb
> Sin' they nailed him to the tree."

The current "Literary Digest" has some queer things about (and by) Pound, and "Current Literature" reprints the "Fere" with all the wrinkles ironed out of it—making a "capon priest" of it.[34] [27]

Travels

> [Insofar as health and finances permitted, Bierce found occasion
> to voyage out of Washington. New York was visited frequently,
> and in the winter of 1907 Bierce undertook a trip to Galveston,
> Texas, to visit his friend S. O. Howes.]

We had fine weather all the time on the gulf, but a pretty rough sea a part of the time. The Lampasas is a washtub for speed; we were exactly 7 1/2 hours getting to Key West and—incidentally—to starvation. I was there only ten hours or I should have perished of famine. But every hour of the sea life was delightful. I chummed with the captain and sat at his table, with that pretty girl between of whom you predicted that she would not lack attention. Did I feel it my duty to confirm your reputation as a prophet? O, well, it was no great trouble. She too disembarked at Key West. I fear she lives there. She says so, but I don't see how anybody can!

From Tampa my journey was devoid of interest. I found Florida the most uninteresting country that I ever saw. Nothing but scrubby pines and sand, except in the cities, where "tropical" plants are cultivated sedulously and, I think, with difficulty. [28]

> [It was in the summer of 1910 that Bierce embarked upon his long-
> delayed return to California. Leaving in late April and traveling by
> way of the Panama Canal, Bierce finally reached the Bay Area in
> mid-May.]

I arrived on Thursday the 19th, but this is the first opportunity that I have had to acknowledge your notes. . . .

I had a pleasant, but rather long voyage. Was three days in Panama and saw something of the canal work—the magnitude whereof transcends expression. If I had taken the right line of steamers from New York (the Panama Railroad's line) it would have cost me eighty dollars less. One pays for one's ignorance and carelessness.

On arrival at San Francisco I gathered up my nephew and his wife[35] and came directly up here to my brother's shack[36] on the mountainside. And, faith! it is a paradise. Right above a beautiful river (we have a canoe) with a half-dozen pretty villages in sight below, and the woods already filled with their summer population from the city. One meets groups of pretty girls in camping attire everywhere—some of whom say that I held them on my knee when they were little (I mean to again) though I fancy it may have been their grandmothers! Ah, my good, good friend, how I pity you in your office, slaving at your oar! (How is that for mixed metaphor?) May the new baby do much to smooth the asperities of the situation. And I pray that its pretty mother may now have passed out of the danger zone.

I don't know when I shall go down to the city, and to Carmel, and to Yosemite. Sterling will probably come up here. [29]

I've got the heave o' the sea out of my bones and am cultivating the mountain element in my legs. Also I parade up to the town in a canoe nearly every day for mail and provisions. Ah, you should see this river, with its wild mountain banks ablaze with flowers. My brother's shack is five hundred feet above—almost over it. . . .

I had a pleasant voyage with a day at Kingston, three at Panama, and a few hours at as many of the dozen Central American and Mexican ports as I cared to see. My health has been excellent. [30]

We went to Yosemite—my brother, his son and his son's wife, and the Sterlings. It (the valley) is too great to write about—the only famous place that has not disappointed me. You *must* see it some day. [31]

I am half-distracted with a lot of friends (and some "lion-hunters") hauling me this way and that. My regular situation is that I'm due in a half-dozen places at once. Gee! it is no joke this returning to one's old home. I'd give much for a week of Washington, or that very quiet village, little old New York. [32]

I'm having too much of a good time, and am almost worn out. I wish you could have been with me to the Bohemian grove play—it was the finest spectacle that I ever saw.[37]

You'll not be sorry to know that my health is pretty good, despite the fact that I've "cut the booze"—mostly. [33]

My departure from California was somewhat hurried and unexpected at the last, but I did steal a day to visit the Grand Cañon of the Colorado; and when you go West again *you* must do so too. You will not regret having its memory always with you.

I had a good time, and saw the greatest three things on the continent—Yosemite, the Grand Cañon and the work on the Panama Canal. But the *best* thing that I saw was your cousin Lora. She is a dear girl.

I went to St. Helena and arranged for a new, large and beautiful lot in the cemetery, where the sun will shine and the grass grow. Your fern is all that grows on the old one, and it is sickly. Even the trees are dying.

The new lot will have a beautiful tall-growing palm in each corner. The lot is 20 ft. by 20. The necessary work will be done at once, and George Fee will see that it is done right. I hope you approve. [34]

You asked me about the relative interest of Yosemite and the Grand Cañon. It is not easy to compare them, they are so different. In Yosemite only the magnitudes are unfamiliar; in the Cañon nothing is familiar—at least, nothing would be familiar to you, though I have seen something like it on the upper Yellowstone. The "color scheme" is astounding—almost incredible, as is the "architecture." As to the magnitudes, Yosemite is nowhere. From points on the rim of the Cañon you can see fifty, maybe a hundred, miles of it. And it is never twice alike. Nobody can describe it. Of course you must see it sometime. I wish our Yosemite party could meet there, but probably we never will; it is a long way from here, and not quite next door to Berkeley and Carmel. [35]

> [In late summer of 1911 Bierce accepted an offer to spend time at the
> home of George Sterling's uncle, Frank C. Havens, in Long Island.]

I'm only a few days back from a month's outing—mostly at Sag Harbor, Long Island. And since returning I've been playing at asthma—beating the game! I saw Percy[38]—he was kind enough to pass a night with me in New York on my way home. We dined and breakfasted together, and missed you.

It was a good time that I had in Long Island, autoing and motorboating most of the time, and getting a succession of skins "under the sun." George Sterling was of the party, all of whom were Californians, male and female. *Now* I'm going to work. [36]

> [The summer of 1912 saw Bierce's second, and last, trip to
> California.]

I've been here nearly a week, but so "programmed" and pulled about that I've had neither time nor heart to write. And we are expecting to set out for Lake Tahoe (see your map) tomorrow morning.

We had a pleasant journey until we were about leaving the Grand Cañon, where we had passed two days of delight. Then Miss Christiansen was handed a telegram that her father was dying. He has since died, but she got home in time to see him and be recognized. Of course she can not be with us at Tahoe, but the irrepressible Priscilla Shipman will be of the party. Also Mrs. Sterling, but the divel a George "of that ilk". My address will remain Oakland, Cal. . . .

Good-bye; I'm awfully sorry you're not with me in this land of the sun and the suffragette. [37]

I am having a glorious good time and find myself wishing every day that you were here to share it. If you *were* here we would go to the Bohemian Club grove play tomorrow. As it is, I have declined a dozen invitations to attend it—it is great, but once was enough. There is really a limit to my capacity for drink. You never found it, but you are only one man—multiply yourself by three hundred and your importunities by one thousand, and you'll see how it would be! [38]

I left California October 21st, the date of your letter now before me, but arrived here on the 30th, having stopped at Bloomington, Illinois, to visit my daughter.

No, I shall not see California again, nor see you (I would rather see you than California) and have said farewell to all my Western friends, suggesting that they put up a headstone appropriately inscribed with all my vices. [39]

I shall not again go to California. Our relatives and their friends there are only a small group in my "social circle", but they disappoint. They are all 'ists of one kind and another: socialists, suffragists—anarchists, too, I think. I have no ill-will toward them, but there is no community of feeling between them and me. I don't like their ways, nor they mine; indeed, they seem rather to resent my existence. You see I have a pretty good opinion of myself as a thinker, take myself pretty seriously, and can have no pleasure in the society of persons who think their fool leaders wiser than I. So I shall not again go where they are. [40]

Preparing for the End?

> [Bierce's "disappearance" toward the end of 1913 has certainly aug-
> mented his popular fascination. Much of that year seemed to be
> occupied in putting his affairs in order. Are these the actions of a
> man who is merely going away on a long voyage, or one who never
> expects to return at all?]

My dear Helen,
    I am transferring to you the ownership of the new lot in the St. Helena cem-
etery. George Fee, who has attended to everything there for me and has taken

much trouble and charged nothing for his services, wanted to buy the old lot. I told him he should have it for nothing. I had forgotten that the deed was in your mother's name and that you were now the owner as her heir. But I know that you will be glad to perform the promise made by me.

If you have the original deed please write at the bottom of it:

"I hereby direct and empower the St. Helena Public Cemetery Association to transfer and set over to George W. Fee all my right, title and interest in and to the above described lot of land."

Sign it and send the deed so amended to me, and I will send it to my St. Helena lawyer (James A. Nowland—maybe you know him) who says that will be sufficient.

If you have *not* the deed, or can not find it, take the enclosed paper to a notary and have it duly "executed," and send me that.

I think it better to have the new lot transferred to you while I am living, though I shall continue to pay the superintendent's bills, as before.

By the way, I do not wish to lie there. That matter is all arranged, and you will not be bothered about the mortal part of

Your Daddy. [41]

I am just loafing my life away here in Washington, eschewing pen-and-ink (never again) and keeping my face clean and my nails evenly pared. Sometimes, by way of variation, I go to my club to look over the foreign magazines and reviews. (I observe that Scheffauer has in "The Fortnightly" an article on the death of satire—I don't care how dead it is.)[39] And every evening after dinner a slender sylph from Georgia, with the most delicious Southern drawl, comes down from the flat above and makes coffee for me. You'd adore her, naturally. That is the history of my life, as it flows along toward the brink of the Cataract. But

> "I shall see, before I die,
> The palms and temples of the south"—[40]

Maybe. [42]

The Neale Publishing Co.,

Gentlemen,

I have sold and assigned to Carrie J. Christiansen, of this city, all my copyrights, and all my right title and interest in the contract (dated the first day of June, 1908) between you and me for publication of "The Collected Works of Ambrose Bierce", and in all royalties or other profits accruing therefrom, both present and future.

This is to notify you of the transaction, in accordance with the terms of said contract. Kindly acknowledge receipt of this notification and that it is satisfactory to you.

    Very truly yours,
        Ambrose Bierce.

September 19, 1913. [43]

> [In recent years much skepticism has been expressed as to whether Bierce really went permanently into Mexico in late 1913, as he repeatedly stated in letters was his wish. What is certain is that he first undertook one final trip to old Civil War battlefields, after which he remained for a time in Texas. After that—silence.]

If I am to hear from you again for a long time you'll have to answer this letter pretty soon. I am going away. My plans are not very definite, but they include a journey into—possibly across—South America. I have arranged for a pretty long absence. If we have trouble with Mexico before I leave I shall probably go there instead—or at least first.

    My health is excellent. [44]

I suppose I shall not see your book[41] for a long time, for I am going away and have no notion when I shall return. I expect to go to, perhaps across, South America— possibly via Mexico, if I can get through without being stood up against a wall and shot as a Gringo. But that is better than dying in bed, is it not? [45]

Thank you for the book. I thank you for your friendship—and much besides. That is to say good-by at the end of a pleasant correspondence in which your woman's prerogative of having the last word is denied to you. Before I could receive it I shall be gone. But some time, somewhere, I hope to hear from you again. Yes, I shall go into Mexico with a pretty definite purpose, which, however, is not at present disclosable. You must try to forgive my obstinacy in not "perishing" where I am. I want to be where something worth while is going on, or where nothing whatever is going on. Most of what is going on in your own country is exceedingly distasteful to me. [46]

The "indefinite region" to which I expect to go for "an indefinite time" (not, I hope, for *all* time) is Mexico and South America. My plan, so far as I have one, is to go through Mexico to one of the Pacific ports, if I can *get* through without being stood up against a wall and shot as an American. Thence I hope to sail for some port in South America. Thence to across the Andes and perhaps across the continent. Isn't all that "indefinite"? Naturally, it is possible—even probable—that I shall not return. These be "strange countries," in which things happen; that is why I am going. And I am seventy-one! [47]

I am about to leave here—shall go on Wednesday, or Thursday, so you'd better not write. In about two weeks I shall probably be in San Antonio, Texas; I want to visit five or six of my old civil war battlefields first. *Then* if I can get into Mexico in a way to suit me I shall do so. It is probably easier to get in than out, but I mean to *try* to pass through the country (mostly on horseback, doubtless) to some Pacific port; thence to South America.

It is a fool plan, of course,—that is why I like it. I want to see (and *be*) "something going on".

Carrie will attend to all my affairs here. I've given her all that I own except the money that I shall carry on my person. She knows what to do if I don't come back, which is, of course, not improbable. If it had not been for Carrie there would have been nothing, not even my books and pictures. She *made* me save enough to keep me while I was compiling my "collected works", which bring in very little. [48]

Good-bye—if you hear of my being stood up against a Mexican stone wall and shot to rags please know that I think that a pretty good way to depart this life. It beats old age, disease, or falling down the cellar stairs. To be a Gringo in Mexico—ah, that is euthanasia! [49]

It would not be prudent to tell you of my plans; this country is full of spies and watchers, and I've no confidence even in the U.S. mails. I mean to go into Mexico; that is all that you need to know. There is good fighting all along the border and everywhere. Maybe I shall see some of it—as an "innocent by-stander."

I visited all my old battlefields—Chickamauga, Chattanooga, Stone's River, Franklin, Nashville and Shiloh—arriving here[42] on Monday last pretty well worn out. Shall stay a few days longer. After that I shall be out of reach of letters, so can not hear from you. [50]

> [The last surviving letter by Bierce, dated December 26, 1913, was
> written from Chihuahua. In spite of many claims by journalists
> and others that they caught sight of Bierce in Mexico or elsewhere,
> there are no reliable reports of the ultimate fate of Ambrose
> Bierce.]

I was . . . impatient of your foolish notion that in the matter of my proposed visit to "the Andes" I was posing. I do not know why you think the Andes particularly spectacular—probably because you have not traveled much. To me they are no different in grandioseness from the Rockies or the Coast Range—merely a geographical expression used because I did not care to be more specific. The particular region that I had in mind has lured me all my life—more now than before, because it is, not more distant from, but more inaccessible to, many of the things of which as an old man I am mortally tired. What "interpretation" you put upon my letters regarding that spot you have not seen fit to inform me, which before rebuking me (I am not hospitable to rebuke) you should have done. I suppose you have a *habit* of "interpretation". You worship a god who (omniscient and omnipotent) has been unable to make his message clear to his children and has to have a million paid interpreters, and you are one of them. (Pardon me; you invited me to "convert you from the error of your ways.") So little do I know of your "interpretation" that I was not even aware that I had written you of my intention to go to "the Andes." If I did, as of course I did, I must also have told you that I intended to go by the way of Mexico, which I am doing, though it looks now as if "the Andes" would have to wait. . . .

I do not know how, nor when, you are to get this letter; there are no mails, and sometimes no trains to take anything to El Paso. Moreover, I have forgotten your address and shall send this to the care of Lora. And Lora may have gone to the mountains. As to me, I leave here tomorrow for an unknown destination. [51]

A Sole Survivor:
An Epilogue

[This essay was first published in the *Oakland Daily Evening Tribune* for October 18, 1890, and reprinted as the final segment of "Bits of Autobiography," and to that degree might be seen as Bierce's epitaph on himself. It discusses how Bierce physically survived the many friends and associates he had known over a long life; but it also suggests his survival from a different age and a different ethos, and in that sense he was a solitary individual indeed.]

Among the arts and sciences, the art of Sole Surviving is one of the most interesting, as (to the artist) it is by far the most important. It is not altogether an art, perhaps, for success in it is largely due to accident. One may study how solely to survive, yet, having an imperfect natural aptitude, may fail of proficiency and be early cut off. To the contrary, one little skilled in its methods, and not even well grounded in its fundamental principles, may, by taking the trouble to have been born with a suitable constitution, attain to a considerable eminence in the art. Without undue immodesty, I think I may fairly claim some distinction in it myself, although I have not regularly acquired it as one acquires knowledge and skill in writing, painting and playing the flute. O yes, I am a notable Sole Survivor, and some of my work in that way attracts great attention, mostly my own.

You would naturally expect, then, to find in me one who has experienced all manner of disaster at sea and the several kinds of calamity incident to a life on dry land. It would seem a just inference from my Sole Survivorship that I am familiar with railroad wrecks, inundations (though these are hardly dry-land phenomena), pestilences, earthquakes, conflagrations and other forms of what the reporters delight to call "a holocaust." This is not entirely true; I have never been shipwrecked, never assisted as "unfortunate Sufferer" at a fire or railway collision, and know of the ravages of epidemics only by hearsay. The most destructive *temblor* of which I have had a personal experience decreased the population of San Francisco by fewer, probably, than ten thousand persons, of whom not more than a dozen were killed; the others moved out of town. It is true that I once followed the perilous trade of a soldier, but my eminence in Sole Surviving is of a later growth and not specially the product of the sword.

Opening the portfolio of memory, I draw out picture after picture—"figure-pieces"—groups of forms and faces whereof mine only now remains, somewhat the worse for wear.

Here are three young men lolling at ease on a grassy bank. One, a handsome, dark-eyed chap, with a forehead like that of a Grecian god, raises his body on his elbow, looks straight away to the horizon, where some black trees hold captive certain vestiges of sunset as if they had torn away the plumage of a flight of flamingoes, and says: "Fellows, I mean to be rich. I shall see every country worth seeing. I shall taste every pleasure worth having. When old, I shall become a hermit."

Said another slender youth, fair-haired: "I shall become President and execute a *coup d'etat* making myself an absolute monarch. I shall then issue a decree requiring that all hermits be put to death."

The third said nothing. Was he restrained by some prescient sense of the perishable nature of the material upon which he was expected to inscribe the record of his hopes? However it may have been, he flicked his shoe with a hazel switch and kept his own counsel. For twenty years he has been the Sole Survivor of the group.

The scene changes. Six men are on horseback on a hill—a general and his staff. Below, in the gray fog of a winter morning, an army, which has left its entrenchments, is moving upon those of the enemy—creeping silently into position. In an hour the whole wide valley for miles to left and right will be all aroar with musketry stricken to seeming silence now and again by thunder claps of big guns. In the meantime the risen sun has burned a way through the fog, splendoring a part of the beleaguered city.

"Look at that, General," says an aide; "it is like enchantment."

"Go and enchant Colonel Post," said the general, without taking his field-glass from his eyes, "and tell him to pitch in as soon as he hears Smith's guns."

All laughed. But to-day I laugh alone. I am the Sole Survivor.

It would be easy to fill many pages with instances of Sole Survival, from my own experience. I could mention extinct groups composed wholly (myself excepted) of the opposing sex, all of whom, with the same exception, have long ceased their opposition, their warfare accomplished, their pretty noses blue and chill under the daisies. They were good girls, too, mostly, Heaven rest them! There were Maud and Lizzie and Nanette (ah, Nanette, indeed; she is the deadest of the whole bright band) and Emeline and ———— but really this is not discreet; one should not survive and tell.

The flame of a camp-fire stands up tall and straight toward the black sky. We feed it constantly with sage brush. A circling wall of darkness closes us in; but turn your back to the fire and walk a little away and you shall see the serrated summit-line of snow-capped mountains, ghastly cold in the moonlight. They are in all directions; everywhere they efface the great gold stars near the horizon, leaving the little green ones of the midheaven trembling viciously, as bleak as steel. At irregular intervals we hear the distant howling of a wolf—now on this side and again on that. We check our talk to listen; we cast quick glances toward our weapons, our saddles, our picketed horses: the wolves may be of the variety known as Sioux, and there are but four of us.

"What would you do, Jim," said Hazen, "if we were surrounded by Indians?"

Jim Beckwourth[1] was our guide—a lifelong frontiersman, an old man "beated and chopped with tanned antiquity."[2] He had at one time been a chief of the Crows.

"I'd spit on that fire," said Jim Beckwourth.

The old man has gone, I hope, where there is no fire to be quenched. And Hazen, and the chap with whom I shared my blanket that winter night on the plains—both gone. One might suppose that I would feel something of the natural exultation of a Sole Survivor; but as Byron found that

> our thoughts take wildest flight
> Even at the moment when they should array
> Themselves in pensive order,[3]

so I find that they sometimes array themselves in pensive order, even at the moment when they ought to be most hilarious.

Of reminiscences there is no end. I have a vast store of them laid up, wherewith to wile away the tedious years of my anecdotage—whenever it shall please Heaven to make me old. Some years that I passed in London as a working journalist are particularly rich in them. Ah! "we were a gallant company" in those days.

I am told that the English are heavy thinkers and dull talkers. My recollection is different; speaking from that, I should say they are no end clever with their tongues. Certainly I have not elsewhere heard such brilliant talk as among the artists and writers of London. Of course they were a picked lot; some of them had attained to some eminence in the world of intellect; others have achieved it since. But they were not all English by many. London draws the best brains of Ireland and Scotland, and there is always a small American contingent, mostly correspondents of the big New York journals.

The typical London journalist is a gentleman. He is usually a graduate of one or the other of the great universities. He is well paid and holds his position, whatever it may be, by a less precarious tenure than his American congener. He rather moves than "dabbles" in literature, and not uncommonly takes a hand at some of the many forms of art. On the whole, he is a good fellow, too, with a skeptical mind, a cynical tongue, and a warm heart. I found these men agreeable, hospitable, intelligent, amusing. We worked too hard, dined too well, frequented too many clubs, and went to bed too late in the forenoon. We were overmuch addicted to shedding the blood of the grape. In short, we diligently, conscientiously, and with a perverse satisfaction burned the candle of life at both ends and in the middle.

This was many a year ago. To-day a list of these men's names with a cross against that of each one whom I know to be dead would look like a Roman Catholic cemetery. I could dine all the survivors at the table on which I write, and I should like to do so. But the dead ones, I must say, were the best diners.

But about Sole Surviving. There was a London publisher named John Camden Hotten. Among American writers he had a pretty dark reputation as a "pirate." They accused him of republishing their books without their assent, which, in absence of international copyright, he had a legal, and it seems to me (a "sufferer") a moral right to do. Through sympathy with their foreign confrères British writers also held him in high disesteem.

I knew Hotten very well, and one day I stood by what purported to be his body, which afterward I assisted to bury in the cemetery at Highgate. I am sure that it was his body, for I was uncommonly careful in the matter of identification, for a very good reason, which you shall know.

Aside from his "piracy," Hotten had a wide renown as "a hard man to deal with." For several months before his death he had owed me one hundred pounds sterling, and he could not possibly have been more reluctant to part with anything but a larger sum.[4] Even to this day in reviewing the intelligent methods— ranging from delicate finesse to frank effrontery—by which that good man kept me out of mine own I am prostrated with admiration and consumed with envy. finally by a lucky chance I got him at a disadvantage and seeing my power he sent his manager—a fellow named Chatto, who as a member of the firm of Chatto & Windus afterward succeeded to his business and methods—to negotiate. I was the most implacable creditor in the United Kingdom, and after two mortal hours of me in my most acidulated mood Chatto pulled out a check for the full amount, ready signed by Hotten in anticipation of defeat. Before handing it to me Chatto said: "This check is dated next Saturday. Of course you will not present it until then."

To this I cheerfully consented.

"And now," said Chatto, rising to go, "as everything is satisfactory I hope you will go out to Hotten's house and have a friendly talk. It is his wish."

On Saturday morning I went. In pursuance, doubtless, of his design when he antedated that check he had died of a pork pie promptly on the stroke of twelve o'clock the night before—which invalidated the check! I have met American publishers who thought they knew something about the business of drinking champagne out of writers' skulls. If this narrative—which, upon my soul, is every word true—teaches them humility by showing that genuine commercial sagacity is not bounded by geographical lines it will have served its purpose.

Having assured myself that Mr. Hotten was really no more, I drove furiously bankward, hoping that the sad tidings had not preceded me—and they had not.

Alas! on the route was a certain tap-room greatly frequented by authors, artists, newspaper men and "gentlemen of wit and pleasure about town."

Sitting about the customary table were a half-dozen or more choice spirits— George Augustus Sala, Henry Sampson,[5] Tom Hood the younger, Captain Mayne Reid,[6] and others less known to fame. I am sorry to say my somber news affected these sinners in a way that was shocking. Their levity was a thing to shudder at. As Sir Boyle Roche might have said, it grated harshly upon an ear that had a dubious check in its pocket.[7] Having uttered their hilarious minds by word of mouth all they knew how, these hardy and impenitent offenders set about writing "appropriate epitaphs." Thank Heaven, all but one of these have escaped my memory, one that I wrote myself . At the close of the rites, several hours later, I resumed my movement against the bank. Too late—the old, old story of the hare and the tortoise was told again. The "heavy news" had overtaken and passed me as I loitered by the wayside.

All attended the funeral—Sala, Sampson, Hood, Reid, and the undistinguished others, including this present Sole Survivor of the group. As each cast his handful of earth upon the coffin I am very sure that, like Lord Brougham on a somewhat similar occasion, we all felt more than we cared to express.[8] On the death of a political antagonist whom he had not treated with much consideration his lordship was asked, rather rudely, "Have you no regrets now that he is gone?"

After a moment of thoughtful silence he replied, with gravity, "Yes; I favor his return."

One night in the summer of 1880 I was driving in a light wagon through the wildest part of the Black Hills in South Dakota. I had left Deadwood and was well on my way to Rockerville with thirty thousand dollars on my person, belonging to a mining company of which I was the general manager. Naturally, I had taken the precaution to telegraph my secretary at Rockerville to meet me at Rapid City, then a small town, on another route; the telegram was intended to mislead the "gentlemen of the road" whom I knew to be watching my movements, and who might possibly have a confederate in the telegraph office. Beside me on the seat of the wagon sat Boone May.

Permit me to explain the situation. Several months before, it had been the custom to send a "treasure-coach" twice a week from Deadwood to Sidney, Nebraska. Also, it had been the custom to have this coach captured and plundered by "road agents." So intolerable had this practice become—even iron-clad coaches loopholed for rifles proving a vain device—that the mine owners had adopted the more practicable plan of importing from California a half-dozen of the most famous "shotgun messengers" of Wells, Fargo & Co.—fearless and trusty fellows with an instinct for killing, a readiness of resource that was an intuition, and a sense of direction that put a shot where it would do the most good more accurately than the most careful aim. Their feats of marksmanship were so incredible that seeing was scarcely believing.

In a few weeks these chaps had put the road agents out of business and out of life, for they attacked them wherever found. One sunny Sunday morning two of them strolling down a street of Deadwood recognized five or six of the rascals, ran back to their hotel for their rifles, and returning killed them all!

Boone May was one of these avengers. When I employed him, as a messenger, he was under indictment for murder. He had trailed a "road agent" across the Bad Lands for hundreds of miles, brought him back to within a few miles of Deadwood and picketed him out for the night. The desperate man, tied as he was, had attempted to escape, and May found it expedient to shoot and bury him. The grave by the roadside is perhaps still pointed out to the curious. May gave himself up, was formally charged with murder, released on his own recognizance, and I had to give him leave of absence to go to court and be acquitted. Some of the New York directors of my company having been good enough to signify their disapproval of my action in employing "such a man," I could do no less than make some recognition of their dissent, and thenceforth he was borne upon the payrolls as "Boone May, Murderer." Now let me get back to my story.

I knew the road fairly well, for I had previously traveled it by night, on horseback, my pockets bulging with currency and my free hand holding a cocked revolver the entire distance of fifty miles. To make the journey by wagon with a companion was luxury. Still, the drizzle of rain was uncomfortable. May sat hunched up beside me, a rubber poncho over his shoulders and a Winchester rifle in its leathern case between his knees. I thought him a trifle off his guard, but said nothing. The road, barely visible, was rocky, the wagon rattled, and alongside ran a roaring stream. Suddenly we heard through it all the clinking of a horse's shoes directly behind, and simultaneously the short, sharp words of authority: "Throw up your hands!"

With an involuntary jerk at the reins I brought my team to its haunches and reached for my revolver. Quite needless: with the quickest movement that I had ever seen in anything but a cat—almost before the words were out of the horseman's mouth—May had thrown himself backward across the back of the seat, face upward, and the muzzle of his rifle was within a yard of the fellow's breast! What further occurred among the three of us there in the gloom of the forest has, I fancy, never been accurately related.

Boone May is long dead of yellow fever in Brazil, and I am the Sole Survivor.

There was a famous *prima donna* with whom it was my good fortune to cross the Atlantic to New York. In truth I was charged by a friend of both with the agreeable duty of caring for her safety and comfort. Madame was gracious, clever, altogether charming, and before the voyage was two days old a half-dozen of the men aboard, whom she had permitted me to present, were heels over head in love with her, as I was myself.

Our competition for her favor did not make us enemies; on the contrary we were drawn together into something like an offensive and defensive alliance by a common sorrow—the successful rivalry of a singularly handsome Italian who sat next her at table. So assiduous was he in his attentions that my office as the lady's guide, philosopher and friend was nearly a sinecure, and as to the others, they had hardly one chance a day to prove their devotion: that enterprising son of Italy dominated the entire situation. By some diabolical prevision he anticipated Madame's every need and wish—placed her reclining-chair in the most sheltered spots on deck, smothered her in layer upon layer of wraps, and conducted himself, generally, in the most inconsiderate way. Worse still, Madame accepted his good offices with a shameless grace "which said as plain as whisper in the ear" that there was a perfect understanding between them. What made it harder to bear was the fellow's faulty civility to the rest of us; he seemed hardly aware of our existence.

Our indignation was not loud, but deep. Every day in the smoking-room we contrived the most ingenious and monstrous plans for his undoing in this world and the next; the least cruel being a project to lure him to the upper deck on a dark night and send him unshriven to his account by way of the lee rail; but as none of us knew enough Italian to tell him the needful falsehood that scheme of justice came to nothing, as did all the others. At the wharf in New York we parted from Madame more in sorrow than in anger, and from her conquering cavalier with polite manifestations of the contempt we did not feel.

That evening I called on her at her hotel, facing Union Square. Soon after my arrival there was an audible commotion out in front: the populace, headed by a brass band and incited, doubtless, by pure love of art, had arrived to do honor to the great singer. There was music—a serenade—followed by shoutings of the lady's name. She seemed a trifle nervous, but I led her to the balcony, where she made a very pretty little speech, piquant with her most charming accent. When the tumult and shouting had died we re-entered her apartment to resume our conversation. Would it please monsieur to have a glass of wine? It would. She left the room for a moment; then came the wine and glasses on a tray, borne by that impossible Italian! He had a napkin across his arm—he was a servant.

Barring some of the band and the populace, I am doubtless the Sole Survivor, for Madame has for a number of years had a permanent engagement Above, and my faith in Divine Justice does not permit me to think that the servile wretch who cast down the mighty from their seat among the Sons of Hope was suffered to live out the other half of his days.

A dinner of seven in an old London tavern—a good dinner, the memory whereof is not yet effaced from the tablets of the palate. A soup, a plate of whitebait be-lemoned and red-peppered with exactness, a huge joint of roast beef, from which we sliced at will, flanked by various bottles of old dry Sherry and crusty Port—such Port! (And we are expected to be patriots in a country where it cannot be procured! And the Portuguese are expected to love the country which, having it, sends it away!) That was the dinner—O, there was Stilton cheese; it were shameful not to mention the Stilton. Good, wholesome, and toothsome it was, rich and nutty. The Stilton that we get here, clouted in tin-foil, is monstrous poor stuff, hardly better than our American sort. After dinner there were walnuts and coffee and cigars. I cannot say much for the cigars; they are not over-good in England: too long at sea, I suppose.

On the whole, it was a memorable dinner. Even its non-essential features were satisfactory. The waiter was fascinatingly solemn, the floor snowily sanded, the company sufficiently distinguished in literature and art for me to keep track of them through the newspapers. They are dead—as dead as Queen Anne, every mother's son of them! I am in my favorite rôle of Sole Survivor. It has become habitual to me; I rather like it.

Of the company were two eminent gastronomes—call them Messrs. Guttle and Swig—who so acridly hated each other that nothing but a good dinner could bring them under the same roof. (They had had a quarrel, I think, about the merit of a certain Amontillado—which, by the way, one insisted, despite Edgar Allan Poe, who certainly knew too much of whiskey to know much of wine, *is* a Sherry.) After the cloth had been removed and the coffee, walnuts and cigars brought in, the company stood, and to an air extemporaneously composed by Guttle, sang the following shocking and reprehensible song, which had been written during the proceedings by this present Sole Survivor. It will serve as fitly to conclude this feast of unreason as it did that:

THE SONG

Jack Satan's the greatest of gods,
        And Hell is the best of abodes.
'Tis reached through the Valley of Clods
        By seventy beautiful roads.
Hurrah for the Seventy Roads!
        Hurrah for the clods that resound
        With a hollow, thundering sound!
Hurrah for the Best of Abodes!

We'll serve him as long as we've breath—
        Jack Satan, the greatest of gods.
To all of his enemies, death!—
        A home in the Valley of Clods.
Hurrah for the thunder of clods
        That smother the souls of his foes!
        Hurrah for the spirit that goes
To dwell with the Greatest of Gods!

Appendix

Visions of the Night

[This remarkable account of various strange dreams Bierce had in the course of his life first appeared in the *Examiner* for July 24, 1887, and was reprinted in volume 10 (1911) of his *Collected Works.* We have appended to it another brief account of a dream found in a "Prattle" column in the *Argonaut* (Oct. 26, 1878).]

I hold the belief that the Gift of Dreams is a valuable literary endowment—that if by some art not now understood the elusive fancies that it supplies could be caught and fixed and made to serve, we should have a literature "exceeding fair." In captivity and domestication the gift could doubtless be wonderfully improved, as animals bred to service acquire new capacities and powers. By taming our dreams we shall double our working hours and our most fruitful labor will be done in sleep. Even as masters are, Dreamland is a tributary province, as witness "Kubla Khan."[1]

What is a dream? A loose and lawless collocation of memories—a disorderly succession of matters once presented in the waking consciousness. It is a resurrection of the dead, pell-mell—ancient and modern, the just and the unjust—springing from their cracked tombs, each "in his habit as he lived,"[2] pressing forward confusedly to have an audience of the Master of the Revel, and snatching one another's garments as they run. Master? No; he has abdicated his authority and they have their will of him; his own is dead and does not rise with the rest. His judgment, too, is gone, and with it the capacity to be surprised. Pained he may be and pleased, terrified and charmed, but wonder he can not feel. The monstrous, the preposterous, the unnatural—these all are simple, right and reasonable. The ludicrous does not amuse, nor the impossible amaze. The dreamer is your only true poet; he is "of imagination all compact."[3]

Imagination is merely memory. Try to imagine something that you have never observed, experienced, heard of or read about. Try to conceive an animal, for example, without body, head, limbs or tail—a house without walls or roof. But, when awake, having assistance of will and judgment, we can somewhat control and direct; we can pick and choose from memory's store, taking that which serves, excluding, though sometimes with difficulty, what is not to the purpose; asleep, our fancies "inherit us." They come so grouped, so blended and compounded the one with another, so wrought of one another's elements, that the whole seems new; but the old familiar units of conception are there, and none beside. Waking or sleeping, we get from imagination nothing new but new adjustments: "the stuff that dreams are made on"[4] has been gathered by the physical senses and stored in memory, as squirrels hoard nuts. But one, at least, of the senses contributes nothing to the fabric of the dream: no one ever dreamed an odor. Sight, hearing, feeling, possibly taste, are all workers, making provision for our nightly entertainment; but Sleep is without a nose. It surprises that those keen observers, the ancient poets, did not so describe the drowsy god, and that their obedient servants, the ancient sculptors, did not so represent him. Perhaps these latter worthies, working for posterity, reasoned that time and mischance would inevitably revise their work in this regard, conforming it to the facts of nature.

Who can so relate a dream that it shall seem one? No poet has so light a touch. As well try to write the music of an Æolian harp. There is a familiar species of the genus Bore (*Penetrator intolerabilis*) who having read a story—perhaps by some master of style—is at the pains elaborately to expound its plot for your edification and delight; then thinks, good soul, that now you need not read it. "Under substantially similar circumstances and conditions" (as the interstate commerce law hath it) I should not be guilty of the like offense; but I purpose herein to set forth the plots of certain dreams of my own, the "circumstances and conditions" being, as I conceive, dissimilar in this, that the dreams themselves are not accessible to the reader. In endeavoring to make record of their poorer part I do not indulge the hope of a higher success. I have no salt to put upon the tail of a dream's elusive spirit.

I was walking at dusk through a great forest of unfamiliar trees.[5] Whence and whither I did not know. I had a sense of the vast extent of the wood, a consciousness that I was the only living thing in it. I was obsessed by some awful spell in expiation of a forgotten crime committed, as I vaguely surmised, against the sunrise. Mechanically and without hope, I moved under the arms of the giant trees along a narrow trail penetrating the haunted solitudes of the forest. I came at length to a brook that flowed darkly and sluggishly across my path, and saw that it was blood. Turning to the right, I followed it up a considerable distance, and soon came to a small circular opening in the forest, filled with a dim, unreal light, by which I saw in the center of the opening a deep tank of white marble. It was filled with blood, and the stream that I had followed up was its outlet. All round the tank, between it and the enclosing forest—a space of perhaps ten feet in breadth, paved with immense slabs of marble—were dead bodies of men—a score; though I did not count them I knew that the number had some significant and portentous relation to my crime. Possibly they marked the time, in centuries, since I had committed it. I only recognized the fitness of the number, and knew it without counting. The bodies were naked and arranged symmetrically around the central tank, radiating from it like spokes of a wheel. The feet were outward, the heads hanging over the edge of the tank. Each lay upon its back, its throat cut, blood slowly dripping from the wound. I looked on all this unmoved. It was a natural and necessary result of my offense, and did not affect me; but there was something that filled me with apprehension and terror—a monstrous pulsation, beating with a slow, inevitable recurrence. I do not know which of the senses it addressed, or if it made its way to the consciousness through some avenue unknown to science and experience. The pitiless regularity of this vast rhythm was maddening. I was conscious that it pervaded the entire forest, and was a manifestation of some gigantic and implacable malevolence.

Of this dream I have no further recollection. Probably, overcome by a terror which doubtless had its origin in the discomfort of an impeded circulation, I cried out and was awakened by the sound of my own voice.

The dream whose skeleton I shall now present occurred in my early youth. I could not have been more than sixteen. I am considerably more now, yet I recall the incidents as vividly as when the vision was "of an hour's age"[6] and I lay cowering beneath the bed-covering and trembling with terror from the memory.

I was alone on a boundless level in the night—in my bad dreams I am always alone and it is usually night.[7] No trees were anywhere in sight, no habitations of men, no streams nor hills. The earth seemed to be covered with a short, coarse vegetation that was black and stubbly, as if the plain had been swept by fire. My way was broken here and there as I went forward with I know not what purpose by small pools of water occupying shallow depressions, as if the fire had been succeeded by rain. These pools were on every side, and kept vanishing and appearing again, as heavy dark clouds drove athwart those parts of the sky which they reflected, and passing on disclosed again the steely glitter of the stars, in whose cold light the waters shone with a black luster. My course lay toward the west, where low along the horizon burned a crimson light beneath long strips of cloud, giving that effect of measureless distance that I have since learned to look for in Doré's pictures,[8] where every touch of his hand has laid a portent and a curse. As I moved I saw outlined against this uncanny background a silhouette of battlements and towers which, expanding with every mile of my journey, grew at last to an unthinkable height and breadth, till the building subtended a wide angle of vision, yet seemed no nearer than before. Heartless and hopeless I struggled on over the blasted and forbidding plain, and still the mighty structure grew until I could no longer compass it with a look, and its towers shut out the stars directly overhead; then I passed it at an open portal, between columns of cyclopean masonry whose single stones were larger than my father's house.

Within all was vacancy; everything was coated with the dust of desertion. A dim light—the lawless light of dreams, sufficient unto itself—enabled me to pass from corridor to corridor, and from room to room, every door yielding to my hand. In the rooms it was a long walk from wall to wall; of no corridor did I ever reach an end. My footfalls gave out that strange, hollow sound that is never heard but in abandoned dwellings and tenanted tombs. For hours I wandered in this awful solitude, conscious of a seeking purpose, yet knowing not what I sought. At last, in what I conceived to be an extreme angle of the building, I entered a room of the ordinary dimensions, having a single window. Through this I saw the same crimson light still lying along the horizon in the measureless reaches of the west, like a visible doom, and knew it for the lingering fire of eternity. Looking upon the red menace of its sullen and sinister glare, there came to me the dreadful truth which years later as an extravagant fancy I endeavored to express in verse:

> Man is long ages dead in every zone,
> The angels all are gone to graves unknown;
> The devils, too, are cold enough at last,
> And God lies dead before the great white throne![9]

The light was powerless to dispel the obscurity of the room, and it was some time before I discovered in the farthest angle the outlines of a bed, and approached it with a prescience of ill. I felt that here somehow the bad business of my adventure was to end with some horrible climax, yet could not resist the spell that urged me to the fulfilment. Upon the bed, partly clothed, lay the dead body of a human being. It lay upon its back, the arms straight along the sides. By bending over it, which I did with loathing but no fear, I could see that it was dreadfully decomposed. The ribs protruded from the leathern flesh; through the skin of the sunken belly could be seen the protuberances of the spine. The face was black and shriveled and the lips, drawn away from the yellow teeth, cursed it with a ghastly grin. A fulness under the closed lids seemed to indicate that the eyes had survived the general wreck; and this was true, for as I bent above them they slowly opened and gazed into mine with a tranquil, steady regard. Imagine my horror how you can—no words of mine can assist the conception; the eyes were my own! That vestigial fragment of a vanished race—that unspeakable thing which neither time nor eternity had wholly effaced—that hateful and abhorrent scrap of mortality, still sentient after death of God and the angels, was I!

There are dreams that repeat themselves. Of this class is one of my own,[10] which seems sufficiently singular to justify its narration, though truly I fear the reader will think the realms of sleep are anything but a happy hunting-ground for my night-wandering soul. This is to true; the greater number of my incursions into dreamland, and I suppose those of most others, are attended with the happiest results. My imagination returns to the body like a bee to the hive, loaded with spoil which, reason assisting, is transmuted to honey and stored away in the cells of memory to be a joy forever. But the dream which I am about to relate has a double character; it is strangely dreadful in the experience, but the horror it inspires is so ludicrously disproportionate to the one incident producing it, that in retrospection the fantasy amuses.

I am passing through an open glade in a thinly wooded country. Through the belt of scattered trees that bound the irregular space there are glimpses of cultivated fields and the homes of strange intelligences. It must be near daybreak, for the moon, nearly at full, is low in the west, showing blood-red through the mists with which the landscape is fantastically freaked. The grass about my feet is heavy with dew, and the whole scene is that of a morning in early summer, glimmering in the unfamiliar light of a setting full moon. Near my path is a horse, visibly and audibly cropping the herbage. It lifts its head as I am about to pass, regards me motionless for a moment, then walks toward me. It is milk-white, mild of mien and amiable in look. I say to myself: "This horse is a gentle soul," and pause to caress it. It keeps its eyes fixed upon my own, approaches and speaks to me in a human voice, with human words. This does not surprise, but terrifies, and instantly I return to this our world.

The horse always speaks my own tongue, but I never know what it says. I suppose I vanish from the land of dreams before it finishes expressing what it has in mind, leaving it, no doubt, as greatly terrified by my sudden disappearance as I by its manner of accosting me. I would give value to know the purport of its communication.

Perhaps some morning I shall understand—and return no more to this our world.

One More Dream

From childhood I have been passionately fond of the heliotrope. The divine plant has had from my heart the devotion that other men give to women, to gold, or to

God; and my loyal fidelity to it has, I think, exercised a wholesome restraint on me in matters of love, business, and religion. As I slept, the other night, a spray of my adored flower on my pillow, I dreamed that I was on a large island in a tropic sea. Close behind me was the trunk of a giant tree—a heliotrope—whose branches covered the whole island and whose top touched heaven. All the fowls of the air built nests and sang in its foliage. Overcome by the ravishing perfume, I sank, swooning with happiness, at its root, yet, gazing dreamily seaward, could not help observing that of the many ships drawn convergent toward the island by the tree's matchless beauty all those beating up from leeward, on arriving within range of the odor which to me was heaven, put about and fled, holding their noses in the brine. Looking upward I then perceived that there was not a flower on the tree; the odor came from the swollen bodies and dropping oils of my literary enemies, one of whom was hanging by the neck from every branch. Filled with inexpressible rapture I awoke, the fragrant spray of heliotrope entangled in my moustache.

Rejoice, O mine enemies, and sing songs, that for once ye were my rivals—in a dream. A dream that was not your own! For in my dreaming I thought your attachment to my beloved mistress, the heliotrope, was stronger than mine, hoped it was more enduring, and felt it better for posterity. I regarded the union without jealousy, favored it without affectation, and remembered it with delight. It was a wild, impossible fancy, and it passed: yet waking I cherish the fond hope that Heaven will some day grant me the paternal satisfaction of seeing you all happily united to a sour-apple tree.

A Rational Anthem

[This poem first appeared in the *Wasp* for September 16, 1882, and was subsequently reprinted in the fifth volume of Bierce's *Collected Works*. It is his most compact encapsulation of his cynicism toward American politics and society.]

My country, 'tis of thee,
Sweet land of felony,
    Of thee I sing—
Land where my fathers fried
Young witches and applied
Whips to the Quaker's hide
    And made him spring.

My knavish country, thee,
Land where the thief is free,

Thy laws I love;
I love thy thieving bills
That tap the people's tills;
I love thy mob whose will's
    All laws above.

Let Federal employees
And rings rob all they please,
    The whole year long.
Let office-holders make
Their piles and judges rake
Our coin. For Jesus' sake,
    Let's *all* go wrong!

Notes

Introduction

1. Bierce to George Sterling, Sept. 12, 1903, *The Letters of Ambrose Bierce*, ed. Bertha Clark Pope (San Francisco: Book Club of California, 1922), 75.
2. Bierce to Blanche Partington, July 31, 1892, *Letters*, 5.
3. Bierce's articles on the subject have been collected in Lawrence I. Berkove, ed., *Skepticism and Dissent: Selected Journalism 1898–1901*, rev. ed. (Ann Arbor, Mich.: UMI Research Press, 1986).
4. As Bierce remarked in a letter, "Here in the East the Devil is a sacred personage (the Fourth Person of the Trinity, as an Irishman might say) and his name must not be taken in vain." Bierce to George Sterling, May 6, 1906, *Letters*, 120.

The Civil War (1861–1865)

1. Italian for "sacred field."
2. The battle of Carrick's Ford took place on July 13, 1861.
3. The battle of Philippi took place on June 3, 1861.
4. The battle of Laurel Hill, near Beverly, (West) Virginia, took place on July 11, 1861. This and other Union victories in 1861 secured the heavily Unionist

northwest corner of seceded Virginia for the Union cause, and elevated Maj. Gen. (U.S. Volunteers [USV]) George Brinton McClellan to national attention as a fighting general. See also note 41.

5. Adj. Gen. (CSA) Robert Selden Garnett (c. 1819–1861) was killed at Carrick's Ford while conducting the retreat from Laurel Hill.

6. Bierce has considerably minimized his own actions here. The *Indianapolis Journal* (July 27, 1861) reported: "Privates A. J. [*sic*] Bierce . . . and Boothroyd . . . Ninth Indiana Volunteers, advanced up the hill to within fifteen paces of the enemy's breastworks when Boothroyd was wounded in the neck by a rifle ball paralyzing him. Bierce, in open view of the enemy, carried poor Boothroyd and his gun without other assistance, fully twenty rods, balls falling around him like hail." Bierce's heroism here probably had much to do with his rapid promotion.

7. Alfred, Lord Tennyson (1809–1892), "The Lotos-Eaters" (1832), l.4.

8. Edgar Allan Poe (1809–1849), "Ulalume" (1847), l.5.

9. The injured Confederate was James E. Hanger, who devised an artificial wooden leg for himself and later went into business making artificial limbs for Southern soldiers.

10. *The Pleasures of Hope* (1799) was published by the Scottish poet Thomas Campbell (1777–1844) when he was twenty-two. The celebrated opening reads: "At summer's eve, when Heaven's ethereal bow / Spans with bright arch the glittering hills below, / Why to yon mountain turns the musing eye, / Whose sunbright summit mingles with the sky? / Why do those cliffs of shadowy tint appear / More sweet than all the landscape smiling near?—/ 'Tis distance lends enchantment to the view, / And robes the mountain in its azure hue."

11. Milton (1608–1674), *Paradise Lost* (1667), 1.293–94.

12. Tennyson, *In Memoriam* (1850), 54.8.

13. *Marplot:* One who hinders an undertaking through officious interference.

14. One would like to think this a deliberate misquotation of a poem by Robert Kelley Weeks (1840–1876), "Possession," in *Poems* (New York: Leypoldt & Holt, 1866), 44 ("And love may be, so it seems to me, / Complete without possession").

15. Cf. Bierce's story "An Affair of Outposts," *San Francisco Examiner,* Dec. 19, 1897 (also in *In the Midst of Life* [1898]). In nineteenth-century American military jargon an *affair* was defined as "an action or engagement not of sufficient magnitude to be termed a battle, but usually of more importance than a skirmish; as the affair of outpost, or the affair of the rearguard." Edward S. Farrow, *Farrow's Military Encyclopedia* (New York: privately printed, 1885).

16. In his story "The Coup de Grâce" (*San Francisco Examiner,* June 30, 1889, and in *Tales of Soldiers and Civilians* [1891]) Bierce supplies a lightly fictionalized version of this event: "Fifty yards away, on the crest of a low, thinly wooded hill, he saw several dark objects moving about among the fallen men—a herd of swine. One stood with its back to him, its shoulders sharply elevated. Its forefeet were upon a human body, its head was depressed and invisible. The bristly ridge of its chine showed black against the red west"; *Collected Works,* 2:128.

17. Confederate field armies were usually named after the states where they were formed.

18. Federal armies were usually named after the rivers near where they were formed.

19. Samuel Taylor Coleridge (1772–1834), "The Rime of the Ancient Mariner" (1798), l.559.

20. Lt. Gen. (CSA) Albert Sidney Johnston (1803–1862), native of Kentucky, Texas loyalist, and prewar U.S. Army Regular with a reputation second only to Robert E. Lee, was fatally wounded the first day of fighting.

21. Maj. Gen. (CSA) Pierre Gustave Toutont Beauregard (1818–1893), native of Louisiana and prewar commandant of Cadets at West Point, commanded the forces that fired on Ft. Sumter. He was Johnston's second in command at Shiloh.

22. Beauregard commanded the first Army of Mississippi (formed from Confederate Western Department No. 2), which was combined with Johnston's Central Army of Kentucky at Corinth on March 29, 1862, forming another Army of Mississippi.

23. An alternate name for the battle.

24. Maj. Gen. (USV) Ulysses Simpson Grant (1822–1885), a native of Ohio, West Point graduate, Mexican War veteran, was selling kindling door to door when the war began. He was the commander of the Army of the Tennessee and the Middle Tennessee Department at Shiloh.

25. Maj. Gen. (USV) Don Carlos Buell (1818–1898) was a lieutenant colonel in San Francisco when the war began. His Army of the Ohio, of which Bierce's division formed a part, had moved from Western Virginia and across most of Tennessee by train, and was making its way to join Grant when the Confederates attacked at Pittsburg Landing.

26. This may have been Ann Wallace, wife of Union Brig. Gen. (USV) William Harvey Lamb Wallace, commander of the 2d Division at Shiloh. She was at the general's side when he died of wounds three days after the battle on April 10, 1862.

27. The morality of whether to put a mortally wounded soldier to death is the subject of "The Coup de Grâce" (see note 16). See also Bierce's "On the Right to Kill the Sick," *New York Journal,* Oct. 1, 1899, 30; *San Francisco Examiner,* Oct. 1, 1899, 14.

28. *Vidette:* more commonly "vedette" in American usage; a sentry, often mounted, moving in advance of the skirmish line.

29. Deut. 1:33.

30. Edwin McMaster Stanton (1814–1869), secretary of war under Lincoln (succeeding Simon Cameron to the post in 1862) and Andrew Johnson (1862–68).

31. Maj. Gen. (USV) William Tecumseh Sherman (1820–1891), West Point graduate from Ohio, was teaching military school in Louisiana when the war began. At Shiloh he commanded the 5th Division of the Army of the Tennessee, and was wounded early in the battle.

32. The reference is to Buell's "The Battle of Shiloh, or Pittsburg Landing," *New York World,* February 19, 1865; Grant's *Personal Memoirs of U. S. Grant* (1885–86; 2 vols.); Sherman's *Memoirs of William T. Sherman* (1875;

2 vols.); and numerous articles and counter-articles from in *Century Magazine* and other publications years after the battle. Historians still argue the question "Buell late, or Grant early?"

33. Often cited as Stone's River.

34. Maj. Gen. (USV) William Starke Rosecrans (1819–1898), Ohioan, West Point graduate, and engineer, commanded the Army of the Cumberland at Stones River.

35. Lt. Gen. (CSA) Braxton Bragg (1817–1876), native of North Carolina, West Point graduate, U.S. Army Regular officer until 1856, and Louisiana planter at the outbreak of the war, was in command of the Confederate Army of the Tennessee at Stones River.

36. Tenth Battery, Indiana Light Artillery, in Crittenden's Division of Wagner's Brigade at Stones River.

37. William Cullen Bryant (1794–1878), "Thanatopsis" (1817), l.74.

38. Col. (Ind.) John Franklin Miller (1831–1886) commanded the 27th Indiana Volunteer infantry in the 2d Division of Thomas's Center Corps at Stones River, where he was wounded on the first day. He later served as a U.S. senator from California (1880–86).

39. This sort of punishment fell out of favor after the war and was banned by 1880.

40. Gen. Henry Wager Halleck (1815–1872), commander of the Department of the Missouri (later the Mississippi) in the early stages of the war.

41. Maj. Gen. George Brinton McClellan (1826–1885), commander of the Army of the Potomac. He ran for president against Lincoln on the Democratic ticket in 1864.

42. Fort Donelson on the Cumberland River in Tennessee fell to the Union forces on February 16, 1862.

43. In the *San Francisco Examiner* appearance of the essay, the following opening paragraph was omitted from subsequent reprints:

> In choosing the Chickamauga National Park as a point of rendezvous for the army the Washington authorities probably had in mind only strategic considerations; yet the place can hardly fail to speak to the hearts of our soldiers in a most impressive way. On that historic ground occurred the fiercest and bloodiest of all the great conflicts of modern times—a conflict in which skill, valor, accident and fate played each its important part, the resultant a tactical victory for one side, a strategical one for the other. At the end of two days of tremendous fighting the Federal force retired from the field to the position at Chattanooga, which it had been the purpose of the campaign to gain and hold.

44. Rosecrans was one of the most respected officers in the Union Army before Chickamauga, having been voted the Thanks of Congress for Stones River (Murfreesboro), one of only fifteen so honored throughout the war. Rosecrans later blamed Crittenden, Thomas, and McCook for the defeat at Chickamauga.

45. Maj. Gen. George Henry Thomas (1816–1870), a Virginian and prewar

captain who stayed loyal to the Union, was Rosecrans's second in command and commander of the XIV Corps at Chickamauga.

46. Col. (later Maj. Gen. USV) Edward Moody McCook (1833–1909), eldest son of the "Tribe of John," the Fighting McCooks of Ohio (seventeen men from the same family who fought for the Union), and a Kansas legislator at the war's start. McCook commanded the 1st Cavalry Division in the Army of the Cumberland's Cavalry Corps at Chickamauga.

47. Maj. Gen. (USV) Thomas Leonidas Crittenden (1819–1893), native of Kentucky and the son of Sen. J. J. Crittenden, commanded the XXI Corps at Chickamauga.

48. In the *San Francisco Examiner* the following text appears here:

> . . . , and as soon as a brigade had marched its length beyond the one immediately preceding, it moved in line bodily off the road to the right and met the enemy in the wood. Imagine a snake lying in a path, its head to the north; imagine the doubling movement that it must make in order to bring its head to the south, without moving it. That is the movement made by our army in that first day's fight, and everywhere we were successful in covering each part of the road before the enemy could strike across it at that point.

49. "Days of danger, nights of waking"; Sir Walter Scott (1771–1832), *The Lady of the Lake* (1810), 1.31.

50. Brig. Gen. (USV) William Babcock Hazen (1830–1887) was teaching tactics at West Point when the war began. He commanded the 2d Brigade, 2d Division, XXI Corps at Chickamauga. Bierce joined his staff as a topographical engineer, or mapmaker, in the spring of 1863. Hazen was perhaps Bierce's closest associate during the Civil War.

51. Brig. Gen. (USV) Thomas John Wood (1823–1906), commander of the 1st Division, XXI Corps at Chickamauga. A Kentuckian and prewar Regular, Wood was Grant's roommate at West Point, and would be the last survivor of the Class of 1845.

52. The telegram to President Lincoln read: "We have met with a serious disaster; extent not yet ascertained."

53. Brig. Gen. (USV) James Abram Garfield (1831–1881), later to become president (1881). Garfield was chief of staff to Rosecrans from July 1863 until Rosecrans's removal after Chickamauga. Much was made of Garfield's actions at Chickamauga during his presidential campaign, and it aided significantly in his electoral victory. He was promoted to major general in the volunteers during the battle. For Bierce's response to Garfield's assassination see page 185.

54. Maj. Gen. (USV) James Scott Negley (1826–1901), brigadier general of Pennsylvania Militia before the war and commander of the 2d Division, XIV Corps at Chickamauga. After the battle he was relieved of duty for alleged cowardice. Although cleared by a court-martial, he was not reinstated to a command and resigned from the army in early 1865.

55. Maj. Gen. (USV) Gordon Granger (1822–1876) of New York, a West Point graduate, lieutenant in the Regular Army when the war began, and com-

mander of the Reserve Corps of the Army of the Cumberland at Chickamauga.

56. Bierce's older brother Albert, whom he variously called Grizzly, Sloots, or Ursus.

57. For his leadership of the refugees and his own troops as rear guard to the collapsing Federal army, Thomas, known in the army before the battle as "Old Slow-Trot" and "Pap," would earn yet another sobriquet: "The Rock of Chickamauga."

58. Brig. Gen. (USV) Jefferson Columbus Davis (1828–1879), a native of Indiana who was at Ft. Sumter when the shelling began, commanded the 1st Division, XX Corps at Chickamauga. Davis had murdered fellow Union brigadier general William "Bull" Nelson in Louisville in 1862, but his only punishment seems to have been denial of his promotion to major general in the volunteers, despite Grant's and Rosecrans's recommendations.

59. Col. (USA) Archibald Gracie (1858–1912) was the son of Brig. Gen. (CSA) Archibald Gracie Jr. (1832–1864), who commanded a brigade in Preston's Division of Buckner's Corps in Longstreet's Left Wing at Chickamauga. His book asserts that the Confederates decisively won the battle, the Union forces fleeing the field; but the most "stupendous blunder of the war" was the failure of the Confederates to pursue the Union army and put a seal on the victory. A year after his book appeared, Gracie sailed on the *Titanic*; although he survived the sinking of the ship, he died several months later.

60. Brig. Gen. (USV) John Milton Brannan (1819–1892), a prewar captain of artillery, commanded the 3d Division of Thomas's XIV Corps at Chickamauga.

61. Lt. Gen. (CSA) Daniel Harvey Hill (1821–1889), commander of the II Corps in Polk's Right Wing of the Army of Tennessee at Chickamauga. He later wrote an article, "Chickamauga: The Great Battle of the West," *Century Magazine* 11 (Apr. 1887): 937–62.

62. R. U. Johnson and C. C. Clough Buel, eds., *Battles and Leaders of the Civil War*, 4 vols. (New York: Century Co., 1884–88).

63. Charles C. Aleshire, who led the 18th Ohio Battery in the 1st Division of the Reserve Corps at Chickamauga.

64. Maj. Gen. (USV) John McAuley Palmer (1831–1900), a Democratic legislator from Kentucky before the war, commanded the 2d Division, XXI Corps at Chickamauga. He was about fifty-seven at the time of this writing.

65. Brig. Gen. (USV) John Basil Turchin (1822–1901), Russian-born veteran of the Russian army, the Crimean War, and commander of the 3d Brigade, 4th Division of the XIV Corps at Chickamauga, also called the "Russian Thunderbolt." His wife personally appealed to President Lincoln after Buell court-martialed him in the summer of 1862 for burning a Georgia town. Lincoln not only had him reinstated but promoted him to brigadier general of volunteers.

66. Brig. Gen. (USV) Charles Cruft (1826–1883), an Indianan, commanded the 1st Brigade, 2d Division, XXI Corps at Chickamauga.

67. Bierce later recanted these statements to some degree: "While on the sub-

ject I should like to do an act of justice. A few weeks ago I showed Colonel
J. P. Jackson to have been in error in supposing himself to have commanded the Twenty-third Kentucky Infantry in the assault on Missionary
Ridge. I then expressed a conviction that his whole military record was a
dream—that he had never been a soldier. In this I was wrong: I find that
as Lieutenant-Colonel he commanded that regiment more than a year
before at Perryville. At Missionary Ridge it was, as I stated, commanded
by Lieutenant-Colonel J. C. Foy. If Jackson had been with it as an officer it
could only have been as Colonel and he would have been in command.
My notion is that he had been reduced to the ranks"; "Prattle," *San Francisco Examiner*, Dec. 23, 1888.

68. The *San Francisco Examiner* appearance of the essay opened with the following paragraph, which was omitted from subsequent reprints.

> History is not only untruthful; it is negligent. It overlooks events
> of importance and relates trifles. Such is the case in the history of our
> great civil war: the military annals of that heroic period are over-
> loaded with a multitude of narratives having only such interest as
> may have been imparted to them by the accident of a sparkling pen
> or some picturesque element not essential to the "action of the
> piece." Greater events, lacking the good fortune to have attracted the
> attention of one who could write what men are willing to read, find
> no permanent place in the record, and perish from the memory of all
> except the rapidly diminishing band of those to whom they were a
> personal experience.

69. Maj. Gen. (USV) Oliver Otis Howard (1830–1909) was teaching mathematics at West Point at the beginning of the war. By the Atlanta campaign he was commanding IV Corps of the Army of the Cumberland.

70. The Union forces moved through Dalton on May 7, Resaca on May 14–15,
Adairsville on May 17, and Kingston and Cassville on May 18.

71. Maj. Gen. (USV) John McAllister Schofield (1831–1906), a prewar Regular
and schoolteacher, commanded XXIII Corps (also called the Army of the
Ohio) in the Atlanta campaign.

72. Lt. Gen. (CSA) Leonidas Polk (1806–1864), West Point graduate, Episco-
pal bishop of Louisiana, and personal friend of Confederate President
Jefferson Davis, commanded a corps in the Army of Tennessee on the
Dallas Line. He was killed at Pine Mountain, three weeks after Pickett's
Mill.

73. Brig. Gen. (USV) David Sloane Stanley (1828–1902) was fighting in Kansas
when the war broke out and refused a commission in an Arkansas regiment in 1861. He commanded the Federal Cavalry Corps at Chickamauga
as commander of the IV Corps under General Sherman.

74. The battle of Chancellorsville (a Union defeat) occurred in Virginia on
May 1–2, 1863, for which Howard, whose IX Corps bore the brunt of
Jackson's flanking attack, was often blamed by his fellow officers and the
press.

75. Lt. Gen. (CSA) John Bell Hood (1831–1879), a prewar Regular from Ken-

tucky who had lost an arm at Gettysburg while commanding the attack on Little Round Top and a leg at Chickamauga only two months later, commanded a corps in Johnston's army on the Dallas Line.

76. Maj. Gen. (USV) Philip Henry ("Little Phil") Sheridan (1831–1888), a prewar Regular in an administrative job in Missouri when the war broke out, was commanding the 3d Division of XX Corps in the Atlanta campaign.

77. Brig. Gen. Patrick Ronayne Cleburne (1828–1864), an Irish-born veteran of the British army who immigrated to Arkansas in the 1840s, rose steadily in the ranks after enlisting as a private in the 15th Arkansas Infantry. By Pickett's Mill, Cleburne was commanding one of the best fighting divisions in the Confederacy and had fought in every battle Bierce had, often in direct opposition. He was sometimes known as the "Stonewall Jackson of the West."

78. Lt. Gen. (CSA) William Joseph Hardee (1815–1873) was on leave from his post as commandant of Cadets at West Point when the war began. He had translated a book from French on infantry tactics used by both sides early in the war. He commanded a corps in the Army of Tennessee during the Atlanta campaign.

79. Gen. Joseph Eggleston Johnston (1807–1891), a prewar Regular, commander of the Army of Tennessee during the Atlanta campaign, and at this time the fourth highest ranking officer in the Confederacy. The quotation is from his *Narrative of Military Operations* (New York: D. Appleton & Co., 1874), 328–29.

80. Maj. Gen. (CSA) Joseph Wheeler (1836–1906) was fighting Indians in the West when the Civil War began. "Fightin' Joe" Wheeler was commanding all the Confederate cavalry in the Western Theater by May 1864.

81. Quoted in Johnston's *Narrative,* 587. See also Hood's *Advance and Retreat* (New Orleans: Hood Orphan Memorial Fund, 1880), 119.

82. On Foy, see page 36.

83. Johnston, *Narrative,* 329–31.

84. Brig. Gen. (CSA) Mark Perrin Lowrey (1828–1885), a Baptist minister before the war, commanded a brigade in Hardee's corps.

85. Colonel Baucum is unidentified.

86. William B. Hazen, *A Narrative of Military Service* (Boston: Ticknor & Co., 1885), 261.

87. Johnston, *Narrative,* 331.

88. The reference is to two competing American lexicographers. Noah Webster (1758–1843) compiled his first dictionary in 1806. His *American Dictionary of the English Language* was first published in 1828. In the next year Joseph Emerson Worcester (1784–1865), a compiler of geographical dictionaries and gazeteers, produced an abridgment of Webster's dictionary and subsequently produced dictionaries rivaling Webster's.

89. The *San Francisco Examiner* appearance of the essay opened with the following headnote, which was omitted from subsequent reprints:

> How the following narrative of personal adventure came into my hands, who was the hero of it and whether in publishing it here I com-

ply strictly with his wishes—these are matters of no importance to the reader. I can vouch for the truth of the story in so far as the memory of a truthful man has served him; for apart from his credibility I have independent evidence of the most unimpeachable kind. Perhaps this assurance is hardly needful, for there is nothing incredible in the tale, which is, indeed, merely a report of such incidents in the life of a soldier as might occur, and frequently did occur, in the civil war without evoking much comment other than good-natured raillery from those having contemporary knowledge of them. It is not impossible that in the feeling of having already experienced as much of that kind of comment as he deserves we may find the narrator's real reason for insisting that under no circumstances shall his name be disclosed.

90. The Union forces overran Atlanta on September 1, 1864.
91. Col. (Ill.) Henry Kumler McConnell (d. 1898), acting brigade commander in the 2d Division, XV Corps of the Army of the Tennessee, now commanded by Gen. William B. Hazen.
92. Andersonville was a large Confederate prison in southwestern Georgia, opened in February 1864. Because of bad sanitation and other deficiencies, at least thirteen thousand prisoners died there.
93. Theodore O'Hara (1820–1867), "The Bivouac of the Dead" (1847), l.4. The poem was written to commemorate the Americans slain in the battle of Buena Vista (Feb. 22–23, 1847).
94. Recall the section heading in Bierce's story, "The Damned Thing" (1893): "A Man Though Naked May Be in Rags."
95. Maj. Gen. (CSA) Nathan Bedford Forrest (1821–1877) was a prewar slave trader. Without any military training "that devil, Forrest," as Sherman called him, was a cavalry genius, commanding an irregular corps in Hood's army at Franklin. After the war he was the first Grand Wizard of the Ku Klux Klan.
96. Col. (Ill.) Philip Sidney Post (1833–1895), a lawyer and editor from New York, brigade commander at Spring Hill.
97. Maj. Gen. (CSA) Benjamin Franklin Cheatham (1820–1886), a major general in the Tennessee State Militia at the beginning of the war, commanded a corps at Spring Hill. Hood accused him of causing the Confederate defeat at Franklin.
98. Brig. Gen. (USV) George Day Wagner (1829–1869), commander of the 2d Division of the IV Corps.
99. Col. (Ohio) Emerson Opdycke (1830–1884) commanded the 1st Brigade, 2d Division, IV Corps and was later credited with saving the Union battle line.
100. An adaptation of Edward FitzGerald's translation of the *Rubáiyát of Omar Khayyám* (1859): "Ah Love! could you and I with Him conspire / To grasp this Sorry Scheme of Things entire, / Would not we shatter it to bits—and then / Remould it nearer to the Heart's Desire!" (stanza 99).
101. Five Confederate generals died at Franklin: Brig. Gen. John Adams (b. 1825), a prewar Regular; Patrick Ronayne Cleburne (see note 77 above);

States Rights Gist (b. 1831), a Texas attorney and county official; Hiram Bronson Granbury (b. 1831); and Otho French Strahl (b. 1831), a Tennessee attorney.

102. Casualty figures in the American Civil War, though staggering to the imagination, were not as great as some have made out. Combined Federal and Confederate casualties (dead, wounded, and missing) at Franklin may have reached eight thousand, but no more. The Franklin/Nashville campaign, conducted in a severe winter, was notorious for exposure injuries, and the starving, often barefoot Confederates suffered far worse than their Yankee counterparts. This could account for some of the exaggerated casualty figures.

103. Gen. Joseph K. Barnes (1817–1882), the Union army's acting surgeon general. The battle of Gettysburg occurred on July 1–3, 1863; Temescal Creek is unidentified.

104. Brig. Gen. (USV) Samuel Beatty (1820–1885), a Mexican War veteran and prewar sheriff, commanded 3d Division, IV Corps at Franklin.

The Aftermath of the War (1865–1867)

1. From Hamlet's soliloquy; *Hamlet*, 3.1.86 ("pitch" in Shakespeare).
2. John Bidwell (1819–1900), author of several works about the exploration of California. Bierce refers to *A Journey to California* (1842), published six years before John W. Marshall discovered gold on the estate of John August Sutter in 1848.
3. *Hardee's Tactics* (1855), the standard military manual of the period, written by Gen. William Joseph Hardee (see "The Civil War," note 78).
4. Thomas Gray (1716–1771), *Elegy Written in a Country Church-yard* (1751), l.12.
5. William Wordsworth (1770–1850), *The Excursion* (1814), 8.461 (also 9.725).
6. [Thomas] Mayne Reid (1818–1883), Irish-American author of many adventure novels. Bierce was acquainted with him (see "A Sole Survivor").
7. Isa. 32:2.
8. Cyrus Townsend Brady (1861–1920), *Indian Fights and Fighters* (New York: McClure, Phillips & Co., 1904), 14–15.
9. Ibid.
10. In the winter of 1845 a group of people in Illinois led by Jacob and George Donner decided to move to California. They left the next spring, but in December became trapped by snow in the Sierra Nevada mountains. A group of fifteen set out in mid-December on foot without food, and they were forced to eat human flesh until at last they reached an Indian village in early January 1847. The party that stayed behind also resorted to cannibalism.
11. Hans Breitmann is the hero of a series of ballads in German-American dialect written by Charles Godfrey Leland (1824–1903). They were collected in *The Breitmann Ballads* (1871) and other volumes.
12. *Macbeth*, 4.3.222 ("cannot" in Shakespeare).

13. Percy Bysshe Shelley (1792–1822), "Ozymandias" (1818), l.2.
14. John Keats (1795–1821), "On First Looking into Chapman's Homer" (1816), lines 11–14.
15. Shakespeare, *1 Henry IV*, 1.3.258 ("have done" in Shakespeare).
16. Shakespeare, *Sonnets,* 62.10.
17. Shelley, "Ozymandias," l.14 ("stretch" in Shelley).

Early Days in San Francisco (1868–1872)

1. The reference is to the *Table Talk* of Samuel Taylor Coleridge (1772–1834), first published in 1836. Henry St. John, Viscount Bolingbroke (1678–1751), English political writer, was known for his eloquence in oratory.
2. There are two cities in the United States named Titusville, one in Florida and one in Pennsylvania.
3. See page 145 for Bierce's defense of Chinese immigrants.
4. For a more serious treatment of the ethics of suicide see page 225.
5. *Nolle prosequi,* indicating that the plaintiff or prosecutor no longer wishes to pursue an action or some part of it.
6. Susan B. Anthony (1820–1906), well-known crusader for female suffrage. In later years her articles were printed in the *San Francisco Examiner* adjacent to Bierce's columns on the editorial page.
7. Shakespeare, *Macbeth*, 1.7.60 ("sticking place" in Shakespeare).
8. This spelling of "height" was accepted in Bierce's day. His friend Joaquin Miller built a house that he called The Hights.
9. Mark Twain married Olivia Langdon on February 2, 1870.
10. Twain had spent the better part of 1864–66, as well as the spring and summer of 1868, in San Francisco, but left on July 7, 1868, for the East.
11. A phrase Bierce repeated on many occasions, most notably in his definition of "Cynic" in *The Devil's Dictionary:* "A blackguard whose faulty vision sees things as they are, not as they ought to be."

The English Jaunt (1872–1875)

1. Washington Irving (1783–1859), "Stratford-on-Avon," in *The Sketch-Book* (1819–20). Irving visited Stratford in 1815.
2. Shakespeare, *Macbeth,* 4.3.175.
3. Both General Sherman and Mark Twain visited Stratford in the fall of 1872.
4. Sir John Franklin (1786–1847) was an English explorer of the Arctic who discovered the northwest passage. David Livingstone (1813–1873) had been found by Henry Morton Stanley in 1871. He would die in Africa two years later.

5. A misquotation ("I left him practising the one hundredth Psalm") of the final line (l.848) of *The Vision of Judgment* (1822) by George Gordon, Lord Byron (1788–1824).

6. Sir Walter Scott, *Kenilworth* (1821).

7. Napoleon III (1808–1873) became emperor by a coup d'état on December 2, 1851; one year later he established the Second Empire. He was captured on September 2, 1870, during the Franco-Prussian War; later released, he joined his family in Chislehurst, a small town in Kent, where he died on January 9, 1873. He had married Eugénie de Montijo (1826–1920) in 1853.

8. Henri Rochefort (Victor Henri, Marquis de Rochefort-Luçay, 1831–1913) was a French polemical writer, first for the left, then for the right. *La Lanterne* published eleven issues in 1868–69. Rochefort was condemned by military law in 1873 for supporting the Commune of Paris and was sentenced to New Caledonia; but he escaped in four months. An amnesty in 1880 allowed him to return to France.

9. Ambrose Bierce, "Loot," *Lantern* 1 (May 18, 1874): 6.

10. Ambrose Bierce, "Le Comte de Luçay," *Lantern* 2 (July 15, 1874): 3, 6. Bierce has quoted the entire article.

11. *Lantern* 2 (July 15, 1874): 3.

12. Walt Whitman (1819–1892), "Song of Myself" (1855), l.4.

13. Alexander Pope (1688–1744), "Epilogue to the Satires" (1738), dialogue 1, l.136 ("Do good" in Pope).

14. Joaquin Miller (1837–1913), California poet and longtime friend of Bierce's, who was also visiting England at this time. He had attained spectacular fame in England upon the publication of his *Songs of the Sierras* (1871).

15. Thomas Hood the Younger (1835–1874), son of the comic poet Thomas Hood (1799–1845) and a prolific writer, editor, and illustrator. He was the editor of *Fun,* to which Bierce contributed voluminously during his entire English stay, and *Tom Hood's Comic Annual,* to which Bierce also contributed.

16. Prov. 23:32.

17. Leigh Bierce was born on April 29, 1874. Bierce's first son, Day, was born in December 1872.

18. The reference is to Bierce's work for *Figaro* (semiweekly), *Fun* (weekly), and the *Lantern* (occasional). The other weekly and the monthly are unidentified.

19. Mollie, pregnant with her third child (Helen, born Oct. 30, 1875), had taken the children back to San Francisco in April.

Return to San Francisco (1875–1879)

1. See the next section.

2. Samuel Woodworth (1785–1842), "The Old Oaken Bucket" (1817), l.2.

3. Byron, *Childe Harold's Pilgrimage* (1812–18), 3.22.

4. Actually "raptures and roses of vice"; Algernon Charles Swinburne (1837–1909), "Dolores" (1866), l.69.

5. Byron, *English Bards and Scotch Reviewers* (1809), l.415 ("monuments" in Byron).

6. Bierce wrote a poem to Harcourt's memory, "T. A. H.," *Wasp* (Feb. 16, 1884); in *Shapes of Clay* (1903).

7. "On with the Dance!," *Californian* (Feb./Mar. 1880); in *Collected Works*, volume 8.

8. This line is not found in the plays of William Congreve.

9. An oft-repeated anecdote about the German poet and critic Heinrich Heine (1797–1856). See Louis Untermeyer, *Heinrich Heine: Paradox and Poet* (New York: Harcourt, Brace, 1937), 307. Hans Ferdinand Massmann was a professor of Latin frequently twitted by Heine.

10. Hector A. Stuart published several books of poems; Bierce is probably referring to *Ben Nebo and Other Poems* (1876).

11. Bierce is repeating a story out of Plutarch's *Life of Alcibiades:* "Alcibiades had a dog which cost him seventy minas, and was a very large one, and very handsome. His tail, which was his principal ornament, he caused to be cut off, and his acquaintances exclaiming at him for it, and telling him that all Athens was sorry for the dog, and cried out upon him for this action, he laughed, and said, 'Just what I wanted has happened then. I wished the Athenians to talk about this, that they might not say something worse of me.'" Plutarch, *The Lives of the Noble Grecians and Romans,* trans. John Dryden, rev. Arthur Hugh Clough (New York: Modern Library, n.d.), 238.

12. Editor of the *Carson* (Nevada) *Appeal.*

13. Cf. Bierce's comment to George Sterling: "I don't share your regret that I have not devoted myself to serious poetry. I don't think of myself as a poet, but as a satirist; so I'm entitled to credit for what little gold there may be in the mud I throw. But if I professed gold-throwing the mud which I should surely mix with the missiles would count against me." Bierce to George Sterling, Oct. 21, 1903; *Letters,* 78.

14. See "The *Examiner* Years," note 53.

15. Frank M. Pixley (1824–1895), founder and editor of the *Argonaut.*

16. Harry J. Widmer's account is as follows:

> I went down to the office of the Argonaut at about 10 o'clock this morning in company with a gentleman who was prepared to testify to the identity of the writer of the slanderous article and inquired for Bierce. He is the individual who edits the tattle or prattle department. He is a debilitated, soured scribbler, well known in the limited circle of his readers, and is remarkable for nothing but his ill temper and his cynical nature. His writings are notorious chiefly for coarse abuse and vulgarity. I was directed to a front room, where

I FOUND BIERCE

> Seated at a table writing. I said: "Are you Mr. Bierce?" Said he: "That is my name." I then said: "Did you write the article referring to

Miss Katie Mayhew in the last issue of the Argonaut?" Bierce, putting
his hand on his hip and rising, said: "I did not write the letters." I replied: "I do not refer to them, but to the editorial comments." Bierce
answered: "If you mean where she was spoken of as 'a charming blackguard,' I did." Before the words were well out of his mouth, I struck
him a violent blow on the temple with my clenched fist, knocking him
backward through the panes of an adjoining window. Previous to hitting him, I noticed that he had drawn his pistol. The noise of the falling glass alarmed the office, and several employes, headed by F. M.
Pixley, rushed into the room.

I DEMANDED A RETRACTION

Of Pixley, who said "We will not retract," and then I let him have it
smack in the face, which caused him to wink, sputter and fall back. A
tall man then stepped between us; and Bierce, who was in another corner of the room quivering like a man attached to a galvanic battery, his
face white with fear, called out in a weak, tremulous voice, "Don't let
him hit me again, and I promise on my word as a gentleman not to
shoot." His attitude was most ludicrous, standing there with a loaded
pistol in his hand, and in mortal fear of an unarmed man. "You are the
boss of this room, and I want you to assert yourself," said Pixley.
Whereupon Bierce made a desperate effort to rally his sinking courage,
and seeing he was surrounded by the attaches and backed by his employer, he pointed his pistol at me and murmured in a hardly audible
tone, "Leave the room instantly, or I'll shoot." Having accomplished
the object of my visit, and chastised him and his employer, I picked up
my hat and cane and left the room, extending an invitation to the pro-
prietor-in-chief to come out on the sidewalk, but Pixley declined the
invitation and remained in his office.

"Katie Mayhew's Husband," *San Francisco Chronicle* 28 (Oct. 2, 1878): 3.
17. Denis Kearney was the rabble-rousing leader of the Workingmen's party;
    it is therefore understandable that he would adopt a virulently anti-Chi-
    nese stance.
18. Loring Pickering, part owner of the *San Francisco Call.*
19. Cf. Bierce's simple comment in "Ashes of the Beacon": "An inherent
    weakness in republican government was that it assumed the honesty and
    intelligence of the majority, 'the masses,' who were neither honest nor
    intelligent"; *Collected Works,* 1:61.
20. Perhaps Bierce is referring to a conversation Boswell had with Johnson on
    March 23, 1783, as recorded in his *Life of Johnson:* "I mentioned politics.
    Johnson. 'Sir, I'd as soon have a man to break my bones as talk to me of
    publick affairs, internal or external. I have lived to see things all as bad as
    they can be.'"
21. Presumably William Cullen Bryant (1794–1878), American poet.
22. See "The Civil War," page 36 and note 67.
23. Leon Donnat, *L'Etat de Californie: Receuil de faits observés en 1877–1878*
    (Paris: Librairie Ch. Delagrave, 1878). It was never translated.

24. Ralph Waldo Emerson (1803–1882), "The Problem" (1840), l.33.
25. Meichel Henry De Young (1849–1925), founder and editor of the *San Francisco Chronicle*. Bierce repeatedly attacked him in both his columns and his verse.
26. Shakespeare, *As You Like It*, 2.7.161.
27. Luke 15:23.
28. Gen. John McComb, later warden of the state penitentiary at San Quentin.

The Black Hills (1880–1881)

1. H. A. Iddings, a secretary to Captain West.
2. Edwin Booth (1833–1893), celebrated American actor whose brother, John Wilkes Booth, was the assassin of Lincoln.
3. Hiram Hale, whose wife, Sophia, was suing West for embezzling her company stock.
4. A flume was being built to convey water from Spring Creek to Rockerville.
5. Evidently a reference to Mrs. Ida Karl, a married woman (whose husband was apparently away) of whom West was unusually fond. Contrary to Bierce's allegations, however, she does not appear to have bestowed her favors upon anyone but West.
6. Charles A. Girdler and William H. Male were stockholders who had come from New York to look into affairs at the mine. L. L. Alexander was superintendent of the Father De Smet mine. Chambers was an accountant.
7. Edward S. Kaufman, a relative of Bierce's San Francisco friend Charles Kaufman.
8. On whom see page 168.
9. F. A. Babcock, superintendent of the Rhoderick Dhu mine.
10. Milton E. Pinney, a Deadwood merchant who had taken over West's duties after the latter's ouster in July.

The *Wasp* Years (1881–1886)

1. Allen Forman, editor of the *Maquereau,* the New York organ of the Pacific Coast Women's Press Association. Forman made several attacks on Bierce in the magazine.
2. Charles Shortridge was a writer for the *San Jose Mercury*. For De Young see "Return to San Francisco," note 25, above.
3. General W. H. L. Barnes, a prominent attorney and Republican politician in San Francisco.
4. William Sharon (1821–1885) was a wealthy bank manager and a senator from Nevada (1875–81). He and his executors were involved in a long drawn-out lawsuit with Sarah Althea Hill, who claimed she had a valid marriage contract with Sharon and therefore a claim to his estate; Hill and his lawyers maintained that the contract was a forgery.

5. Shakespeare, *Macbeth*, 4.1.111.

6. "by dispensing with, not changing, me."

7. The Reverend Mr. Stiggins is a hypocritical cleric in Dickens's *Pickwick Papers*. Bridlegoose is an English rendering of a character (Bridoye) in François Rabelais' *Gargantua et Pantagruel*. He is a corrupt judge who decides lawsuits by a toss of the dice.

8. *Crœsus:* A spectacularly wealthy king of Lydia in the sixth century B.C.E.; later the name was used for any wealthy individual. *Impecu:* adaptation of "impecunious," or a poor person advocating violence against the rich. *Parvenu:* newly rich. *Latronus:* adaptation of the Latin *latro*, "robber."

9. Nauvoo is a small town in Illinois where Joseph Smith and the Mormons settled in 1839. Smith was murdered there in 1844 and the Mormons left for Utah (Ogden is a city in Utah).

10. George Q. Cannon, "Utah and Its People," *North American Review* 132 (May 1881): 451–66.

11. Coleridge, "The Rime of the Ancient Mariner," l.125.

12. A reference to three celebrated prime ministers of England: Robert Walpole (1715–17, 1721–42), Benjamin Disraeli (later Earl of Beaconsfield) (1868, 1874–80), and William Ewart Gladstone (1868–74, 1880–85, 1886, 1892–94). Bierce's writings during his English stay contain many discussions of Disraeli and Gladstone.

13. The poet James Russell Lowell (1819–1891) was appointed minister to Great Britain by President Rutherford B. Hayes in 1880; he served until 1885.

14. Probably a reference to Lowell's "Campaign Epigrams," published in two installments in the *Nation* (Sept. 14 and Oct. 12, 1876).

15. Shakespeare, *Hamlet*, 3.4.135.

16. James Harrison Wilson, "Reminiscences of General Grant," *Century Magazine* 8 (Oct. 1885): 947–54. The entire issue was devoted to articles about Grant.

17. General Grant was the victor of the battle of Vicksburg in Mississippi on July 4, 1863.

18. A reference to St. Paul, who was called Saul before his conversion to Christianity (see Acts 9:3–8).

19. Erastus F. Beadle (1821–1894), who formed the publishing company Beadle and Adams in 1858 and in 1860 began publishing dime novels; it was the leading publisher of dime novels until the emergence of Street and Smith in the last decade of the nineteenth century.

20. A snide reference to Frank M. Pixley, who had evidently spoken on the subject in the *Argonaut*. Ulysses S. Grant had commanded the Union forces in their disastrous loss at Cold Harbor, Virginia, on June 3, 1864. The reference to the Column Vendôme alludes to Grant's month-long visit to Paris in late 1877.

21. A reference to the ancient legend of the colossus of Memnon (a mythical king of Ethiopia), whose stones were said to sing at dawn.

22. The "eminently practical man" in *Hard Times* (1854) who wanted only "facts."

23. There is some mention of Wilde's personal character in Longfellow's late letters, but no mention of his poetry.
24. Tennyson, "The Lotos-Eaters," l.24.
25. Hugh Dalziel, "Dogs and Their Management," *Harper's* 72 (Mar. 1886): 583–94.
26. Gen. George Stoneman (1822–1894), who served as governor of California (1883–87), defeating Morris Estee.
27. Henry J. Dam, "Practical Penology," *North American Review* 144 (May 1887): 514–23.
28. Black Bart was the nickname of Charles E. Boles (c. 1830–1917), a notorious stagecoach robber. Bierce wrote a poem about him, "'Black Bart, Po8,'" *San Francisco Examiner,* January 29, 1888 (also in *Black Beetles in Amber* [1892]).
29. The article apparently was published as an unsigned editorial, as no mention of the matter appears in Bierce's regular "Prattle" column.
30. George Hamlin Fitch, a longtime book reviewer for the *San Francisco Chronicle.*
31. W. C. Bartlett, editorial writer for the *San Francisco Bulletin.*

The *Examiner* Years (1887–1905)

1. A reference to the turmoil resulting from the American Railway Union's boycott of the Pullman Company in California from July to September 1894. Bierce's "Prattle" column was suspended for the issues of July 29 and August 5 after he had strongly condemned the labor unions in his "Prattle" columns of July 8 and July 15.
2. The Amalgamated Association of Street Railway Employes in St. Louis waged a series of strikes in 1900.
3. In a contested election William Goebel (1854–1900) was declared governor of Kentucky. An assassin tried to take his life on January 31, 1900, the day of his inauguration; he died on February 3.
4. "The Passing Show," *New York Journal,* Feb. 4, 1900, 26. The column also appeared in the *San Francisco Examiner,* February 4, 1900, 26.
5. President William McKinley was shot by Leon Czolgosz on September 6, 1901; he died eight days later.
6. Hearst ran unsuccessfully for governor of New York in 1906. Elihu Root (1834–1937) became President McKinley's secretary of war in 1899. He was later secretary of state under Theodore Roosevelt (1905–9) and senator from New York (1909–15).
7. A reference to the Homestead strike of July–November 1892. Bierce wrote about it in "Prattle," *San Francisco Examiner,* July 24, 1892, 6.
8. The Theosophical Society was founded in 1875 by Helena P. Blavatsky, Henry Steel Olcott, and William Q. Judge. For Bierce's satiric fable on the society, see "The Ashes of Madame Blavatsky" in *Fantastic Fables* (1899).
9. The Italian soprano Adelina Patti (1843–1919) and the celebrated clergy-

man Henry Ward Beecher (1813–1887) were both accused of adultery; the latter, it appears, unjustly.

10. "And, in the lowest deep, a lower deep," Milton, *Paradise Lost,* 4.76.

11. Bierce had attacked Greer Harrison in his "Prattle" column (*San Francisco Examiner,* Oct. 13, 1895); Harrison had responded in "The Degeneracy of Ambrose Bierce," *San Francisco Call,* October 20, 1895. Bierce had tangled with Arthur McEwen, another editorial writer for the *Examiner,* on several occasions, most recently in May and June 1895. On that occasion McEwen claimed that he had given Bierce a "caning" (see "Bierce and McEwen," *San Francisco Examiner,* Nov. 11, 1895).

12. Shakespeare, *Timon of Athens,* 5.4.72–73 ("gait" in Shakespeare").

13. See "The End," note 37.

14. Probably Ina Coolbrith (1842–1928), a noted California poet whose work Bierce had been praising since his *Argonaut* days.

15. John O'Hara Cosgrave, editor of the *Wave.*

16. A reference to the English writers Thomas Carlyle (1795–1881) and Thomas Babington Macaulay (1800–1859), and the French writers Hippolyte Taine (1828–1893), author of a celebrated history of English literature (1863), and Anne-Louise-Germaine Necker, Madame de Staël (1766–1817), novelist and critic.

17. Byron, *English Bards and Scotch Reviewers,* l.6.

18. The term "mugwump" was applied to Republicans who deserted their party to vote for Grover Cleveland in the election of 1884. James G. Blaine (1830–1893) was the Republican candidate for president that year.

19. Rutherford B. Hayes, who ultimately won the contested presidential election of 1876.

20. Levi Parsons Morton (1824–1920), Benjamin Harrison's vice president.

21. Allen Granberry Thurman (1813–1895), Cleveland's vice-presidential running mate.

22. Robert Browning (1812–1889), "Caliban upon Setebos" (1864), lines 209–10.

23. Andrew Carnegie (1835–1919), who, as a wealthy industrialist, would naturally have supported the Republicans.

24. See "The Civil War," note 27.

25. Eliza D. Keith (1854–?), author of stories, histories, and textbooks.

26. Sutro was an important businessman and the mayor of San Francisco from 1894 to 1896.

27. *Mi todita:* Spanish for "my whole (thing)."

28. Gertrude Atherton (1857–1948), California novelist. For her piquant account of meeting Bierce in the early 1890s, see her *Adventures of a Novelist* (New York: Liveright, 1932), 202–6.

29. Charlotte Perkins Stetson (later Gilman) (1860–1935), political activist and author of "The Yellow Wall Paper" (1892); Emily Tracy Y. Parkhurst, a suffragette.

30. "Di Vernon" is derived from Diana Vernon, a character in Scott's *Rob Roy.*

31. Presumably a reference to "A Dissertation upon Roast Pig," in *Elia* (1823; later in *The Essays of Elia*) by Charles Lamb (1775–1834).

32. Col. Dan Burns, a California politician frequently attacked by Bierce. Burns was the secretary of state of California at the time.
33. "Ouida" is the pseudonym of English novelist Marie Louise de la Ramée (1839–1908).
34. Ellen Gosse, "The Tyranny of Woman," *New Review* 10 (May 1894): 615–25.
35. "Ouida," "The New Woman," *North American Review* 158 (May 1894): 610–19.
36. Robert Browning (1812–1889), "Caliban upon Setebos" (1864), lines 209–10.
37. Bierce has here listed several advocates for women's rights: Elizabeth Cady Stanton (1815–1902); Susan B. Anthony (see "Early Days in San Francisco," note 6); and Charlotte Perkins Stetson (see note 29 above). Sarah Grand is the pseudonym of Frances Elizabeth (Clarke) M'Fall (1854?–1943), chiefly known as a novelist.
38. Clara S. Foltz (1849–1934), a California suffragette.
39. *Mark Twain's Library of Humor* (New York: Charles L. Webster & Co., 1888). Actually edited anonymously by William Dean Howells. It included six fables (from "The Fables of Zambri, the Parsee" [1872–73]) by Bierce.
40. Shakespeare, *1 Henry IV*, 5.4.146. The concluding word in Shakespeare is "lying."
41. One of Bierce's "Little Johnny" sketches from the *Wasp* was reprinted in the *New York World* in July 1881.
42. See Ambrose Bierce, "Full of Nothing: Holes in the Universe for Tapping Strays," *Oakland Daily Evening Tribune*, Sept. 27, 1890, 1. The article refers to a German scientist's article in a volume entitled *Verschwinden und Seine Theorie*.
43. Howells (1837–1920) had a column, "The Editor's Study," in *Harper's* from 1886 to early 1892; he was a coeditor of *Cosmopolitan* for four months, later in 1892.
44. The contents of the May 1892 *Harper's* included: "Jane Field" (815–31) by Mary E. Wilkins Freeman (1852–1930); "The World of Chance" (856–68) by Howells; "Malouin" (910–13) by William McLennan; and "Jessekiah Brown's Courtship" (933–41) by Ruth McEnery Stuart (1849–1917). It does not appear as if Bierce ever read Wilkins Freeman's book of weird tales, *The Wind in the Rose-bush and Other Stories of the Supernatural* (1903).
45. Latinized vocative form of Henry James.
46. Milton, *Paradise Lost*, 12.644.
47. Milton, *Paradise Lost*, 4.682–84.
48. Tennyson, *In Memoriam*, 55.10.
49. W. C. Morrow (1853–1923), *The Ape, the Idiot and Other People* (Philadelphia: Lippincott, 1897), a collection of horror and suspense tales, many of which had appeared in the *Argonaut* and the *San Francisco Examiner*. Morrow was a longtime friend of Bierce.
50. Bierce does not mean that he taught in a school, but rather that he informally instructed a number of individuals in the art and technique of writing. Among his more noted pupils are the poets George Sterling

(1869–1926) and Herman George Scheffauer (1878–1927). He also gave instruction to Myles Walsh, Amy L. Wells, Eleanor (Vore) Sickler, and others.

51. See "War Topics," *San Francisco Examiner,* July 22, 1898, 6.

52. The incident to which Bierce alludes is unidentified.

53. François, Duc de La Rochefoucauld (1613–1680), *Maximes Supprimées,* 18.

54. Actually from Jean de La Fontaine (1621–1695): "Ventre affamé n'a point d'oreilles"; *Fables,* bk. 9 (1678–79), fable 17.

55. Characters, respectively, in Shakespeare's *Much Ado about Nothing* and *Romeo and Juliet.*

56. The reference is to a variety of American humorists who all wrote pseudonymously: Artemus Ward (Charles Farrar Browne, 1834–1867); John Phoenix (George Horatio Derby, 1823–1861); Josh Billings (Henry Wheeler Shaw, 1818–1885); Bill Nye (Edgar Wilson, 1850–1896); and Mark Twain (Samuel Langhorne Clemens, 1835–1910). Nye's work was printed in the *Examiner.*

57. The reference is to an unsigned review of *Tales of Soldiers and Civilians* in the *New York Sun* 59 (Mar. 12, 1892): 7. It is probably by M. W. Hazeltine, the *Sun*'s staff reviewer.

58. The references are to "A Watcher by the Dead" and "The Affair at Coulter's Notch."

59. The article, entitled "A Cry for Peace in Fable-Land" and signed "Dorch," appeared in *Life* 739 (Feb. 18, 1897): 128.

60. Fitz-James O'Brien (1828–1862), "What Was It?" *Harper's* (Mar. 1859); reprinted in O'Brien's *Stories and Poems* (1881) and many subsequent collections. O'Brien, born in Ireland but living in the United States since at least 1852, fought in the Civil War on the Union side. He was wounded on February 26, 1862, and died on October 6 of that year.

61. John P. Irish (1843–1923), editor of the *Oakland Times* and *Alta California.*

62. Fleet Strother, a California politician. See Bierce's poem "Fleet Strother" in *Black Beetles in Amber* (1892).

63. William Wallace Bowers (1834–1917) and James George Maguire (1853–1920), both representatives from California.

64. Grove Johnson (1841–1926), representative from California.

65. John Tyler Morgan (1824–1907), senator from Alabama (1877–1907).

66. William Pierce Frye (1830–1911), senator from Maine (1881–1911).

67. Thomas Brackett Reed (1839–1902), Speaker of the House in 1889–90 and 1894–96.

68. Horace Henry Powers (1835–1913), representative from Vermont and chairman of the House Committee on Pacific Railroads.

69. William Cowper (1731–1800), "Olney Hymns" (1774), 35.1. The reference, of course, is to God.

70. Byron, *Manfred,* 1.243.

71. James Lawrence Pugh (1820–1907), senator from Alabama (1880–1907).

72. Stephen Benton Elkins (1841–1911), secretary of war (1891–95) and senator from West Virginia (1895–1901).

73. Shakespeare, *Hamlet,* 3.4.179.

74. John Henry Gear (1825–1900), senator from Iowa (1895–1900) and chairman of the Senate Committee on Pacific Railroads.
75. Samuel Greeley Hilborn (1834–1899), representative from California (1892–94, 1895–99).
76. Sen. John Percival Jones (1829–1913) of Nevada.
77. Oliver Goldsmith (1730?–1774), *The Traveller* (1764), l.10.
78. Unsigned. "Thanks to Congressmen, Hisses [f]or Huntington," *San Francisco Examiner*, June 30, 1896, 1.
79. Adm. George Dewey (1837–1917) destroyed the Spanish fleet at Manila on May 1, 1898.
80. Rear Adm. William Thomas Sampson (1840–1902), commander of the North Atlantic Squadron (1898–99); Rear Adm. Winfield Scott Schley (1839–1911), commander of the South Atlantic Squadron (1899–1901). The latter came in for vigorous attack from Bierce during the entire war with Spain.

The End (1905–1913)

1. Byron, *Manfred*, 3.4.40–41.
2. In the August 1905 *Cosmopolitan* Bierce published his satire, "The Jury in Ancient America" (later incorporated into "Ashes of the Beacon").
3. S. S. Chamberlain, an editor for Hearst's newspapers.
4. Rudolph Block (1870–1940), journalist and short-story writer who also wrote under the pseudonym Bruno Lessing.
5. In "Prattle" for August 9, 1896, Bierce attributes the phrase "heard to cease" to Joaquin Miller.
6. Max F. Ihmsen, Hearst's political manager.
7. Arthur Brisbane (1864–1936), one of Hearst's leading editors and writers.
8. Presumably a reference to "Bits of Autobiography."
9. Alfred Henry Lewis (1857–1914), one of Hearst's star reporters and a prolific contributor to *Cosmopolitan*.
10. Probably "The Stranger," *Cosmopolitan* (Feb. 1909).
11. George d'Utassy, a Hearst executive in New York. Norcross is unidentified.
12. John Brisben Walker was editor of *Cosmopolitan* in early 1905. Casamajor is unidentified.
13. Bierce was fond of riding a canoe on the Potomac.
14. Albert Bierce, Bierce's older brother.
15. Walter Neale (1873–1933), publisher of Bierce's *Collected Works* and later the author of a memoir/biography, *Life of Ambrose Bierce* (1929).
16. Herman Scheffauer, *Looms of Life* (New York: Neale Publishing Co., 1908). Bierce took note of the book in his "Small Contributions" column for June 1908.
17. Isa. 53:3.

18. For Sterling see "The *Examiner* Years," note 50. Sterling had six sisters, so it is unclear which one is noted here.

19. In "A Poet and His Poem" (*Cosmopolitan*, Sept. 1907), Bierce had highly praised Sterling's "A Wine of Wizardry." In the subsequent controversy (conducted largely in the pages of the *San Francisco Examiner*) many old enemies of Bierce chose the occasion to attack both him and Sterling. Bierce replied to the attacks in "An Insurrection of the Peasantry" (*Cosmopolitan*, Dec. 1907).

20. Charles William Doyle (1852–1903), author of *The Taming of the Jungle* (1899) and *The Shadow of Quong Lung* (1900).

21. Neale reprinted *Can Such Things Be?* in 1903.

22. Chatto and Windus reprinted *Tales of Soldiers and Civilians* in 1892, retitling it *In the Midst of Life.*

23. Neale eventually did issue a thirty-two-page prospectus of the *Collected Works* in early 1909, containing extracts from material for all the planned volumes.

24. The following scheme underwent many changes over the course of the next several years, as space considerations forced Bierce to shift various items from one volume to another.

25. A reference to *The Shadow on the Dial* (1909), a book of Bierce's "essays" (actually extracts from newspaper columns) assembled by S. O. Howes.

26. *Write It Right: A Little Blacklist of Literary Faults,* a small book on solecisms issued by Neale in 1909. It was not included in the *Collected Works.*

27. Bierce apparently refers to the use of the serial comma, which he did not favor.

28. Carrie Christiansen, Bierce's longtime secretary.

29. Evidently a review of the first volume of the *Collected Works* in a London magazine or newspaper. Reviews have been found in the *Athenaeum* (July 8, 1909), *Saturday Review* (July 31, 1909), and *T.P.'s Weekly* (Sept. 17, 1909), but none seem to be the item discussed here.

30. Unsigned, "The Underground Reputation of Ambrose Bierce," *Current Literature* 47 (Sept. 1909): 279–81.

31. The reference is to Bierce's "Ashes of the Beacon," in *Collected Works,* volume 1.

32. Hildegarde Hawthorne, "Bearer of Evil Tidings" (a review of *The Shadow on the Dial*), *New York Times Saturday Review of Books,* Aug. 14, 1909, 491. Harrison Gray Otis was owner and editor of the *Los Angeles Times.* His review has not been found.

33. Ezra Pound, "The Ballade of the Goodly Fere," one of "Three Poems," *English Review* 3 (Oct. 1909): 382–84; in Pound's *Exultations* (1909).

34. An anonymous article discussing Pound ("Current Poetry") appeared in *Literary Digest* 40 (Feb. 26, 1910): 402–4. "The Ballade of the Goodly Fere" was reprinted in *Current Literature* 38 (Mar. 1910): 342–43.

35. Carlton and Lora Bierce.

36. Albert Bierce, father of Carlton.

37. Every summer the members of the Bohemian Club in San Francisco put on an elaborate "grove play" written by one of their members. Many of the early plays were published in a three-volume set, *The Grove Plays of*

the Bohemian Club, ed. Porter Garnett (San Francisco: Bohemian Club/ H. S. Crocker Co., 1918).

38. Percival Pollard (1869–1911), novelist and critic. He had written about Bierce in a collection of his essays, *Their Day in Court* (Washington, D.C.: Neale Publishing Co., 1909).

39. Herman Scheffauer, "The Death of Satire," *Fortnightly Review* 99 (June 1913): 1188–99.

40. Tennyson, "You ask me, why, tho' ill at ease" (1833), lines 27–28.

41. Josephine Clifford McCrackin, *The Woman Who Lost Him and Tales of the Army Frontier* (Pasadena, Calif.: George Wharton James, 1913). Bierce contributed an introduction to the volume.

42. San Antonio, Texas.

A Sole Survivor

1. Bierce wrote several half-fictional stories about Beckwourth for *Fun* in 1873–74.
2. Shakespeare, *Sonnets*, 62.10.
3. Byron, *Manfred*, 3.4.43–45.
4. Hotten had published Bierce's first book, *The Fiend's Delight* (1873).
5. The reference is to two British journalists of the period, George Augustus Sala (1828–1896) and Henry Sampson (1841–1891), the owner of *Fun* from 1874 to 1878.
6. For Mayne Reid see "The Aftermath of the War," note 6.
7. Sir Boyle Roche (1743–1807), Irish politician known for the flamboyancy of his speeches.
8. Henry, Lord Brougham (1778–1868), English politician, historian, and man of letters. The episode to which Bierce refers is unidentified; presumably it is found in Brougham's *The Life and Times of Henry Lord Brougham* (1871).

Appendix

1. "Kubla Khan" (1816) is a fantastic poem by Coleridge. After taking opium, Coleridge dreamed that he had composed a poem of two to three hundred lines; upon awakening, he could remember only a little over fifty lines of it.
2. Shakespeare, *Hamlet*, 3.4.135.
3. Shakespeare, *A Midsummer-Night's Dream*, 5.1.8.
4. Shakespeare, *The Tempest*, 4.1.260–61.
5. The following dream was incorporated into "The Death of Halpin Frayser," *Wave* (Dec. 19, 1891); in *Can Such Things Be?* (1893).
6. Shakespeare, *Macbeth*, 4.3.175.

7. This dream appears to have been the nucleus of "An Inhabitant of Carcosa," *San Francisco News Letter* (Dec. 25, 1886); in *Tales of Soldiers and Civilians* (1891).

8. Gustave Doré (1832–1883), French illustrator, engraver, painter, and sculptor, best known for his fantastic engraved illustrations of such works as the Bible, *Paradise Lost,* and "The Rime of the Ancient Mariner."

9. "Finis Æternitatis," *Black Beetles in Amber* (1892).

10. "At my suggestion the late Flora Macdonald Shearer put this drama into sonnet form in her book of poems, *The Legend of Aulus*" (note by Bierce).

Sources

The Civil War (1861–1865)

"A Bivouac of the Dead." *New York American,* Nov. 22, 1903,
    22. Rev. *The Collected Works of Ambrose Bierce* (Wash-
    ington, D.C.: Neale Publishing Co., 1912), 11:395–98.

"Battlefields and Ghosts." Bierce to Alexander L. Whitehall,
    corresponding secretary, 9th Regiment Indiana Vet-
    eran Volunteer Infantry Association. Sept. 30, 1904. In
    *Ninth Indiana Veteran Volunteer Infantry Association:
    Proceedings of the Eighteenth Annual Reunion* (N.p.,
    1904), 13–18. Rpt. as *Battlefields and Ghosts* (Palo Alto,
    Calif.: Harvest Press, 1931).

"On a Mountain." *Collected Works,* 1:225–33.

"What I Saw of Shiloh." [1] *Wasp* 282 (Dec. 23, 1881): 408–9;
    283 (Dec. 30, 1881): 442–43. Rev. *San Francisco Exam-
    iner,* June 19, 1898, magazine section, 7; June 26, 1898,
    magazine section, 11; Rev. *Collected Works,* 1:234–69.
    "Appendix": [2] "Prattle," *San Francisco Examiner,*
    Dec. 4, 1898, 12.

"Stones River and Missionary Ridge." [1] "Prattle," *San
    Francisco Examiner,* May 5, 1889, 4. [2] "Prattle," *San
    Francisco Examiner,* Dec. 29, 1895, 6. [3] "Prattle,"
    Wasp 498 (Feb. 13, 1886): 5.

"A Little of Chickamauga." [1] *San Francisco Examiner,* Apr.
    24, 1898, 18 (as "Chickamauga"). In *Collected Works,*
    1:270–78. "Appendix": [2] "War Topics," *San Fran-
    cisco Examiner,* May 8, 1898, 18. [3] Bierce to Archibald

Gracie, Mar. 9, 1911. MS, Bancroft Library, Univ. of California at Berkeley. [4] "Prattle," *San Francisco Examiner,* Nov. 11, 1888, 4.

"The Crime at Pickett's Mill." [1] *San Francisco Examiner,* May 27, 1888, 9. In *Collected Works,* 1:279–96. "Appendix": [2] "Prattle," *San Francisco Examiner,* Oct. 7, 1894, 6.

"A Letter from the Front Lines." Bierce to Clara Wright, June 8, 1864. Printed in Carey McWilliams, "Ambrose Bierce and His First Love," *Bookman* 75 (June–July 1932): 257–58.

"Four Days in Dixie." *San Francisco Examiner,* Nov. 4, 1888, 9. In *Collected Works,* 1:297–314.

"What Occurred at Franklin." [1] *Cosmopolitan Magazine* 42 (Dec. 1906): 223–36 (as "What May Happen Along a Road"). In *Collected Works,* 1:315–27. "Appendix": [2] "Prattle," *San Francisco Examiner,* Aug. 19, 1888, 4. [3] "Prattle," *San Francisco Examiner,* Dec. 23, 1888, 4.

"The Battle of Nashville." [1] "Prattle," *Wasp* 363 (July 14, 1883): 5. [2] "War Topics," *San Francisco Examiner,* June 5, 1898, 18.

"Further Memories of the Civil War." [1] "Prattle," *Argonaut* 3 (Dec. 21, 1878): 17. [2] "Prattle," *Wasp* 295 (Mar. 31, 1882): 182. [3] "Prattle," *San Francisco Examiner,* Dec. 8, 1889, 6. [4] "The Passing Show," *San Francisco Examiner,* Dec. 2, 1900, 30.

"The Hesitating Veteran." *San Francisco Examiner,* Aug. 16, 1901, 14. In *Collected Works,* 4:115–18.

The Aftermath of the War (1865–1867)

"'Way Down in Alabam'." *Collected Works,* 1:328–48.

"Across the Plains." *Oakland Daily Evening Tribune,* Nov. 8, 1890, 1 (as "Lieutenant Bierce"). In *Collected Works,* 1:360–69.

"The Mirage." *San Francisco Examiner,* Aug. 14, 1887, 11. In *Collected Works,* 1:370–82.

"An Unexpected Encounter." "Prattle," *San Francisco Examiner,* Apr. 10, 1887, 44.

Early Days in San Francisco (1868–1872)

All items from "Town Crier" (*San Francisco News Letter*), except where indicated: [1] Nov. 27, 1869, 9. [2] Dec. 19, 1868, 9. [3] Mar. 20, 1870, 9. [4] Mar. 9, 1872, 9. [5] July 10, 1869, 11. [6] Oct. 1, 1870, 9. [7] Jan. 14, 1871, 9. [8] Nov. 4, 1871, 9. [9] Jan. 30, 1869, 9. [10] Feb. 6, 1869, 9. [11] July 17, 1869, 11. [12] Aug. 21, 1869, 11. [13] Dec. 18, 1869, 9. [14] Feb. 3, 1872, 9. [15] Apr. 10, 1869, 9. [16] Apr. 23, 1870, 9. [17] Jan. 6, 1872, 9. [18] Aug. 6, 1870, 9. [19] Aug. 13, 1870, 9. [20] Feb. 24, 1872, 9. [21] Dec. 17, 1870, 9. [22] Feb. 4, 1871, 9. [23] "Female Suffragers and the Town Crier," *San Francisco News Letter* (Dec. 30, 1871): 5 (as by "Almira Faircheek"). [24] Feb. 19, 1870, 9. [25] June 18, 1870, 9. [26] Aug. 20, 1870, 9. [27] Apr. 23, 1870, 9. [28] Sept. 24, 1870, 9. [29] Apr. 8, 1871, 9. [30] Jan. 27, 1872, 9. [31] Mar. 9, 1872, 9.

The English Jaunt (1872–1875)

"First Impressions of England." All items from *Daily Alta California,* except
where indicated: [1] "Letter from London," July 21, 1872, 1. [2] "Letter
from London," Oct. 11, 1872, 1. [3] "Letter from London," Oct. 21, 1872, 1.
[4] "Letter from London," Oct. 11, 1872, 1. [5, 6] "Letter from England,"
Oct. 30, 1872, 1. [7, 8] "Letter from England," Dec. 6, 1872, 4. [9, 10] "Notes
Written with Invisible Ink by a Phantom American," in *Nuggets and Dust*
(London: Chatto & Windus, 1873), 54–57.
"Working for an Empress." *Wasp* 334 (Dec. 23, 1882): 830 (as "How I Worked
for an Empress"). In *Collected Works,* 1:349–59.
"The English Literati." Letters to Charles Warren Stoddard. MS, Huntington
Library and Art Gallery, San Marino, Calif. [1] Mar. 16, 1873. [2] Sept. 28,
1873. [3] July 4, 1874. [4] June 2, 1875.
"That Ghost of Mine." *Argonaut* 2 (Apr. 6, 1878): 6.

Return to San Francisco (1875–1879)

All items from "Prattle" (*Argonaut*), except where indicated: [1] June 30, 1877, 5.
[2] July 14, 1877, 5. [3] Nov. 2, 1878, 9. [4] Apr. 1, 1877, 5. [5] June 23, 1877, 5.
[6] Sept. 29, 1877, 1. [7] Oct. 6, 1877, 5. [8] "Prattle," *San Francisco Examiner,* Feb. 5, 1888, 4. [9] May 26, 1877, 5. [10] June 2, 1877, 5. [11] June 16,
1877, 5. [12] July 7, 1877, 5. [13] Sept. 22, 1877, 5. [14] Oct. 6, 1877, 5. [15] Apr.
6, 1878, 5. [16] Sept. 15, 1877, 5. [17] Oct. 5, 1878, 9. [18] Oct. 12, 1878, 9. [19]
Oct. 13, 1877, 5. [20] Dec. 29, 1877, 5. [21] Mar. 9, 1878, 9. [22] July 27, 1878,
9. [23] May 24, 1879, 1. [24] Oct. 19, 1878, 9.

The Black Hills (1880–1881)

All items, except where indicated, derived from letters included in Paul Fatout's
Ambrose Bierce and the Black Hills (Norman: Univ. of Oklahoma Press,
1956). [1] Bierce to John McGinnis Jr., July 15–16, 1880, 62–65. [2] Bierce to
John McGinnis Jr., Aug. 2, 1880, 74–75. [3] Bierce to John McGinnis Jr.,
Aug. 8, 1880, 55–56, 80–81. [4] Bierce to S. B. Eaton, Sept. 2, 1880, 89–92.
[5] Bierce to S. B. Eaton, Sept. 6, 1880, 97, 102–3. [6] Bierce to S. B. Eaton,
Sept. 14, 1880, 105–6, 111–13. [7] Bierce to S. B. Eaton, Sept. 24, 1880, 116–20.
[8] Bierce to S. B. Eaton, Sept. 24, 1880, 122. [9] Bierce to S. B. Eaton, Oct.
7, 1880, 136–37. [10] Bierce to the Editor, *Black Hills Journal* 4 (Jan. 15,
1881): 4. [11] "Prattle," *San Francisco Examiner,* Apr. 17, 1892, 6.

The *Wasp* Years (1881–1886)

All items from "Prattle" (*Wasp*), except where indicated: [1] "To My Liars," *Wasp*

328 (Nov. 11, 1882): 709; in *Black Beetles in Amber* (1892). [2] 349 (Apr. 7, 1883): 5. [3] 409 (May 31, 1884): 5. [4] 416 (July 19, 1884): 5. [5] 243 (Mar. 26, 1881): 196. [6] 280 (Dec. 9, 1881): 374. [7] 452 (Mar. 28, 1885): 5. [8] 243 (Mar. 26, 1881): 196. [9] 248 (Apr. 29, 1881): 276. [10] 296 (Mar. 31, 1882): 198. [11] 251 (May 20, 1881): 324. [12] 252 (May 27, 1881): 340. [13] 258 (July 9, 1881): 19. [14] 269 (Sept. 23, 1881): 197. [15] 476 (Sept. 12, 1885): 5. [16] 481 (Oct. 17, 1885): 5. [17] 264 (Aug. 19, 1881): 115. [18] 266 (Sept. 2, 1881): 149. [19] 386 (Dec. 22, 1883): 5. [20] 296 (Mar. 31, 1882): 198. [21] 297 (Apr. 7, 1882): 214. [22] 298 (Apr. 14, 1882): 229. [23] 353 (May 5, 1883): 5. [24] 502 (Mar. 13, 1886): 5. [25] "Prattle," *San Francisco Examiner*, Jan. 6, 1889, 4.

The *Examiner* Years (1887–1905)

"A Thumb-Nail Sketch." *Collected Works*, 12:305–15. All other items taken from "Prattle" (*San Francisco Examiner*), except where indicated: [1] May 15, 1892, 6. [2] June 28, 1891, 6. [3] May 26, 1889, 4. [4] June 2, 1889, 4. [5] Aug. 7, 1892, 6. [6] Nov. 3, 1895, 6. [7] July 8, 1888, 4. [8] Oct. 28, 1888, 4. [9] Jan. 19, 1890, 6. [10] July 5, 1891, 6. [11] "The Passing Show," July 15, 1900, 26. [12] Oct. 4, 1891, 6. [13] June 24, 1894, 6. [14] Dec. 23, 1894, 6. [15] "Joaquin Miller on Joaquin Miller," *San Francisco Examiner*, Jan. 30, 1898: magazine section, 7. [16] Aug. 26, 1888, 4. [17] Jan. 22, 1893, 6. [18] May 22, 1892, 6. [19] "The Passing Show," Aug. 27, 1899, 13. [20] "The Passing Show," Sept. 17, 1899, 13. [21] "Concerning Wit and Humor," *San Francisco Examiner*, Mar. 23, 1903, 12. [22] June 26, 1892, 6. [23] Mar. 1, 1897, 6. [24] May 27, 1894, 6. [25] "Bierce on the Funding Bill," *San Francisco Examiner*, Feb. 1, 1896, 1. [26] "His Deal with Pacific Mail," *San Francisco Examiner*, Feb. 15, 1896, 1. [27] "Huntington under Morgan's Lash," *San Francisco Examiner*, Feb. 18, 1896, 1. [28] "Morgan to Offer His Own Measure," *San Francisco Examiner*, Feb. 22, 1896, 1. [29] "Bierce to Huntington," *San Francisco Examiner*, Mar. 21, 1896, 14. [30] "Funding Foes Court a Fight," *San Francisco Examiner*, Apr. 22, 1896, 1. [31] "Another Thieves' Scheme on the Pacific Coast," *New York Journal*, May 4, 1896, 4. [32] "Funding Dealt Its Death Blow," *San Francisco Examiner*, May 7, 1896, 7. [33] "Funding Is Dead Until December," *San Francisco Examiner*, May 27, 1896, 1. [34] "War Topics," *San Francisco Examiner*, May 29, 1898, 18. [35] Dec. 4, 1898, 12. [36] Bierce to Myles Walsh, Apr. 2, 1901, MS, Ambrose Bierce Correspondence, Archives and Rare Books Dept., Univ. of Cincinnati. [37] Bierce to George Sterling, May 2, 1901, MS, New York Public Library.

The End (1905–1913)

All items derived from letters by Bierce as follows: [1] To Bailey Millard, Jan. 19, 1906, MS, Bailey Millard Papers, Ax 431, Dept. of Special Collections and Univ. Archives, Knight Library, Univ. of Oregon, Eugene. [2] To Mr.

Casamajor, Apr. 22, 1906, MS, Bancroft Library, Univ. of California at Berkeley. [3] To S. O. Howes, May 11, 1906, MS, Huntington Library, San Marino, Calif. [4] To S. O. Howes, May 22, 1906, MS, Huntington Library, San Marino, Calif. [5] To Mr. Maxwell, Nov. 23, 1906, MS, Bancroft Library, Univ. of California at Berkeley. [6] To William Randolph Hearst, July 8, 1907, MS, Bancroft Library, Univ. of California at Berkeley. [7] To William Randolph Hearst, July 13, 1907, MS, Bancroft Library, Univ. of California at Berkeley. [8] To William Randolph Hearst, Mar. 30, 1908, MS, Bancroft Library, Univ. of California at Berkeley. [9] To William Randolph Hearst, May 18, 1908, MS, Bancroft Library, Univ. of California at Berkeley. [10] To William Randolph Hearst, Mar. 7, 1909, MS, Bancroft Library, Univ. of California at Berkeley. [11] To George Sterling, Apr. 20, 1906, MS, Berg Collection of English and American Literature, New York Public Library, Astor, Lenox, and Tilden Foundations. [12] To George Sterling, May 6, 1906, MS, Berg Collection of English and American Literature, New York Public Library, Astor, Lenox, and Tilden Foundations. [13] To Edward F. Cahill, June 20, 1906, *The Letters of Ambrose Bierce,* ed. Bertha Clark Pope (San Francisco: Book Club of California, 1922), 123. [14] To Herman Scheffauer, Mar. 31, 1908, MS, Berg Collection of English and American Literature, New York Public Library, Astor, Lenox, and Tilden Foundations. [15] To Herman Scheffauer, Jan. 10, 1909, MS, Berg Collection of English and American Literature, New York Public Library, Astor, Lenox, and Tilden Foundations. [16] To Walter Neale, Apr. 28, 1908, MS, Huntington Library, San Marino, Calif. [17] To Walter Neale, June 7, 1908, MS, Bancroft Library, Univ. of California at Berkeley. [18] To James D. Blake, Oct. 23, 1909, MS, Bancroft Library, Univ. of California at Berkeley. [19] To Walter Neale, Mar. 22, 1911, MS, Huntington Library, San Marino, Calif. [20] To Walter Neale, Sept. 16, 1908, MS, Huntington Library, San Marino, Calif. [21] To Walter Neale, Aug. 25, 1910, MS, Huntington Library, San Marino, Calif. [22] To Walter Neale, July 15, 1911, MS, James S. Copley Library Collection, La Jolla, Calif. [23] To Walter Neale, Jan. 23, 1913, MS, Huntington Library, San Marino, Calif. [24] To Walter Neale, Sept. 1, 1909, MS, Huntington Library, San Marino, Calif. [25] To S. O. Howes, Sept. 6, 1909, MS, Huntington Library, San Marino, Calif. [26] To George Sterling, Jan. 29, 1910, MS, Berg Collection of English and American Literature, New York Public Library, Astor, Lenox, and Tilden Foundations. [27] To George Sterling, Mar. 7, 1910, MS, Berg Collection of English and American Literature, New York Public Library, Astor, Lenox, and Tilden Foundations. [28] To S. O. Howes, Nov. 30, 1907, MS, Huntington Library, San Marino, Calif. [29] To Walter Neale, May 24, 1910, MS, Huntington Library, San Marino, Calif. [30] To S. O. Howes, June 1, 1910, MS, Huntington Library, San Marino, Calif. [31] To S. O. Howes, July 10, 1910, MS, Huntington Library, San Marino, Calif. [32] To Walter Neale, July 15, 1910, MS, Huntington Library, San Marino, Calif. [33] To S. O. Howes, Aug. 11, 1910, MS, Huntington Library, San Marino, Calif. [34] To Helen (Bierce) Cowden, Nov. 4, 1910, MS, Bancroft Library, Univ. of California at Berkeley. [35] To Lora Bierce, Nov. 14, 1910, *The Letters of Ambrose Bierce,* ed. Bertha Clark Pope (San Francisco: Book Club of California, 1922), 165. [36] To S. O. Howes, Sept. 17, 1911, MS, Huntington Library, San Marino, Calif. [37] To Walter Neale, July 2, 1912, MS, Huntington Library, San Marino, Calif. [38] To Walter Neale, Aug. 9, 1912, MS, Huntington Library, San Marino, Calif. [39] To Ruth Robertson, Nov. 3, 1912, MS, Ella Strong Library, Scripps College, Claremont, Calif. [40] To Helen (Bierce) Cowden, Nov. 6, 1912, MS, Yale Collection of American Literature, Beinecke Rare Book and Manuscript Library, Yale Univ., New Haven, Conn. [41] To Helen (Bierce) Cowden, Jan. 27, 1913, MS, Yale Collection of American Literature, Beinecke Rare Book and Manuscript Library, Yale Univ., New Haven, Conn. [42] To Amy Wells, Aug. 5, 1913, MS, Bancroft Library, Univ. of California at Berkeley. [43] To the Neale Publishing Co., Sept. 19, 1913, MS, Rare Book Collection, Univ. of Louisville, Ky. [44] To Helen (Bierce) Cowden, Sept. 10, 1913, MS, Special Collections, Univ. of Pennsylvania Library. [45] To Josephine McCrackin, Sept. 10, 1913, *The Letters of Ambrose Bierce,* ed. Bertha Clark Pope (San Francisco: Book Club of California, 1922), 195. [46] To Josephine McCrackin, Sept. 13, 1913, *The Letters of Ambrose Bierce,* ed. Bertha Clark Pope (San Francisco: Book Club of California, 1922), 195–96. [47] To Eleanor (Vore) Sickler, Sept. 21, 1913, MS, Bancroft Library, Univ. of California at Berkeley. [48] To Helen (Bierce) Cowden, Sept. 29, 1913, MS, Yale Collection of American Literature, Beinecke Rare Book and Manuscript Library, Yale Univ., New Haven, Conn. [49] To Lora Bierce, Oct. 1, 1913, *The Letters of Ambrose Bierce,* ed. Bertha Clark Pope (San Francisco: Book Club of California, 1922), 196–97. [50] To Helen (Bierce) Cowden, Oct. 30, 1913, MS, Ella Strong Library, Scripps College, Claremont, Calif. [51] To Blanche Partington, Dec. 26, 1913, MS, Bancroft Library, Univ. of California at Berkeley.

A Sole Survivor

"A Sole Survivor," *Oakland Daily Evening Tribune,* Oct. 18, 1890. In *Collected Works,* 1:383–402.

Appendix

"Visions of the Night." *San Francisco Examiner,* July 24, 1887, 11. In *Collected Works,* 10:122–33.
"One More Dream." "Prattle," *Argonaut* 3 (Oct. 26, 1878): 9.
"A Rational Anthem." *Wasp* 320 (Sept. 16, 1882): 581.

Further Reading

[Aside from major books on Bierce, this bibliography concentrates on biographical works on Bierce and on critical works that discuss his writings in the context of his life.]

Aaron, Daniel. "Ambrose Bierce and the American Civil War." In *Uses of Literature,* edited by Monroe Engel. Cambridge, Mass.: Harvard Univ. Press, 1973.

Berkove, Lawrence I. "Ambrose Bierce's Concern with Mind and Man." Ph.D. diss., Univ. of Pennsylvania, 1962.

————. "The Impossible Dreams: Ambrose Bierce on Utopia and America." *Huntington Library Quarterly* 44 (Autumn 1981): 283–92.

————. "The Man with the Burning Pen: Ambrose Bierce as Journalist." *Journal of Popular Culture* 15 (Fall 1981): 34–40.

Bierce, Helen. "Ambrose Bierce at Home." *American Mercury* 30 (Dec. 1933): 453–58.

Bosse, David. "From Maps to the Macabre: Ambrose Bierce as a Topographer." *Geography and Map Division Bulletin* 144 (June 1986): 2–15.

Brazil, John R. "Behind the Bitterness: Ambrose Bierce in Text and Context." *American Literary Realism* 13 (Autumn 1980): 225–37.

Brooks, Van Wyck. "The Letters of Ambrose Bierce." In *Emerson and Others.*
New York: Dutton, 1927.
———. "San Francisco: Ambrose Bierce." In *The Confident Years 1885–1915.*
New York: Dutton, 1952.
Couser, Thomas G. "Writing the Civil War: Ambrose Bierce's 'Jupiter Doke,
Brigadier-General.'" *Studies in American Fiction* 18 (Spring 1990): 87–98.
Davidson, Cathy N. *The Experimental Fictions of Ambrose Bierce.* Lincoln: Univ.
of Nebraska Press, 1984.
———, ed. *Critical Essays on Ambrose Bierce.* Boston: G. K. Hall, 1982.
de Castro, Adolphe (G. A. Danziger). *Portrait of Ambrose Bierce.* New York:
Century, 1929.
Fatout, Paul. *Ambrose Bierce: The Devil's Lexicographer.* Norman: Univ. of Okla-
homa Press, 1951.
———. *Ambrose Bierce and the Black Hills.* Norman: Univ. of Oklahoma Press,
1956.
Francendese, Janet M. "Ambrose Bierce as a Journalist." Ph.D. diss., New York
Univ., 1977.
Goldstein, J. S. "Edwin Markham, Ambrose Bierce, and 'The Man with the
Hoe.'" *Modern Language Notes* 58 (Mar. 1943): 165–75.
Grattan, C. Hartley. *Bitter Bierce: A Mystery of American Letters.* Garden City,
N.Y.: Doubleday, 1929.
Grenander, M. E. *Ambrose Bierce.* New York: Twayne, 1971.
———. "Ambrose Bierce, John Camden Hotten, *The Fiend's Delight,* and *Nug-
gets and Dust.*" *Huntington Library Quarterly* 28 (Aug. 1965): 353–71.
Hayden, Brad. "Ambrose Bierce: The Esthetics of a Derelict Romantic." *Gypsy
Scholar* 7 (1980): 3–14.
Klein, Marcus. "San Francisco and Her Hateful Ambrose Bierce." *Hudson Re-
view* 7 (Autumn 1954): 392–407.
McWilliams, Carey. *Ambrose Bierce: A Biography.* New York: A. & C. Boni, 1929.
———. "Ambrose Bierce and His First Love." *Bookman* (New York) 35 (June
1932): 254–59.
Mencken, H. L. "Ambrose Bierce." In *Prejudices: Sixth Series.* New York: Knopf,
1927.
Millard, Bailey. "Personal Memories of Amborse Bierce." *Bookman* (New York)
40 (Feb. 1915): 643–58.
Morris, Roy, Jr. *Ambrose Bierce: Alone in Bad Company.* New York: Crown,
1995.
Neale, Walter. *Life of Ambrose Bierce.* New York: Neale Publishing Co., 1929.
Noel, Joseph. *Footloose in Arcadia: A Personal Portrait of Jack London, George
Sterling, Ambrose Bierce.* New York: Carrick & Evans, 1940.
O'Brien, Matthew C. "Ambrose Bierce and the Civil War: 1865." *American Lit-
erature* 48 (Nov. 1976): 377–81.
Owens, David M. "Bierce and Biography: The Location of Owl Creek Bridge."
American Literary Realism 26 (Spring 1994): 82–89.
Saunders, Richard. *Ambrose Bierce: The Making of a Misanthrope.* San Francisco:
Chronicle Books, 1985.

Solomon, Eric. "The Bitterness of Battle: Ambrose Bierce's War Fiction." *Midwest Quarterly* 5 (Winter 1964): 147–65.

Starrett, Vincent. *Ambrose Bierce.* Chicago: Walter M. Hill, 1920.

Sterling, George. "The Shadow Maker." *American Mercury* 6 (Sept. 1925): 10–19.

Walker, Franklin. *Ambrose Bierce: The Wickedest Man in San Francisco.* San Francisco: Colt Press, 1941.

Wilson, Edmund. "Ambrose Bierce on the Owl Creek Bridge." In *Patriot Gore: Studies in the Literature of the American Civil War.* New York: Oxford Univ. Press, 1962.

Wilt, Napier. "Ambrose Bierce and the Civil War." *American Literature* 1 (Nov. 1929): 260–85.

Index

A Sole Surviror was designed and typeset on a Macintosh computer system using PageMaker software. The text is set in Minion, and the titles in ITC Officina. This book was designed by Kay Jursik, composed by Kimberly Scarbrough, and manufactured by Thomson-Shore, Inc. The recycled paper used in this book is designed for an effective life of at least three hundred years.